LIVING WORDS

AAR

American Academy of Religion
Reflection and Theory in the Study of Religion

Editor
David E. Klemm

Number 12
LIVING WORDS
Studies in Dialogues about Religion

by
Terence J. Martin

LIVING WORDS

Studies in Dialogues about Religion

by
Terence J. Martin

Scholars Press
Atlanta, Georgia

LIVING WORDS
Studies in Dialogues about Religion

by
Terence J. Martin

Library of Congress Cataloging in Publication Data

Martin, Terence J., 1951–
    Living words : studies in dialogues about religion / Terence J. Martin.
        p.   cm. — (AAR reflection and theory in the study of religion ; no. 12)
    Includes bibliographical references and index.
    ISBN 0-7885-0512-2 (pbk. : alk. paper)
    1. Dialogue—Religious aspects. 2. Religions—Relations.
I. Title. II. Series.
BL410. M37   1998
291.1'72—dc21
                            98-37407
                            CIP

Printed in the United States of America
on acid-free paper
∞

In gratitude to my parents

Terence and Barbara Martin

Table of Contents

Part II: Irony and Religion

Part III: An Ethic of Discourse

Preface

This book is about dialogue over religion. Its pages spring from three things. First, it arises from a recurring perception that efforts to speak about religion regularly get mired in confusion and conflict. Talk about religion is anything but easy. Indeed, misunderstanding and rancor are common results. Second, this work is animated by the dogged hope that such talk might go better if participants adopted certain postures and practices of speech—in particular, the habits of *critical* thinking, a sense of *irony*, and an *irenic* approach to opposition. Third, this book takes its method from the conviction that literary dialogues on religious topics are useful tutors regarding both the problems and the possibilities of religious discussions. A turn to the genre of dialogue just might shed light on living dialogue about religion.

The work that follows emerges from prolonged conversation with colleagues and friends. As Horace reminds us, critical discourse can be honest, free, and most fruitful among friends. In this regard, I am indebted to local colleagues like Thomas Bonnell, Kevin McDonnell, and Herold Weiss for their insights and suggestions on various chapters. No venue for conversation has been more helpful than that provided by members of the Theology and Ethics Colloquy. Richard B. Miller, Charles A. Wilson, Douglas F. Ottati, David E. Klemm, and Lois K. Daly provided years of critical commentary and constructive encouragement; to each I am thankful. I am especially grateful to William Schweiker, whose enthusiasm for dialogue and keen insight made it possible for me to find and focus the central issues of my project; I am fortunate to have such a friend and critic.

Many of the dialogues discussed in the following chapters revel in irony and humor, sometimes at the expense of religion, sometimes to its benefit. As Horace aptly puts it, no law is violated if someone "laughs while speaking the truth." Almost every ironic twist and humorous point found below has been discussed (and laughed at) with John R. Shinners; I greatly appreciate his gift for humor and his instinct for irony. Far too much talk about religion is uncritical and humorless. The dialogues treated in this book seek to counter this tendency by illustrating the importance of criticism and irony in speaking the truth about religion. There is no reason, however, that speaking such truth should not be hospitable. The chapters on Hume and Erasmus highlight the need and the possibility of wedding hard criticism and comic irony to a civil and irenic regard for opposition. I am thankful to Phyllis Kaminski for encouraging me to pursue and to practice this Erasmian imperative.

This book has been dreadfully long in the making. In this regard, I stand in debt to assorted Road Lobsters and Road Dogs. Mile after mile, their healthy amazement and persistent chiding forced me to keep this project in proper perspective. Lastly, I am fortunate to have had the editorial help of Tawni Toth.

1

Religious Dialogue
and Dialogues on Religion

"What do you suppose is our purpose when we use words?"

—Augustine's initial question in *De Magistro*[1]

"Once when I was sitting with my brothers and they were asking questions and I was answering them, many things had been put forward for discussion. At length our talk came to a point where we all began to sigh, and to wonder greatly at the instability and unquietness of the human heart."

—Hugh of St. Victor[2]

It is a commonplace of popular wisdom that it is better to avoid discussing religion and politics in public settings.[3] These subject matters, while so important and so fascinating, are known to breed a great deal of confusion and enmity. People's passions become inflamed, their understanding dims, and furious conflict can result. There is a good chance that participants in the exchange will not even speak on the same wave-length. What is obvious to one person may be unintelligible for another; what counts as a good reason for one may be irrational to another. It is better—so the wisdom goes—to leave these subjects alone. And yet there is no shortage of talk about religion and politics, and not surprisingly, there is no shortage of misunderstanding and trouble.

Popular wisdom's counsel appears to hold for discourse about all sorts of basic commitments and fundamental loyalties. By "discourse" I mean any attempt to interact through language.[4] The event of discourse may be about anything, it may be with anyone, and its results may or may not bear fruit. The difficulties people encounter with religion or politics seem to stem from the inherent gravity of these issues, from the depth of the speakers' personal or group investment, and from the inescapable fact that what people care about so deeply, what they revere and hold to be sacred, is peculiar unto each person. These topics, consequently, are natural hotbeds for strained and contentious communication. In this regard, religion and politics have earned their reputation time and time again.

In what follows I want to take a close look at what happens in discourse on religion. By "religious discourse," I mean any attempt by people to talk with each other about "religious" questions. Such a description is—admittedly—terribly broad, perhaps even nebulous. At least initially, however, I think it best to set the parameters of what will count as "religious" discourse as liberally as possible, both in terms of *what* is discussed and in terms of *who* participates. They should be broad enough, for instance, to include things commonly recognized as belonging to an organized religion (talk about the doctrines, moral tenets, and ritual prescriptions of specific institutions), as well as more general phenomena which are "religious" without being connected to a known religion (independent queries on the mysterious powers and ultimate ends which shape the course and quality of human life).[5] The religious should be conceived of with sufficient breadth to incorporate everything: from the simplest act of worship to the most complex liturgical performance; from the most nervous popular superstition to the most arcane of speculative theories; from the most abstract of mystical experiences to the most concrete programs for building a better world; from the purest of moral ideals to the most sordid of actual practices.

Discourse on religion, moreover, is not restricted to those people who self-consciously and deliberately profess religious beliefs or commitments. Nor is it confined to those who happen to hold the "same" religious views. Religious discourse, here understood, includes all who find themselves engaged in the practice of talking and listening about what generally are considered questions of religion—whether their participation is intentional, accidental, or forced; whether they regard themselves as religious or renounce any and all affiliation with religion; whether they profess allegiance to one tradition or to another. It encompasses, therefore, the contribution of the skeptic as much as the believer, the dissident as the orthodox, the Buddhist as the Christian, and so on. While this delineation of what counts as "religious" discourse may disconcert both religious insiders (who would exclude those not like themselves) and outsiders (who would resist being included), I think it important to keep both in the picture. Discourse on religion, after all, is the way it is—full of possibilities and yet tenuous and unstable—in large part because it brings together such a disparate pool of interlocutors.

Defined this broadly, discourse on religion is both natural and widespread; but, regrettably, so too are the undesirable consequences about which popular wisdom warns us. Though similar problems arise in other varieties of discourse—not only political, but also moral, economic, and philosophical—talk about religion seems unusually and characteristically susceptible to problems with intelligible and rational communication. This is the upshot of popular wisdom's admonition: religion has acquired a reputation for troublesome and acrimonious discourse.

(1) Four Examples and Three Issues

A series of examples will help us see the soundness of popular wisdom's warning.

(a) Voltaire, the great eighteenth century wit and critic, had an unusual ability to depict the workings of religious discourse in a way which would both help people understand their failures and exhort them to do better. In one little dialogue, for instance, Voltaire plays with the hermeneutical problems generated when residents of two self-absorbed cultures encounter each other.[6] The setting is an Amsterdam bookstore, where a Chinese man is engaged in conversation with several Dutch intellectuals about the books for sale in the store. At one point, their discussion turns to a book bearing the title *Universal History*. This intrigues the Chinese man because he hopes to hear stories about his homeland. When they tell him about the book's contents, however, things go sour. The Chinese man has never heard of the Roman empire. He thinks he has heard of Caesar, but he has confused him with a Turk. He finds it hard to believe that a puny little country like Palestine could be so important. Bit by bit, he begins to distrust the Dutchmen: could they be making all these things up? This so-called *Universal History* includes nothing about China. The Chinese man leaves, disgusted. All communication has broken down. It is not even clear that they are from the same world. Voltaire's little dialogue is, I think, a parable of what can happen in discourse over fundamental perspectives and values. As James Boyd White puts it, all too often, words lose their meaning and worlds splinter.[7] In cross-cultural discourse like that portrayed by Voltaire, clear and rational communication can be shaky.

As Voltaire knew all too well, religious discourse frequently degenerates into open hostility, but he also knew that the keys to amicable communication were quite simple. The "Japanese Catechism," published in Voltaire's *Philosophical Dictionary*, provides a good example. A brief colloquy between a Japanese and an Indian, the former narrates how his land has managed to overcome the disputes among the many "cooking factions" in his country. In the past, he tells the Indian, "we persecuted, lacerated, devoured one another, for nearly two centuries."[8] Each faction, it seems, intolerantly insisted on its own dietary habits: the Breuxeh renounce "blood pudding or lard"; the pispates, "on certain days of every week, and even during a considerable part of the year, would a hundred times sooner eat turbot, trout, sole, salmon, sturgeon, for a hundred *écus*, than feed themselves with a veal stew that wouldn't come to more than four *sous*"; the Terluh, the Vincal, the Batistapenes, and the Diestes each had their own specialties and standards as well—only the Quekars seem exempt from this culinary fury.[9] Sounding like one of his beloved Quakers, Voltaire ends his parody of religious factionalism with an exhortation to tolerance. As the Japanese speaker reports, the dissension among the kitchen factions at long last has ended. Now, "all quarrels at table are carefully curbed, in accordance with the precept of our great Japanese cook, SUTI RAHO CUS FLAC" (alias Horace), who wisely taught concerning a divisive issue like food, that "Dinner was made for collective and decent joy, and we must not throw glasses at each others' heads."[10] Such wise counsel apparently was enough to quiet the passions and ease the tensions of the Japanese speaker's society. The advice given—that we should not throw glasses at each other over dinner—rings with so much self-evident truth that it must bring a smile of recognition to the faces of

Voltaire's readers. And that, I take it, is Voltaire's point. Rational and tolerant talk between religious sects is as simple as it is rare. Unfortunately, discord and strife frequently prevail despite reason's counsel.[11]

(b) Rational communication becomes a problem in other spheres of religious discourse as well. The meaning of words shifts and understanding easily becomes blocked, for instance, in exchanges between the affluent and the poor. One of Ernesto Cardenal's dialogues between some Nicaraguan *campesinos* and an international banker provides a case in point. Their topic is the meaning of Jesus' saying in *Luke* 16: 13, "You cannot serve God and mammon." The banker suggests that these words must be understood in the context of "the economy of the times, which was a slave system." This outrages one of the *campesinos*: for him, capitalism is a slave system, and "the money that goes from hand to hand . . . [is] like a long, long chain that links everybody's necks together and winds up on Wall Street, which is where all money ends, as you know."[12] The banker wants to know what they think the bank should do with its money, "according to the Gospel." "It's very clear," retorts Marcelino; "give it out." "But," the banker exclaims, "then there won't be any money to lend to people in need." If this counsel were taken seriously, "the banks would be ruined." To this worry, one of the *campesinos* replies: "And the banks, as you know just as well as we do, are a great big shit!"[13] In this exchange, there is no linguistic bridge available to allow mediation between the banker's capitalist practicality and the *campesinos'* unmitigated denunciation of capitalistic slavery. What seems normal to the banker is evil to the Nicaraguans; what seems just to the latter seems revolutionary to the former. The *campesinos'* moral indignation and the banker's sense of practical rationality collide. Discourse is fractured. All hope of understanding, much less persuasion, fades away.

(c) Of course, not every effort to talk with others about religion results in such stark impasses. Many exchanges on religion, in fact, achieve a fair degree of mutual understanding. Yet even apparently balanced and civil exchanges reveal just how tenuous discourse on religion can be. An early dialogue of Augustine's— "Against the Academics"—provides a perfect example. Superficially, the discourse pictured by Augustine is both productive and gracious. Secluded in their philosophical retreat at Cassiciacum, Augustine and his young interlocutors test the view held by the skeptical Academics (notably Cicero) that wisdom is "not merely the knowledge but also the quest of those divine and human things which pertain to a happy life."[14] It is Licentius (and later Alypius) who defends this position against the criticisms of Trygeticus, who is later replaced by Augustine in the front against the Academics. For Licentius, the wise man withholds assent from claims to knowledge, since only probability and not truth can be apprehended by the human mind. The wise man is the one who searches for truth, not the one who claims to possess it. Showing his own earlier affiliation with Ciceronian thought, Augustine concedes that few people seem to achieve wisdom; and he acknowledges that his arguments against the Academics are not meant to detract from the value of "a thorough search for truth."[15] Still, there must be some real measure of wisdom, Augustine maintains, or else the wise man would contradictorily be called wise without in fact possessing wisdom. The skeptical Academic foolishly doubts that anyone is wise (and for that is called wise!), while Augustine simply is uncertain who is wise and who is not.[16]

As Peter Brown notes in his biography of Augustine, this dialogue is hardly noteworthy for the depth of its arguments.[17] What is significant about this text is the rhetorical contour Augustine gives to the interlocutors' conversation. On the one hand, their discourse is remarkably civil: they pledge to cooperate with each other, avoiding the trap of a "mere verbal controversy."[18] Being friends, they will graciously allow each other to "revoke what has been thoughtlessly conceded" in their discussion, since "finding the right and the true" is far more important than victory in disputation.[19] Their dialogue will be playful and good-spirited. On the other hand, their interaction frequently is strained by more serious and competitive passions. Throughout the text, in fact, dialogue is described in militant terms: speakers attack and defend positions, wilt under assaults, and relish victories. Thus, for example, midway through the dialogue, Augustine squares off with Alypius, challenging him to forge ahead in more serious inquiry: "Do you understand what I am saying? Let us at once fling those trifles away from us: 'For an eager warrior, weapons must be forged.'"[20] This use of militant imagery, however, is not mere decoration. Rather, it points up the many ways in which Augustine's imaginary discourse is shaped by aggressive passions and contentious interests: regarding the other as adversary, assuming intimidating stances, undertaking manipulative maneuvers, feeling embarrassment for mistakes, and harboring resentment for being outmatched—to name just a few.[21]

At key points, their language shows the stress of these tensions: first, their words become mutually unintelligible; and second, they come to find each other's efforts at persuasion to be irrational. The former occurs in a conflict between Alypius and Augustine over what question they are addressing. When Augustine insists that a wise man must possess wisdom or not be called wise, Alypius suggests that *seeming to know* and *knowing* are not the same thing. Wisdom is only the investigation, not the possession, of truth. Augustine responds in a scolding tone: "You are not extricating yourself by complicating matters. In fact, I think you are disputing merely for the sake of exercise." For his part, Augustine appears to be disputing for the sake of victory, and to this end, he presses his argument relentlessly: even for the person who seems to himself to be wise, wisdom must be something and not nothing. When Alypius humbly responds that it still seems to him "that there is a difference in meaning between 'it seems to him that he knows' and 'he knows'," Augustine replies amicably (but also a bit wearily) that perhaps "neither of us understands what the other is saying."[22] This is exactly correct.

They are not understanding each other because each is posing a different question. Alypius champions the Academic ideal of Socratic ignorance—never claiming to be wise and always suspecting those who seem to themselves to be wise. Augustine, for his part, wishes to secure the possibility of definite knowledge; his new-found Christian sensibilities must be protected against skeptical erosion. Their communication, in short, has splintered, since the key terms of their respective philosophical positions are unintelligible and illicit to the other.

When they resume the debate after lunch, however, Augustine is back on the offensive. For him it is not simply a matter of asking *different* questions, but of Alypius deviously answering *his* question with another (rival) question. He chides Alypius for being indirect and evasive. And when Alypius concedes under pressure that something is known by the wise man, Augustine gloats over his victory.[23] Shortly thereafter, he launches into a long, uninterrupted monologue, in which he gives the correct view on these questions while the others simply listen.[24] They have been silenced. It is Augustine alone who speaks.

In place of their voices, he now substitutes what he imagines philosophical opponents might say to him, thereby constructing an imaginary conversation with interlocutors of his own making. The irony, of course, is that this is precisely what Augustine has done as the author of the entire dialogue. Now, however, the power of the author to have his own way has intruded on the text. It is as if Augustine has become impatient with the tiresome process of persuasion through dialogue. His arguments with his interlocutors, therefore, have become heavy-handed (something resented first by Licentius and later by Alypius); and consequently, his communication with his readers becomes magisterial and didactic. Augustine, it seems, speaks as the wise one (thereby personifying the position he has defended), while the others only search. The dialogue among them, it turns out, is something of a playpen, in which Augustine confidently toys with his immature interlocutors.[25] The power of the master has replaced the argumentative processes of philosophical dialogue. It is no wonder, therefore, that his interlocutors complain that his method of persuasion is less than rational.

(d) Cultural differences, economic disparities, and personal power contort the attempts to discuss religion in situations like those depicted in these three dialogues. Sometimes, however, the difficulties stem from nothing more than differences in personality and the not uncommon failure to keep a cool head while talking about religion. Such is the case in a dialogue by Iris Murdoch, entitled "Above the Gods: A Dialogue about Religion." Murdoch imaginatively recreates a Socratic dialogue dealing with the essence of religion and its relation to morality. Various views are offered by the speakers—to wit, that "religion is superstition, that it's socially useful, that it's the love of goodness, and . . . that it's the harmony of good and evil"[26]—all under the close examination of Socrates. What is interesting for my purposes is the way that each character's personality (their strengths, natural tendencies, commitments, blind spots, etc.) effects the course of the dialogue. When, for instance, Antagoras suggests that nationalism and patriotism are practical substitutes for religion, Timonax can only respond with anger. He becomes, in Murdoch's words, "incoherent with annoyance and conviction," and their brief exchange suffers from the infusion of his rage.[27] Acostos enters the discussion with great reticence. Unlike Antagoras and Timonax, however, he wants to defend a positive view of religion. For him, religion is "absolute seriousness" about life and the "perpetual work" that goes with it.[28] Acostos, however, is less confident than the others, and his timidity gives way to confusion when Socrates presses him to develop his position further.

> **Socrates:** Now gather yourself together for a final assault.
> **Acastos** (struggling): I can't—
> **Socrates:** Can there be religion without mythology, without stories and pictures? Should we be trying now to think of it like that?
> **Acastos:** I don't know!
> **Socrates:** Is a certain opaqueness, a certain *mystery*, necessary to it?
> **Acastos:** I don't know!
> **Socrates:** Would you say that religion is something natural?
> **Timonax:** Socrates, do stop, let's have an interval, let's drink and not think! Acastos says there is no time off from religion, but do let's have some time off from philosophy!

At which time, drinks are served and Acastos is let off the hook. Sometimes, it seems, philosophical dialogue is too much for an ordinary mind to handle.

The most dramatic clash of personalities occurs between Plato (who, as Timonax says, "gets so cross when he can't explain his ideas")[29] and Alcibiades (who stumbles into the discussion drunken, flirting with Socrates, and teasing the others). Alcibiades angers Plato initially by claiming to agree with Plato's views on religion:

> **Socrates:** Plato has been telling us about being in love.
> **Alcibiades:** My subject too!
> **Timonax:** He's in love with Good.
> **Alcibiades:** Is it mutual?
> **Antagoras:** He thinks that goodness is the same as knowledge.
> **Alcibiades:** But I think that too!
> **Plato** (tense, very hostile): No, you don't. We can't possibly be agreeing. Religion is the love and worship of goodness and truth, it's a magnetic power, it's absolute, and if we really love what's good we become good, and—
> **Alcibiades:** Oh Pusskins—
> **Plato:** You're drunk!

When pressed to be serious, Alcibiades defines religion in a manner true to his character; it is the "love and worship of power" and the knowledge that "good and evil are not enemies, they are friends."[30] Such a view infuriates Plato, and the passion of his commitments drives him beyond language to violence.

> **Plato** (furious): That's a damned lie, the worst lie of all, Good must never make peace with evil, never, never! It must kill evil!
>
> **Alcibiades:** You are bloodthirsty! Don't you want harmony, don't you want to make something creative out of all that warfare that's going on inside you? Why be always tearing yourself to pieces? Don't you want human life to work, to function?
>
> **Plato:** That's perfect muck! Good must be pure and separate and—absolute—and—only what's completely good can—save us—
>
> **Alcibiades:** But your perfectly pure good thing does not exist, that's the trouble, dear, all the world proves that!
>
> **Plato:** It does, it must—it's more real—I can't explain—
>
> **Alcibiades:** My dear little one, I can see that you can't![31]

In reaction, Plato "hurls himself at Alcibiades"! Socrates separates the two (slapping Plato!), and then proceeds to give a view which reconciles the other positions, cutting through the impasses which infected their exchange. Only Socrates seems immune from the bickering and flashes of temper which repeatedly threaten the dialogue's progress. He keeps his eyes fixed on the question at hand, tempering his interlocutors' outbursts and mediating their disputes. For the average interlocutor, however, talk about religion is infected with passion and fury—leading, all too often, to acrimony and even violence.

To say the least, these dialogues yield vivid evidence of the strains and stresses experienced when people gather to talk about religion. Popular wisdom's warning about discussing religion in public seems well founded. Any number of factors—cultural, economic, and personal—may conspire to make talk about religion unintelligible or irrational.

What becomes evident when reading these dialogues is the interpersonal or social nature of talk about religion. Such talk—as with any form of discourse—takes place among people. It is a social and dialogical undertaking. This may seem obvious, and indeed, I think it is. But it is a point too often ignored by advocates and scholars of religion alike, both of whom have a tendency to regard simpler or more controlled forms of language as the most elemental. Other genres of religious language—prayer, soliloquy, homily, declarative propositions ("I believe that God exists"), creedal confessions, and narrative—in one way or another all step away from the intricate tangles which crop up in real life exchanges. They conceal the dialogical give and take of living discourse, or they abstract from the broader social context in favor of simple units of utterance, or finally they seek to domesticate the sociality of discourse through a narrator's control. Certainly the artistic recreations of dialogue written by Voltaire, Cardenal, Augustine, and Murdoch suggest otherwise. Discourse on religion occurs within a social, interpersonal context, and for that very reason, is liable to be complex, messy, and uncontrollable. Every achievement of understanding and persuasion arises through the complicated nexus of voices and interests collected for discussion, and concomitantly, every failure to be intelligible and rational emerges within the same setting. It is precisely the social or interpersonal nature of religious discourse, in other words, which makes it so intriguing yet so arduous.

When seen in this light, two key features stand out as central to discourse. In the most diverse manners and with varying degrees of success, speakers intend to be understood and they hope to persuade. The first feature is communicative: speakers commit their words to others in order to communicate their ideas, feelings, and actions. The second dimension is probative: speakers hope to effect and move listeners to think or feel or do something. For communication to succeed, language must be intelligible. For persuasion to succeed, arguments and warrants must be rational. The problem, of course, is that a great deal of discourse stumbles on both scores. Interlocutors fail to understand each other (thus raising hermeneutical problems) and they falter in their efforts to convince each other (thus raising rhetorical questions). The hermeneutical issues concern communicative intelligibility (what interlocutors take their words and those of others to mean, either agreeing or finding themselves face to face with the unintelligible). The rhetorical problems center around issues of probative rationality (what interlocutors take to be reasonable, either agreeing to or dissenting from a line of argument).

Religious discourse, certainly, is not exempt from the hermeneutical and rhetorical difficulties which attend these two sides of all discourse. Indeed, the dialogues described earlier give ample evidence of how easily discussions on religion become unintelligible or irrational. If anything, talk about religion intensifies the strain on understanding and persuasion. Religious discourse characteristically opens up venues for discussion and introduces topics for exchange which stretch the communicative and probative fiber of linguistic activity. When these fibers break, rancor and brutality often follow. Popular wisdom, of course, has long known this.

By nature, talk about religion takes up inherently allusive, even mysterious topics. Religion deals with "limit-experiences" (to borrow David Tracy's phrase): it refers to life-shaping and world-grounding realities which lie dimly at the very edges of human comprehension and apprehension.[32] Religious forces and values, in other words, pose the "limits to" human life (they define it and shape it), even as they stand at the "limits of" understanding (they evade definition and clarity). But despite the opacity of religious phenomena, people tend to invest themselves with great personal commitment (even passion) in their tradition's language for these fundamental realities. Though ontologically murky, religious beliefs frequently are treated with the utmost certainty, or they are assumed to be beyond question. On both counts—the obscurity of the object and the surety of the commitment—religion is a terribly difficult topic for discussion.

But there is more. Religion is difficult to talk about not only because its questions are ontologically allusive, and not only because people invest so much in their religions, but also because the social venues for talking about religion are highly diversified. People have different experiences, different perspectives, and different languages; and consequently, any attempt to talk about religious questions must cope with the social gaps and clashes created by these differences. Religious plurality, to say the least, poses formidable obstacles to intelligible communication and rational persuasion. And since religious language lives discursively—socially, among people—it has no choice but to proceed within the highly diversified terrain of this plurality. As a result, interlocutors must operate on the brink—struggling to make sense and to convince each other in that liminal space created by their differences. On this count too—the fact of religious plurality—religion pushes interlocutors to points of discourse where understanding and persuasion teeter on the edge of collapse. It is these facts about religious discourse which warrant popular wisdom's warning. Talk about religion is characteristically unstable.

Though much more will follow on this subject, it is important to underscore from the very beginning that religious discourse reaches the point of communicative and probative instability from the most diverse causes—including, as I have said, the ontological opaqueness of its referents, the fervent degree of its underlying commitments, and the inescapable fact of diversity. There is no simple explanation for the difficulties of talking about religion. They cannot be blamed on a certain kind of religious language (e.g., mystical), nor attributed to one set of motives rather than another (e.g., orthodoxy versus reform). Religious language, in fact, is driven to these points by interlocutors who want to defend religion and by those who seek to attack it, by those seeking to expand its horizons or by those intent on containing them, by those using religion to re-enforce existing orders or by those planning to overturn them. All who participate—friend and foe alike—appear implicated in the delicate balance between success and failure to communicate clearly and argue rationally. This seems to be—as popular wisdom tells us—a fact of religious life.

It is precisely this fact about religious discourse which motivates the present study. My purpose in this book is to explore and describe the deep-seated and pervasive forms of tension present in religious discourse. What happens when people of different stripes meet to talk about religion? How does it happen that intelligible communication and rational persuasion prove so tenuous when it comes to religion? What, exactly, are some of the ways in which efforts to speak with others about religion arrive at the point of discursive instability? What, moreover, are the forces at work which generate these problems about which popular wisdom speaks? Why does so much stress and strain accompany discourse on religion? And finally, where does that leave those of us who will—by choice or by chance—find ourselves involved in discourse on religious questions? How should we proceed?

In what follows, I want to approach these questions using the method already employed in this introduction—namely, by taking up literary dialogues on religious topics as models of religious discourse. As we have seen already, these dialogues—like those of Voltaire, Cardenal, Augustine, and Murdoch discussed above—provide an appropriately focused, but wide-ranging resource for observing and reflecting on what people do when they talk with each other about God and other religious issues. These dialogues are highly stylized but nonetheless very revealing portraits of attempts to converse about religious issues. In choosing this genre, an author has accepted the challenge to work within the social limits of an imaginative conversation, creating a world of discourse with its own peculiar situations, purposes, strategies, and achievements. Whether the dialogues portray conversations between skeptics and believers, Christians and non-Christians, defenders of orthodoxy and heretics, etc., they provide graphic test cases for critically examining the possibilities, the obstacles, and the achievements of religious conversation. They can, therefore, teach us something about the peculiar ambiguities which effect people's attempts to speak with others about religion.

I propose in the following chapters to look at some of the classic dialogues in Western religious thought. Turning back to these texts will yield three main benefits. First, re-reading classic writers in light of their choice of the dialogue genre sheds fresh light on these authors' substantive concerns. The literary form is not incidental—in fact, it is crucial—to the message advanced. Anselm of Canterbury and David Hume, for instance, speak in original ways when we as readers pay attention to the *way* they speak to us, something all too frequently ignored in philosophical interpretation of these authors. Their policies and methods for dealing with the complexities of discourse—through which and by means of which they articulate their messages—are woven into the literary fibers of the dialogues they bequeath to us. Attending to their uses of the dialogue form, therefore, will allow us to glean something of these authors' attitudes toward the social demands and dialogical possibilities of religious discourse; and consequently, it will bring a new perspective to bear on their views religion, since they rarely are thought to have been sensitive to these aspects of religious language.

Second, paying close attention to the uses of this genre yields several philosophical dividends. Tending to the choice of genre makes it possible, in a word, to better understand the variable and complicated workings of religious discourse. As literary models of conversations on religion, these dialogues feature different locales for exchanges, each demanding (but also offering) different rhetorical possibilities to the interlocutors. As a result, they instantiate many facets typical of religious discourse—including the precarious ambiguity between rational and irrational discourse so common to such exchanges. Consequently, they offer useful models for philosophical reflection. But literary dialogues bear other philosophical fruits as well. As will become clear, these texts not only imitate religious discourse; more importantly, dialogues allow authors to participate in living discourse with readers by means of their literary imitations. Dialogues, in other words, directly engage readers in discourse with an author, and the product of this discourse is of great philosophical value both for coming to terms with an author's position on the tensions endemic to religious language and for initiating ethical reflections on norms and ideals for discourse.

And third, the turn to literary genre for the sake of philosophical reflection on religion also addresses the reigning concerns of today's post-modern academic culture as they are reflected in religious and theological studies. Whatever else the term "post-modern" means, and it has come to mean many different things, it points out certain basic concerns about human language and culture. For someone affected by post-modern sensibilities, human communication (the practice of talking and understanding each other civilly and rationally) appears fragmented and precarious. On the one hand, communicative discourse and the cultural constructs designed to assure it appear terribly fragile, threatened by an unbridled plurality of voices. On the other hand, what counts as "rational" appears intractably ambiguous, concealing passionate and possibly tyrannical interests. What authors like Voltaire, Cardenal, Augustine, and Murdoch portray so vividly—the instability of discourse, the ubiquity of confusion and irrationality, and the imperative of coherent and civil communication—remains at the heart of post-modern life. Indeed, issues of communicative intelligibility and probative rationality stand at the center of the methodological debates across the study of religion today, as they do for the humanities generally. Consequently, critical re-reading of selected classical dialogues for the sake of philosophical understanding of religious discourse speaks directly to the questions plaguing post-modern culture.

In the remainder of this introduction, I want to follow up on these initial remarks with some propadeutic reflections on the three main planks of this study: (a) the importance of dialogue as a problem for contemporary religious studies, and in particular, for current post-modern dilemmas arising in the world of Christian theological discourse; (b) the usefulness of looking at the genre of literary dialogue as a major artistic medium for portraying and participating in religious discourse; and c) the philosophical significance of descriptively examining the forces which make religious language so fundamentally ambiguous.

(2) Dialogue in Contemporary Religious Studies

Talk of dialogue abounds across the field of religious studies. Indeed, concern for dialogue—its urgency, its difficulties, and its promises—has become one the reigning motifs in current discourse on religion. This is the first plank on which the following study rests.

A few specific examples may help to illustrate both how pivotal yet exacting dialogue has become in contemporary religious discourse. In each case, speakers face situations where understanding is strained and persuasion is stretched to the breaking-point. Consider the following representative examples: first, in the encounter of major world religions; second, from the third world; and third, from within a first world church.

(a) The open encounter of the world's religions represents one of the most promising, yet also one of the most pressing contexts for contemporary religious discourse. Religious plurality is inescapable. Facing up to this fact appears to offer rich opportunities for dialogue, but it is by no means an easy road to travel.

The landscape has changed in the last few decades. The longstanding strategies for maintaining traditional divisions, re-enforcing doctrines of superiority, or claiming revelatory uniqueness have all but eroded. No one in any religious tradition can evade the fact of religious plurality—not without, that is, the most hardened self-delusion. It is no longer possible (and it was possible in former days) to be indifferent to the existence and value of other traditions, or to maintain an uncritical air of superiority. The fundamental question posed by the fact of religious plurality is now unavoidable: what does it mean and how should we live when we fully recognize that our own religious tradition is but one among many? In the Christian world, the old dogmas of revelatory supremacy simply appear counter-factual and the turn inward and away from encounter with others—under the guise of private spirituality or under a sectarian banner—appears increasingly impractical. Even the relatively recent language of progressive theologians like Karl Rahner—to wit, that non-Christians are "anonymous Christians" and hence can and should be respected by Christians—proves shaky and untenable, if not hegemonic and imperialistic.[33] The problems are no less exigent for other religions. How feeble claims of special election (Judaism), finality (Islam) or all-encompassing universality (Hinduism) look in the midst of the unbridled religious plurality in the world.[34] It is in this changed religious environment that we hear calls for new—more open and respectful—ways of discourse, replacing centuries of religious arrogance, contempt, neglect, and paternalism.

This new, world-wide context for religious discourse has emerged for several reasons. First, the demands on religious consciousness arise at least in part because of the rapidly changing technological and political scene. Instantaneous world-wide communications, for instance, not only bring people closer to each other; they also create an atmosphere of political immediacy quite different from that formerly imposed by European colonialism. Second, the new context for discourse issues from a new form of western universalism, now articulated through liberal academic forums under the title of multiculturalism. The ideals of diversity, criticism, open exchange, etc. reflect the linguistic mentality of academic life in a liberal culture, and this mentality has mandated adjustment on the part of the world's religions. Third, the shifting context for religious discourse also has arisen from the recognition by some Christian theologians that open and respectful dialogue is itself a faithful (and hence, necessary) enactment of Christian love. This amazingly belated recognition has led to some very creative postures toward interreligious dialogue—to wit, that faithfulness to Christ lies precisely in the self-emptying openness of dialogue.[35] Fourth, dialogue between the religions has arisen because of the infusion of non-Christian voices into western societies, including the academic world of religious studies. And finally, dialogue among the religions is made imperative and urgent by threats of violence and war. As Hans Küng puts it, "the most fanatical, the cruelest political struggles are those that have been colored, inspired, and legitimized by religion."[36] Certainly the list of wars fueled by religious-ethnic hatred in this *fin de siècle* period underscores Küng's point. Dialogue, consequently, becomes an act of global responsibility.

Interreligious dialogue can bring significant and striking discoveries. Even here, however, there is disagreement. There are those who find dialogue leading to the discovery of broad commonalities among religions. John Hick, for instance, speaks of the "universe of faiths" centering upon a common God. In his words, "he is the sum, the originative source of light, whom all the religions reflect in their own ways."[37] Others are more cautious, making only tentative proposals for language that might be shared between two traditions. Gordon Kaufman, for example, is deliberately experimental in putting forth the hypothesis that the Christian idea of God's self-emptying love strikes a common chord with the Buddhist notion of emptiness.[38] A third result of interreligious dialogue has to do with what interlocutors discover about their own traditions (the "intrareligious dialogue") after encountering the claims of someone else's religion. For many, the discovery of the alien and the encounter with another tradition casts a new light on one's own tradition.[39] This can produce new forms of self-examination within a religious world, including novel and controversial reassessments of key doctrines. The debate within Christian theology over the uniqueness of Jesus is a case in point.[40] There is, finally, another less noticed but still important repercussion of interreligious dialogue: it has mandated a new, closer working relationship between historians of religion and theologians. Theologians now find themselves informed by the history of religions; and historians find themselves pulled from their position as neutral observers into discussions of truth with advocates of different traditions.[41]

What is important about all this for my purposes are the effects interreligious dialogue has on the life and practice of religious discourse. In the dialogue among representatives of different traditions, there is the stark realization of the urgency and importance of dialogue, mixed with the unsettling perception of the difficulties and complexities at hand in this form of discourse. Interreligious dialogue is at once compelling in its possibilities and overwhelming in its challenges. A clear sign of this creative tension is that dialogue has become an issue in its own right. The imperative to dialogue, consequently, mandates that participants step back and reflect on the nature, the methods, and the criteria for engaging in dialogue. A considerable bulk of the literature concerned with interreligious dialogue, in fact, now is devoted to these kinds of theoretical and methodological questions: what is the point of dialogue? how should dialogue proceed? what will adjudicate differences between speakers? The practice of dialogue, in other words, has engendered a corresponding theory of dialogue.[42]

This development, I suggest, is crucial: it signals the recognition of the communicative and probative problems at hand in this venue for religious discourse. Dialogue among the religions takes interlocutors to the limits of understanding and rationality. Ironically, the prospects and the obstacles lie just there.

(b) Perhaps the most revolutionary development in Christian studies over the last two decades has occurred in the midst of third world struggles for human dignity and social justice. Religious leaders and theologians in Latin America, Africa, and Asia have rekindled awareness of the call to liberating action and the preferential option for the poor—two features of Hebrew and Christian scriptures long buried in the lethargy of first world, institutional Christendom. The unifying challenge of these liberation theologies, despite the different cultural contextualizations behind them, is to participate in the emergence of the kingdom of God through concrete forms of personal, social, and political activity.

One of the most striking leitmotifs of these theologies is their brutal encounter with the brokenness of human discourse, including religious discourse. In this regard, concern with religious discourse is anything but a barren academic exercise. Apartheid South Africa provided a good case in point. An ecumenical evaluation of the apartheid system in South Africa, titled "The Kairos Document; Challenge to the Church," succinctly captures what apartheid meant for the majority in that country:

> Apartheid is a system whereby a minority regime elected by one small section of the population is given an explicit mandate to govern in the interests of, and for the benefit of, the white community. Such a mandate or policy is by definition hostile to the common good of all the peoples. In fact because it tries to rule in the exclusive interests of whites and not in the interests of all, it ends up ruling in a way that is not even in the interests of those whites. It becomes an enemy of all the people. A tyrant. A totalitarian regime. A reign of terror.[43]

Apartheid radically divides human beings to serve the economic, political and cultural interests of a small minority. The majority suffer the degradation of powerlessness and marginalization. Apartheid dehumanizes by division.

What is so interesting about the "Kairos Document" is its analysis of how the church in South Africa embodies apartheid in itself. As it notes, "the Church is divided."

> More and more people are now saying that there are in fact two Churches in South Africa—a White Church and a Black Church. Even with the same denomination there are in fact two Churches. In the life and death conflict between different social forces that has come to a head in South Africa today, there are Christians (or at least people who profess to be Christians) on both sides of the conflict—and some who are trying to sit on the fence![44]

Those who profess the "same" religion dwell on either side of apartheid. Christian discourse is divided and splintered.

In the document's analysis, there are three "theologies" or forms of discourse within the "Christian" churches of South Africa: 1) There is a state theology which shrouds itself in selective biblical exegesis in order to sanctify its own privileges in the name of a "law and order" ordained by God.[45] Statements from Andres Treurnicht, the leader of the pro-apartheid Conservative Party, provide vivid evidence of this form of Christian discourse, notably his contention that there is biblical legitimation for apartheid.[46] 2) There is also a "church theology," a perspective common among the leadership of the "so-called 'English-speaking' Churches," which preaches reconciliation and peace in South Africa, while remaining silent about the justice and repentance necessary for true peace. 3) Finally, the "Kairos Document" describes and endorses a "prophetic theology." Rooted in the biblical memory of suffering and promise of liberation, and grounded in social analysis of South African divisions, this form of Christian discourse engages in a "confrontational" denunciation of apartheid and a hope-filled, pastoral annunciation of liberation.

The divisions of discourse described by the "Kairos Document" represent what Jon Sobrino calls an "epistemological break."[47] This term carries two meanings for Sobrino, both of which shine through the Kairos Document's rhetorical analysis of the divisions within the South African churches. There, is on the one hand, a descriptive point: the way the world is known through the resources of biblical tradition is broken apart and held in opposition, leaving communication between these different "theologies" incoherent and futile. On the other hand, the epistemological break speaks evaluatively of the different ways scriptural resources are marshaled to speak to the world of apartheid. That is, the prophetic theology claims title to an "epistemological privilege": it knows and speaks accurately and correctly to the situation in South Africa. Both descriptively and evaluatively, therefore, the "Kairos Document" points up a rupture in the way Christians speak their perceptions and judgment of the world around them. Reminiscent of Ernesto Cardenal's dialogue discussed earlier, the dialogue between these Christian languages (theologies) appears impossible.

Given the severity marking this venue for religious discourse, it is truly amazing to find anyone speaking of dialogue without compromising the majority's demands for justice. Yet this is precisely what Desmond Tutu did. The General Secretary of the South African Council of Churches (SACC) since 1978 and winner of the Nobel Peace Prize in 1984, Tutu persisted in his call for critical but rational dialogue between the White apartheid government and leaders of the majority community. His address to the Eloff Commission—a government commission investigating charges that the SACC illegally received funds from abroad for the purpose of instigating unrest in South Africa—speaks directly to his commitment to dialogue. Speaking for the SACC, he told the white ministers: "We believe in negotiation, discussion and dialogue." Speaking for himself, he underscored his faith in "dialogue and meeting" by chronicling his many efforts to engage white officials. But he concedes that with each effort "to engage them in dialogue, . . . we have been rebuffed."[48]

In the situation described by the "Kairos Document," of course, Tutu is walking a dangerous road. Even to speak about dialogue cannot help but look naive and compromising. Because of this, it is important to be precise about just what kind of discourse Tutu has in mind. Like many liberation theologians, Tutu rejects the idea of neutral ground between the oppressive minority and the oppressed majority. There are no easy form of "reconciliation and forgiveness" without fundamental conversion and the establishment of justice. So too, Tutu speaks uninhibitedly of God taking the side of the oppressed. There is, therefore, no sense of uncritical compromise or neutrality in Tutu's sense of dialogue. Indeed, his proposals for dialogue with the different parties influencing events in South Africa are decidedly critical and demanding; he is fully aware of the obstacles attendant on dialogue in this situation, as he salts his appeals with repeated warnings of violence. For Tutu, dialogue is the last non-violent chance for the White community. It is—literally—either dialogue or bloodshed. Fully cognizant of the rigidity of apartheid, and yet stubborn in his hopes for rational discourse leading to just and peaceful change in South Africa, Tutu grasps at dialogue. It remains, however, a precarious possibility.

What the case of South African Christianity suggests, I believe, is something very basic about religious discourse. In this venue, discourse appears radically and irremediably fractured. Rifts of enormous proportions—at once racial, economic and religious—make intelligible and rational dialogue all but impossible. What a religious leader like Desmond Tutu demands, therefore, stands at the very outreaches of possibility.

(c) Another rupture in discourse has appeared in the United States over the issue of abortion. I think, in particular, of the attacks and ultimatums from the Roman Catholic right (including some powerful prelates) directed against Catholic politicians and voters in recent elections. Here, once again, we find the hermeneutical and probative fibers of religious discourse stretched to the breaking-point. Dialogue appears imperative, but unlikely if not impossible.

The American presidential race of 1984 provides a case in point. During the campaign, democratic vice-presidential candidate Geraldine Ferraro came under attack from then Archbishop O'Connor for her views on abortion. Ferraro claimed to be against abortion personally, but unwilling to take a public stand against access to abortion. Her views were private and they would not affect her decisions as an elected official. O'Connor lambasted Ferraro for this distinction. Catholic public officials, he claimed, must carry Catholic teaching on abortion into the realm of public policy. Ferraro, for her part, appeared unprepared to argue her position persuasively.

At this point the discourse broadened. New York Governor Mario Cuomo entered the debate, attempting to offer a more articulate defense of Ferraro's position. Cuomo began with a plea for rational conversation: all will benefit, he argued, "if suspicion is replaced by discussion, innuendo by dialogue."[49] Given this, Cuomo speaks about abortion as a person with dual commitments—at once faithful to his Catholic tradition and responsible to the electorate which put him in office. Privately, he renounces abortion. Publicly, however, the matter is more complex. As a citizen he is legally free to hold that his "religious beliefs would serve well as an article of our universal public morality." But as an elected official he has other responsibilities to consider. There are, he notes, limits to responsible public advocacy for an elected official. Unrestricted advocacy of religious values, possibly leading to legislation affecting all citizens, would constitute a dangerous assault on the freedom of those who hold differing religious values. Cuomo concludes, therefore, that the struggle to have the political system "adopt certain articles of our belief as part of public morality is not a matter of doctrine: it is a matter of prudential political judgment." Sometimes religious beliefs must remain private, not finding public and legal expression. The key, for Cuomo, is to find ways of expressing religious beliefs (e.g., reverence for life), while at the same time respecting the pluralistic democracy in which we live.

Cuomo's position met with some fiery criticisms. O'Connor, for his part, answered that Catholic voters have the obligation to vote for candidates who would work to legislate those values at the heart of Catholic doctrine. Religious teaching must issue in public policy. Less stridently, Representative Henry J. Hyde of Illinois rejected the Ferraro-Cuomo distinction between private morality and public policy. In his words,

> The question today is not whether a Roman Catholic commitment is compatible with American public office; the question is whether the American experiment can survive the sterilization of the public arena that takes place when religiously based values are systematically ruled out of order in the public discourse.[50]

The Catholic public official, Hyde contends, bears the responsibility to lead the effort to establish a public consensus against abortion. The first step to that end is to allow "appeal to religiously based values" to have a place in "the public debate over the public business." Until that happens, he contends, "the abortion debate will remain a case of barely restrained 'civil war carried on by other means.'"[51]

Hyde's image of "civil war" is fully apt, given the enmity and rancor fueling this Catholic exchange. Despite their substantive differences, Hyde and Cuomo prove the exception to the rule when they plead for rational and civil discourse over these questions. The same appeal for dialogue is heard in Joseph Cardinal Bernadin's efforts to articulate a "consistent ethic of life." His purpose is to show "that success on any one of the issues threatening life requires a concern for the broader attitude in society about respect for life."[52] As he puts it, "the viability of a principle depends on the consistency of its application." The power of this statement is the challenge it makes to Catholics on both the political right and left. It demands, for instance, that conservative Catholics who are opposed to abortion also think seriously of how respect for life applies to the nuclear arms race or to welfare policy; and it requires liberal Catholics who are resolute in their opposition to war and in their support of social welfare programs to think seriously of how respect for life applies to the unborn. Bernadin hopes, in other words, to initiate public dialogue on these life issues. He prods Catholics to learn the art of dialogue. Thus, for example, Catholics should share their vision with the wider society, but do so "in nonreligious terms which others of different faith convictions might find morally persuasive." Moreover, he insists, Catholics "should maintain and clearly articulate our religious convictions but also maintain our civil courtesy."[53] Given the sharpness of most public discourse on abortion in recent years, Bernadin's plea for rational dialogue is astonishing.

What this debate between Catholic politicians and bishops illustrates is just how essential and yet precarious public discourse on abortion has become. Indeed, the issue at hand is not simply abortion, but also communication and dialogue. Just as the trials of interreligious dialogue give rise to theoretical reflection on the nature and criteria of such discourse, so too here, the "civil war" of religious words over abortion engenders reflection on the place of religious discourse in the public setting. In what ways and to what degree can religious values be brought to bear on problems in the public arena? Can religion speak rationally in the open venue of political discourse? Or more basically, should it do so?[54] These questions, as yet, remain unanswered—or I should say, the many answers to these questions remain unresolved. As in the other two examples of contemporary religious discourse, the possibility of intelligible and rational discourse remains in question.

These three examples arise in widely varied contexts of contemporary religious discourse. One takes place between different religions, one within a single religion, and one within an individual church. Despite the differences in venue, they share three key things which are important for this study.

First, each takes place where religious discourse reaches its limits. Those who enter into such discussions—by chance or by fate—find themselves at the edge of possibility. What might be achieved appears of great value, but what can be achieved seems very tenuous. In these situations, interlocutors find themselves entering open and uncontrolled situations for discourse. They are called to speak in contexts in which what Richard Rorty calls "normal discourse" breaks down. For Rorty,

> normal discourse is that which is conducted within an agreed-upon set of conventions about what counts as relevant contribution, what counts as answering a question, what counts as having a good argument for that answer or a good criticism of it. Abnormal discourse is what happens when someone joins in the discourse who is ignorant of these conventions or who sets them aside.[55]

If these three cases of religious discourse are at all typical, and I think they are, then a great deal of contemporary religious discourse is abnormal in Rorty's sense. In each instance, discourse occurs where perspectives, practices and standards are unclear and up for grabs. Certainly this is the case where Buddhists engage Christians or when Jews encounter Muslims. So too this abnormality holds in the tense and nebulous discourse between an oppressive South African government and the majority population, even though both are "Christian." And finally it seems equally unclear how Catholics opposed over the morality of abortion can and will speak with each other, despite the fact that they are members of the same ecclesial community. Nothing is obvious or easy about discourse in any of these situations. Interlocutors are expected to speak intelligibly and to argue rationally where the very meaning of intelligibility and the scope of rationality are unsettled. And, like the literary dialogues mentioned earlier, discourse in these living situations is driven to the limits of possibility by a number of different factors. Cultural gaps, racial prejudices, economic inequalities, and differences in moral sensibility conspire in one combination or another to stretch discourse to the breaking-point. And violence looms on the horizon.

Second, each of these cases of religious discourse gives rise to methodological reflections on the intelligibility and rationality of discourse. In response to these cases, religious discourse becomes a problem for itself. It is true, of course, that scholars of religion have long been aware of the problems attending religious language. Many of the classics of Western religious thought from Augustine's *On Christian Doctrine*, through Aquinas' reflections on analogy, to twentieth century philosophical debates on the verifiability of religious words have puzzled over the workings of religious language. Most of these works, however, deal with semantic problems (how words refer) and questions of truth (whether and how propositions correspond to reality). Only occasionally did rhetorical or herme-neutical concerns take center stage, as in Augustine's discussion of the weariness which arises from the inability to communicate clearly to catechumens or in Schleiermacher's reflections on biblical hermeneutics.[56] Today, the concerns with religious language are social and communicative. How can people of different stripes talk with each other intelligibly and rationally? Why does so much re-ligious discourse degenerate into misunderstanding and raillery? What principles or norms, if any, might guide talk about religion? These questions constitute the starting point for this book: the communicative and probative problems, tasks, and ideals for religious discourse.

These kinds of reflections have been at the center of much philosophical and theological literature of late. The debates on rationality and relativism in phi-losophy of science and cultural anthropology have set the terms for investigating the continuities and discontinuities of understanding through history and across different cultures. Philosophers like Richard Rorty and Richard Bernstein have pursued the hermeneutical implications of these debates—Rorty emphasizing the contingency of all human vocabularies and advocating a conversational (as opposed to a foundationalist) approach to philosophical inquiry; Bernstein ad-dressing the social and political bases for understanding and communication. Behind Rorty and Bernstein, the philosophical hermeneutics of Hans-Georg Gada-mer and the theoretical sociology of Jürgen Habermas have provided the philo-sophical categories for understanding the nature of understanding and for de-limiting the scope of rational communicative action. Drawing on all of the above, Christian theologians like David Tracy and Edward Schillebeeckx have explored the hermeneutical landscape of theological discourse; while others, like Elizabeth Schüssler Fiorenza, Juan Luis Segundo, and Johannes Baptist Metz, have focused more specifically on the ideological distortions which plague theological interpre-tation and discourse.[57]

While I have no wish to circumscribe this literature too narrowly, I think it is safe to point out just how central the ideas of dialogue and communication are to these authors. Certainly this is in large part due to the influence of Gadamer's philosophical hermeneutics (which gives dialogue center stage) and of Haber-mas' theoretical sociology (which makes communication its central concern). Along these same lines, the philosophy of dialogue forwarded by Martin Buber and the theory of dialogical imagination found in the works of M. M. Bakhtin have played a central role in highlighting the importance of dialogue in human existence and culture.[58] At the same time, the analytical schools of contempo-rary philosophy increasingly have developed the social and discursive views of language at play in the later Wittgenstein.[59] Under all of these influences, the "linguistic turn" in academic culture has itself turned dialogical. It is no accident, therefore, that religious and theological studies have tapped into this literature, since the problems of discourse and the possibilities of dialogue are exactly what is at stake in contemporary efforts to speak with others about religion.

Third, the concern with discourse and the appeal to dialogue heard in each of these three venues for contemporary religious discourse bespeaks certain fundamental anxieties which mark post-modern culture. As these examples make plain, there are two basic fears present in contemporary venues for religious discourse. On the one side there is the fear of fragmentation and chaos. From this perspective, interreligious dialogue portends a relativistic confusion of voices, third world religious discourse threatens irreparable divisions, and discourse on abortion presages moral anarchy. On the other side, there is a prevalent anxiety about the effects of power and domination on discourse. From this point of view, interreligious dialogue may yet harbor patronizing stances and surreptitious strategies of conquest, extra weight must be given to third world prophetic voices of liberation in order to counter the tyrannical power of the oppressor's voice, and the continuing danger in the Catholic debate over abortion lies with the authoritarian intrusion of the Roman hierarchy. Religious discourse today bears all of the symptoms of post-modernity.

Though fundamentally different stances, these two contemporary perspectives share a common reality: they both are keenly aware of the fragility and precariousness of religious discourse. Both are wary of the irrational forces at work in religion. Each fears the breakdown of language and the outbreak of violence—albeit from opposite causes. The appeal for dialogue in each case, therefore, reflects the sense of importance and urgency operating in contemporary religious life and study. Dialogue has taken center stage. This constitutes the first plank upon which this study rests.

(3) Dialogue as Literary Genre

The literary dialogue—in its many and varied forms—represents an important but often overlooked artistic analogue to the actual practice of living dialogue. Thinking about the problems and possibilities of dialogue, therefore, can be enhanced by a turn to literature in dialogue form. This is the second plank upon which this study is built.

My claim—that a literary turn can serve philosophical ends—needs some explanation, since the dominant strains of current philosophical thinking about religion regularly ignore the relevance of literary genre. My approach builds upon what Martha Nussbaum calls the "organic connection" between a text's form and its content. The choice of genre serves an expressive function. In her words,

Style itself makes claims, expresses its own sense of what matters. Literary form is
not separable from philosophical content, but is, itself, a part of content—an integral
part, then, of the search for and the statement of truth."[60]

A text's form not only conveys the author's conception. It also gives a demeanor
to the point, colors the message with character, puts a twist on its meaning, and
loads the ideas with implications. In these various ways, the author expresses
something to the reader which is not reducible to the content stripped of all form.
The content, after all, is nothing without its expressive form, any more than Aristotelian "matter" is conceivable aside from form. The literary form, in other
words, is integral to the author's act of communication. Without it, nothing is said
at all. And, moreover, without a form which fits (or suits) the intended content,
nothing is said adequately. Certain genres, as Nussbaum observes, have a larger
capacity for expressing the content. Those forms which are "more complex, more
allusive, more attentive to particulars," for instance, more "fully and fittingly" express complex and ambiguous notions, while genres which are intentionally
simple, direct and formal prove ill-suited to express such messages.[61]

On the other hand, the choice of genre also performs a "statement-making"
function. A text's style, in other words, is not simply a vehicle for a content which
could just as readily be conveyed through alternative genres; rather, the author's
decision about style and form itself makes a statement to the reader about the
world and what to expect in it. A text speaks as much by showing as by saying.
Again in Nussbaum's language,

> That telling itself—the selection of genre, formal structures, sentences, vocabulary,
> of the whole manner of addressing the reader's sense of life—all of this expresses a
> sense of a life and of value, a sense of what matters and what does not, of what
> learning and communicating are, of life's relations and connections."[62]

Nussbaum's contention is that certain genres (for her, certain forms of narrative)
are more adequate than others at signaling to their readers that life is complex, allusive, and filled with surprises. While the first function of style affects the expression of content, the second speaks directly to the reader in its own right. The
reader, therefore, must listen attentively not only to what is said, but also to how
the author makes the point. Both functions of genre—expressive and statement-
making— make a text's style an integral part of the author's power to speak.

What Nussbaum claims for narrative forms of literature holds true for literary
dialogues as well.[63] To make this connection clear and convincing, of course, will
require a great deal of evidence from close reading of actual texts—something I
will provide in the chapters to follow. The proof, as they say, lies in the pudding.
For the moment, however, I want to offer a preliminary sketch of how form and

content function together in literary dialogues—looking initially at the genre's expressive function; then treating its statement-making value; and lastly, offering some initial illustrations of the dialogue's literary range and form.

(a) *Dialogue's Expressive Function.* As a working definition, I understand a "dialogue" to be a form of discourse established with a reading audience through imitative textual discourse. What this definition immediately suggests is that there are two layers of discourse at work in a dialogue: one between author and reader, and another between the characters within the text. A literary dialogue, then, is a dialogue by means of dialogue.

The first layer of discourse is primary and ultimate (since the dialogue is written to express what an author wants to say), but it depends upon the second layer of discourse (what goes on within the text) for its fruition. What an author has to say to a reading audience, in other words, may be prior in intention and purpose, but the author only speaks through the discourse as it is portrayed in the written text. Moreover, it is this textual discourse that the audience encounters through reading. This is what the reader sees. This is the discourse first requiring interpretation, for there is no direct access to the author except through the interlocutors' discourse. The author and reader meet only through the complex prism of the fictional discourse. Because of this, the form and style of discourse portrayed within the dialogue, plays a crucial, even basic, role in shaping—and hence, expressing—what the author says and what the reader understands.

The expressive power of the dialogue, therefore, lies in the text's capacity to represent or portray actual discourse. The dialogue is an imitative genre. Its composition requires an "imitative art." Nothing is more fundamental to its literary nature. And what an author imitates in composing a dialogue is the discursive exchanges of living interlocutors. Writers of dialogues, therefore, take Horace's advice to heart: as he puts it in "The Art of Poetry," those who practice an "imitative art" must "look to life and manners for a model, and draw from thence living words."[64] When, consequently, a dialogue represents conversation on a vexing topic like religion, the text mimes the give and take of different voices in dialogue, replete with all the forces and pressures which bring religious discourse to the edges of intelligibility and rationality. They mime—as we saw from the dialogues of Voltaire, Cardenal, Augustine and Murdoch—the complex and fragile contour of living discourse. In so doing, the dialogue's mimetic capacity yields a literary form which fits the hermeneutical and probative texture of actual religious discourse. The mimetic form, in short, suits the content up for discussion.

Though countless dialogues on a great variety of issues have been written over the centuries, the genre's imitative nature rarely has been understood. Aristotle, for instance, was puzzled about how to classify the dialogue. He regarded the "conversations of Socrates" as a nameless "form of imitation" to be grouped with the mime-like "farces of Sophron and Xenarchus."[65] Dialogues perplexed Aristotle because they combine an imitation of real life with high-flown metaphysical speculations and didactic interests. They "imitate by language alone" and thus are "poetic," yet they share substantive theoretical concerns, like a "theory of medicine or physical philosophy," and thus are not purely mimetic. Dialogues become, in the words of K. J. Wilson, "incomplete fictions." So categorized, Aristotle says nothing more about this genre, thereby imprisoning "dialogue categorically in the silence of a nameless art."[66]

But what puzzled Aristotle was celebrated by later masters of dialogue. Witness Erasmus boasting that "whereas Socrates brought philosophy down from heaven to earth; I have brought it even into the games, informal conversations, and drinking parties."[67] Erasmian dialogues, as will be evident in chapter six, revel in reflecting the down-to-earth ways in which weighty philosophical and religious questions get bandied about by the most various and ordinary of characters. Conversations typically occur, therefore, in the most mundane contexts (at roadside inns or festive gatherings) and between undeniably common speakers (monks, soldiers, harlots, butchers, and scholars). The same holds for the dialogues dealt with at the beginning of this chapter: Voltaire's dialogue occurs in a bookstore; Cardenal's in a *campesino* village; Augustine's in a country villa; and Murdoch's at one interlocutor's home. Each conversation mimes living voices. Dialogues— as M. M. Bakhtin argues—resist the dominating force of a single, authorial voice, even when such domination is the author's rhetorical intention. Instead, they mandate that an author work within the social limits of actual opposition, where a plurality of voices must be faced squarely in the nitty-gritty give and take of ordinary conversation. As a result, they reflect the achievements of insight and mutual understanding as well as the unseemly maneuvering and heavy-handed ploys for position, all of which are the stuff of living discourse. In both ways, dialogues imitate living conversation.

Still, Aristotle's distrust of the poetic purposes written into literary dialogues was not unfounded, for dialogues are far more orderly and intellectual than living discourse. Although dialogues do portray human interaction, with speakers and listeners acting and reacting to each other, the mimetic quality of these texts is acutely specialized. They copy the interaction of disparate voices, yet they are cleaned up; or as one commentator on dialogue put it, they are "purged of [life's] chaos and its intemperance."[68] Even a dialogue like Arthur Schopenhauer's "On Immortality; A Dialogue," which vividly reflects the sharp and stinging flavor of actual conversation, allows the interaction of ideas of self and death to take center stage. When, for instance, Philalethes characterizes the question of personal immortality as "childish and most ridiculous"—since personal existence is in truth the "universal will to live"—Thrasymachos responds with acrimony: "You're childish yourself and most ridiculous, like all philosophers!"[69] Schopenhauer captures the belligerence which can infest living conversation, but the dialectic of ideas is not overtaken by the characters' passions. The conversation portrayed in dialogues like this is heavily formalized to reveal certain things (e.g., the unfolding of an argument, the process of persuasion, or the genesis of confusion) that would not be so pronounced in living discourse.

In this regard, dialogues try to do two things at once, and the expressive function of the genre depends on maintaining the tension of this combination. They are fictional, and hence, they imaginatively emulate the drama of living conversation; but, unlike drama for the stage, the drama of dialogue hangs predominantly on the dialectic of ideas and words. They are, therefore, realistic in portrayal, though the portrayal is truncated and somewhat idealized by the concern with the intellectual drama of ideas and theories. Yet for all this intellectual weight, the dialogue persists with enough characterization to call to the reader's mind the image of personal speakers interacting in conversation. This is true even in dialogues in which the characters are rendered impersonally—even anonymously—with names like "A," "B," or "C".[70] As a genre, therefore, dialogues are mimetically incomplete. They imitate the confusing and often confused nature of living conversation, even while they attempt to articulate and highlight the ideas at stake in the conversation. In its varied ways, the genre lives in and for this tension. It is precisely this aspect of the dialogue that serves to express the author's intended content with both intellectual pointedness and artistic realism.

The peculiar mimetic form of the literary dialogue makes the genre especially well suited to represent discourse on religious questions and issues. In Nussbaum's terms, the dialogue's complex and allusive form proves especially "fitting" to express the complex and ambiguous results of peoples' efforts to speak about religion. In a preliminary way, the dialogues of Voltaire, Cardenal, Augustine and Murdoch illustrate both the expressive fit between the dialogue form and the basic tensions affecting the intelligibility and rationality of religious discourse. A more sustained argument for this use of the dialogue form will appear in the chapters to follow. For the present, suffice it to say that the mimetic portrayal of living discourse which is peculiar to the dialogue provides ample space and sufficient form to capture expressively the ambiguities of meaning and truth at play in religious discourse. The expressive function of the dialogue, consequently, warrants careful examination of the workings of discourse portrayed within the texts of literary dialogues.

(b) *Dialogue's Statement-Making Function.* As Nussbaum tells us, literary genre not only contributes to an author's power of communication by imaginatively expressing the intended content; it also makes a statement in its own right to the reader. This clearly holds true for dialogues.

In choosing to write in dialogue form, an author both imitates living voices (through the discourse portrayed in the text) and participates in dialogue (by engaging an audience who reads the text). What we have in the dialogue is at once two layers of discourse: first, that among the characters; and second, that between the author and the intended readers. The first layer tells the reader something about the activities of living voices. The interlocutors' discourse mimes actual discourse, and, thereby, expresses to the reader something about the reality of that which is represented. This is, as I have said, the expressive value of the dialogue form. By this feature of the text, the reader is directed to think about the reality of discourse. At the same time, however, the written dialogue constructs and facilitates a dialogue between author and audience. In this respect, the genre directs the reader not outward toward reality but back to the author standing behind the text. As a result, readers must approach the written text not only to learn something about real discourse, but also to learn what the dialogue's author has to say to them.

The author makes a statement to readers through the choice and use of genre. In a sense, this function of the text's form was already apparent when we considered the expressive value of the dialogue genre. For while it is the author who imitates living discourse through the dialogue, it is also the author who makes these fictions incomplete. The author, after all, creates the world of the dialogue, moves the speakers and orchestrates their interaction, and directs the movement to its preappointed end. Dialogical mimesis is bent toward the purposes of the author. Dialogues, therefore, reveal an author's imagination at work through the ways opposition is perceived, portrayed, and managed within the written dialogue. They render public traces of the author's dialogical imagination. Consequently, they establish a dialogue between author and audience, with the artistic text's imitation of living voices standing in the middle. The mimetic power of the dialogue (portrayed in the interlocutors' discourse) invites the reader into an actual (non-mimetic) dialogue with the author; or, put another way, the incompletely fictional character of the dialogue, caused by the author's control over the characters' discourse, throws the reader back into the dialogue searching to glean the author's message.

In this dialogue between author and reader, it is the form, once again, that is instructive. In the first place, the way in which the genre is deployed reveals something about what the author perceives to be at stake in religious discourse. Authors of dialogues not only speak to readers about specific religious topics, the existence of God, for instance, or the meaning of redemption. They also say something about the activities and processes of discourse on these topics, and they make this statement about the discourse through the crafting of the interlocutors' dialogue. They are sensitive, in other words, to the rhetorical and probative processes of discourse on religious questions, and they convey their perceptions through the particular shape given to the written dialogue. Voltaire, as we saw, was particularly concerned with the genesis of misunderstanding in his cross-cultural dialogue; and Augustine aims not only to refute the Academics' skepticism, but to show how impossible it is to speak with someone who denies that anyone (even a wise person) ever possesses wisdom. Both tell their readers something vital about the possibilities and the difficulties of communication and persuasion, and they accomplish this not through direct (textual) statement, but by showing their point happening in and through the interlocutors' conversation.

The reader of a dialogue, therefore, must pay special attention to this statement-making function of the dialogue form. Failing to do so would mean reading the text as if it were a verbatim representation (like an audio recording) of actual discourse, thereby missing the fact that what the dialogue means is not reducible to what is represented. A taped recording merely repeats what is said: it does not create the conversation, it does not embellish it, and it does not offer its own interpretation, even though it does confront the listener with something novel—both by detaching the subject from its original environment and by calling attention to parts and forms of speech not always noticed by the naked ear.[71] The art of dialogue calls for something different. Like the recording it imitates living words, but unlike the recording it deliberately is creative and interpretive. The polemical dialogue, for instance, does not merely repeat verbatim what an adversary has to say; it is designed, rather, to let the reader see just how demented and ludicrous the opponent is. It accomplishes this not by saying it outright and not by simply repeating the enemy's words, but by showing the vacuity and folly of their position when confronted with those who uphold true and correct belief. Something similar occurs in ironic dialogues, as will be evident in chapters four and five. The ironic use of the dialogue form depends on indirection, where the author's voice may directly conflict with what is represented in the interlocutor's words. The presence of an author, therefore, is a disadvantage only if one seeks pristine duplication of reality. What authorship contributes to the dialogue is a distinct benefit, however, if one values the nuances of meaning and the subtleties of design at work in what Horace calls the "imitative arts." What is lacking in the exactitude of imitation is gained back in the author's artistic statement, which in turn allows us to glean something new in what the text imitates. Dialogues are both imitative and artistic, and their value lies in the tension of these elements.[72]

But, in the second place, reading these texts with an eye on the author's use of the dialogue form also lets us see their authors in a fresh light. Too often the interpretation of philosophical and theological authors—whether Anselm, Hume, or Diderot—fastens onto positions and arguments without giving the least consideration to the form of writing used by these authors. Rarely has attention been devoted to the significance of these writers' option for the dialogue. The importance of genre is ignored. David Hume, for instance, most frequently is read either through his non-dialogical texts (the *Treatise on Human Nature* or the *Enquiries*, for instance); or, worse yet, his *Dialogues Concerning Natural Religion* is read as if it were a treatise forwarding a purely logical critique of the argument from design. The same thing occurs in readings of Plato as a systematic thinker. Given the importance of genre for an authors' statement about the workings of discourse, this neglect of the dialogue genre is not only unwarranted; it also is detrimental to a well-rounded and adequate understanding of these authors.

To put this point more positively, we can learn something new about an author, can see their work in a new and fresh light, if we as readers learn to listen to the statements they make through the use of the dialogue form. If, as I have argued, a text's genre allows an author to say something about the world of discourse, something which is not said either directly or in what is represented in the text, then we will learn to hear their voices in a novel manner if we learn to attend to their uses of literary form.

(c) *The Range of Literary Dialogues: A Sketch.* The form, as we have seen, plays two decisive roles in speaking about religion: it expresses the complexities and ambiguities typical of conversations on religious questions, and it allows the author to make a statement about the possibilities and difficulties at work in such discourse. What follows in the remainder of this section is a brief sketch of the literary range of the dialogue form. As a genre, the dialogue is richly varied—in history, style, topic, structure and purpose.

The ancient roots of the genre may well lie in the fifth century mimes of Sophron or Xenarchus, if Aristotle is correct. Classical Greek and Roman culture creates the models for all later writers of dialogues in the west: Plato crafting the dialectical arguments typical of Socratic conversation; Cicero creating the more gentle and spacious art of oratorical dialogue; and Lucian of Samasota perfecting the comic practice of satirical dialogue. Dialogues abound across the middle ages, reflecting their classical roots but put to the service of Christian theological inquiry. The sixteenth century witnesses a profusion of dialogues, some in the service of reformation debates (e.g., the works of Ulrich von Hutten) and many devoted to the aspirations of renaissance humanism (e.g., in the works of Erasmus of Rotterdam, Thomas More, and Lorenza Valla). The enlightenment of seventeenth and eighteenth century Europe constitutes one of the most prolific periods for the dialogue genre: Fontenelle, Voltaire, and Denis Diderot in France; George Berkeley, John Locke, and David Hume in England; and in Germany, Gotthold Lessing, Johann Gottfried Herder, and Christoph Wieland. Dialogues continue to be written today: think, for instance, of Iris Murdoch's work already mentioned, as well as the dialogues by Peter Gay, Clodovis Boff, and Paul Feyerabend. What this brief list indicates is the great historical range in which dialogues have been composed. But suggestive as it is, it fails entirely to document the vast number of dialogues written across the ages—some by famous philosophers, theologians, or scientists, but most by writers long forgotten in the annals of western culture.[73]

Dialogues also differ greatly in style, from finely crafted and polished texts like Diderot's *Rameau's Nephew* or Erasmus' "A Pilgrimage for Religion's Sake" (both of which will be examined below) to rough-edged street pamphlets and one column notes in newspapers.[74] Some dialogues bear the stamp of artistic excellence: characters are developed with depth and contour, the discourse is balanced and multi-leveled, and the author either refrains from dominating the opposition or remains hidden behind one or more characters' voices. Others give evidence of the debt they owe to a classical model, and frequently their imitation gives new life and force to their classical paradigm. Such is the case, for instance, in the dialogues of Nicolas Malebranche (rightly called the "French Plato"), where rigorous argumentation and dialectical finesse are represented with vivid clarity.[75] The same holds for the lively and trenchant dialogues of the dead written by H. D. Traill in the manner of Lucian.[76] Many other dialogues are stylistically bound by their author's didactic interests. Some are charming enough, but of little substance (like Erasmus' earliest colloquies, designed, as he says, to attract young boys to the study of letters and to assist them in learning Latin); others are long-winded treatises, arranged as lengthy answers from the master prompted by student questions (as in John the Scot's *Peripheson; On the Division of Nature*).[77] Far too many dialogues, however, are the work of hacks. They are banal, tedious and boring. Characterization, balance of discourse, development—in a word, all the virtues possible to the genre—are laid aside. Such works, naturally, evoke weariness in readers.

Dialogues portray conversations of all kinds, and any topic is fair game—politics, literature, cuisine, and the vagaries of human behavior. In almost every case, a dialogue works where some opposition or difference exists. Thus we find dialogues depicting discourse between Tories and Whigs, between men and women, between Europeans and "savages," between different gods, etc. Literally any opposition can give rise to a dialogue. As we will see in chapter five, there are no limits to who can meet and talk together in the literary dialogue, since people from all cultures and time periods—rich and poor, mighty and weak, famous and common—can be brought together in discussion. It doesn't even matter if the speakers are no longer among the living; they speak again in "dialogues of the dead." In stranger cases, the partner in discussion may not be human at all: thus we find Benjamin Franklin, talking with his gout![78] Or the author's interlocutor may be himself, as is the case in the narcissistic dialogues of Rousseau.[79] When the issue is religion, exchanges occur between faithful believers and resolute skeptics; staunch defenders of orthodoxy and independently minded heretics; Christians of different stripes; Christians and non-Christians; gods and mortals; and so on. The world of discourse is open to anyone who can speak.

Dialogues begin with encounter. Speakers address each other, and, in so doing, they begin the process of constructing a context for their interaction. Even where the speakers' discourse is framed by an introductory narrative (e.g., as in Cicero's *The Nature of the Gods*), it is only through the speakers' encounter that a space for dialogue is established.[80] This initial world-building usually issues from the interlocutors' mutual address and from their references to their surroundings.[81] A world is opened for communicative interaction. Although individual speakers are at home in their respective worlds, they now enter into a new, undeveloped context, to which each will contribute but none may claim. In dialogues, this new context is usually a space apart (in a den, outside a city, etc.); it also tends to be an insular time, an autonomous period (e.g., between high noon and sunset), for chronology is not marked, even though arguments follow one another sequentially. So Cicero's *The Nature of the Gods* takes place at a friend's house during the Latin Festival; Abelard's *Dialogue of a Philosopher with a Jew and a Christian* commences as Abelard is "looking around in a dream"; and Martin Heidegger's "Discourse on Thinking" occurs on a country path.[82] Frequently, the spatial and temporal insularity of the discourse is ensured by omitting any mention of context whatsoever.

As we have seen, the primary mark of dialogical situations is the difference between the speakers. Even where interlocutors are familiar with each other, some contrast appears, some gap arises between them. Extreme cases present speakers entirely unable to communicate with each other. Earlier, we saw an outrageous example of this in Voltaire's little colloquy between a Chinese man and some Dutch intellectuals. The difference between speakers, however, is not always a product of cultural distance. Schopenhauer's dialogue "On Religion" pits two rationalists, who, for all practical purposes, represent two sides of the same view of religion. For both, philosophy surpasses religion in theoretical and practical value. Demopheles, however, argues that religion remains a practical substitute for the masses. Philalethes cannot accept this concession to what is false; for him, religious education "produces a kind of partial paralysis of the brain" leading to "lifelong imbecile bigotry." Religion may be practical, but a fraud is still a fraud.[83] Their dialogue is a fiery exchange, ending in impasse, sarcasm, and a tenuous, seemingly insincere accord. More often, talk about religious issues is marked by less severe forms of opposition, but they are nonetheless formidable. The most common obstacle to religious speech and understanding are situations in which something shared becomes the issue of opposition. Much of Justin Martyr's "Dialogue with Trypho, a Jew," for instance, is occupied with argument over the proper interpretation of Hebrew scripture, a normative resource claimed by Jew and Christian alike.[84] What Jews and Christians share is in dispute. No one in this situation can bridge their opposition.

Dialogues are animated, above all, by the posing of a question. Questions initiate the dynamic flow of the conversation and they sustain this movement once begun. In Hans Georg Gadamer's language,

> To ask a question means to bring into the open. The openness of what is in question consists in the fact that the answer is not settled. It must still be undetermined, in order that a decisive answer can be given."[85]

A question marks the first moment of understanding, as Gadamer says, "when something other, with its own validity, addresses us, becoming questionable."[86] In so doing, the *other* is imagined as *something*, and hence is brought into an analogical relation with the speaker. This imaginative construct takes many forms in religious dialogues. The *other* may be encountered with esteem, as is the case in Klaus Klostermaier's dialogue between a Hindu and a Christian; or the *other* may be envisaged pejoratively, as Theodoret of Cyrus does by conceiving his dialogue partner ("Eranistes") as a patchwork of heresies.[87] There is, in either case, a fundamental openness to the other; but this basic form of social relatedness need not mean they are accepting or even respectful. The Marquis de Sade's traditional priest and the dying hedonist talk and listen to each other, but their mutual communicative openness is a minimal social engagement which is filled in with tension and disdain as the dialogue proceeds.[88] The openness initiated by a question is a beginning, but it is not a principle, much less a principle of respect determining the shape of discussion. In the course of conversation, the way the other is construed is open to constant revision.

Questions build on questions. They invite, prompt, or mandate answers or further questions. The speakers are caught up in this to and from movement; their dialogue is the performance of the movement itself. Gadamer's analysis of play is particularly apt for understanding the dynamics of conversation, since the interlocutors, in a very real sense, are caught up in the cumulative dialogical process which they have initiated. Insofar as the cumulative processes of the dialogue shape the development of individual contribution, Gadamer is correct to say that "all playing is being-played,"[89] for in some conversations, the speakers lose themselves as the subject matter takes over. But this is a rare event, and, if literary dialogues are accurate and vivid portraits of human conversations, it is not the norm. Indeed, speakers rarely lose themselves in the play of talk; rather, they assert themselves in an attempt to effect the course of conversation. The subject matter (e.g., the nature of God, the utility of religion, etc.) is usually up for grabs in the variously competitive assertions of different voices. The playful exchange is charged with the active, probative moves of its players. Speakers and listeners are actively engaged in constructing arguments and marshaling evidence for the positions they uphold. Whatever the opposition involved, dialogues portray a range of strategies, depending upon the author's agenda or goal: some mime Socratic *elenchus*; others practice satire in the spirit of Lucian; many model disputations or become downright polemical; still others are purely didactic; and only a few stage an irenic meeting of the minds.[90]

The argumentative play of religious dialogue transforms every speaker who enters. No one speaks without being transformed by the process. Interlocutors, occasionally, are uplifted and enlightened by sharing each other's traditions, as is the case in Klaus Klostermaier's interreligious dialogue, in which the Hindu and the

Christian are illuminated by the discovery of how much the two traditions share, and humbled by the common insight that Absolute Truth lies beyond each religious tradition.[91] Dialogue can, however, have the opposite effect. In Lucian's "Zeus Catechized," for example, Zeus is humbled by a series of questions, each leading closer to the conclusion that even the gods are subject to fate. Zeus begins as a mighty god, becomes frustrated and indignant at the devastating effect of Cyniscus' seemingly innocent questions ("just this one question"), and finally is exposed as helpless.[92] These two dialogues display extreme forms of transformation: the first is apotheotic; the second deicidal. A more intricate, common, and hence interesting effect of dialogue is the conversion of an interlocutor. Anselm's "Why God Became a Man," which I will treat in chapter two, vividly portrays this kind of transformation. Boso begins, confident in his original assumptions which make anything like a divine incarnation incongruous; he becomes anxious and distressed when he finds that his scheme of justice is too meager to describe God's love for sinners; and, finally, he is overjoyed at the dialogue's end, as anyone might be when relieved of a frightful anxiety. He has been converted, and joy is the natural response.[93]

Dialogues typically portray conversations which do not end with a firm conclusion. The play of question and answer finds provisional resting places, but no finality. The closing exchanges of Herder's *God, Some Conversations*, for instance, ends with just such a note of caution.[94] Similarly, after lengthy discussion, Erasmus' Catholic fish-eater and Protestant butcher resolve to end their discourse, but without any pretension to finality, for the dispute they are engaged in is obviously endless.[95] They agree, ironically, to have further conversations over dinner—veal at the butcher's on Thursday, fish at the fish-eater's on Friday. The same provisional closure occurs in dialogues in which the author seems intent on settling the issue once and for all. Justin's "Dialogue with Trypho," once again, is clearly bent on subduing the Jewish objections of Trypho, yet, curiously, the conversation ends with Trypho intrigued but not at all convinced; room is explicitly left open for future encounters.[96] Moreover, where dialogues do end conclusively, it is usually in sharp division, not agreement, meaning that the dialogue did not achieve any sort of shared finality. The Marquis de Sade's "Dialogue between a Priest and a Dying Man" ends in this kind of sharp division, but, for that very reason, it can make no claims to finality. The prudish priest leaves horrified and disgusted; the libertine dies in the arms of "six women lovelier than the light of day."[97]

Schleiermacher's *Christmas Eve*, perhaps more than any other literary dialogue, illustrates the provisionality, the interminability, but also the opportunity of discourse on religious issues. The evening opens in warmth, beauty, and gaiety; a fitting context for celebrating "the children's festival."[98] The first interpretation of Christmas belongs to the innocent and precocious Sophie, who expresses her joy through sacred music and an imaginative nativity scene. The initial conversations (Ernestine calls it "idle controversy") compare the exterior and interior, the masculine and feminine, and the particular and the universal sides of Christmas; but the preference in each dyad highlights the centrality of the child in Christmas. In Eduard's words, Christmas celebrates "the serene joy of living in the new world we owe to the Child we celebrate," something said in deeds (not words) through Ernestine's meticulous arrangement of the room, through the playful exchange of gifts, through Ernst's rapturous expectation of a "new life" with Friedrike, through Eduard and Ernestine's testimony to the "pure revelation of the divine in my [their] daughter," but, above all, in Sophie's joy and innocence.[99] An extended reflection by the adults follows, the women offering stories which capture their sense of Christmas, the men putting forth their theories of the incarnation. The dialogue ends not with resolution of the different views of Christmas, but with Josef's late entry, berating the men (especially Leonhardt, "this contriving, reflective, dialectical, superintellectual man") for their "tedious and cold" speech-making, and calling everyone back to the "speechless joy" of the child's Christmas:

> Eyes sparkle and dance again, the sign of a beautiful and serene existence within. To my good fortune, I too have become just like a child again. As a child stifles his childish pain, . . . when something is done to arouse his childish joy, so it is with me today.[100]

The closing is, thus, not a conclusion, for in the end we are hurled back from adult abstractions to the immediacy of child-like joy. In this discourse, there is no end, only a beginning and a continuing conversational process. Such is the life of dialogue.

These, then, are some of the prominent features of discourse at work in literary dialogues. Both as imitative works of art and as vehicles for an author's dialogue with a reading audience, the enormous range of discourse captured in these texts provides helpful models for thinking about living discourse, even as the texts themselves engage readers in dialogue. This literary genre, therefore, can teach us a great deal about the nature of religious discourse. This constitutes the second plank of my study.

(4) Dialogues as Philosophical Tutors

This book is about dialogue—that practiced by living people and that imitated in written texts. It is the relationship between the two—between life and art, that is—which offers an important opportunity for understanding something of the nature of religious discourse, as well as providing an occasion for better understanding those classic voices which produce lasting artifacts of religious discourse. Religious dialogue and dialogues on religion go hand in hand.

This confluence of life and art makes for some tricky problems of interpretation, but it also offers up valuable opportunities for the careful reader. The purpose of this book is to address these problems and seize upon those opportunities. The challenge is to read dialogues on several different levels at once. Each level of reading brings its own questions to the text.

It is important, in the first place, to be clear about the intellectual and cultural motivations for turning to dialogues. As I said earlier, post-modern academic culture is plagued by problems surrounding human communication. Those affected with post-modern sensibilities are struck with the confusing plurality of voices that fragments human communities and makes claims to reason and order precarious and ambiguous. Earlier, I cited the difficulties entailed in interreligious dialogue, the challenge for productive dialogue within a third world church, and the divisive issue of abortion as examples of these post-modern conditions. They raise serious questions about the possibility, the shape, and the outcome of religious dialogue: is dialogue possible across cultural divides, between militant adversaries, or in the passionate world of moral commitments? For that matter, is it desirable? Or, does dialogue mean abandonment of identity and compromise of principle? If there is to be dialogue in these situations, how will it proceed? What are its goals? Who will adjudicate the exchange? These are heady questions. It is little wonder that they have spawned methodological investigations in religious and theological studies concerned with the dialogical nature of human understanding. My first contention is that literary dialogues address these questions directly: dialogues portray and participate in the very practices that vex the post-modern academic study of religion.

But it is equally vital, in the second place, to attend to the artistic origin and literary form of the dialogue. Literary dialogues are the product of an "imitative art." The written discourse they display mimes the living words of real speakers in a way that fittingly expresses the fragility of communication and the ambiguities of persuasion typical of actual religious discourse. At the same time, however, the written text is the medium for the author's dialogue with a reading audience: through the dialogue's form, the author conveys his or her perceptions of the nature and range of discourse. Concretely, dialogues represent a number of features characteristic of living discourse: the social nature of dialogue, the role of questioning and argumentation, the precariousness of understanding, the strategies of persuasion, the open-endedness of truth, and so on. These literary phenomena demand attention. In response, we must ask: why do different authors in different cultures and historical periods choose to write in the genre of dialogue? What does the form contribute to their message? What more do we hear when we listen to classic authors through their option to speak through dialogue? How does the dialogue form affect an author's dialogue with readers? I suggest, in the second place, that paying attention to the literary genre of dialogue makes possible a fresh engagement with the concerns and claims of authors writing these texts.

The third plank of this study follows directly from the second. Reading dialogues in a genre-conscious manner yields ample philosophical dividends. Dialogues (a) shed light on the nature of religious discourse; (b) engage readers in reflecting on the fundamental ambiguities and limit situations common to different forms of religious discourse; and (c) prompt normative considerations of desirable possibilities for this kind of discourse. Each of these philosophical topics will find a place in the chapters to follow.

(a) At the most basic level, dialogues provide relatively stable models for phenomenological description of the contour and practices of discourse. Because dialogues imitate living discourse in written form, they allow readers to eavesdrop on the conversation of others. Consequently, they provide answers to basic, descriptive questions about the essence of religious discourse: what happens when people engage each other over such issues? What transpires? How does discourse proceed? Where does it lead? What norms do interlocutors perceive as guiding them? As indicated in the sketch at the end of the previous section, dialogues furnish answers to these rudimentary questions. They embody—and hence they evidence—the role of context, the function of difference, the kinds of strategy and interaction, and the range of outcomes possible in dialogue. Attending to the discourse within the text, therefore, can yield a rudimentary phenomenology of religious discourse.

(b) There is, however, a more valuable philosophical premium at hand from a study of dialogues. That is, dialogues permit us to observe (and hence, come to understand) what ultimately is at stake in people's attempts to converse over religious issues; they give concrete form to the various ambiguities which swirl around religious discourse, making it at once so difficult and yet so compelling. As we saw earlier in the works of Voltaire, Cardenal, Augustine and Murdoch, literary dialogues illustrate the aspiration to communicate intelligibly and to persuade rationally, but they also show the stresses and strains which undercut speakers' efforts. Voltaire's interlocutors, for instance, embark on an amicable conversation aimed at common understanding, only to discover the destructive impact of their cultural narrow-mindedness. What we as readers witness is the dialectic of unity (the one world history they presume to share) and plurality (their cultural differences). Understanding appears possible, then it is threatened, and finally it crumbles. The intelligibility of their dialogue hovers at the edge where their presumptions meet their prejudices. If understanding is to occur, then it must happen in that liminal region—but, alas, the undertow of their cultural biases puts a quick end to such a goal. For my purposes, the key philosophical issue here is the dialectic of aspiration and limitation as it affects the quest for understanding. The idea of a common world attracts the speakers into dialogue, but they are unable to sustain intelligible communication at the edge of their individual experiences.

Something similar happens in Augustine's dialogue, but there the issue is persuasion, not understanding. Each participant hopes to come out on top, offering reasons for his view, while tearing away at his opponents. As we saw, however, the goal of rational persuasion gives way to Augustine's magisterial posturing and heavy-handed argumentation. What we as readers witness is the dialectic of wisdom and skepticism, but the outcome in favor of Augustine's wisdom is not won through rational means of persuasion. The rationality of this dialogue hangs in the gulf between intentions and convictions. If persuasion is to occur, then it must take place on the boundaries of the two positions—but, for Augustine, this proves too frustrating to pursue. At stake here is a dialectic between intention and practice as it affects efforts at rational persuasion. The very idea of wisdom (including, of course, knowledge of God) proves inviting to all involved, but the disparity in their views erodes the possibility of sustained rational argumentation.

With these dialectics we come right to the heart of the matter. In religion, discourse is brought to the limits of intelligibility and rationality. As I discussed in the first section of this introduction, interlocutors are—by the nature of the subject—compelled to enter that boundary area between understanding and misunderstanding, and between rationality and irrationality. The dialectical tensions that ensue come in a great variety of forms, depending on the venue for conversation. But what seems sure, and certainly what is philosophically interesting, is that religious discourse hovers ever so brilliantly and yet precariously on the edge of insight and disaster. Popular wisdom regards the dangers as more significant than the rewards. What seems evident, however, is that human beings will continue to engage each other precisely at these tenuous points. Indeed, I believe they must. Yet they will certainly also falter. That much is evident not only from these dialogues, but also from the history of religions.

This phenomenon has long been recognized as endemic to religion. Rudolf Otto's famous work *The Idea of the Holy* is especially valuable for its analysis of the dialectical nature of religious experience. For Otto, the essence of religion lies in a combination of contrasting feelings or valuations of the holy. The source and object of religious experience—what he calls the "numinous"—is a mystery at once tremendous and fascinating. The numinous is the *mysterium*, the "wholly other,"

> that which is quite beyond the sphere of the usual, the intelligible, and the familiar, which therefore falls quite outside the limits of the 'canny,' and is contrasted with it, filling the mind with blank wonder and astonishment.[101]

The mysterious is, first of all, the *tremendum*: it is experienced as something uncanny and terrifying, evoking a "feeling of peculiar dread," a "terror fraught with inward shuddering."[102] It is "majestic" and "absolutely unapproachable." It provokes a "feeling of one's own submergence, of being 'dust and ashes' and nothingness." It is overpowering, "a force that knows not stint nor stay, which is urgent, active, compelling, and alive."[103] At the same time, however, as the holy is experienced as that which is "aweful" and uncanny, it is experienced as "uniquely attractive and fascinating," bearing the power to "entrance" and "transport" the person toward itself.[104] For my purposes, what is crucial in Otto's analysis is the ambiguity of terror and attraction at the heart of religious experience. In Otto's words,

> These two qualities, the daunting and the fascinating, now combine in a strange harmony of contrasts, and the resultant character of the numinous consciousness, to which the entire religious development bears witness, at any rate from the level of 'daemonic dread' onwards, is at once the strangest and most noteworthy phenomenon in the whole history of religion.[105]

Religious experience, and the language used to express it, live within this "strange harmony of contrasts."

My analysis of dialogues points up similar ambiguities at the heart of religious life. Unlike Otto, however, who concentrates on the contrasts of language used to *refer* to the holy, I have shifted my focus to the social sphere of human communication. There, I suggest, the same "harmony of contrasts" is at work. On one hand, people feel compelled to speak of the ultimate horizons of their lives: the issues are alluring, they compel attention, they entice interest. All this is clearly evident in the dialogues discussed at the beginning of this chapter. The idea of a common world, the conflict of wealth and religion, the meaning and possibility of wisdom, and the very idea of religion—each of these topics evokes interest, arouses passions, and animates conversation. On the other hand, as we saw, the effort to speak intelligibly and rationally with others on these issues proves tenuous at best. Thus, interlocutors become overwhelmed, their language becomes mutually unintelligible, their efforts at persuasion appear irrational. In a word, they are driven back, even as they come forward to speak. Discourse on religion, therefore, seems designed to operate on the boundaries of intelligibility and rationality, and not simply because the object of religious experience is mysterious and ominous. Discourse on religion rises and falls—and it appears designed to do both—precisely because the venues for talking about religion stretch and strain the communicative and probative fibers of linguistic activity. It offers great opportunities for understanding (e.g., between religions) and persuasion (e.g., between skeptics and believers), but it also is a place where understanding and persuasion teeter on the edge of collapse. This situation may appear tragic, and to a certain extent it is. It also can be comical, as we will see in some of the chapters to follow. Regardless of how this "strange harmony of contrasts" is interpreted, it demands careful scrutiny as something central to religious life.

Still, the matter is more complex than I have indicated. Dialogues are not merely textual show-cases; they are more than models of living discourse. They are also artistic means of *engaging* an audience in a dialogue of writing and reading. Authors speak with readers and evoke the response of interpretation through the written text. Because of this, the dialectics evident within the text also reverberate throughout this broader exchange with the reader. Dialogues are written, in other words, not only to show but also to engage readers *in* the specific dialectics perceived as crucial by the author and embedded in the text. At this point, then, the "strange harmony of contrasts" typical of religious discourse becomes a dimension of the dialogue between author and reader. As a result, these contrasts become not only a topic for observation, but also a subject of self-scrutiny. Readers must ask what dialectics are at work in different venues for religious discourse; but they must also inquire how we are to understand them and to find our way through them. As we will see in the chapters to follow, each dialogue opens up a distinct venue for discourse, and, within that dialogical space, proposes and develops a distinctive dialectical movement. Each dialogue—as I will introduce shortly—takes discourse to the limits of intelligibility and rationality. Consequently, each text engages readers in precisely that boundary area where understanding and persuasion are at stake and at risk over a religious question.

(c) There is, finally, a third philosophical dividend to be won from careful reflection on the dialectical tensions at play in dialogues on religion. In a word, literary dialogues either implicitly or explicitly raise questions about how discourse should be practiced. That is, they illustrate and provoke discourse on ideals or norms for dialogue on religion: for instance, by portraying an ideal form of discourse (respectful or conducive to understanding) in contrast to undesirable forms (fractured or divisive); by illustrating the movement or transition to what is perceived to be an ideal form of discourse (promoting unity, order, or freedom, for instance); or, lastly, by engaging readers in reflection on the kind of discourse necessary even to begin talking about the difference between good and bad forms of discourse. Dialogues provoke normative questions: how should people speak with each other? how should conversation on religion go? And they can instigate second-order questions on the possibility and the shape of discourse about ideal discourse: how are we to begin talking about the best way to talk about religious issues? Some dialogues make these normative questions their specific focus. But even dialogues which place other concerns at center-stage tacitly carry a normative trajectory. Thus we find Voltaire experimenting with the contrast between ethnocentric discourse and the possibility of broad-mindedness; and Cardenal posing the contrast between a wealthy man's self-justifying practicality and a revolutionary community's strident protest against economic oppression; and Augustine and Murdoch—in different ways—juxtaposing the open but scattered discourse of friends with the perspective and wisdom of a master. Each dialogue, in short, initiates reflection on norms for discourse.[106]

In several important ways, therefore, literary dialogues on religion yield valuable philosophical lessons. This is the third plank on which this work is built. Dialogues provide insight into the nature of religious discourse—its contour, its strategies and practices, and its outcomes. They engage readers directly in a dialogue with the author, thereby sparking reflection on the dialectical tensions at work in talk about religious questions. And, lastly, they prompt normative reflection on ideals for discourse. The chapters that follow seek to capitalize on these three philosophical dividends.

(5) Criticism, Irony, and Irenicism

The bulk of this book consists of separate studies of major dialogues on religious questions. In my coverage of this material, I make no pretense of treating the genre in a comprehensive manner. This is not a history of dialogue. Instead, each chapter pursues the more modest goal of focusing on the dialogue or dialogues of a single author. Only chapter five takes up the works of more than one author, in order to flush out the range of a certain type of literary dialogue. My aim, throughout the course of the book, is to offer a series of readings of literary dialogues on religion, in response to post-modern quandaries in religious and theological studies, for the sake of understanding something of the peculiar but fascinating drama of religious discourse.

Each chapter, therefore, builds upon the three planks I have laid out in this introduction. In a nutshell, once again, the aim in each of these studies is (a) to address current difficulties facing religious discourse, (b) by means of a literary turn to study the genre of dialogue, (c) for the sake of philosophically exploring and understanding something of the possibilities and limits of religious discourse. The book as a whole, consequently, is governed by a contemporary motive. I hope, in particular, to speak to the kinds of questions concerning the intelligibility and rationality of discourse under debate in contemporary religious and theological studies. That means tending to the prevailing post-modern anxieties about the fragility and domination of discourse and to the deep yearnings in religious and academic culture for coherence and civility in human communications. In order to contribute to these lines of debate, each chapter will assume a literary focus on the genre of dialogue as it has been deployed by some of the most prominent authors in the philosophical and theological literature of western culture. I turn to the written genre because the form stands in organic relation to authorial message, expressing the content with indispensable tone and color, and making an independent statement about the world of discourse. I turn specifically to dialogue because this genre uniquely serves to convey the ambiguities of living words exchanged, in this case, over religious topics; and, by that means, to engage a reading audience in the same processes of discourse. More particularly, I turn to classic dialogues because these texts have proved able—generation after generation—to capture and represent the peculiar dialectics and limit situations of religious discourse. This book, finally, is driven by a fundamental, philosophical interest in the workings of religious discourse. I hope that the following studies will shed some light on how different forms of discourse take religious dialogue to the limits of intelligibility and rationality; simultaneously, I hope they point out certain promising pathways for discourse over religion.

This book contends, in sum, that perennial philosophical lessons culled by a genre study of classic dialogues will prove instructive (and possibly corrective) for the kind of discursive anxieties infecting late twentieth century religious and theological studies. To this end, my choice of authors and texts for discussion is designed to point up what I take to be three of the most promising (and requisite) paths open to religious discourse. Before people's efforts to communicate and argue with each other about religious questions can proceed intelligibly and rationally—avoiding thereby the pitfalls so evident in the conversations depicted by Voltaire, Cardenal, Augustine and Murdoch—the following criteria must be met. First, discourse must embrace the habits of *criticism*. Understanding might be promoted and truth might be served if interlocutors subjected religious concerns and claims (whether their own or someone else's) to open examination by question, counterpoint, and experimentation. Second, interlocutors also need to gain the perspective of *irony*. Passions are cooled and civility is promoted when interlocutors achieve the balance of mind and self-critical humor which comes with ironic detachment. Talk about religion sorely needs the gentle leveling provided by ironic wit. Third, discourse should embody an *irenic* spirit. The ideal of open and respectful dialogue requires commitment to pacifying the passions of division, supplemented by efforts to reconcile opposed minds and worlds.

Criticism, irony and irenicism—as styles of discourse over religion—offer up the possibility that talk about religion, at least temporarily and in certain locales, might avoid the abuses and excesses common wisdom associates with talk about religion. If people are to talk with each other about religious questions in an amicable and productive manner—which is, to say the least, extremely rare—then they would be wise to listen and learn about these lines of discursive activity. In praising these forms of discourse, however, I am not foreclosing the idea that there may be other helpful pathways to intelligible and rational communication over religious questions. I hope that there are. Nor am I suggesting that these three styles of talk are failsafe. Quite the opposite. As will be readily apparent in the following chapters, they also lead inevitably, but perchance also productively, to the limits of intelligibility and rationality. Indeed, what makes them so intriguing and so compelling is that they operate in the very midst of the confusions and ambiguities which swirl around conversations about religion, even as they hold open the possibility of intelligible, rational, and civil dialogue.

The chapters to follow work in pairs. Each pair takes up one of these three lines of discourse, while each chapter within the pair offers an alternative practice of this style of discourse.

The first pair of chapters explores dialogues which accent the place and role of criticism in religious discourse. Chapter two looks at the dialogues of Anselm of Canterbury, in order to show that Anselm's classic project of "faith seeking understanding" is a dialogical process, and that this methodological vision lives prominently through his frequent choice of the dialogue form. In Anselm's hands, the attempt to harness rational argumentation in the service of faith's self-understanding pushes the outer limits of doctrinal language to the point of discovering something novel and surprising about religious life, only to be pulled back by the constraints of orthodox doctrine. For Anselm, consequently, religious discourse works in the tension of rational discovery and orthodox conservation.

Chapter three turns to the vastly different dialogues of Denis Diderot, the eighteenth century editor of the *Encyclopedia*. Like Anselm, Diderot is devoted to the spirit of dialogue, and this commitment finds a recurring and highly effective literary outlet in the dialogue genre. Unlike Anselm, however, Diderot employs the tool of reason as a critical weapon against the superstition and barbarism found throughout the religious world. In Diderot's texts, dialogue becomes the venue for uninhibitedly experimental engagement with the most diverse sources of disorder and irrationality—the shocking novelty of scientific discoveries; the unsettling otherness of non-European societies; and, especially, the oppressive intolerance of organized religion. Diderot's beloved critics (and hence his readers too) stand at the edges of familiarity, flirting with the uncanny oblivion which lies at the frontiers of rational criticism. For Diderot, discourse on religion takes place in the dialectical tension of rational criticism and discursive chaos. Together, but in opposition, the dialogues of Anselm and Diderot confront readers with the alternative trajectories and distinctive limits embedded in the dialectic of faith and reason—now seen as a function of discourse.

The second pair of chapters attends to critical discourse over religion that is laced with an ironic tone and satiric wit. Chapter four offers a reading of David Hume's *Dialogues Concerning Natural Religion*, without doubt one of the most sophisticated yet elusive philosophical dialogues ever written. In essence, Hume showcases the myriad rhetorical entanglements which affect each and every attempt to speak with others about God. Hume plays the benevolent ironist, standing above the fray of religious voices, playfully shifting back and forth between opposing advocates of theism, coyly orchestrating their mutually nullifying encounter, marveling at the duplicity and shiftiness between them, and all the while attempting to cure his theistic partners in conversation of their illusions and hostilities. In this regard, the dialogue form proves ideal. It allows Hume to stand "in between"—skeptically defending no position, ironically miming religious hypocrisy and theistic duplicity, and irenically working to instill a sense of humility and tolerance in the practice of religious discourse. Hume shows readers, therefore, just how hypocritical, duplicitous, and fractious discourse with religion can become, all the while demonstrating through the voice of Philo and through his authorship of the *Dialogues* the urgency and the desirability of amicable and civil conversation. For Hume, in the end, religious discourse is played out in the shifting alternative of raillery and civility.

Chapter five turns back the clock to consider Lucian of Samasota's dialogues of the dead. In this unusual use of the dialogue form, discourse is transferred to the realm of the dead, where persons of all sorts and from all centuries are brought together for open and frank evaluations of the ways of the living. What Lucian introduces by this means is a form of discourse which is both outrageously comical and profoundly serious. Like those of Hume, Lucian's dialogues introduce an ironic tone to the criticism of religion; but, unlike the civil spirit at work in Hume, Lucian turns satirical, giving expression to a dissident, even subversive reason, aimed at the self-serious and the arrogant. In yet a second way, Lucian's ironic posture differs from Hume's: where Hume's skepticism leaves theism in suspense, Lucian's satire re-enacts what is typically religious—an act of imaginative transcendence and a breakthrough from blindness to a new way of seeing life. In Lucian's dialogues, religious discourse operates in the ironic play of serious criticism of religion and a comic farce laced with its own religious dimension.

The final two chapters are devoted to an ethics of discourse. Chapter six takes up the dialogues and colloquies of Erasmus of Rotterdam, while chapter seven focuses on Plato's *Phaedrus*. What Erasmus' dialogues illustrate so vividly is the delicate art of conversation required to turn adversaries toward each other in mutual understanding and rational persuasion. Through his use of the dialogue form, therefore, Erasmus holds up the ideal of an amicable and cooperative form of conversation, where critical and irenic discourse makes possible the formation of public communities of rational dialogue. The importance of Erasmus' dialogues for my purposes lies exactly here. He illustrates through his texts and he engages readers in reflecting on the virtues of discourse necessary to sustain intelligible and rational dialogue on religion. In doing this, of course, Erasmus also takes us to the limits of religious discourse—to those rare but desirable points where people of different stripes and loyalties manage to speak together amicably and productively. For Erasmus, therefore, discourse on religion takes place in the contrast between existing forms of discursive adversity and the realizable ideal of irenic conversation.

Plato's *Phaedrus* takes a different but complementary approach to that of Erasmus. Like Erasmus, Plato puts forward a set of guidelines for normatively evaluating discourse. Through the voice of Socrates, he pushes beyond a merely technical evaluation of rhetoric in order to consider ethical questions and normative standards for the use of persuasive language. Unlike Erasmus, however, Plato also introduces second-order questions dealing with the very possibility of ethical discourse. As we will see, Plato loads the *Phaedrus* with structures and devices which seem to undercut his own assertions about ethical speech. The structure of the dialogue, indeed, has led some interpreters (notably, Jacques Derrida) to conclude that Plato's philosophical project is caught in a web of self-dissolving contradictions. I come to the opposite conclusion. What is significant about Plato's *Phaedrus* is that it provides an ethical measure for discourse without seeking exemption from its distortions and perversions. For Plato, therefore, discourse on the ethically best discourse hovers ever so precariously between the passion for clarity and rationality and the inevitability of ambiguity and deception.

But first things must come first. In the next two chapters, I consider dialogues devoted to *criticism* of religious concerns and claims. And, for this purpose, there is nowhere better to begin than the classic dialogues of Anselm of Canterbury.

Notes

[1] Augustine, "The Teacher," trans. John H. S. Burleigh, *Augustine: Earlier Writings* (Philadelphia: Westminster, 1953) 69.

[2] Hugh of St. Victor, translation quoted from G. R. Evans, *Anselm and Talking About God* (Oxford: Clarendon, 1978) 76.

[3] A saying with a likely origin in a letter of Lord Chesterfield, the eighteenth century British statesman, who writes: "religion is by no means a proper subject of conversation in a mixed company; it should only be treated among a very few people of learning, for mutual instruction. It is too awful and respectable a subject to become a familiar one." The same caveat holds for talk about politics. If conversation over religion and politics proves unavoidable, Chesterfield counsels "coolness" and "great good-humour." See the undated letter to his godson in Lord Chesterfield, *Letters of Lord Chesterfield to His Son* (London and Toronto: J. M. Dent; New York: E. P. Dutton, 1929) 298.

[4] Paul Ricoeur: *Interpretation Theory; Discourse and the Surplus of Meaning*, (Fort Worth, Texas: Texas Christian University, 1976).

[5] See John Dewey, *A Common Faith* (New Haven: Yale, 1934) for this distinction between religion and the religious.

[6] Voltaire, "A Conversation with a Chinese," *The Works of Voltaire* Vol. 4, trans. William F. Fleming (Paris and London: E. R. DuMont, n.d.) 28–32.

[7] James Boyd White: *When Words Lose Their Meaning; Constitutions and Reconstitutions of Language, Character, and Community* (Chicago: University of Chicago, 1984).

[8] Voltaire, "Japanese Catechism," *Philosophical Dictionary*, trans. Peter Gay (New York: Harcourt, Brace and World, 1962) 151.

[9] Voltaire, "Japanese Catechism," *Philosophical Dictionary,* 152–53.

[10] Voltaire, "Japanese Catechism", *Philosophical Dictionary,* 154. The reference is to Horace's Odes. See *The Odes and Epodes of Horace*, trans. Joseph P. Clancy (Chicago: University of Chicago, 1960) I. 27: "Cups are for pleasure: to use them as weapons is a Thracian trick. Stop behaving like savages, and spare Bacchus your brawls and bloodshed: he prefers moderation."

[11] Consider, for instance, the hard-headed realism about religious fanaticism portrayed in Voltaire's *Mahomet the Prophet or Fanaticism. A Tragedy in Five Acts*, trans. by Robert L. Meyers (New York: Frederick Ungar, 1964).

[12] Ernesto Cardenal, *The Gospel in Solentiname* Vol. 1, trans. Donald D. Walsh (Maryknoll, New York: Orbis, 1984) 225.

[13] Cardenal, *The Gospel in Solentiname,* 1: 233 and 235.

[14] Augustine, "Answer to the Skeptics" ("Contra Academicos"), *Writings of Saint Augustine* Vol. 1 (New York: CIMA Publishing, 1948) I. 8. 23.

[15] Augustine, "Answer to the Skeptics," II. 1. 1 on the rarity of wisdom; compare III. 5. 12. On the value of searching for truth, see III. 3. 1.

[16] Augustine, "Answer to the Skeptics," III. 8. 17.

[17] Peter Brown, *Augustine of Hippo; A Biography* (Berkeley: University of California, 1969) 120.

[18] Augustine, "Answer to the Skeptics," II. 10. 24.

[19] Augustine, "Answer to the Skeptics," I. 3. 8.

[20] Augustine, "Answer to the Skeptics", II. 9. 24; see II. 12. 27–28 for similar language.

[21] See for example, Trygeticus' resentment over the smooth but swift rhetorical moves of Licentius (I.5.15). Trygeticus is similarly embarrassed in I.3.7.

[22] Augustine, "Answer to the Skeptics," III. 3. 6.

[23] Augustine, "Answer to the Skeptics," III. 5. 12.

[24] See Augustine, "Answer to the Skeptics," III. 15–20. 44. The same thing happens in Augustine, *On Free Choice of the Will* (Indianapolis: Bobbs-Merrill, 1964). Augustine's extended monologue silences Evodius through the last quarter of the dialogue.

[25] Augustine, "Answer to the Skeptics," II. 13. 29 for the image of the playpen.

[26] Iris Murdoch, "Above the Gods; A Dialogue about Religion," in *Acostos; Two Platonic Dialogues* (New York: Penguin, 1987) 118.

[27] Murdoch, "Above the Gods," 80.

[28] Murdoch, "Above the Gods," 87–89.

[29] Murdoch, "Above the Gods," 70.

[30] Murdoch, "Above the Gods," 114 and 116.

[31] Murdoch, "Above the Gods," 116–117.

[32] David Tracy, *Blessed Rage for Order* (New York: Seabury, 1975) 92–94. See also David Tracy, *The Analogical Imagination: Christian Theology and the Culture of Pluralism* (New York: Crossroad, 1981) 160–161.

[33] Karl Rahner, "Christianity and the Non-Christian Religions," *Theological Investigations* vol. 5, trans. Karl-H. Kruger (New York: Seabury, 1966) 115–134; "Anonymous Chris-

tians," *Theological Investigations* vol. 6, trans. Karl-H. and Boniface Kruger (New York: Seabury, 1974) 390–398; and "Observations on the Problem of the 'Anonymous Christian'," *Theological Investigations* vol. 14, trans. David Bourke (New York: Seabury, 1976) 280–294. On the notion of anonymous Christianity, see Karl-Heinz Weger, *Karl Rahner: An Introduction to His Theology* (New York: Seabury, 1980) 95–101 and 112–141.

[34] On the challenge of pluralism to the world's religions, see Harold Coward, *Pluralism; Challenge to World Religions* (Maryknoll, New York: Orbis, 1985).

[35] See, for instance, Paul Tillich, *Christianity and the Encounter of the World's Religions* (New York: Columbia, 1963); and Raimundo Panikkar, *The Unknown Christ of Hinduism* (Maryknoll, New York: Orbis, 1981) 61.

[36] Hans Küng, *Christianity and World Religions*, trans. Peter Heinegg (Garden City, New York: Doubleday, 1986) 442.

[37] John Hick, *God Has Many Names* (Philadelphia: Westminster, 1980) 71.

[38] Gordon D. Kaufman: "God and Emptiness: An Experimental Essay," *Buddhist-Christian Studies* 9 (1989): 175–187. See the Buddhist responses by Rita M. Gross and Ryusei Takeda, as well as transcriptions of their dialogue, in the same volume.

[39] See the marvelous Hassidic parable of the Jewish rabbi who ventures far from home in search of a treasure, only to find a treasure buried in "the neglected corner of his [own] house." Heinrich Zimmer: *Myths and Symbols in Indian Art and Civilization* (New York: Harper and Row, 1946) 220–21. Sometimes it takes a stranger—a voice from another world—to let us see the riches in our own traditions. Zimmer takes the tale from Martin Buber, *Tales of the Hasidim; The Later Masters* (New York: Schocken, 1848) 245–246. See Wendy Doniger O'Flaherty's discussion in *Other People's Myths* (New York: Macmillan, 1988) 137–141. Interestingly, Doniger notes how her discovery of this tale replicates the tale's message: she "had to read a book about India, . . . to find that parable from my own Jewish tradition." *Other People's Myths*, 192, footnote 3.

[40] See, for example, Paul F. Knitter's creative efforts to conceive a christology without claims of uniqueness in Knitter, *No Other Name? A Critical Survey of Christian Attitudes Toward the World Religions* (Maryknoll, New York: Orbis, 1985) 171–204. Other Christian theologians—including progressive thinkers like Hans Küng—resist such revisions of christic uniqueness. Hans Küng, *On Being a Christian*, trans. Edward Quinn (Garden City, New York: Doubleday, 1976) 98–116; and, more recently, *Christianity and World Religions*. See Knitter's challenge to Küng, "Hans Küng's Theological Rubicon," ed. Leonard Swidler, *Toward a Universal Theology of Religion* (Maryknoll, New York: Orbis, 1987) 224–230; and a restatement by Küng, "What is True Religion? Toward an Ecumenical Criteriology," *Toward a Universal Theology of Religion*, 231–250. See also S. J. Samartha, *One Christ—Many Religions; Toward a Revised Christology* (Maryknoll, New York: Orbis, 1991); and Gabriel Moran, *Uniqueness: Problem or Paradox in Jewish and Christian Traditions* (Maryknoll, New York: Orbis, 1992).

[41] On the tensions which result from close working proximity of the history of religions and theology, see P. Joseph Cahill, *Mended Speech: The Crisis of Religious Studies and*

Theology (New York: Crossroad, 1982). For constructive efforts to think theologically within the context of interreligious dialogue, see Wilfred Cantwell Smith, *Towards a World Theology* (Philadelphia: Westminster, 1981); and, more recently, Paul F. Knitter, "Dialogue and Liberation: Foundations for a Plurality Theology of Religions," *The Drew Gateway* 58 (Spring 1988).

[42] The theoretical literature on interreligious dialogue is vast. For important and representative works, see Raimundo Panikkar, *The Intra-Religious Dialogue* (New York: Paulist, 1978); Leondard Swidler, John B. Cobb, Jr., Paul F. Knitter, and Monika K. Hellwig, *Death or Dialogue: From the Age of Monologue to the Age of Dialogue* (London: SCM; Philadelphia: Trinity Press International, 1990); David Tracy, *Dialogue with the Other; The InterReligious Dialogue* (Louvain: Peeters; Grand Rapids: William B. Eerdmans, 1990); and Paul J. Griffiths, *An Apology for Apologetics; A Study in the Logic of Interreligious Dialogue* (Maryknoll, New York: Orbis, 1991). For efforts to conceive interreligious dialogue on Buddhist principles, see Sallie B. King, "Toward a Buddhist Model of Interreligious Dialogue" in *Buddhist-Christian Studies* 10 (1990): 121–126; and Masao Abe, "The Impact of Dialogue on My Self-Understanding as a Buddhist," *Buddhist-Christian Studies* 9 (1989) 63–70.

[43] *The Kairos Document: Challenge to the Church*, second edition (Grand Rapids: Eerdmans, 1986) 23.

[44] *Kairos Document*, 1.

[45] *Kairos Document*, 3–8.

[46] Roger Thurow, "Charismatic Politician Rejuvenates Apartheid As South African Force," *Wall Street Journal*, October 21, 1988, 1.

[47] Jon Sobrino, *The True Church and the Poor* (Maryknoll, New York: Orbis, 1984) 33–35.

[48] Desmond Tutu, *Hope and Suffering* (Grand Rapids: Eerdmans, 1984), 181–183. See also Desmond Tutu, *Crying in the Wilderness: Struggle for Justice in South Africa* (Grand Rapids: Eerdmans, 1982); and *The Words of Desmond Tutu* (New York: Newmarket Press, 1989). On Tutu, see Shirley Du Boulay, *Tutu: Voice of the Voiceless* (Grand Rapids: Eerdmans, 1988); and *Hammering Swords into Ploughshares: Essays in Honour of Archbishop Mpilo Desmond Tutu* (Grand Rapids: Eerdmans; Trenton, New Jersey.: Africa World Press, 1987).

[49] Mario Cuomo, "Religious Belief and Public Morality: A Catholic Governor's Perspective," address given September 17, 1984, at the University of Notre Dame.

[50] Henry J. Hyde, "It's Time Religious Values Trickled Down Into Politics," *National Catholic Reporter*, October 19, 1984, 13.

[51] Henry J. Hyde, "It's Time Religious Values Trickled Down Into Politics," 13. Jeffrey L. Sheler speaks similarly of the "abortion battle" taking place within the Christian churches over the same canonical and traditional resources. "The Theology of Abortion," *U. S. News and World Report*, March 9, 1992: 54–55.

[52] Joseph Cardinal Bernadin, "A Consistent Ethic of Life: An American-Catholic Dialogue", *Thought* 59 (March 1984) 104.

[53] Joseph Cardinal Bernadin, "A Consistent Ethic of Life," 106. For a discussion of the abortion controversy of the 1984 American presidential race, see Richard P. McBrien, *Caesar's Coin; Religion and Politics in America* (New York: MacMillan, 1987) 135–168.

[54] See the essays in ed. Robin W. Lovin, *Religion and American Public Life* (New York: Paulist, 1986).

[55] Richard Rorty, *Philosophy and the Mirror of Nature* (Princeton: Princeton University, 1979) 320.

[56] Augustine, "On the Catechising of the Uninstructed," *Nicene and Post-Nicene Fathers*, ed. Philip Schaff (New York: Scribners, 1900) 292–293. Friedrich Schleiermacher, *Hermeneutics: The Handwritten Manuscripts* (Missoula, Montana: Scholars Press, 1977).

[57] Richard Rorty, *Consequences of Pragmatism* (Minneapolis: University of Minnesota, 1982); *Contingency, Irony, and Solidarity* (Cambridge: Cambridge University, 1989); and *Objectivity, Relativism, and Truth; Philosophical Papers* vol. 1 (Cambridge: Cambridge University, 1991). Richard J. Bernstein, *Beyond Objectivism and Relativism; Science, Hermeneutics, and Praxis* (Philadelphia: University of Pennsylvania, 1983); and *Philosophical Profiles* (Philadelphia: University of Pennsylvania, 1986). Hans-Georg Gadamer, *Truth and Method* (New York: Crossroad, 1982); *Reason in the Age of Science*, trans. Frederick G. Lawrence (Cambridge, Massachusetts: MIT, 1981); *Philosophical Hermeneutics*, trans. David E. Linge (Berkeley: University of California, 1976). Jürgen Habermas, *The Theory of Communicative Action; Reason and the Rationalization of Society*, trans. Thomas McCarthy (Boston: Beacon, 1981); *The Philosophical Discourse of Modernity; Twelve Lectures*, trans. Frederick Lawrence (Cambridge, Massachusetts: MIT, 1987), especially ch. 11; and *Moral Consciousness and Communicative Action*, trans. Christian Lenhardt and Shierry Weber Nicholsen (Cambridge, Massachusetts: MIT, 1990). For discussion of the issues of interpretation and communication in Gadamer and Habermas, see Fred R. Dallmayr, *Language and Politics; Why Does Language Matter to Political Philosophy?* (Notre Dame: University of Notre Dame, 1984), 115–147; and *Polis and Praxis; Exercises in Contemporary Political Theory* (Cambridge, Massachusetts: MIT, 1984); and ed. Robert Hollinger, *Hermeneutics and Praxis* (Notre Dame: University of Notre Dame, 1985). For theological contributions to these discussions, see David Tracy, *The Analogical Imagination*; Edward Schillebeeckx, *The Understanding of Faith: Interpretation and Criticism*, trans. N. D. Smith (New York: Seabury, 1974); and *Christ: The Experience of Jesus as Lord*, trans. John Bowden (New York: Seabury, 1980) 30–79. Elizabeth Schüssler Fiorenza, *In Memory of Her: A Feminist Theological Reconstruction of Christian Origins* (New York: Crossroad, 1983); and *Bread Not Stone: The Challenge of Feminist Biblical Interpretation* (Boston: Beacon, 1984). Juan Luis Segundo, *Faith and Ideologies*, (Jesus of Nazareth Yesterday and Today, vol. 1), trans. John Drury (Maryknoll, New York: Orbis, 1984). Johannes Baptist Metz, *Faith in History and Society: Toward a Practical Fundamental Theology*, trans. David Smith (New York: Seabury, 1980).

[58] Martin Buber, *I and Thou*, second edition, trans. Ronald Gregor Smith (New York: Scribners, 1958). M. M. Bakhtin, *The Dialogic Imagination; Four Essays*, trans. Caryl

Emerson and Michael Holquist (Austin: University of Texas, 1981); and Mikhail Bakhtin, *Problems of Dostoevsky's Poetics*, trans. Caryl Emerson (Minneapolis: University of Minnesota, 1984).

[59] See, for instance, the pieces in ed. Richard Rorty, *The Linguistic Turn: Recent Essays in Philosophical Method* (Chicago: University of Chicago, 1967).

[60] Martha C. Nussbaum, *Love's Knowledge; Essays in Philosophy and Literature* (New York and Oxford: Oxford University, 1990) 3.

[61] Nussbaum, *Love's Knowledge*, 3.

[62] Nussbaum, *Love's Knowledge*, 5.

[63] See, for instance, Nussbaum's treatment of Plato's "artful" supercession of "tragic theatre" with the theatre of "inquiry"—what she calls "a pure crystalline theatre of the intellect"—in Martha C. Nussbaum, *The Fragility of Goodness; Luck and Ethics in Greek Tragedy and Philosophy* (Cambridge: Cambridge University, 1986) 122–135.

[64] Horace, *Satires, Epistles and Ars Poetica*, trans H. Rushton Fairclough (Cambridge: Harvard University, 1978) 477; the classical pagination is 317–320.

[65] Aristotle, *Poetics*, in Richard McKeon, *The Basic Works of Aristotle* (New York: Random House, 1941) 1447b.

[66] K. J. Wilson: *Incomplete Fiction; The Formation of English Renaissance Dialogue* (Washington: Catholic University, 1985) 5.

[67] Erasmus, "The Usefulness of the *Colloquies*", in *The Colloquies of Erasmus*, trans. Craig R. Thompson (Chicago: University of Chicago, 1965) 630.

[68] Goldsworthy Lowes Dickinson, "Dialogue as a Literary Form," *Essays by Divers Hands* (London: Oxford University) 4.

[69] Arthur Schopenhauer, "Immortality: A Dialogue," in *Essays of Arthur Schopenhauer*, trans. T. Bailey Saunders (New York: A. L. Burt, n.d.) 404.

[70] Voltaire, "A, B, C," *Philosophical Dictionary*, trans. Peter Gay (New York: Harcourt, Brace and World, 1962) 497–606.

[71] As Walter Benjamin reminds us, even the "techniques of reproduction" significantly alter the object represented, effectively liquidating a thing's "uniqueness and permanence" for the sake of making them universally available. Walter Benjamin, "The Work of Art in the Age of Mechanical Reproduction," *Illuminations*, trans. Harry Zohn (New York: Schocken, 1969) 220–223. The mimetic function of literary dialogues differs significantly—not least by the fact that the deliberately crafted literary dialogue gives order and coherence to speakers' words, whereas verbatim reproductions reveal all the rough and tumble starts and stops which occur in living discourse. See Keir Elam, *The Semiotics of Theatre and Drama* (London: Methuen, 1980) 178–182.

[72] As Torquato Tasso put it in his sixteenth century "Discourse on the Art of Dialogue," dialogue "occupies middle ground between poet and dialectician." Torquaato Tasso, *Tasso's Dialogues: A Selection with the Discourse on the Art of Dialogue* (Berkeley: University of California, 1982) 33.

[73] The most comprehensive work on the history of dialogue to date remains Rudolf Hirzel, *Der Dialog; ein literarhistorischer Versuch*, 2 vols. (Leipzig, 1895), although Hirzel's study focuses primarily on classical dialogue. Other helpful studies include Michel Ruch, *Le Préambule dans les oeuvres philosophiques de Cicéron: essai sur la genese et l'art du dialogue* (Paris and Strasbourg, 1958); Jean Andrieu, *Le Dialogue antique; structure et présentation* (Paris, 1954); Gottfried Niemann, *Die Dialogliteratur der Reformationszeit nach ihrer Entstehung und Entwicklung* (Leipzig, 1905); K. J. Wilson, *Incomplete Fictions; The Formation of English Renaissance Dialogue* (Washington: Catholic University of America, 1985); David Marsh, *The Quattrocento Dialogue; Classical Tradition and Humanist Innovation* (Cambridge, Massachusetts: Harvard University, 1980); Jean Laborderie, *Le dialogue platonicienne de la maturité* (Paris, 1978); and Elizabeth Merrill, *The Dialogue in English Literature* (Hamden, Conn.: Archon, 1969). See the notes in the chapters to follow for historical studies of dialogues by specific authors.

[74] Denis Diderot, *Rameau's Nephew and Other Works* (Indianapolis: Bobbs-Merrill, 1964). Erasmus of Rotterdam, "A Pilgrimage for Religion's Sake," in *The Colloquies of Erasmus*, trans. Craig R. Thompson (Chicago: University of Chicago, 1965). See chapter three on Diderot and chapter six on Erasmus.

[75] Nicolas Malebranche, *Entretiens sur la Métaphysique; Dialogues on Metaphysics*, trans. Willis Doney (New York: Abaris, 1980).

[76] H. D. Traill, *The New Lucian; Being a Series of Dialogues of the Dead* (London: Chapman and Hall, 1900).

[77] John The Scot (Joannes Scotus Eriugena), *Periphyseon; On the Division of Nature*, trans. Myra L. Uhlfelder (Indianapolis: Bobbs-Merrill, 1976).

[78] Benjamin Franklin, "Dialogue Between Franklin and the Gout," *A Benjamin Franklin Reader*, ed. Nathan G. Goodman (New York: Thomas Y. Crowell, 1945) 731–737.

[79] Rousseau: *Judge of Jean-Jacques: Dialogues, The Collected Writings of Rousseau*, ed. Roger D. Masters and Christopher Kelly (Hanover and London: University Press of New England, 1990).

[80] Cicero, *The Nature of the Gods*, trans. Horace C. P. McGregor (Harmondsworth, England: Penguin, 1972).

[81] Keir Elam, *The Semiotics of Theatre and Drama* (London: Methuen, 1980) 143.

[82] Peter Abelard, *A Dialogue of a Philosopher with a Jew, and a Christian*, trans. Pierre J. Payer (Toronto: Pontifical Institute of Mediaeval Studies, 1979); Martin Heidegger, *Discourse on Thinking* (New York: Harper and Row, 1976).

[83] Arthur Schopenhauer, "On Religion: A Dialogue" in *Schopenhauer: Essays and Aphorisms* (Baltimore: Penguin, 1970) 98 and 107.

[84] Justin Martyr, "Dialogue with Trypho, a Jew" in Alexander Roberts and James Donaldson, eds., *The Ante-Nicene Fathers* vol. 1 (Grand Rapids: Eerdmans, 1979).

[85] Hans-Georg Gadamer, *Truth and Method* (New York: Crossroads, 1982) 326–327.

[86] Gadamer, *Truth and Method*, 266.

[87] Klaus K. Klostermaier, "A Hindu-Christian Dialogue on Truth," *Journal of Ecumenical Studies* 12 (Spring 1975) 157–171; Theodoret, "Dialogues (Eranistes)" in Philip Schaff and Henry Wace, eds., *Nicene and Post-Nicene Fathers*, vol. 3 (Grand Rapids: Eerdmans, 1953) 160–244.

[88] Marquis de Sade, "Dialogue between a Priest and a Dying Man" in Richard Seaver and Austryn Wainhouse, eds., *The Marquis de Sade* (New York: Grove Press, 1965) 163–175.

[89] Hans-Georg Gadamer, *Truth and Method*, 93–95.

[90] For discussion of the kinds of argumentation modeled in literary dialogues, see Ch. Perelman and L. Olbrechts-Tyteca, *The New Rhetoric; A Treatise on Argumentation*, trans. John Wilkinson and Purcell Weaver (Notre Dame: University of Notre Dame, 1969); and Stephen Toulmin, *The Uses of Argument* (Cambridge: Cambridge University, 1969).

[91] Klaus Klostermaier, "Hindu-Christian Dialogue."

[92] Lucian, "Zeus Catechized" in A. M. Harmon, trans., *Lucian*, vol. 2 (Cambridge: Harvard University, 1960) 60–87.

[93] Anselm of Canterbury, "Why God Became a Man" in ed. and trans. Jasper Hopkins and Herbert Richardson, *Anselm of Canterbury*, vol. 3 (Toronto and New York: Edwin Mellen, 1976) 43–137.

[94] Johann Gottfried Herder, *God, Some Conversations*, trans. Frederick H. Burkhardt (Indianapolis: Bobbs-Merrill, 1940) 92.

[95] Erasmus, "A Fish Diet" in *The Colloquies of Erasmus*, 357.

[96] Justin Martyr, "Dialogue with Trypho, A Jew," 270.

[97] Marquis de Sade, "Dialogue between a Priest and a Dying Man," 175.

[98] Friedrich Schleiermacher, *Christmas Eve: A Dialogue on the Incarnation*, trans. Terrence N. Tice (Richmond, VA: John Knox, 1967) 31. For two helpful readings of this dialogue, see Terrence N. Tice, "Schleiermacher's Interpretation of Christmas: 'Christmas Eve,' 'The Christian Faith,' and the Christmas Sermons," *Journal of Religion* 47 (April 1967) 100–126; and Dawn De Vries, "Schleiermacher's *Christmas Eve Dialogue*: Bourgois Ideology or Feminist Theology?," *Journal of Religion* 69 (April 1989) 169–183.

[99] Schleiermacher, "Christmas Eve," 45 and 36.

[100] Schleiermacher, "Christmas Eve," 85–86.

[101] Rudolf Otto, *The Idea of the Holy*, trans. John W. Harvey (London and Oxford: Oxford University, 1958) 26.

[102] Otto, *The Idea of the Holy*, 13 and 14.

[103] Otto, *The Idea of the Holy*, 19, 20, and 24.

[104] Otto, *The Idea of the Holy*, 31.

[105] Otto, *The Idea of the Holy* 31.

[106] For a broad-based discussion of ethical criticism of literary works, see Wayne C. Booth, *The Company We Keep: An Ethics of Fiction* (Berkeley: University of California, 1988); see especially Booth's helpful bibliographies.

PART ONE

FAITH AND REASON IN DIALOGUE

2

Faith Seeking Understanding Through Dialogue: Anselm's Paradigm

"Now, issues which are examined by the method of question-and-answer are clearer, and so more acceptable, to many minds—especially to minds that are slower."

—Anselm in "Why God Became a Man"

"I do not know why it is that just when I was hoping to come to the end of our inquiry, I see instead other questions arising, as though sprouting forth from the roots of the questions we have felled."

—Student in "The Fall of the Devil"

When people talk about God and religion, is their discourse at all rational? Answers to this question vary, depending on what "rationality" is taken to mean. In Western religious traditions the different responses to this question pivot on three ways of construing what is rational. One traditional view links rationality with certain special truths; those, for instance, which find their source in the natural order of things. Such truths provide their proponents an ontological measure that resists the erosion of change, holds across cultural boundaries, or offers an unshakable point of reference. Rooted in reality, this notion of rationality is defined by invariance, universality, and objectivity. Another long prevailing view associates rationality with certain procedures for securing knowledge, so that, for instance, a claim is considered to be rational if it arises from the use of accepted modes of argumentation or procedures of weighing evidence, or again if it can be defended by assuming impartial or scientific standpoints. In this case, rationality is determined by the use of correct methods. In more recent times, the notion of rationality has taken on linguistic and social connotations. A claim is deemed rational only insofar as it is fully open to the scrutiny of public discourse. This view ascertains what is rational by social consensus.

Debates over the rationality of religious discourse—what Pierre Bayle called the "great contest of faith and reason"—have pivoted on each of these standards. Critics have found religion to be irrational ontologically (there is no god, no natural law exists, etc.), procedurally (beliefs do not hold logically or scientifically), and socially (religious claims are incurably private and intramural). In response, advocates of religion have taken two different and opposed routes. Oddly enough, some gladly concede the irrationality of religion. Drawing on purely subjective, affective, or private warrants, they shun all metaphysical claims, they offer no cogent argumentation, and they abdicate public dialogue. Of their own admission, these people have nothing to say to anyone else. Other proponents of religion, however, engage their critics directly. Religion, they insist, tells us something important about the natural and moral order, its claims can be argued persuasively (at least to a point), and its tenets can be made intelligible and credible in the public arena. For these people, reason serves the religious life.

Among those committed to this latter opinion, few have equaled the efforts of Anselm of Canterbury, the eleventh century monk, scholar and bishop, whose reflections on the rational basis of his faith have long functioned as a beacon for philosophers and theologians working in the orbit of Christian intellectual culture. Anselm's writings stand as "classics"—to use David Tracy's key term.[1] They continue, throughout the ages, to challenge and provoke readers into thinking freshly and more deeply about the meaning and truth of religious claims. It is not the nostalgia of archaic minds but the power and complexity of his textual legacy that prompts and rewards a re-reading of Anselm: the boldness with which he attempts to think and speak at the edges of conceivability about what is most real and most good; the passionate intensity discovered by those who venture past anthologized excerpts of the "Proslogion" to encounter the meditative side of Anselm the monk; the rigorous analysis of language and the methodical crafting of arguments directed at the most obtuse theological topics; the openness to questioning and conversation, most prominently with loyal students but also with believing critics, renegade theologians, other Christian confessions, and even with non-Christians; and, finally, the unshakable confidence that church teachings are unqualifiedly correct, and thus—with the aid of reason—may be understood clearly and indubitably to be true. Indeed, the power of Anselmian classics resides in the distinctive combination of all these characteristics, for it is in their confluence that Anselm pursued his fundamental goal of securing and defending the rationality of religious discourse.

My aim in this chapter is to take a close look at the Anselmian paradigm for theological inquiry, and, specifically, at Anselm's own discursive efforts to probe critically the rationality of religious language. What stands out in Anselm's discourse is its inherent complexity—something hinted at already in the blend of characteristics mentioned in the last paragraph. Nothing is simple or one-dimensional in Anselm. In fact, his entire project is built around certain basic oppositions between the commitments of religious faith and the interests of reasoned inquiry: he favors the introspective life of personal meditation, but he lives and works in social discourse with monks and friends; he is most at home directing and conversing with his monks, though his writings regularly transcend the intramural limits of monasticism to answer the challenge of other voices; his theology takes its start from the everyday language of common belief, but his analytical commitment to the proper signification of terms carries him beneath the surface of language and beyond common usage; and, finally, he thrives on the excitement of speculative (even mystical) discovery, while his conservative impulses warn him not to overstep the bounds of ecclesial orthodoxy. The contrast between faith and reason, in short, is ultimately a distinction between different forms and venues for discourse.

Faith	*Reason*
personal, meditative search for God	social discourse: struggling with the questions of others
monastic privacy and the abbot's discipline	broader publics: challenges from beyond the monastery
common Christian belief and expression	grammatically proper ("correct") use of terms
orthodox church doctrine	speculative inquiry and discovery

These oppositions, I should add, arise not from some shortcoming in Anselm, but from the very nature of the enterprise. He cannot think and speak as he does without participating in the cross-pull of these discursive tensions. They are the warp and woof of his project to rationally understand the life of faith. My purpose is to show how these dyadic structures—personal and social, private and public, common and correct, conservative and speculative—propel Anselm's theological discourse, even as they generate stresses and strains which reverberate throughout the entire project. They are, in the end, permanent and ineluctable features of the kind of critical discourse on religion he wishes to practice.

Though usually overlooked, Anselm's discourse on religion is marked by a fundamental and consistent investment in dialogue. Faith seeking understanding, in other words, proceeds in and through dialogue. Living dialogue with fellow monks proves indispensable for the cultivation of the monastic life which Anselm prized above all. Dialogue through correspondence allows Anselm to converse at a distance with a much larger group—monks, friends, advisees, kings, popes, etc. Textual dialogue—the give and take of arguments with good-willed critics like Gaunilo or with theological irritants like Roscelin—marks almost every Anselmian treatise and essay. And literary dialogue, finally, serves as a vital genre of theological composition, linking the actual practice of conversation and the method of composition in a single literary performance. It is this latter genre of dialogue, I suggest, which provides a unique opportunity for examining the tensive logic at play in Anselm's discourse. Anselm wrote five such dialogues spanning his career: an early dialogue on grammatical questions, three monastic dialogues written between 1085 and 1090, and his long-celebrated masterpiece

"Why God Became a Man."[2] Though by no means his only vehicle for theological expression, these dialogues provide a uniquely transparent window for observing their author's sense of what is fitting, possible, and likely in discourse on religion. In all these respects, Anselm's literary dialogues participate in—even as they reflect and express—their author's struggle with the tensions created from rationally probing the meaning and truth of religious faith.

In the first section of this chapter I will take a look at Anselm's three monastic dialogues. Written in the relatively sheltered environment of the monastery at Bec, these texts are at once meditative and tutorial. The "teacher" confidently resolves a barrage of student questions so that the latter may understand what he professes to believe already. Together they ponder various linguistic conundrums lurking on the surface of popular belief; in each case, the matter is resolved through painstaking grammatical analysis which deepens and magnifies the language of belief until the correct understanding is secured. Anselm's theory of language and his interest in grammar come into sharpest focus in his first dialogue—"De Grammatico." I will examine this text and its importance for Anselm's theological program in the second section. Upon leaving Bec for Canterbury, Anselm finds himself faced with broader and more demanding public forces. Now he must cope with the turbulent world of church-state politics, and he must answer the challenge of ever-widening circles of theological conversation. As we will see, Anselm's technique of grammatical meditation becomes bolder and more speculative in this wider discursive environment, even while his magisterial confidence that church teachings are utterly correct and simply need explication still stands. All four levels of faith and reason stand in creative tension when Anselm returns to the dialogue form in "Why God Became a Man." The third and fourth sections of this chapter will be devoted to this consummate dialogue.

(1) Meditation and Conversation

For over thirty years (roughly between 1060–1092), Anselm lived and worked in the Benedictine monastery at Bec—first as a monk, then as prior, and finally as abbot. No higher earthly life existed in his eyes. The goal of monastic life—service of God and peace in the kingdom of heaven—warranted complete self-abandonment and unqualified discipline. It is true that Anselm sometimes spoke positively about those who did not opt for the monastery. Thus, for instance, he exhorted his monks (upon his departure for Canterbury) always to exercise the "virtue of hospitality" and to show "kindness to all"; he saw real, but relative, value in those lay-people who practiced the "secular equivalent of monastic vows—justice, alms-giving and self-denial"; and he credited secular institutions (and their aristocratic functionaries) with a limited integrity, as long as they served and supported the higher goals of the monastery. Nonetheless, the locus of religious life lay essentially *within* the walls of the monastery. The outside world was dangerous to religious vocation, and those living in it (Jews and nonbelievers) surely would be doomed.[3] Lay Christians have a slightly better chance for salvation, Anselm concedes, but they are fickle in their commitments, like the mercenary soldier who abandons the cause upon the first sign of trouble.[4] Much of Anselm's energies during these years, therefore, are spent encouraging monks to persist in their monastic vows: "stay steadfastly in port," Anselm counseled, "do not risk your eternal safety among the shipwrecks and storms of the world."[5] The true monk should give up "every thought of migrating" from the privacy of the monastery, thus giving "himself up entirely to the diligent performance of the exercises of a holy life."[6]

In Anselm's monastic world, the "exercises of a holy life" centered on the intensely introspective discipline of personal meditation in which the individual magnified an image or experience until it bursts into insight. Among his earliest writings, Anselm's "Prayers and Meditations" go to great lengths to amplify the supplicant's depravity, even while this exercise in self-degradation is intended finally to magnify the contrasting splendor of the saint to whom the prayer is addressed. Anselm's first prayer to Mary is a perfect example: "Life-bearer, mother of salvation, shrine of goodness and mercy, I long to come before you in my misery, sick with the sickness of vice, in pain from the wounds of crimes, putrid with the ulcers of sin."[7] Intensity is the key here, and Anselm is unrelenting. The more vividly he can depict the "smell and foulness" of human sinfulness, the more magnificent the saint's gracious mercy will seem. This goes on page after page, prayer after prayer. The same process of intensification, however, reappears in better known Anselmian works, only now the scope and purpose of meditation is broadened. It is the purpose of the "Monologion," for instance, to intensify language for God, bringing the reader to the outer limits of theological insight. As R. W. Southern nicely puts it, what was formerly a "sin-disclosing introspection" is now an "essence-detecting, God-directed, introspection."[8] Both forms of meditation, in fact, continue to play a crucial role in Anselm's work—including the dialogues, and nowhere more dramatically than in "Why God Became a Man."

Though the monastery was a private world and meditation a highly personal undertaking, monastic existence was neither solitary nor quiet. Within its walls the monastery appears intensely social, with Anselm the abbot at the center of its conversation. No motif is more frequently stressed in Eadmer's biography than Anselm's penchant for conversation. Anselm's life cannot be understood fully, Eadmer insists, without going beyond his actions to see "how he appeared in his talk."[9] Most often we find Anselm in dialogue with his monks (e.g., at dinner), taking their questions and resolving their confusions. In these settings, Eadmer relates, Anselm "never scorned to give a reason when anybody asked for one."[10] But the same openness to dialogue also appears in more public settings. Anselm, we are told, "admitted to his conversation all who wished to hear him without regard to who they were"—including, apparently, non-Christians.[11] Anselm's frequent correspondence with people living outside the monastery is another expression of this openness to discourse on religious life. There is, however, an additional side to Eadmer's portrait of Anselm's life of dialogue, for Anselm was not well-adapted to nor apparently did he enjoy the "controversies and altercations" typical of public exchanges. Such discourse overwhelmed Anselm, Eadmer tells us. The only antidote was to draw him aside and put to him "some question of Holy Scripture"—that is, to engage him in the smaller, more private, and focused colloquies common within the monastery.[12] Eadmer's point is this: Anselm found peace in the world of monastic conversation, especially when he conversed privately "with the more intelligent among them, raising deep questions concerning both sacred and secular books, and giving his answers to their problems."[13] Though open to questions from abroad, Anselm's preference rests with the intramural dialogue of the monastery.

The distinctive quality of this dialogue clearly reflects the social structure of the monastic environment. For Anselm, the monastery was a community of friends guided by the abbot's sympathetic but dominant authority. He could, therefore, address his monks with strikingly intimate language and "apparently boundless emotion," even while maintaining the paternal authority dictated by his position.[14] Both notes are struck in Eadmer's portrait of Anselm's monastic discourse. Eadmer relishes the "charming sweetness which proceeded from his conversation," but this never diminishes the "fatherly authority" Anselm holds for him.[15] What lies beneath Anselm's intimate language is a matter of debate.[16] But what is certain is the paternal character of Anselm's discursive interaction with his monks. "For Anselm," as Southern puts it, "the model of all authority was the paternal authority of the abbot in his monastery, advising, commanding, informing, and labouring for the good of all members of the community."[17] This means two things: Anselm is the confident source of knowledge to whom the monks must turn for answers *and* he is the benevolent tutor who will condescend to their needs and abilities. The combination, once again, is crucial. As Eadmer describes it, Anselm approaches the education of the young men in the monastery not with the severity of "blows and chastisement alone," but with the "encouragement and help of fatherly sympathy and gentleness."[18] Each student must be fed according to his capacity. Anselm's pedagogical discourse, in sum, was both adaptive and patient, even as it exuded confidence and commanded respect. This was the style of his talk, as he guided and exhorted the monks in the meditative practices conducive to the "holy life" desired by those taking up a monastic vocation.

The three literary dialogues written during the years at Bec and grouped together as "treatises pertaining to the study of Sacred Scripture" clearly reflect and embody the conduct of living, monastic discourse.[19] They imitate, in other words, the process of meditative intensification carried on through the peculiarly private and paternal exchanges of monastic conversation.

(a) *Publicity and Privacy*. As literary dialogues go, Anselm's three monastic dialogues portray remarkably insulated conversations. There are, first off, no temporal markings to frame the discussion. Talk simply commences with a question and it ends when the last question is answered, without any promise of sessions to follow. There is, similarly, a complete lack of references to the setting or to the spatial surroundings. Unlike so many of the dialogues treated in the following chapters, the interlocutors' discourse is shielded from any and all designations of location. Finally, the discussion, too, is stripped of any specific personalities. Though the reader begins to associate certain stances with the "teacher" (confidence) or with the "student" (inquisitiveness), no speaker is recognized by name. The insularity of these dialogues' discourse is a natural (and, I think, an intentional) expression of the privacy of Anselm's monastic world. They mimic the detached and secluded venue of living monastic dialogue.

In another sense, however, these works of literary imitation are not private in the least—for what happens within the dialogue is not the same as what happens through the text. Indeed, Anselm's monastic dialogues are a public exercise by means of which Anselm speaks to a reading audience beyond the monastery. The existence of this larger audience shines through in a couple of passages from "The Fall of the Devil." In the first, the student notes that "some persons" who are vexed by the seeming incompatibility of free choice and divine foreknowledge may "perish under a wave of unbelief" by assuming one-sided views, while "many others" are "endangered" by "holding back" from any view whatsoever. Similarly, in a second text, the student appeals for the teacher's patience in replying to his "foolish question" about the origin of evil, for he wants to know "how to answer those who ask me about the same thing."[20] The student interlocutor stands in between Anselm and the reading public; he shares the foolish questions of Anselm's audience and he wants to share in Anselm's answers. The student interlocutor, in other words, functions as a "means of communication" (to borrow Brian Stock's term) between Anselm's living monastic dialogue and a wider reading public.[21] The remarkable thing about these dialogues, therefore, is how they replicate the privacy of the monastery in a text which will and does reach a more public world.

But there is one more twist to Anselm's literary conjunction of the private and the public. And this brings us back once again to Anselm's peculiarly insular handling of the dialogue genre. It is clear, in many respects, that Anselm is interested in the theological questions alive in the secular schools. The student in "The Fall of the Devil," to cite just one of many examples, acknowledges that the issue of divine foreknowledge is a "very celebrated question"—meaning, I take it, that this traditional theological problem remains under debate.[22] Anselm, however, will not enter into a public disputation with the masters of the schools; nor will he produce a literary rendition of such a formal dispute. He *will* speak to this extra-monastic audience, but he will do so only on his own terms. This means that the literate public must enter *his* world of discourse through the lens of his deliberately chosen and carefully crafted literary work.[23] And this work, as we have seen, bears all the private and insular marks of the monastery. We are left, therefore, with a delicate tension between monastic privacy and public discourse. Anselm's monastic dialogues imaginatively imitate (and, thus, inscribe in the text) the insularity of the monastery, yet engage a literate audience living beyond these confines. For this larger public to encounter Anselm, however, they must (as it were) hermeneutically participate in the authors' preferred style of discourse—and that is, as we have seen, distinctly monastic.

(b) *Meditation and Grammar*. Anselm tells us that all three dialogues pertain to the study of scripture. After reading this in the preface, most readers will be taken aback by the discussion to follow, since these texts appear to have very little to do with the bible. "On Truth" examines the nature of truth and its various forms; "Freedom of Choice" investigates the connection between free will and "uprightness-of-will"; and "The Fall of the Devil" explores how the devil can be said to have sinned, even though God did not give him perseverance. None of these texts has a clear connection to the bible. They are not commentaries on biblical texts (like those of Ambrose or Augustine, with which Anselm was familiar); and they are not sustained reflections on biblical themes. There are, granted, numerous biblical allusions and references sprinkled throughout the dialogues; but, more often than not, these function negatively as the source of the student's questions and confusions.[24] How, for instance, if *John* 8: 44 speaks of the devil as a liar by nature, can he be culpable for his fall? Or again: if God is truth (according to *John* 14: 6), how is it that other things (like statements) are said to be true? The bible serves as the common store of authoritative images and beliefs for the monastic community, and, hence, as the student says, "it must not at all be doubted on the basis of human reasoning." But that does not exclude all sorts of questions and confusions, since frequently the teachings of biblical faith "seem incompatible from the point of view of rational reflection."[25] And that is where the dialogues begin. Anselm uses the questions and confusions common to a faith rooted in the bible as the occasion—a negative point of departure—for exploring the fullest and most correct sense of biblical belief.

The bible serves, in other words, as a springboard for meditative inquiry and exploration.[26] But, unlike the solitary searchings of Anselm's "Prayers," meditation now proceeds through the give and take of dialogue; and unlike the earlier emphasis on self-analysis, the techniques of introspective intensification now are directed to the language of common faith. Indeed, the distinguishing mark of these three dialogues is the way that Anselm fuses together the techniques of grammati-

cal (or linguistic) analysis with the monastic practices of meditative intensification. The point is to cut through the inadequacies of common language in order to
arrive at the fully correct formulation of the truth, even if this process of analysis
may seem to deviate from the letter of the text. So the teacher tells the student:

> Be careful not at all to think—when we read in Scripture, or when in accordance
> with Scripture we say that God causes evil or causes not-being—that I am denying
> the basis for what is said or am finding fault with its being said. But we ought not to
> cling to the verbal impropriety concealing the truth as much as we ought to attend to
> the true propriety hidden beneath the many types of expression.[27]

When the language of everyday biblical faith suggests misleading or unfitting
things (say, about God), it is necessary to look into the various meanings of
the words involved, and then to probe intensely for the fullest and most correct expression of the belief in question. It is the endpoint of this introspective
inquiry—that *to which* the bible leads upon intense meditation conducted through
dialogue—that Anselm chiefly has in mind when he says that his dialogues pertain
to the study of scripture. He means, in short, that they pertain to the truth.

I will look more closely at Anselm's grammatical theory of language in the next
section; at this point, however, I want only to outline a few basic steps involved in
Anselm's linguistic analysis. Again and again in the dialogues, the student and
teacher begin their investigation from the common usage of words. At the start
of "On Truth," for instance, the teacher invites the student to investigate the nature
of truth by examining "the various things in which we say there is truth."[28] Repeatedly thereafter, they take their bearing from "our common way of speaking"—
what is "usually said" about the truth or correctness of a statement, or what people
mean when "we call" a thought true or false, and so on.[29] Sometimes, however,
common usage can be misleading, even concealing the truth; in such cases, it is
necessary to push beyond customary ways of speaking. After the teacher says
enigmatically that "before the world existed, it was both possible and impossible
[to be]," the following dialogue ensues:

> **Student:** I am unable to contradict your reasoning; but our common way of speak-
> ing does not agree [with your statement].
> **Teacher:** It is not surprising. For in our common way of speaking many things are
> said improperly. But when it is necessary to search out the very core of truth, it is
> necessary to analyze the troublesome impropriety as far as the subject-matter
> requires and allows.[30]

Religious language, in short, does not always mean what it says—as when it is
said that God leads someone into temptation. The grammatical task, in such cases,
is to distinguish between proper and improper locutions, in order to cull out the
true (correct) sense of the words hidden beneath the surface of familiar language.[31]

One of the most provocative points in Anselm's dialogues occurs precisely here—where the rational examination of the apparent improprieties of common faith leads beyond familiar language to what he insists are grammatically correct locutions. In each of his dialogues, this quest for linguistic rectitude brings discourse to the outer limits of speech. "On Truth," for instance, opens and then later returns to explain a passage from the "Monologion" which challenges anyone "to conceive of when it began to be true, or was ever not true, that something was going to exist"; "Freedom of Choice" struggles to explain why "nothing is more impossible than for God to remove uprightness-of-will" from a person; and "The Fall of the Devil" puzzles over how "the name 'nothing' is significative."[32] Such unusual language—high-flown, speculative, even daring—cannot help but kindle new problems for the student interlocutor, for he has never before heard these kinds of claims.[33] The student's demand, of course, is actually a sign of Anselm's own awareness that the move from the surface to the depths of religious language may appear unorthodox. Several times, therefore, Anselm guards himself from possible criticism by having the student (interestingly) affirm that the teacher's points are "neither incorrect nor uncommon," much less "against right faith."[34] With that, we arrive at the fulcrum of Anselm's project. His meditative quest for linguistic rectitude by means of grammar moves beyond the familiar lines of everyday belief into uncharted territory, even as he reaffirms his deep-seated commitment to the order of orthodox church teachings. In Anselm's eyes, no discrepancy exists between the novelties discovered by grammatical exploration and the common language of orthodox faith. But signs of tension are evident nonetheless.

(c) *Teacher and Student.* The movement between the surface and the depth of language, for Anselm, occurs through the give and take of dialogue. Meditative grammar, in other words, proceeds through dialogue. The style of this dialogue, as we have seen, mirrors the privacy of monastic conversation, even as it invites more public participation. At the same time, however, it also imitates the paternalistic relationship and tutorial discourse of abbot and monk. In this latter respect, as Southern says, Anselm's dialogues are "a tribute to his debt" to the young men with whom he regularly conversed.[35] But what may have been a tribute to his living interlocutors becomes a hermeneutical requirement for later readers. Anselm's use of the dialogue genre invites readers to identify with the student, raising their questions and relating their confusions for the teacher to answer and resolve. The paternal tenor of these exchanges between teacher and student, therefore, represents a textual demand that readers imaginatively accept this tutorial framework for discussion. Anselm's dialogues are designed, curiously, to turn readers into surrogate monks.

Though the teacher is open to any and all questions, his authority is never in question. "Lead the way, I will follow," the student gladly (and somewhat obsequiously) declares.[36] Only rarely does the master's severity show forth—when, for instance, he chastises the student for needing to have points repeated.[37] Most often, in fact, the teacher is ready and willing to lead the student along the way to a fuller understanding of the language of belief. Usually this means answering the student's questions, responding to his objections, and removing obstacles to understanding. At other times it involves a series of complicated distinctions and elaborate explanations; but even seemingly constructive moves put forth by the master are designed entirely to allay the student's intellectual uncertainties, and, hence, to help the student understand what he previously believed without understanding.[38] Above all, the teacher exudes confidence. He is the one with the knowledge and authority necessary to assist the student in his quest. He speaks—naturally—for Anselm.

In many ways, however, the student plays the more significant role in the discursive movement of these dialogues. It is the student, after all, who initiates each dialogue with a question; and it is the student who continues to propel the discourse forward with more and more questions. As he puts it,

> I do not know why it is that just when I was hoping to come to the end of our in-quiry, I see instead other questions arising, as though sprouting forth from the roots of the questions we have felled.[39]

He will, certainly, "believe without doubting" whatever is "said by Divine Authority"—but belief cannot stop the continual flow of questioning. The student is *unsatisfied* intellectually with previous accounts he has read about the devil's freedom; a "solution to this puzzle," he tells the teacher with real urgency, is "exceedingly necessary."[40] He is, similarly, "quite *troubled*" about the source of the devil's disordered will: "why did God create such a nature?"[41] Frequently we find the student simply *confused* over the logical conundrums he finds in Christian belief: how was it ever possible to sin, he asks, if "freedom" means not being able to turn away from God?[42] The student is, in short, intellectually *restless*—without, however, ever doubting the truth of church teachings. As he tells his mentor several times, "I believe, but I desire to understand."[43] In this statement, we hear the undeniable echo of Anselm's own intellectual quest to understand rationally what he believes by faith. Thus, while the teacher's magisterial confidence reflects Anselm's authoritative position as abbot, it is the student who gives voice to his existential thirst for understanding.

But what Anselm concedes to the student in intellectual drive does not alter in the least the paternal (even paternalistic) framework for monastic discourse. Indeed, more often than not, the student functions as nothing more than a voice of acclamation for the teacher's wisdom. Consider, for instance, the student's words of thanks and praise at the end of almost every chapter in "On Truth." There and throughout, the student stands in thankful dependency on the teacher's theological superiority. Only occasionally does the student show some intellectual acuity (when he equates justice and rightness, for instance); and very rarely does he display any argumentative backbone (as when he presses his question how the will simultaneously can be free and in servitude).[44] For the most part he yields to the paternal authority of the teacher. He is pleased, satisfied and grateful for the teacher's definitive resolution of his quandaries. Outside of the monastic world, of course, Anselm's projection of dependency and gratitude into his interlocutor's voice cannot help but appear self-serving, even unctuous. What teacher cannot be tempted to imagine his or her students being so appreciative and eager? But within Anselm's environment, there could be absolutely no embarrassment over this relationship; the monastery does not promote disputations between equals, but question and answer sessions between curious but ignorant monks and a confident but beneficent abbot.

It is only in "The Fall of the Devil" that we begin to see something of a shift in the student's discursive behavior. In this, the last of Anselm's monastic dialogues, the student repeatedly presses his questions with vigor and challenges the teacher's answers. He even complains at one point—imagine the audacity—that the teacher's solution about the devil's culpability is not very convincing.[45] As is not the case in the other two dialogues, here the student actually contributes to the flow of the discussion. When, for instance, the teacher says that the devil sinned because he "willed inordinately to be like God," the student retorts artfully (and in fine Anselmian fashion):

> If God can be conceived only so uniquely that nothing else can be conceived to be like Him, how was the Devil able to will what he was not able to conceive? For he was not so obtuse as not to know that nothing else can be conceived to be like God.[46]

This response forces the teacher to concede that the devil "did not will to be altogether equal to God"; and then to shift his line of argument, claiming now that the devil "willed something by an autonomous will, which was subject to no one else," and this is proper to God alone.[47] The student, in short, has contributed to the progress of their shared search for understanding. The question then becomes whether this development in the student's role in any way alters the paternalistic flavor of Anselmian dialogue.

Even more startling are a couple of passages in "The Fall of the Devil" in which the student appears especially savvy, maybe even ironic. In the first instance, the student juxtaposes his typical approbation of the teacher's insight with an immediate introduction of another problem:

> Your argument is so bound together by true, necessary, and clear reasons that I do not in any respect see how what you say can be undone—*except* that I do see something to be implied which I do not believe ought to be said, but which I do not see how to deny if what you say is true.[48]

Similarly in another passage, he says: "I do not see that your reasoning can be invalidated. *But* nevertheless, a certain question does seem to arise from it."[49] The reader has to wonder how something which is so certain—rock solid, above all question, invulnerable to dispute—can so quickly be called into question, especially by a mere student.

The quickness of these juxtapositions—approval succeeded by exception, acceptance followed by doubt—would suggest that the student may be ironically simulating subservience or feigning approval when he sees clearly the teacher's weaknesses. Certainly if we came across this language in a dialogue by Plato, Lucian, Erasmus, or Hume, we would immediately and for good reason discern irony in the student's words. But that is largely because these authors consistently prompt their readers to read suspiciously, to watch for concealed currents, and to listen for double entendres. Anselm does none of this. Indeed, what we know of Anselm's monastic environment, and what recurs for the most part in the flow of his dialogues, discourages an ironic reading of these passages. It is far more likely that these unusual sections reflect Anselm's experience of an increasingly demanding, highly spirited group of young monks, who brought ever more questions and ever more rigorous demands to the feet of the abbot. When the student says that questions keep arising from the answers to prior questions, and when Anselm inscribes this intellectual hunger in the student's discursive behavior, we as readers are confronted with Anselm's sense of just how intense, incessant, and demanding the process of faith seeking understanding can be, especially from the abbot's perspective. And all of this occurs, it is important to note, within the paternalistic framework of Anselm's beloved monastic world. The paternal arrangement stands firm and fixed. In fact, it is enhanced for Anselm by the increased energy in the student's discourse, especially since every query is answered—in the end—with the teacher's unswerving surety, followed—once again—by the student's reverent thanks.

(d) *The Point of Dialogue.* The two voices in Anselm's dialogues—one magisterial and one inquisitive—converge in their shared definition of the goal of dialogue. Most often it is the student's comments that identify the end-point of their discussion. Above all he seeks "clarity" of understanding; he wants to "see" the truth, and see it clearly.[50] When such clarity is achieved, he can exclaim with great fervor, "I see this so clearly that I cannot fail to see it."[51] And this achievement, he says repeatedly, is "pleasing" and "satisfying." This emotive language, in fact, is Anselm's primary marker to indicate the point of dialogue. He returns to it again and again in order to depict what the student wants from dialogue. Having gained understanding, the student is pleased and satisfied. "I see," he says, "and I am pleased because I see."[52] Whereas his questions troubled him, now the teacher's answers "satisfy" him.[53] And it is satisfaction that he desires. "You so satisfy me regarding the things about which I ask," he tells the teacher, "that neither in what you set forth nor in the outcome of your argument does my mind see any truth to totter."[54] What really proves satisfying, in other words, are answers that are "in no way mistaken," conclusions that can be held "unreservedly," and reasons that are unshakable.[55] Only rock-solid truth can allay the student's confusions and quandaries. But happily, what the student seeks, the teacher delivers.

Anselm gives two different, but complementary, accounts of the kind of certainty that satisfies the student's intellectual thirst. In both cases, it is linguistic closure which the student seeks and the teacher provides. The first description is grammatical. The end of "Freedom of Choice" affords a good example. Throughout this dialogue, the teacher has struggled to lessen the student's confusions by framing a complete and accurate definition of freedom. When the teacher finishes his task (clarifying freedom as "the ability to keep uprightness-of-will for the sake of this uprightness itself"), the student applauds the grammatical results. "The definition seems to me to be complete," he declares. Or, in the teacher's words, this definition is "so complete that it includes neither more nor less than the freedom we are examining." It is "neither too broad nor too narrow."[56] It is exactly right; it fits the reality of freedom perfectly. This grammatical completion, however, naturally leads to a second kind of closure, and this is dialogical. What the student yearns for is a state of satisfaction, and that state is realized when there are no questions or objections left. At the close of "Freedom of Choice," for instance, the student is happily "satisfied" with the teacher's lessons. As he puts it, "I can find nothing which I must ask regarding them."[57] Again in "The Fall of the Devil," he equates satisfaction with the elision of questions: "You have so satisfied me about the evil which is injustice that every query which used to be in my mind regarding evil has now been settled."[58] In practical terms, therefore, the student's desire for complete definitions and unshakable reasons is defined dialogically as that which stands beyond question and objection.[59] He wants to put questions (and the agitation caused by them) behind him. Correspondingly, the teacher consistently is open to the student's queries, but he has no interest in encouraging further exploration once the correct sense of belief has been confirmed. For both, therefore, the aim of dialogue is fulfilled by ending the need for dialogue.

With this, we come face to face with another basic tension at work in Anselm's dialogues. In one sense, theological discourse is exploratory. The teacher wants to lead the student "from the more familiar to the less familiar" dimensions of belief.[60] Grammatical meditation on the meaning of religious language, we have seen, leads the student to see new, uncommon things about his faith. Having made these discoveries, however, it becomes clear that what appeared as novelties were—all along—simply the proper sense of belief buried beneath the surface of common language. As the student puts it in "The Fall of the Devil," "What I earlier believed without knowing, you have caused me, still believing, to know."[61] The teacher, in other words, has uncovered the hidden but correct sense of belief for the student to see. So the student says in "On Truth": "I now see clearly what I had not noticed before."[62] The crucial point here is that the truth in question was always already there—only implicitly. Of that, the teacher is without a doubt. No new truths have been introduced, only new understandings and formulations of the things believed from the beginning. In another sense, therefore, theological discourse is explicative. Anselm has, in Southern's words, only to explicate the "conclusion [which] is implicit in his beginning."[63] The student's experience of discovery, therefore, is carefully and strictly limited by the teacher's paternal confidence that dialogue can only lead back to the truths already held in faith. Like one of Socrates' interlocutors, the student is disaffected from his presumption of knowledge ("I see that I did not understand what I was saying"), and then led maieutically to the latent truths carried in the common language of their shared faith.[64]

I will return in the third and fourth sections of this chapter to see how the dyadic structures of Anselm's project surface in his most famous literary dialogue, namely "Why God Became a Man." In the next section, however, I want to pause briefly to take a look at Anselm's interest in grammar, since his use of linguistic analysis plays such a crucial part in the development of his theological program.

(2) Anselm's Linguistic Turn

Anselm's discourse on religion—it is apparent—is through and through concerned with language. He turns the reader's attention to the improprieties of common religious language, he proceeds by grammatical analysis which creates distinctions between proper and improper locutions, he thereby moves his interlocutors (and hence, his readers) toward what he considers to be correct definitions, which he hopes (and expects) are identical with orthodox church teachings, even while the entire process frequently (at times, brilliantly) leads to the outer fringes of metaphysical conceivability. The entire enterprise turns on questions and answers about language—that is, on dialogue over language.

Anselm's turn to language came early in his monastic career; immediately, in fact, upon his encounter with Lanfranc at the Benedictine monastery at Bec in 1059. By the time the young Anselm came to Bec, the abbot Lanfranc had a long-established and widespread reputation as a renowned lawyer, a churchman important to Rome for relations with Normandy, and, most importantly for present purposes, a master of logic and linguistic studies. The latter role was carried on by means of the "school for external pupils" attached to the monastery, where Lanfranc taught an amalgam of rhetoric, grammar, and dialectic culled from Latin translations of Aristotle's "Categories." Driven by the need for "skilled clerks" to serve administrative functions, "notable men in all parts of Europe, from the pope downwards, were glad to send their aspiring relatives to Lanfranc's school, not to become monks, but to learn grammar, rhetoric and logic, and to return to their native lands with these useful accomplishments."[65] Indeed, as Southern observes, Lanfranc enjoyed "extraordinary success in raising a small, poor, and undistinguished monastic community to a state of some prosperity" by means of this appendage to the monastery.[66] It was in this context that Anselm became immersed in critical attention to argument and language—first (no doubt) as an intellectually curious monk, later as Lanfranc's assistant, and finally as teacher within the secular school. More specifically, it was the place in which he appropriated the tools of Aristotelian logic which would help to give shape to the grammatically slanted method of meditative reflection found in both the monastic dialogues and his mature writings. Anselm's introduction to linguistic analysis, therefore, arises in the secular wing of a monastic community, a venue designed to meet the interests of the larger public world, but sponsored by a community dedicated to more private religious concerns. Soon after the completion of "De Grammatico," Anselm steps inward to pursue the religious questions at the heart of the monastery, thereby leaving the affairs (and the existence) of the external school behind him, though by no means abandoning its grammatical concerns.

In addition to initiating Anselm to the world of Aristotelian logic, Lanfranc also provided Anselm with a fine model for turning grammatical investigation to the benefit of theological inquiry. Indeed, the abbot was widely known for his application of grammar and logic to the interpretation of biblical literature and to the conduct of theological controversy. On the first score, Lanfranc broke new ground by turning grammatical and rhetorical analysis to some of the more convoluted reasoning found in the letters of Paul.[67] A noteworthy letter from Pope Nicholas II, however, shows that this turn to biblical studies was not always valued as much as the secular service provided by the external school. Though he is aware that Lanfranc is "now fully occupied with the study of the Bible," Nicholas orders him to tend immediately to the instruction of the pope's "well-beloved imperial and papal chaplains" who were sent to Bec to learn "the arts of dialectic and rhetoric." One can assume that Anselm found Lanfranc's biblical work more rewarding. On the second score, Lanfranc was a key player in the eucharistic debate with Berengar at the Easter Council in 1059, thereby providing Anselm with a practical example of how logical analyses might be applied fruitfully to theological matters. Interestingly, both Lanfranc and Berengar sought to uphold the real presence of Christ's body and blood in the eucharist, and both did so with a common store of terms, distinctions, and moves taken from Aristotle's "Categories." The argument pivoted on a grammatical hinge—specifically, how and what nouns and pronouns signify in a phrase like "This is my body." Berengar denied a change of substance in the Aristotelian sense on the grounds that the pronoun in the liturgical proposition (referring to the bread) would be annulled by the predicate nominative (my body); this "manifest grammatical impossibility" dictates, therefore, an alternative, spiritual mode of signification for the key liturgical words.[68] Lanfranc countered (with orthodox support) by affirming a substantial change in Aristotle's sense; he argued by means of "equipollent" redefinition of terms that the signification of the pronoun ("this") is changed over (identified with) the noun ("body") which is predicated in the liturgical pronouncement.[69] Though Anselm may very well have dissented from Lanfranc's position in this controversy, and perhaps even been sympathetic with Berengar on grammatical grounds, it remains true that he found in Lanfranc a master who was both fundamentally committed to religious exploration of scripture and yet fully adept in the secular arts. As Southern observes, Anselm "could not have hit upon a happier combination: in dialectical skills and theological literature, Lanfranc had provided all that he needed."[70]

We first find Anselm delving into discussions of grammar and logic in the dialogue which has come to be known as "De Grammatico."[71] Originally titled "How [an] Expert-in-Grammar is Both a Substance and a Quality," this text addresses a series of logical puzzles stemming from Aristotle's discussion of paronymous names in the later chapters of the "Categories." As Aristotle notes, there are times when something is named by reference to a certain quality; in such cases, "the name of that which is qualified is derived from that of the quality."[72] Such derivative (or "paronymous") names perplex the student of Anselm's dialogue because—as we will see shortly—they wreak havoc with the construction of sound syllogisms. He wants the teacher, therefore, to clear away the grammatical problems which impede good, logical reasoning. Within Anselm's works, and certainly compared with the texts for which Anselm is most famous, this piece is highly unusual both in style and in content. Though posed in the same teacher-student framework as the monastic dialogues, the discourse is strictly technical, the interaction is terse, and the student is blunt and demanding. And unlike the monastic dialogues, the topics taken up for discussion are purely secular. The religious questions about God, the devil, and freedom of choice—those things which perplex his student interlocutors in the monastic writings—have not yet surfaced. In their place stand questions of logic stemming from students' struggles to make sense of Aristotle. As Southern notes, the "content and temper" of "De Grammatico" are "wholly secular," cut off from the concerns of the cloister.[73] What we see in this first dialogue from Anselm's hand, therefore, is the kind of discourse that reflects the intellectual life of the external school rather than that of the cloister. It is from this environment—at once monastic and yet far more in tune with public intellectual concerns that will occupy him in coming years—that Anselm's concern with linguistic matters arises.

It is the student who initiates the dialogue. The problem he faces is that incompatible conclusions apparently can be drawn logically, depending on whether names are taken to refer to a substance or a quality. The entire matter turns grammatically on the ambiguity of "*grammaticus*," which may mean either an expert in grammar or expertise in grammar; the same kind of ambiguity is carried in the

English word "expert," which may refer to either a substance or a quality. As the student reasons, from the premises "Every/Everything expert-in-grammar is a man" and "Every man is a substance," it follows that "(an) expert-in-grammar is a substance." But, he argues, this conclusion can be contested with two sets of alternative premises, both of which exclude "expert-in-grammar" from being a substance (i.e., a man). First,

> "No/Nothing expert-in-grammar can be conceived without conceiving of expertise-in-grammar.

Any man can be conceived without conceiving of expertise-in-grammar"; and second,

> "Every/Everything expert-in-grammar admits of more and less.
> No man admits of more and less";

both sets of premises lead to the same conclusion: namely, that "No/Nothing expert-in-grammar is a man." Upon some interrogation and prompting from the teacher, the student draws a parallel (but equally untenable) syllogism:

> "Any animal can be conceived without conceiving of rationality.
> No man can be conceived without conceiving of rationality.

Moreover,

> No animal is necessarily rational.
> Every man is, necessarily, rational."

From these premises, the student concludes that "No man is an animal."[74] As the student notes, there seems to be a great deal of "deception" here, for "although the premises are seen to be true and to be conjoined according to the rules for syllogisms, nevertheless truth does not support their conclusions."[75] Logic and truth are out of synch.

The teacher proceeds to clear up the student's confusion by focusing his attention on the key terms of his syllogism. When the student declares that "any man can be conceived without conceiving of expertise-in-grammar," the teacher presses him, asking "what do you say that a man can be conceived *as* without conceiving of expertise-in-grammar?" "Say what you mean," he demands; to which the student responds with more precision, that "any man can be conceived *as a man* without conceiving of expertise-in-grammar." So too with the minor premise, the student must say what he means precisely, which yields a new and improved "no expert-in-grammar can be conceived *as (an) expert-in-grammar* without conceiving of expertise-in-grammar." The important demand here is that the student "say what he means." By pressing the student in this way, the teacher underscores the grammatical underpinnings of syllogistic reasoning. Though the original syllogisms may appear to have common terms allowing for inferences, it is not enough for the "common term of a syllogism" to be common merely in "verbal form," since crucial ambiguities may be concealed in these words. The common terms of syllogisms must also be common in meaning. Indeed, the teacher declares, "the meaning—rather than the word—determines a syllogism."[76] As the discussion proceeds, it becomes more and more clear why the student is generating obviously false conclusions from just as obviously true premises. He simply is not tending to the full and proper meaning of the words he is using, and, hence, is oblivious to the "sophism which is deceiving [him] under the guise of correct reasoning."[77]

What the teacher insists upon is that the student become more sensitive to the differing ways in which words signify things. For example, the words "man" and "expertise-in-grammar" signify differently, one referring to a substance and the other to a quality. "It is not strange," the teacher concludes, "to say that with respect to being a man (an) expert-in-grammar is a substance . . . , but with respect to expertise-in-grammar expert-in-grammar is a quality."[78] Both are equally appropriate ways of speaking, provided the words are understood in their different significations. But there is more. Consider, the teacher says, how differently "man" signifies "the things of which a man consists" and "expert-in-grammar" signifies both "man *and* expertise-in-grammar." "Of and by itself the name 'man' signifies as a single thing those things of which the whole of (a) man consists"; but though it captures all these things at once—in a "single signification, and with a single name"—the name 'man' "principally signifies, and is appellative of, the substance." The case is quite different for the name "expert-in-grammar," which does not signify "as a single thing man and expertise-in-grammar." Rather, "of and by itself it signifies expertise-in-grammar, and *on the basis of something else* it signifies man."[79] One must, therefore, be cognizant of the "proper" signification of names, even though "the customary course of speaking" may glide over these differences.

In other words, the student must come to appreciate the complex (or derivative) manner of signification that occurs with paronymous names (like, for instance, "expert-in-grammar"). If, for example, someone were to say, "In this building there is whiteness," there would be no reason to think that a horse was inside. All one could rightly imagine would be the color white, and "white" would not in any way indicate something else. But, the teacher continues, if you were faced with a white horse and a black ox, and someone said, "poke it," "but did not indicate by a gesture which one he was speaking of," there would be no way to know which animal to poke, until, that is, he said "the white one."

Student: On the basis of the name "white" I would understand that the horse was meant.

Teacher: Therefore, the name "white" would signify to you the horse.

Student: Yes, it certainly would.

Teacher: Do you not see that [the name "white" would signify the horse] in a way other than does the name "horse"?

Student: I see it. Surely, even before I would know that the horse is white, the name "horse"—of and by itself, and not on the basis of anything else—would signify to me the substance of the horse. But the name "white" would not of and by itself signify [to me] the substance of the horse, but would signify it on the basis of something else, viz., on the basis of the fact that I know the horse to be white.[80]

The same distinction—between "signification of and by itself" and "signification on the basis of something else"—helps to clear up the student's initial perplexity over "(an) expert-in-grammar" as well. Referring once again to Aristotle's "Categories," "expert-in-grammar" signifies in and of itself a quality; "and yet with respect to appellation, (an) expert-in-grammar is really a substance."[81] The latter name signifies a substance only indirectly, on the basis of its primary signification of the quality, though common parlance ignores such distinctions. Logical accuracy, however, mandates more careful attention to the manners of signification.

The analysis of "De Grammatico" is—to say the least—not the most intellectually gripping of Anselm's writings. It lacks both the philosophical richness of a dialogue like "On Truth" and the theological depth of Anselm's better known doctrinal works. It is, however, the very first, complete expression of Anselm's budding interest in language, and, hence, the gateway to the kind of religious discourse which he will practice throughout his career. Despite the dryness of this text, however, two important lessons stand out. First, though the student is concerned with valid syllogisms, the teacher is intent on elucidating the grammatical underpinnings of logic. If the student is to grow in the practice of good reasoning, in other words, then he must (as Southern puts it) "penetrate the surface of words and appearances to reach the reality to which they refer."[82] The teacher drives home his points, therefore, not by ironclad syllogism but by scrutinizing the forms of sentences and clarifying the proper meaning of words. Here we see Anselm's initial turn to grammatical criticism—a move which plays a central part in the monastic dialogues (as we have seen already) and in the further development of Anselm's later theological works. Second, while the teacher spots and resolves logical incongruities by grammatical analysis, Anselm presents this first grammatical lesson by means of a literary dialogue. Dialogue becomes the means by which the grammatical diagnosis and resolution are applied to logical logjams. In opting for this genre of presentation, Anselm is not simply falling in line with literary convention. He is also, and more importantly, making a statement (to recall Nussbaum's point) about the workings of discourse; in particular, he is telling us something more about language—especially the social dimensions—than what the teacher says (in the dialogue) about grammar.

At first glance, "De Grammatico" appears very similar to the monastic dialogues. The dialogue opens with the same signs of insularity: the student raises questions, the teacher answers them, and the entire exchange proceeds without mention of a world beyond the conversation itself. But though the exchanges reflect the segregated atmosphere of the monastery, the analysis of language which follows takes—as we have seen—a purely secular turn. What the student cares about, after all, are problems of logic stemming from debates over Aristotle. He is worried, for instance, what the "expositors of dialectic" have written in their books, and how what they teach (about names for substances and qualities) conflict with use in ordinary conversation.[83] There is not even a hint of religious sensibility or interest. As noted already, the dialogue reflects the linguistic concerns of those students working in the external school; hence it mirrors the interests of the larger public world that sent these young men to study at Bec. Anselm's first dialogue, in sum, has one foot in the monastery and one in the secular world—though it leans to the latter side. One sign of this straddling of contexts is the discursive behavior of the student, who from the outset is boldly demanding: "make me certain" and "show me the truth," he commands.[84] Indeed, as Southern notes, when compared with the monastic dialogues, the pupil is consistently "less respectful, less willing to accept the master's view of any question, almost truculent."[85] And corresponding to the student's impudent stance, the teacher becomes merely a provider of answers. As the student defines their relation, "it is up to me, who am in doubt, to disclose what troubles me [about (an) expert-in-grammar being both a quality and a substance], and it is up to you to show the tenability of each disjunct and the compatibility of both."[86]

Despite this distinctive context, however, the kind of discursive relation Anselm paints between teacher and student remains tutorial, and consequently, shares a common trajectory with the monastic dialogues. The flow of conversation is driven by the student's intellectual anxiety and frustration. From the beginning, the student is *frustrated* by logical conflicts caused by paronymous names. When the teacher attempts to shed light on the "sophism which is deceiving [the student] under the guise of correct reasoning," the latter becomes *impatient*. He is caught in unwieldy syllogisms. As he puts it, the teacher's clarifications do not "satisfy my mind in such a way that my mind rests tranquil, as if what it was seeking had been found." And that—tranquility of mind—is precisely what he seeks. Unable to untangle himself from his *perplexity*, he brashly accuses the teacher of impeding his progress: "For you seem to me as if you did not care about teaching me, but to care only about impeding my arguments."[87] In addition, the student is *anxious* that what the "expositors of dialectic" have "so often and so studiously written in their books" stands in conflict with ordinary usage. If, for instance, he were to speak in public and say "(A) useful expertise is expert-in-grammar" or "This man has expert-in-grammar," "then not only would the experts-in-grammar be furious but even the unlearned would jeer."[88] The conflict, as he observes, is that the "customary usage of all speakers" regards (an) expert-in-grammar as a substance, yet the dialecticians refer to it as a quality. Even after the teacher instructs him in the differing modes of signification, the student is still "*not without qualms.*"[89]

Throughout all of this, the teacher remains calm, unflappable, and obliging. Slowly but surely, he leads the student along toward the answers he seeks. One ought not to let the dialecticians "disquiet us," he assures his pupil, since (as Aristotle teaches) "(an) expert-in-grammar" strictly speaking signifies a quality, though "with respect to appellation, (an) expert-in-grammar is really a substance."[90] With this the student appears at ease. He becomes happy only when the teacher's explanations do not "allow [him] to doubt" any further. His questions are answered and he can think of no more objections. The whole point of dialogue, consequently, is determined by the removal of doubts and the satisfaction of an anxious mind. The teacher has served his function, and he has done so in precisely the same paternal manner as will occur in the monastic dialogues. Like these religiously oriented dialogues, the point of "De Grammatico" is to answer objections and to allay intellectual anxieties. The point of dialogue is the contentment of a closed inquiry. But though the intellectual closure enjoyed by the student spells the end of their conversation, the teacher unexpectedly interjects a note of open-endedness. Because the dialecticians so vigorously "contend" with these problems today, it is best (the teacher counsels) not "to cling so tightly to the points we have made that you would hold to them with stubborn persistence even if by weightier arguments someone else could destroy them and could prove something different. But should this destruction occur, you would not deny that at least our discussion has benefitted us in the practice of argumentation."[91] And with that note, the dialogue ends with a note of tolerance that Anselm will not be able to maintain when he takes up doctrinal questions. For matters of religion, the magister graciously will entertain as many questions as arise, but he will leave no doubt that—when the conversation ends—the correct understanding of doctrine is an absolutely settled matter.

For the purposes of the present discussion, "De Grammatico" is important because it marks the start of Anselm's linguistic turn—and with that, the consolidation of the fundamental oppositions which constitute the shape and tenor of Anselm's theological enterprise. It is true, of course, that this little dialogue stands in glaring contrast to Anselm's other work; it shows no concern for religious issues, nor does it advance speculatively to novel theological insights. But what is already present in this early, quite non-theological dialogue—the attention to grammar and the option for dialogue—provide Anselm with precisely those tools he will soon carry to the labor of theological inquiry. In this sense, "De Grammatico" is the first step toward Anselm's mature theological investigations.

On the one hand, it firmly establishes grammar as Anselm's "primary mode of thought."[92] Though concern with the interpretation of Aristotle soon disappears from Anselmian texts, the analysis of words and sentences and the imperative to attend to the proper signification of words takes on lasting importance in Anselm's theological investigations. From this point onward, truth is defined grammatically as proper (though not common) signification—a measure of truth we have seen repeatedly in the monastic dialogues, and one that becomes omnipresent in the rest of Anselm's work, most famously perhaps in the so-called ontological argument.[93] As Stock rightly notes, the issue in the famous chapters of the "Proslogion" is not so much God's existence (Anselm assumes that), but the "manner in which meaningful statements could be made in language about [ultimate] reality."[94] What is demonstrated, in other words, is not the existence of God, but a grammatical lesson about common, Christian language for God—namely, that it contains within it a full and correct manner of signification which is both fully ontological (it does refer to God's being) and radically self-transcending (it always points beyond any settled signification). As Southern aptly puts it, "since words and sentences are mirrors of reality, their analysis is the first step towards an account of the ultimate reality."[95] This grammatical premise governs every step of the "Proslogion," as Anselm plumbs the surface layers of the grammar of belief to glean what he hopes will be the full but still intelligible signification of language for radically transcendent being. This premise remains basic to much of Anselm's corpus.

On the other hand, this little dialogue launches Anselm on a course which is fundamentally committed to dialogue. Differences notwithstanding, the trajectory and the tenor of Anselmian discourse remains the same from this early text, through the monastic dialogues, all the way to "Why God Became a Man." From "De Grammatico" forward, truth is defined dialogically as the elision of doubt, which yields intellectual closure and satisfaction. In many of Anselm's texts not written in dialogue form, where Anselm is faced with a "world of confrontations," he works aggressively to correct (ultimately, to silence) the wrong-headed constructions of his opponents.[96] Thus, for instance, we find him castigating Roscelin (the master of a secular school in northern France who linked his heterodox trinitarian views with Lanfranc and Anselm) for daring to "question the truth of what the Catholic Church believes in its heart and confesses with its mouth".[97] As he puts it in some surprisingly harsh rhetoric, men like Roscelin have grown " 'horns' of self-confident knowledge"; they "plunge rashly into complex questions concerning divine things without first striving in firmness of faith for earnestness of life and of wisdom."[98] In response, Anselm sets out to arrest (what he perceives to be) the perpetrator's theological arrogance, and thereby, relieve the unease of his anxious brethren by closing the matter firmly and finally. Thus he warns Roscelin not to "toss his horns in strife but let him bow his head in reverence."[99] In Anselm's dialogues, however, where he is writing in a more amicable setting for his monks and pupils, the point of discourse is consistently a mind at rest, and that condition of tranquility is generated by the teacher confidently fielding the student's objections and questions. Dialogue, in the end, must (nonetheless) remain open to further inquiry (since new questions and doubts can always arise for the student interlocutor), even while the central impulse of the conversation is embodied in the teacher's magisterial and paternal ability to shut down all current sources of uncertainty.

(3) Anselm's Penultimate Dialogue

Anselm returns to the dialogue genre, once again, but for the final time, with the writing of "Why God Became a Man." By the time of its composition (between 1095 and 1098), Anselm's life has changed dramatically. As archbishop of Canterbury, he now faces the demanding and distracting responsibilities of administering the Canterbury properties, and, more significantly, he finds himself unwittingly embroiled in political disputes between Rome and the English kings, especially concerning the monarchial right of investiture and the demand for clerical homage to the king. He has, at the same time, entered a new and larger venue of theological discussion. As already mentioned, he engages in theological controversies on matters of doctrine in works like "The Incarnation of the Word," a piece written by Anselm to defend himself against the unsolicited and unappreciated approbation of Roscelin; and he agrees (with the writing of "The Procession of the Holy Spirit") to defend the Roman church's doctrine of the Holy Spirit against Greek orthodox views at the Council of Bari in late 1098.[100] Both works reflect a very different (and far more public) world than the monastic environment which gave birth to the early dialogues and the "Proslogion."[101] Anselm, in short, has stepped from the monastery onto the stage of European politics and theology, and this shift in venue bears an immediate and significant impact on his theological project.

Of great importance for the purposes of this chapter, the drafting of "Why God Became a Man" represents the meeting-point of Anselm's ideals for monastic dialogue with a new, more demanding public environment for discourse—the confluence of which reproduces the oppositions which constitute the fiber of his theological program. Indeed, the challenges facing Anselm are greater than ever, his aspirations to maintain the style of discourse possible in the monastery accordingly are raised to new heights, and, consequently, the tensions at the very heart of his work are magnified as never before. All of this Anselm inscribes in the discourse of his dialogue.

At first glance, "Why God Became a Man" appears to be just as insulated as Anselm's monastic dialogues. There is, for instance, no mention of the time or place for the dialogue. Following a brief statement by Anselm, discourse simply begins with Boso's request that Anselm assist him in understanding the reasons behind his faith in God's redemptive incarnation; and it ends with a prayer of thanksgiving for God's guidance. The dialogue is stripped of worldly realism. There are no social points of reference to orient the reader and there are no overt marks of engagement with recognized groups or individuals. Clearly, Anselm still conceives of optimal theological conversation as taking place within the serene privacy of the monastery.

A deeper look, however, reveals three significant shifts since the monastic dialogues. First, Anselm replaces the "teacher" with his own name. With this move Anselm shuns the personal anonymity of the monastery. Instead, he explicitly connects the dialogue's dominant positions with himself as a recognized churchman, and thereby brings his public, theological reputation to bear on the discourse within the dialogue. Anselm, in short, has gone public in a new and more pronounced way. Second, Anselm gives credit to a real person as his interlocutor. The recognition of Boso by name also breaks the longstanding tradition of anonymity in monastic dialogues, and consequently gives authentic and tangible form to the position of an educated Christian who lives within the monastery but is in touch with wider currents of thought. Third, though the dialogue between Anselm and Boso retains much of the insulated flavor of the early texts, there are signs that Anselm is increasingly conscious of a broader, extra-monastic audience. This was evident already in "The Fall of the Devil," in which the student refers to people outside the monastery who trouble him with their questions, and again in "The Incarnation of the Word," in which Anselm acknowledges that "there are many who are struggling with the same problem."[102] In "Why God Became a Man," however, these references are multiplied. Thus we find Anselm, from the beginning, acknowledging that the problems and questions raised by "unbelievers" to faithful Christians have played a large part in motivating the writing of this dialogue; and Boso, as we shall see presently, makes constant reference to the nonbelievers who confront him with their objections and criticisms.[103] In each of these ways, Anselm is turning ever more consciously and explicitly to engage an extra-monastic public in dialogue, even while he persists with the insular format of his earlier dialogues.

Anselm, in short, is of two minds, and the discourse within the dialogue reflects this split in purpose. In statement and in practice, he now wishes to pursue two distinct but interconnected aims, each apparently designed to meet the demands of a different audience: (a) to help believers understand their faith in the Christ event, and (b) to argue persuasively with nonbelievers without appealing to assumptions which depend upon Christian faith. He hopes, in his words, to help the faithful "delight in the comprehension and contemplation of the doctrines which they believe" *and* "to give satisfactory answer to everyone who asks of them a reason for the hope which is in us."[104] What is crucial here is the fact that Anselm intends to engage both groups through the same text, so that two discursive agenda converge in a single exchange. The dialogue with Boso, consequently, must fulfill two functions at once, shifting back and forth with distinct argumentative strategies to meet the discursive interests of each group. The decisive point is *how* Anselm chooses to combine these distinct discursive practices.

In order to argue successfully with nonbelievers, Anselm declares that he will shun all reference to Christ. He wants to demonstrate to the nonbeliever "by rational necessity—Christ being removed from sight, as if there had never been anything known about Him—that no man can be saved without Him."[105] These are bold words, indeed; and thus it is understandable that Anselm would want to concede immediately the immensity of his task.[106] What he fears, however, has nothing to do with the possibility or impossibility of argumentatively persuading skeptical nonbelievers of this article of Christian faith. He worries, rather, whether someone might think that he was departing from "true doctrine," or that they might become indignant that he would treat "such an elegant topic by an inelegant and contemptible discourse."[107] What Anselm has in mind, clearly, are objections coming from within the Christian community. Nonbelievers, in other words, are not foremost on his mind. Nor, for that matter, are they named and confronted in the dialogue of his text. Given their absence, therefore, one has to wonder what exactly Anselm means when he says that he will demonstrate truths of Christian doctrine with rational necessity to nonbelievers.

As Southern and others have observed, Anselm perceived two significant sources of public debate over the doctrine of the incarnation. One source came from within Christianity but from outside the monastery—in the secular (nonmonastic) schools of northern France. Anselm was especially cognizant of the controversies brewing at the cathedral school of Laon around the work of Ralph of Laon. Another source of criticism originated from the Jewish community living in London. Anselm knew from his student Gilbert Crispin's experience with such critics that Jewish intellectuals were raising profound questions about the compatibility of the incarnation with the transcendent dignity of God.[108] Given his awareness of these public currents of theological discussion, it certainly is remarkable that they remain overtly absent from the discourse represented in "Why God Became a Man." Anselm will not confront them directly, even in fictional form, as Gilbert did in two literary dialogues—one between a Christian and Jew, and another between a Christian and a pagan philosopher.[109] He will address them, but only indirectly through the questions brought to him by the faithful Christians who are left insecure in their beliefs due to these public controversies. Thus we find Boso echoing a theory of Ralph of Laon's (to wit, that the salvation of humankind depends on tricking the devil into overstepping the bounds of justice by killing an innocent man); we also find him giving voice to Jewish objections that the incarnation of God in human form is unfitting to the dignity of God.[110]

Anselm's very specific use of the dialogue form serves his real but limited public aims perfectly. He wants to speak publicly on current theological questions, and he does so: first, by means of the written and copied text (with his name given as author and as speaker) which becomes a publicly available document (insofar as that was possible in the twelfth century); and second, within the dialogue by attempting to use forms of argumentation and criteria which would prove to be publicly persuasive. But Anselm speaks and argues with this wider public only through the privacy of a personal conversation between himself (still functioning as abbot) and Boso (a bright and beloved monk). The selection of a private venue may, in part, reflect Anselm's distaste for public controversies. But, more significantly, it also reflects Anselm's abiding notion of the proper order for Christian inquiry into matters of faith. As Boso puts it, echoing an Anselmian sentiment, "right order requires that we believe the deep matters of the Christian faith before we presume to discuss them rationally." Unlike the nonbeliever, therefore, the Christian must begin with the confidence of strong belief. So Boso declares that he is "holding so steadfastly to faith in our redemption that even if I were not in any respect able to understand what I believe, nothing could wrest me from firmness of faith."[111] Nothing that transpires in dialogue with nonbelievers, therefore, can change the initial and persisting assumption that Christian faith is true.

Given this point of procedure, public dialogue need only go so far. On the one hand, it is not necessary at all, either to persuade outsiders (Anselm has no interest in that) or to help believers find the truth (they already possess the truth through belief). On the other hand, it just may prove helpful to believing Christians (since, as Boso says, it would be "an instance of carelessness if, having been confirmed in faith, we do not eagerly desire to understand what we believe").[112] What Boso wants from his dialogue with Anselm is to be made "joyful in the understanding of [the] truth" of his faith. From Anselm's perspective, consequently, it is not only acceptable but also proper that public questions of theology be handled in the manner of a private conversation among like-thinking Christians. Such is the discourse he imaginatively crafts in "Why God Became a Man."

Pursuant to this kind of exchange, Anselm selects Boso as his interlocutor. A bright and inquisitive monk, Boso had come to Bec in 1085, as Eadmer reports, seeking "an interview with the abbot." Eadmer's account of his arrival is highly instructive—especially with respect to Boso's suitability as an interlocutor for Anselm. In Eadmer's words, Boso

> had a very acute mind, and he was perplexed by many intricate problems which no-one whom he had been able to meet had unravelled to his satisfaction. He talked therefore to Anselm and laid bare the perplexities of his heart; and he received from him all the answers he required without leaving a shadow of uncertainty. As a result he was moved to admiration and captivated by profound love for Anselm; and as he came to enjoy the intimacy of his conversation, he was led on to despise the world, and in a short time became a monk at Bec.[113]

All that Anselm requires in the way of an interlocutor is captured in this account of Boso. The latter is not only intelligent and philosophically inclined; more importantly, he comes to Anselm perplexed by certain theological questions encountered elsewhere, likely at the cathedral school of Laon. As Southern notes, this public experience makes Boso the perfect interlocutor to assist Anselm in thinking through the arguments and counter-arguments he will need for his dialogue.[114] For good reason, therefore, Anselm beckons Boso to join him at Canterbury as he prepares the text of "Why God Became a Man."[115] But there is another side to Eadmer's report which is equally important, for Boso comes to share in the intimacy of Anselm's private conversations precisely because he submits his questions (and his heart) to the power and authority of Anselm's mind. Boso is not only the thoughtful intellectual in touch with wider currents of theological debate, but also the faithful monk who shares in the privacy of the abbot's discourse by obediently submitting himself to his paternal authority.

Within the dialogue, therefore, Anselm's public interests and private method converge in his discursive interaction with Boso. Anselm could not wish for a more suitable interlocutor, for Boso offers him the opportunity to address public theological questions, but to do so within the privacy of a monastic conversation. Just how intimately these two agenda are bound up with each other is immediately evident in Boso's request to Anselm:

> Allow me, then, to use the words of unbelievers. For since we are fervently seeking the rational basis of our faith, it is fair that I should present the objections of those who are altogether unwilling to approach our faith without rational argumentation. Although they seek a rational basis because they do not believe whereas we seek it because we do believe, nevertheless it is one and the same thing that we and they are seeking.[116]

Boso will play a double discursive role. A steadfast believer himself, he proceeds nonetheless to raise and press the questions and criticism of nonbelievers. Is not the idea of God being born of a woman and enduring the frailties of humanity an insult to God? Would it not have been easier and wiser for God to redeem humanity by a direct act of mercy? Is God truly omnipotent if he cannot save human beings except through the condemnation of a just man?

All of these questions reflect the world of nonbelievers—and probably, as we have seen, the very specific perspectives on Christianity put forward by Jewish intellectuals in London. But they also, and more importantly for Anselm's purposes, serve the interests of believers. Boso is, in this regard, the linchpin for Anselm's whole project; in playing the outsider who demands reasons for everything, Boso the man of faith is given reasons for what he believes. Although not stated explicitly, Boso's double role is possible only because the difficulties raised by critics are also difficulties for the faithful. Indeed, Boso may profess to be certain of a doctrine, but he is as interested in hearing the reason for a belief as any non-believer would be. In this very specific sense, it is "one and the same thing" both believers and nonbelievers seek; they share confusion ("perplexity") and they desire rational explanation. Thus, for instance, when Anselm insists that the God-Man could never exist without "His power, might, and wisdom," even as a child, Boso expresses gratitude for receiving a reason for what he has believed firmly all along. As he puts it, "often we are certain that something is the case but nevertheless do not know how to prove it rationally."[117] Boso's faith may be *held* with certainty, but it is also a faith that has grown perplexed from contact with the incisive questions of outsiders. The religious lives of faithful Christians, consequently, will be enhanced by facing the challenges of nonbelievers, for in explaining the faith to critics, the faithful will be helped to better understand their faith—that is, they will be less perplexed.[118]

But this positive value granted to public dialogue does not mandate an actual and direct encounter with outsiders, much less a literary address through the medium of a fictional dialogue, because the sole reason for entertaining the objections and criticisms of nonbelievers is to serve the self-understanding of believing Christians. Believers and nonbelievers may seek the same thing, but that is no reason in Anselm's mind, to engage nonbelievers in a fully open exchange of views. It is, merely, sufficient reason to entertain their points, insofar as this input—when fully and rationally explained by Anselm—proves useful for Christians seeking to understand their faith. Anselm's public overtures do not change the fundamentally private purpose of this dialogue. In fact, they enhance it. Faith seeking understanding, even that which opens itself to the perplexities of a nonbelieving public, remains for and among Christians.

The intramural character of the discourse appears, again and again, in the dialogue, even as Anselm and Boso attempt to pursue an exchange which supposedly is to be free from Christian assumptions about Christ. That Anselm would feel free to return to a Christian orientation at the end of the first book, where he feels that he is capitalizing on the negative part of his argument (showing that there is no escape for humanity either by the rule of justice or by God's mercy), is perfectly understandable. It seems less in keeping with the spirit of public argumentation, however, when Anselm and Boso agree on working assumptions for their conversation. They agree, for instance, not only to attribute "nothing that is in the least degree unfitting" to God (that assumption could be held by Anselm's nonbeliever) and to accept anything that is "in even the slightest degree reasonable unless something more reasonable opposes it" (that assumption could be held by anyone), but also to agree upon various philosophical and theological assumptions taken from the Christian world (about the intended purpose of creation, the sinfulness of humanity, and the need for forgiveness), including "the other things which we must believe if we are to have eternal salvation."[119] The text does not detail what these other things include, but from the discourse which follows, it becomes vividly apparent that Anselm and Boso are conversing well within the orbit of their Christian beliefs. To engage in this dialogue, one must be a believing Christian.

The intramural complexion of the discourse becomes even more explicit in the uninhibited use of the Christian grammar of belief and in the frequent intrusion of biblical descriptions of Jesus into lines of argument which supposedly are developed with Christian beliefs about Christ bracketed. Early in the dialogue, for instance, Boso echoes an external criticism which finds the very idea of divine incarnation inappropriate to the dignity of God. In response, Anselm immediately turns to defend the rationality of Christian doctrine. *"Those* who say this do not understand what *we* believe," he tells Boso. *"We* affirm that the Lord Jesus Christ is true God and true man," so that any "lowliness or weakness" is attributed not to "His immpassible [divine] nature" but to "the weakness of the human substance which He assumed."[120] There follows a lengthy discussion in which Anselm works to show that "the Son" freely chose his death, and thus was not compelled to die by "the Father"—language which is amply supported by biblical references and quotations. Similarly, in other places, Anselm reverts to biblical descriptions of the life of Jesus in the midst of what purport to be strictly rational demonstrations about certain aspects of the God-man's existence. When, for instance, Boso raises questions about the sinlessness of the God-man, he does so by citing a biblical saying of Jesus (*John* 8:55), and Anselm answers accordingly by specifying what *"we* can say of Christ" on this matter. As if to acknowledge that this discussion was a digression from the argument with nonbelievers, Boso immediately beckons Anselm back to "our investigation about Him as if He did not yet exist— just as we began to do."[121] In yet another instance, Anselm breaks into a detailed description of the self-sacrificial life of the biblical Jesus to confirm what he and Boso have just discovered according to reason—to wit, that the greatest possible payment to God for the sins of humanity would be for someone to "hand himself over to death for the honor of God."[122] While arguing rationally with outsiders, Anselm cannot resist making biblical correlations which can only be for the consumption of an insider like Boso.

None of this discursive slippage is problematic, of course, as along as the intent of dialogue is self-consciously and intentionally to promote the self-examination of faith by and for Christians. What is startling, however, is the juxtaposition of apparently distinct theological agenda—indeed, the shifting back and forth between carefully reasoned argumentation designed to answer the objections of nonbelievers (with all Christian beliefs about Christ removed from sight) and to clarify expressly intramural beliefs within the world of Christian assumptions. The reasons for this movement, I think, are clear from the above discussion. "Why God Became a Man" repeats the pattern of discourse which inheres in the very fibers of Anselm's project of faith seeking understanding. He hopes—as was evident above—to promote an examined religious life through publicly available texts, but his preference remains for private, intramural discourse to achieve this goal. The tension between public inquiry and private self-understanding is heightened and intensified, because Anselm wants (and needs) to extend Christian discourse into the public realm. He will entertain the views of outsiders and he will answer them by reasoned argument, but he will not (and apparently cannot) turn away from the fundamentally private purpose of his project. Theology now may be more public, but in the end it has no other purpose than to alleviate the confusions and questions of committed Christian believers. It is an intramural project.

The tension between the publicity and privacy of Anselm's theological discourse becomes clearly evident in the use of his standard techniques of inquiry—namely, grammatical analysis of the language of belief, and, by that means, meditative intensification of common Christian belief to the limits of its correct signification. This quintessentially Anselmian approach to theological inquiry, as we will see in the next section, is deeply affected by the increasing tensions between Anselm's willingness to consider questions arising from the extra-monastic world and his enduring preference to handle these matters in the sheltered and paternal style of monastic conversation.

(4) The Fitting and the Necessary

True to the methodological orientation used in his earlier works, Anselm returns once again in "Why God Became a Man" to grammatical analysis of the language of common faith. The starting point for inquiry remains the confusions surrounding the ordinary language of belief; and the aim continues to be the clarification of language until the proper (or "fitting") sense of words can be secured. But because Anselm now pursues two distinct agendas, at once addressing the challenge of nonbelievers, and, by that means, serving the self-understanding of believers, the analysis of language becomes considerably more complicated.

At times Anselm's grammatical inquiry is purely intramural, as when he puzzles over the trinitarian implications of saying that Christ offered himself for "God's" honor. In Anselm's words,

> that honor belongs to the whole Trinity. Therefore, since He Himself is God—viz., the Son of God—He offered Himself to Himself (just as to the Father and the Holy Spirit) for His own honor. That is, [He offered] His humanity to His divinity, which is one and the same divinity common to the three persons. Nevertheless, in order *to say more clearly* what we mean, while still abiding within this truth, *let us say (as is the custom)* that the Son freely offered Himself to the Father. For in this way *we speak most fittingly.*[123]

In this case, the ordinary language for belief is found to be confusing when considered in the context of trinitarian teaching; but the same language, Anselm assures Boso, can be used properly, if the more precise (i.e., trinitarian) sense of the words is kept in mind. In other passages Anselm concerns himself with clarifying misleading biblical language by drawing analogies with forms of speech which are used by both believers and nonbelievers. When, for instance, Boso questions the justice and reasonableness of God's allowing (or perhaps, even compelling) an innocent man to die,[124] Anselm launches an extended linguistic analysis in order to show the propriety of saying that Christ was obedient unto death. Appealing to a principle of double effect, Anselm insists that the Father fittingly can be said to have willed the Son's death, since "we often say" that someone wills one (immediate) thing by means of which something higher is willed. This is not an "unusual expression." Anselm insists,

> It is as if He were to say: "Since You, Father, *do not will* that the reconciliation of the world be accomplished in any other way, I say that in this sense You *will* my death. Therefore, let this will of Yours be done—i.e., let my death occur—so that the world may be reconciled to You."[125]

Again, the common language of belief must be made more precise if the customary form of expression is not to send misleading (or, as Anselm would say, "unfitting") signals. In other places, finally, Anselm addresses the language of belief in an even broader fashion—as he does, for instance, when Boso wonders whether it was not necessary for God to complete his original design for creation or be dishonored. Again aiming to overcome apparent improprieties in language, Anselm responds that

> God does nothing by necessity, because He is not in any way compelled to do anything or prevented from doing anything. And *when we say* that God does something as if under the necessity of avoiding dishonor (which, surely, He is in no danger of encountering) we must, rather *interpret this to mean that* He does it under the necessity of maintaining His honor. Indeed, this necessity is nothing other than the immutability of His honor—an immutability which He has from Himself and not from another, and which therefore is *improperly called* necessity.[126]

Here, as in the earlier examples, Anselm aims to establish linguistic rectitude by reinterpreting the central terms of belief, thereby clearing away improper meanings and arriving at more appropriate or "fitting" locutions for faith.

The concept of the "fitting" is central to Anselm's religious and philosophical world, and it naturally plays a pivotal part in "Why God Became a Man." The root meaning of the term for Anselm is grammatical, but, as we saw earlier, this is—for him—no reason to restrict the scope of the term. Within this dialogue, in fact, the fitting use of language frequently carries ontological weight, as in the many instances in which Anselm rejects one of Boso's objections to the incarnation as being improper to the dignity and power of God. For Anselm, Christian doctrine must not introduce anything which would demean or degrade the being of God. It would be unfitting, for example, were God to create "another man who had no sin" in order to redeem human beings, for that would make humanity the servant of that new man, which is contrary to (does not fit) God's original design.[127] Along the same lines, Anselm consistently seeks to establish the rationality of Christian doctrines by placing them in what he perceives to be the proper balance of things. Nowhere does this aesthetic notion of rationality become more apparent (and more far-fetched) than in Anselm's explanation to Boso why it was fitting for the God-man to be born of a woman. Since God already had used the other three forms for creating a human being (from a man and a woman; from neither man nor woman; and from a man without a woman), "nothing is more fitting than that He assume from a woman without a man *that* man about whom we are inquiring." The same kind of reasoning applies to the "fittingness of the God-man's being born of a virgin": "If a virgin was the cause of all the evil to the human race, then it is much more fitting that a virgin would be the cause of all the good for the human race."[128] Such beliefs are rational, for Anselm, precisely because they are fitting, and they are fitting because they correctly signify the proper order (or balance) of reality.

Indeed, there is nothing more basic to Anselm's philosophical and theological sensibilities than this sense of correct or fitting order. It governs every step and every level of his thinking.[129] From the cultural environment of the day, Anselm inherited both political "patterns of right ordering"[130] (between lord and servants, for instance) and ecclesial models of authority (between pope and bishop, for example). On both counts, Anselm clung steadfastly to the reigning hierarchical system of authority. From Augustine, Anselm absorbed a religious sense for the proper ordering of earthly goods under the unifying principle of the one Good. Thus we find Anselm counseling his readers in the "Proslogion" to "love the one Good in which are all goods. . . . Desire the simple Good which itself is every good, and it shall be enough for you."[131] Human life is rightly ordered, in short, when it subordinates its desires under the ultimate delight in God. And finally, from Aristotle, as we have seen, Anselm picks up a commitment to grammatical precision and logical rigor. Grammatical correctness means tending to the fitting significations of words for things.[132] The important point to note here is that all these senses of order work together for Anselm. As Southern nicely puts it, while "Anselm's programme was Augustinian, his operating system was Aristotelian": with Augustine, he saw all things united in God; and with Aristotle, he insisted upon grammatical correctness.[133] And so too, consequently, in his written work, he wanted to display the "correspondence between the ordering of words and the ordering of every part of Creation."[134] Every aspect of discourse—including, therefore, the choice and use of words, the very order taken in theological inquiry, the genre employed to distribute his insights, and the relationship thereby established between author and readers—is to be designed so as to be fitting and correct. It is not surprising, therefore, that "Why God Became a Man" is so thoroughly dominated—in substance and in form—by the quest for correct order. The entire dialogue pivots around his perception of what is fitting or appropriate.

But though images of right order and fitting language recur throughout the dialogue, Boso moves on to demand more rigorous demonstrations. The non-believers whose objections he raises to Anselm will not be moved, after all, by aesthetic appeals to the fitting. So, he says,

> All of these things must be acknowledged to be beautiful and to be pictures, as it were. However, if there is not a solid foundation upon which they rest, they do not seem to unbelievers to suffice for showing why we ought to believe that God was willing to suffer these things of which we are speaking.[135]

Boso wants more than fitting pictures and balanced language. He wants a "rational foundation" and "cogent reasoning which proves that God should or could have humbled Himself" in the way Christians believe. As if to defend the argumentative force of his linguistic search for appropriate or fitting locutions, Anselm counters with what he considers "a very cogent argument"—to wit, that "it was not fitting that God's plan for man should be completely thwarted."[136] In his response, Boso misses the fact that Anselm has answered his objection with yet further appeal to the "fitting"—the very language to which he had objected. It is not long, however, before Anselm adjusts his line of argument to meet the demand for more persuasive forms of reasoning. What is important to note here is the manner in which he forges this reasoning without abandoning the basic designs of his linguistic analysis.

To answer Boso's request for more rigorous argumentation, Anselm moves to construct what he calls "necessary reasons" for the incarnation in a God-Man. This term, admittedly, carries a number of different meanings; and Anselm frequently allows the term a certain ambiguity. Anselm approaches a definition of what he means by 'necessary reasons' when he contracts with Boso on the terms of their exchange. They agree, in short, to "reject nothing that is in even the slightest degree reasonable unless something more reasonable opposes it." So "necessity accompanies any degree of reasonableness, however small, provided it is not overridden by some other more weighty reason."[137] There are two important implications of this statement, neither of which find their way into standard readings of Anselm: first, his requirements for "necessity" must be understood discursively rather than logically. In a logical sense, a stronger argument always outweighs a weaker one (that is obvious); but, in a discursive sense, an argument (weak or not) may demand assent (hold with necessity), unless and until it is countered with an objection or criticism which undercuts it. As will be shown presently, Anselm aims for the latter kind of proof. Second, the term "necessity" is the more public fruit of Anselm's enduring interest in the techniques of meditative intensification, now fully translated into an argumentative strategy. Just as the so-called ontological argument of the "Proslogion" carries the force of necessity by taking a limit concept ("that than which nothing greater can be conceived") to the point at which Anselm's imaginary interlocutor (the "fool") can raise no further objections, so, too, in "Why God Became a Man," Anselm's argument seeks to magnify Boso's words or assumptions, effectively generating superlative phrases (limit concepts), the implications of which will not allow dissent. "Necessary reasons," in short, issue from grammatical intensification taken to the limits of dispute.

Nowhere is Anselm's method of intensification more fully developed than in "Why God Became a Man." Again and again, Anselm takes Boso's assumptions to their limits. He proceeds by questioning the implications of Boso's objections, trying to generate conflicts and intensify predicaments until Boso's assumptions burst into absurdity and yield a new, unexpected insight. On the negative side, Anselm traps Boso in the absurd implications of his own notion of divine justice. Every element of Boso's notion of justice is magnified (the gravity of sin; the extent of human culpability; the magnitude of the debt to God; the impossibility of paying this debt) until what Boso deems necessary (satisfaction to God "according to the measure of sin") is seen to be impossible.[138] This leaves only the horrible conclusion that, "if God is guided by the principle of justice, then there is no way for this unhappy, insignificant man to escape. . . ."[139] The same intensification strategies are later used constructively in the famous argument for the necessity of a God-Man and in the argument for a proxy recipient of the God-Man's reward.[140] At every juncture Anselm generates a superlative phrase (akin to the formula of perfection in the "Proslogion"): sin is a dishonor "than which nothing is tolerated more unjustly"; the debt owed God is "something greater than is that for whose sake you ought not to have sinned"; the payment to God must be "something greater than every existing thing besides God"; the gift presented by the God-man to God must be "something greater than whatever is inferior to God"; a wrong done to the God-man "surpasses, incomparably, all conceivable sins which are not against His person"; and, finally, God's mercy is "so great and so harmonious with His justice that it cannot be conceived to be greater or more just."[141] In each of these cases, Anselm magnifies a notion to such a degree that Boso cannot make a comparison, cannot raise an objection, and cannot formulate a criticism.

In Anselm's mind, this argumentative strategy carries the full force of rational necessity. Now, however, he claims to have secured more than aesthetic rationality—the "beautiful and reasonable" pictures he and Boso enjoyed in their quest for fitting theological language.[142] Now, indeed, Anselm even dares to speak of "inescapable" conclusions![143] What he means by such a claim is inscribed in Boso's responses to Anselm's arguments. Again and again, reason describes the power of an argument to arrest all further objections and questions. Thus Boso says, characteristically: "Since we have proposed to follow reason, I have nothing which I can say against you on all these matters, even though you alarm me a bit."[144] Anselm's arguments are rational in as much as Boso can no longer oppose the master's reasoning. "You remove from me all objections which I thought could be raised against you," admits Boso.[145] The same thing occurs when Anselm seeks to show Boso that "no one can honor or dishonor God as He is in Himself"; Boso can only exclaim in typical fashion, "I do not know what I can say against this conclusion."[146] Or again, when Anselm claims that "reason leads us inescapably to conclude" that the divine and human natures unite in one person, the full force of this claim is discursively explained in Boso's response: "The route by which you lead me is so completely fortified by reason that I do not see how I can veer from it either to the right or to the left."[147] Something is reasonable—indeed, reasonable with necessity—it seems, precisely where an interlocutor cannot but give assent. Reason is defined by lack of escape, by exclusion of all possible objections, by silencing counter-arguments.

What this means for Anselm's entire enterprise is terribly important. He is, most certainly, ready and willing to take on questions and respond to objections. Theology, in Anselm's hands, *is* open to argument. Indeed, Anselm's readiness to take on all sorts of questions—from students, and, by means of them, from beyond his own monastic circle—is written into the civil but paternal style he gives to the dialogue form. "Why God Became a Man," in particular, shows Anselm more than willing to engage all kinds of questions, objections, and criticisms—something evident in the uniquely spirited role given to Boso. But, just as surely, the point of this discursive engagement is—in the end—to close off further question and objection. Like the monastic dialogues, Anselm here again allows doubts and anxieties to be raised precisely so that he can set them to rest. He strives, therefore, for a kind of rationality which is measured by discursive closure. Reason, in short, is defined by the exhaustion of Anselm's interlocutors.

In addition, Anselm's meditative-linguistic quest for necessary reasons reintroduces and magnifies one more of the central tensions inherent in Anselm's theological discourse—specifically, that between the sense of discovery in theological inquiry and the fundamental Anselmian conviction that critical discourse on faith never does more than explicate truths already possessed. On the one hand, since the arguments by dialogical intensification are designed to be persuasive to believers affected by the unsettling questions coming from the public world, Anselm seems to have generated new insights for a nonbeliever and, hence, for confused believers as well about God and world. The public dimension of

Anselm's discourse appears to generate theological novelties. It is evident, for instance, that Anselm leads Boso to a *new* understanding of the incarnation. Boso, it is true, already "possesses" faith, but it is a faith wrapped in misconceptions (not unlike the nonbeliever's) and it is an uncertain faith (something like the anxious faith in chapter one of the "Proslogion"). Anselm's rhetoric tries to show Boso something new, leading him to surprising and elevating discoveries, clearing away obstacles so that Boso will not be able not to conceive the superlative justice and mercy of God. All this is new to Boso, as it would be to the outsider, and Boso's great delight is etched in his reactions: his fright, despair and confusion at the destructive part of Anselm's strategy give way to excitement and joy as he begins to understand the incomparable splendor of the Christ event.[148]

But, since Anselm's discursive aims fundamentally remain intramural, and because his interest remains that of answering questions and closing off objections, what appears to be discovery turns out to be confirmation. What approaches the novel (at the speculative limits of discourse) by speaking at the edges of the public world (at once within and outside the monastery), in the end, remains a confirmation of orthodox beliefs. Theology's exploration, therefore, serves an explicative function. As bold as Anselm can be in searching out the fittingness and the necessary reasons for the incarnation of God in Christ (and he *is* bold in taking Boso and his reader's to the outer edges of coherent discourse), Anselm remains equally conservative (and fully confident) that what he will find is always no more than a more proper way of articulating the truth lying within the common language of faith.[149] The whole point of critical discourse on religion, in other words, is to confirm the truth of religious belief.

The evidence for this point lies in another example of Anselm's commitment to right order and fitting speech. Anselm's notion of fitting language extends not only to what is said, but equally to how something is said, and, therefore, to the discursive exchange portrayed in the dialogue. Linguistic rectitude, in short, is not only an object but a feature of Anselm's theological discourse. First, the "right order" for Christian theological inquiry (Anselm insists) not only mandates a point of departure (begin with belief) and a format for proceeding (discuss them rationally through questions and answers); it also demands a return to the original starting point. So Boso declares that he is "holding so steadfastly to faith in our redemption that even if I were not in any respect able to understand what I believe, nothing could wrest me from firmness of faith."[150] Nothing that transpires in dialogue with nonbelievers, therefore, can change the initial and persisting assumption that Christian faith is true. Second, the proper discursive order between abbot and monk likewise requires a fitting conclusion to dialogue in the correct answers possessed by the abbot. Though Boso plays an active and crucial role (initiating discussion and pressing home well-targeted questions) and though he at times seems downright savvy (like the student in "The Fall of the Devil," he frequently lauds Anselm's answers, only to question them immediately),[151] the paternalistic complexion of the dialogue assures that exploration will—in due time— rediscover and confirm Christian belief. This means, interestingly, that the "fitting" (as a feature of intramural, monastic discourse between abbot and monk) leads inevitably to Anselm's quest for "necessary reasons"—that is, to explanations which confirm belief and close down the need for further dialogue. And third, right order for dialogue also requires right teaching—and that, for Anselm, means submission to the authority of orthodox doctrine.[152] What both Anselm and Boso seek, finally, is the "satisfaction" of correct belief. What they find so satisfying, in other words, is the comfort and assurance that the Christian view of the world—specifically, Anselm's view of the human situation before God—is correct, and therefore beyond question.

To sum up this chapter's key points, Anselm's dialogues reveal the presence of certain dyadic structures at the heart of the attempt to understand the contents of Christian faith. His theological project is bound up with opposing venues, mixed interests, and rival criteria, all of which results in discourse stretched by its constituent oppositions. To speak as Anselm does (both within the text and by means of the text) is to be pulled in several different directions at once—inward to the private assumptions of like-thinking Christians and outward to the public challenge of alternative voices; toward the common language of faith and downward to the hidden depths of this same language; forward in speculative discovery of new ideas and backward under the constraints of orthodox teaching authority. Anselm's commitment to grammatical analysis and dialogue, we saw in the second section, generates these discursive tensions. The search for the proper meaning of religious terms moves with novelty away from the assumptions of common usage, even as it claims to be nothing more than explication of orthodox teachings; and this same grammatical project intends to mollify the doubts and questions of faithful Christians, even as it indirectly aspires to answer the challenges of those persons not starting from the assumptions of faith. Through and through, Anselm invites and encourages open inquiry, while he struggles to achieve a level of certitude which will exhaust all possible questions. Anselm, in sum, faces a multifaceted yet internally generated quandary: his discourse is sundered (by audience, strategy, and criteria), yet he will not (and, apparently, cannot) give up on either side. Theology, for Anselm, is and must be both private and public, speculative and orthodox, exploratory and explicative, open and closed. That is the nature of his discourse.

In as much as centuries of Christian theologians have operated under the umbrella of Anselm's paradigm for religious discourse, I suggest that these same quandaries have cropped up in Christian theology generally. And, in as much as many Christian theologians—from conservative to progressive—continue to this day to practice the kind of critical discourse on religion found classically in the dialogues of Anselm, these same discursive oppositions (and hence, the stresses and strains generated by them) recur in contemporary theology. Such discourse lives ineluctably and intractably in the midst of tensions created of its own designs and interests—speaking at once publicly and privately; committed to the language of common faith but more concerned with proper (albeit unusual) locutions; interested in speculative discovery yet haunted by the voice of orthodoxy; open to inquiry yet finally hungry for closure.

Such discourse, granted, can and does take on many forms. But wherever someone practices the kind of critical discourse on religion classically modeled on Anselm, to that extent they will come to participate in the same kind of cross-tensions. This does not mean—once again—that theological labor is bankrupt. Indeed, these tensions are precisely what make it work. In the end they are permanent, they are unavoidable, and they are irreparable features affecting this kind of discourse on religion.

Notes

[1] David Tracy, *The Analogical Imagination*, ch. 3.

[2] The unfinished "Philosophical Fragments" shows evidence of dialogue form as well; though the majority of the text abandons the give and take of dialogue. See *Anselm of Canterbury*, vol. 2, ed. and trans. Jasper Hopkins and Herbert Richardson (Toronto and New York: Edwin Mellen, 1976) 3–29.

[3] For a portrait of Anselm's monasticism, see R. W. Southern's splendid *Saint Anselm; A Portrait in a Landscape* (Cambridge: Cambridge University, 1990). On the points mentioned here, see 160, 163, 182 and 223.

[4] Anselm's simile of the mercenary soldier is found in Eadmer, *The Life St. Anselm; Archbishop of Canterbury*, trans. R. W. Southern (London: Thomas Nelson and Sons, 1962), 223.

[5] Anselm frequently uses the image of the dangerous sea. I take it from Southern, *Saint Anselm*, 236. As Southern notes, Anselm likely appropriated this image from Horace. See *The Odes and Epodes of Horace*, trans. Joseph P. Clancy (Chicago: University of Chicago, 1960) i, 14.

[6] Anselm's words from a letter to Lanzo, a monk at Cluny. See Eadmer, *Life*, 33. The monk should "stick to God through thick and thin." *Life*, 96. For Anselm, only the angels have a more desirable existence than a monk—for they apparently are immune from the dangers of the world. See Southern, *Saint Anselm*, 223. The severity of Anselm's division between lay and monastic life is clearly evident in his chastisement of Ermengard for not seeing the wisdom of her husband's decision to abandon her for the monastery. See Letter 134; reference from G. R. Evans, *Anselm* (Wilton, Connecticut.: Morehouse-Barlow, 1989) 12.

[7] Saint Anselm, *The Prayers and Meditations of Saint Anselm*, trans. Benedicta Ward (Harmondsworth: Penguin, 1973) 107.

[8] Southern, *Saint Anselm*, 121. The *Monologion* originally was titled "an example of meditating about the rational basis of faith." See *Anselm of Canterbury*, vol. 1, ed. and trans. Jasper Hopkins and Herbert Richardson (Toronto and New York: Edwin Mellen, 1974) viii. The *Proslogion* repeats both forms of meditation as well—the first, highly passionate chapter magnifies the limits of human ability, while the chapters to follow strive to magnify that which lies finally beyond human words.

[9] Eadmer, *Life*, 36. In the end, he laments, there was just too much talk to be reported in a single book.

[10] Eadmer, *Life*, 73 and 80.

[11] Eadmer, *Life*, 107 and 111. The mention of pagans conversing with Anselm refers to Arab troops employed by Roger, count of Sicily, at the siege of Capua in 1098.

[12] Eadmer, *Life*, 80.

[13] Eadmer, *Life*, 50. See Southern, *Saint Anselm*, 445.

[14] Southern, *Saint Anselm*, 143. Anselm's letters are packed with romantic energy. Thus, for instance, Anselm writes to Gundulf: "Everything I feel about you is sweet and pleasant to my heart; whatever I desire for you is the best that my mind can conceive. . . . And so, wherever you go, my love follows you; and wherever I may be, my desire embraces you." Southern, *Saint Anselm*, 144. Or again: "Most beloved. . . since I do not doubt that we both love the other equally, I am sure that each of us equally desires the other, for those whose minds are fused together in the fire of love, suffer equally if their bodies are separated by the place of their daily occupations. . . ." Southern, *Saint Anselm*, 145. As Southern observes, Anselm intended these letters to be shared with other readers, making them at once very intimate and openly public.

[15] Eadmer, *Life*, 59 and 25. Interestingly, Eadmer speaks of Anselm as both "a very dear father" and "the gentlest of mothers." Eadmer, *Life*, 22 and 23.

[16] John Bosworth finds in it evidence of homosexual love. See John Boswell, *Christianity, Social Tolerance and Homosexuality: Gay People in Western Europe from the Beginning of the Christian Era to the Fourteenth Century* (Chicago: University of Chicago, 1980). In response, Southern argues that monastic friendships for Anselm were purely "intellectual realities, passionately conceived and vividly expressed"—even if they oftentimes are expressed in highly romantic (even erotic) terms. For Southern's response, see *Saint Anselm*, 148–165. The evidence is confusing at best.

[17] Southern, *Saint Anselm*, 164.

[18] Eadmer, *Life*, 38. Anselm regarded "the youth and young man, aptly tempered between the extremes of softness and hardness" as the ideal student. See *Life*, 20–21.

[19] Anselm, "Preface," *Anselm of Canterbury*, vol. 2, 73. These dialogues are titled "On Truth," "Freedom of Choice," and "The Fall of the Devil." On these three dialogues, see G. R. Evans, *Anselm and Talking About God* (Oxford: Clarendon, 1978) 76–96.

[20] Anselm, "The Fall of the Devil," *Anselm of Canterbury*, vol. 2, 166–167 and 175. What seems like a literary device without objective reference in the "Proslogion" (where Anselm argues with the hypothetical "fool" from the *Psalms* about the existence of God), here takes on concrete reference to troubled believers outside the monastery who are affecting the faith of his monks. Much later, in "The Incarnation of the Word," Anselm similarly writes "to satisfy the requests of my brethren" who are unsettled by "the many [outside the monastery] who are struggling with same problem." See Anselm, *Anselm of Canterbury*, vol. 3, ed. and trans. Jasper Hopkins and Herbert Richardson (Toronto and New York: Edwin Mellen, 1976) 11.

[21] Brian Stock, *The Implications of Literacy; Written Language and Models of Interpretation in the Eleventh and Twelfth Centuries* (Princeton: Princeton University, 1983) 361.

[22] Anselm, "The Fall of the Devil," 166.

[23] In this sense, Southern correctly observes that Anselm employs the dialogue form "only between friends" (or at least between the abbot and monks). Dialogue provides Anselm with an ideally sheltered and controlled "pedagogical device," and thus does not reflect "a real division of opinion." See Southern, *Saint Anselm*, 115.

[24] Roughly eight indirect references in "On Truth," three in "Freedom of Choice," and seven in "The Fall of the Devil"—according to the notes of Jasper Hopkins and Herbert Richardson, editors of *Anselm of Canterbury*, vol. 2.

[25] The student's words in Anselm, "The Fall of the Devil," 166.

[26] See Southern, *Saint Anselm*, 70–71.

[27] Anselm, "The Fall of the Devil," 133.

[28] Anselm, "On Truth," *Anselm of Canterbury*, vol. 2, 77.

[29] Anselm, "On Truth," 79–80 and 81. See also 83, 89, 94 and 98. "Freedom of Choice" and "The Fall of the Devil" follow the same pattern of analysis.

[30] Anselm, "The Fall of the Devil," 152.

[31] Above all, the student is not to "cling to inappropriate words that merely conceal truth, but rather seek to discover the proper truth of philosophical reality hidden beneath the many-faceted usages of everyday speech." Stock, *Implications of Literacy*, 359.

[32] See Anselm, "On Truth," 77 and 92; "Freedom of Choice," *Anselm of Canterbury*, vol. 2, 118 and following; and "The Fall of the Devil," 147.

[33] See, for example, Anselm, "Freedom of Choice," 118.

[34] Anselm, "The Fall of the Devil," 165 and 175.

[35] Southern, *Saint Anselm*, 446.

[36] Anselm, "On Truth," 91. In this same dialogue, the student wishes to be no more than a "good listener": "you conduct the investigation," he tells the teacher, "and I will heed whatever you find out." "On Truth," 77 and 78.

[37] Anselm, "Freedom of Choice," 123.

[38] Anselm, "The Fall of the Devil," 161.

[39] Anselm, "The Fall of the Devil," 143.

[40] Anselm, "The Fall of the Devil," 167.

[41] Anselm, "The Fall of the Devil," 144.

[42] Anselm, "Freedom of Choice," 107.

[43] Anselm, "Freedom of Choice," 110. See also "The Fall of the Devil," 141.

[44] For the first, see Anselm, "On Truth," 93. See also 91. For the second, see "Freedom of Choice," 121.

[45] Anselm, "The Fall of the Devil," 136–138 and 139.

[46] Anselm, "The Fall of the Devil," 140.

[47] Anselm, "The Fall of the Devil," 140. Later the student presses the teacher on the proper signification of the word "nothing," since he was not satisfied with the teacher's first answer. See 146–149.

[48] Anselm, "The Fall of the Devil," 164, my italics.

[49] Anselm, "The Fall of the Devil," 169, my italics.

[50] Anselm, "On Truth," 84 and 91, for instance.

[51] Anselm, "On Truth," 101.

[52] Anselm, "The Fall of the Devil," 135. See also "On Truth," 90: "What you say pleases me"; and "The Fall of the Devil," 174: the teacher's wisdom is "pleasing to me."

[53] Anselm, "On Truth," 86 and 81. See also, "The Fall of the Devil," 141 and 150.

[54] Anselm, "The Fall of the Devil," 141.

[55] Anselm, "On Truth," 141, 86, and 82.

[56] Anselm, "Freedom of Choice," 124–125.

[57] Anselm, "Freedom of Choice," 126.

[58] Anselm, "The Fall of the Devil,"175.

[59] Anselm, "On Truth," 92; and "The Fall of the Devil," 168.

[60] Anselm, "On Truth," 90.

[61] Anselm, "The Fall of the Devil," 161.

[62] Anselm, "On Truth," 91.

[63] Southern, *Saint Anselm*, 115.

[64] Anselmian dialogue is Socratic in this sense, though as Evans notes, "the master's method is gentler. The pupil is challenged and encouraged to think for himself and put right when he is on the wrong track, but is not made a fool of." See Evans, *Anselm*, 39–40.

[65] Southern, *Saint Anselm*, 29.

[66] Southern, *Saint Anselm*, 29.

[67] On Lanfranc's turn to biblical studies with the help of grammar and logic, see Southern, *Saint Anselm*, 39–43.

[68] Marcia Colish, *The Mirror of Language; A Study in the Medieval Theory of Knowledge* (New Haven: Yale University, 1968) 105.

[69] See Colish, *Mirror of Language*, 105–107. See also Southern, *Saint Anselm*, 24–28.

[70] Southern, *Saint Anselm*, 59. On Anselm's silence concerning the eucharistic debate and the similarity of Berengar's grammatical method and the argument for the existence of God in Anselm's "Proslogion," see Southern's remarks in *Saint Anselm*, 45–46.

[71] On "De Grammatico," see Colish, *Mirror of Language*, 108–110; and Desmond Paul Henry's *Commentary on De Grammatico; The Historical-Logical Dimensions of a Dialogue of St. Anselm's* (Dordrecht and Boston: D. Reidel Publishing Co., 1974).

[72] Aristotle, *Categories*, ch. 9: 26 to ch.10: 4.

[73] Southern, *Saint Anselm*, 63.

[74] Anselm, "De Grammatico," *Anselm of Canterbury*, vol. 2, 39–41.

[75] Anselm, "De Grammatico," 42.

[76] Anselm, "De Grammatico," 43.

[77] Anselm, "De Grammatico," 49.

[78] Anselm, "De Grammatico," 51–52.

[79] Anselm, "De Grammatico," 54–55, my italics.

[80] Anselm, "De Grammatico," 59.

[81] Anselm, "De Grammatico," 64.

[82] Southern, *Saint Anselm*, 64.

[83] Anselm, "De Grammatico," 53.

[84] Anselm, "De Grammatico," 39–40.

[85] Southern, *Saint Anselm*, 63.

[86] Anselm, "De Grammatico," 40.

[87] Anselm, "De Grammatico," 53.

[88] Anselm, "De Grammatico," 53.

[89] Anselm, "De Grammatico," 60, my italics.

[90] Anselm, "De Grammatico," 64.

[91] Anselm, "De Grammatico," 69.

[92] Colish, *Mirror of Language*, 92.

[93] For examples of Anselm's move from common to proper signification of religious language, see Evans, *Anselm*, 43–44. As Colish notes, this grammatical tool is precisely what "he used in his famous proof and throughout his theological writings as a whole." See *Mirror of Language*, 107.

[94] Stock, *The Implications of Literacy*, 350. Karl Barth makes the same point in *Anselm: Fides Quaerens Intellectum*, trans. Ian W. Robertson (Cleveland and New York: World Publishing, 1962) 78.

[95] Southern, *Saint Anselm*, 65.

[96] Southern, *Saint Anselm*, 180.

[97] Anselm, "The Incarnation of the Word," *Anselm of Canterbury*, vol. 3, 11–13.

[98] Anselm, "The Incarnation of the Word," *Anselm of Canterbury*, vol. 3, 11–13.

[99] Anselm, "The Incarnation of the Word," *Anselm of Canterbury*, vol. 3, 11–13. On Anselm's dispute with Roscelin, see Evans, *Anselm*, 57–58; and Evans, *Anselm and Talking About God*, 97–111.

[100] Anselm, "The Procession of the Holy Spirit," *Anselm of Canterbury*, vol. 3.

[101] As Southern observes, Anselm drops the dialogue form when "real enemies appeared." See Southern, *Saint Anselm*, 115.

[102] Anselm, "The Fall of the Devil," 166–167 and 175; "The Incarnation of the Word," 11.

[103] See Anselm, "Why God Became a Man," *Anselm of Canterbury*, vol. 3, I.1, 49–50. References are to book I or II, then the standard section number, followed by the page number in the Hopkins and Richardson edition.

[104] Anselm, "Why God Became a Man," I.1, 49.

[105] Anselm, "Why God Became a Man," preface. For similar language, see I.20, 88 and I.25, 96; and II.10, 109.

[106] Anselm, "Why God Became a Man," I.1, 50.

[107] Anselm, "Why God Became a Man," I.1, 50.

[108] Southern, *Saint Anselm*, 197–205.

[109] See Southern, *Saint Anselm*, 371–372.

[110] Anselm, "Why God Became a Man," I.7, 56–58, for an echo of Ralph's theory, and I.3–6, 52–55, for representative Jewish objections.

[111] Anselm, "Why God Became a Man," I.1, 50.

[112] Anselm, "Why God Became a Man," I.1, 50.

[113] Eadmer, *Life*, 60–61.

[114] Southern, *Saint Anselm*, 202–203. See also Evans, *Anselm and Talking About God*, 161.

[115] Southern, *Saint Anselm*, 202. Anselm pays his respects to his "brother and beloved son Boso" in the opening of "The Virgin Conception and Original Sin," *Anselm of Canterbury*, vol. 3, 143.

[116] Anselm, "Why God Became a Man," I.3, 52.

[117] Anselm, "Why God Became a Man," II.13, 115.

[118] See John McIntyre, *St. Anselm and His Critics* (Edinburgh and London: Oliver and Boyd, 1954) 16 and 48.

[119] Anselm, "Why God Became a Man," I.10, 66–67.

[120] Anselm, "Why God Became a Man," I.8, 58–59, my italics.

[121] Anselm, "Why God Became a Man," II.10, 109.

[122] Anselm, "Why God Became a Man," II.11, 113.

[123] Anselm, "Why God Became a Man," II.18, 133, my italics.

[124] Anselm, "Why God Became a Man," I.8, 59.

[125] Anselm, "Why God Became a Man," I.9, 63.

[126] Anselm, "Why God Became a Man," II.5, 101–102, my italics.

[127] Anselm, "Anselm of Canterbury," I.5, 54.

[128] Anselm, "Why God Became a Man," II.8, 104–106.

[129] See Evans, *Anselm*, 47.

[130] Evans, *Anselm*, 47.

[131] Anselm, "Proslogion," ch. 25, 109.

[132] As Colish remarks, "rectitude"—as the "correct relation of the sign to the thing it signifies"—is "the real criterion of . . . epistemological validity." See *Mirror of Language*, 113.

[133] Southern, *Saint Anselm*, 82.

[134] Southern, *Saint Anselm*, 75. See also Evans, *Anselm*, 46.

[135] Anselm, "Why God Became a Man," I.4, 53.

[136] Anselm, "Why God Became a Man," I.4, 53.

[137] Anselm, "Why God Became a Man," I.10, 66–67.

[138] Anselm, "Why God Became a Man," I.20, 88.

[139] Anselm, "Why God Became a Man," I.24, 95.

[140] Anselm, "Why God Became a Man," II.6, 102–103 and II.19, 133–135.

[141] See Anselm, "Why God Became a Man," I.13, 71; I.20, 90; II.6, 102; II.11, 112; II.14, 116; and II.20, 135, respectively.

[142] Anselm, "Why God Became a Man," II.8, 106.

[143] Anselm, "Why God Became a Man," II.9, 107.

[144] Anselm, "Why God Became a Man", I.11, 68.

[145] Anselm, "Why God Became a Man," I.12, 69–70.

[146] Anselm, "Why God Became a Man," I.15, 74. Compare I.21 and II.11.

[147] Anselm, "Why God Became a Man," II.9, 107.

[148] Compare the transformation of Boso from I.20–24 to II.19.

[149] The tension between the novelty of discovery and the explicative function of theology for Anselm is reflected in the secondary literature. Thus, for instance, we find Southern accenting how both the method and the conclusions of "Why God Became a Man" were "new". Southern, *Saint Anselm*, 205. And, also correct, we find Evans stressing Anselm's "calmer certainties" in this dialogue, not his excitement over new discoveries. Evans, *Anselm and Talking About God*, 136.

[150] Anselm, "Why God Became a Man," I.1, 50.

[151] See, for instance, "Why God Became a Man," I.12; I.15; I.19; II.10; II.15; and II.18.

[152] Anselm, "Why God Became a Man," I.1 and 2, 49–52. As Evans writes, "Behind every one of his arguments is the imperative need to show that there is no discrepancy between doctrinal orthodoxy and the conclusions [that] reason can draw from its independent reflections." *Anselm and Talking About God*, 96.

3

Eclectic Criticism and the Art of Dialogue:
The Example of Diderot

"Conversations are peculiar things, especially when several people are involved. Just look at the roundabout ways we went. It is as strange a mixture as the dreams of a sick and delirious man. Nevertheless, just as there is nothing unconnected in the mind of a dreamer or a madman, so everything hangs together in a conversation, though it would sometimes be very hard to reconstruct all the tenuous links which join up so many disparate ideas. . . . Madness, dreaming, and the disorder to conversation consists in going from one subject to another by way of a common attribute."

—Diderot, in a letter to Sophie Volland, October 20, 1760[1]

The birth of modernity opened a new chapter in the dialectic of faith and reason. Whereas reasoned argument and rational dialogue with challengers serve to promote the self-understanding of orthodox Christian faith in Anselm's eleventh century monastic world, new demands were placed on religion by the intellectual developments of eighteenth century enlightenment Europe. Once the faithful servant of correct religious belief, reason now took critical aim at religion itself. This was, in Kant's words, "the age of criticism"—and "to criticism everything must submit."[2] Armed with the experimental nerve of rapidly developing physical and social sciences, the revolutionary call for freedom from despotism in political philosophy, and the respect for the practical knowledge of ordinary craftsmen typical of the *Encyclopedia*, the spirit of criticism took its stand against the scourge of religious superstition and intolerance. Discourse on religion, consequently, became the venue for a critical assault on the ignorance, narrowness, and barbarity stemming from religion.

This was to be an age of enlightened reason, as Kant proclaimed in 1781. People should "dare to know"—a piece of counsel borrowed from Horace—without lazy and cowardly reliance on the tutelage of would-be authorities.[3] As it turns out, Kant's shibboleth for an "age of enlightenment" was more modest than his charge to readers would suggest; his interest lay chiefly in securing the turf of the philosophical faculty in the university system of his day.[4] But many others were more forthright in their vision for an enlightened humanity. Thus we hear Johann Gottfried von Herder—early on Kant's student, but later his critic—confidently extol "the unwearied zeal of ever-growing Reason," relentlessly promoting the progressive building up of enlightened humanity.[5] Similarly, on the French scene, Denis Diderot does not flinch in confessing his confidence in "the progress of knowledge, that immense river which grows larger every day and which no power (unless it be another Flood) can any longer presume to stop."[6] Even the judicious David Hume could speak with pride of the advances in learning made possible in the political climate of European civilization.

As naive and uncritical as this trust in reason may sound to the more sober sensibilities of post-modern ears, we should not underestimate the critical self-awareness of these progressive and adventurous minds. They are not—despite post-modern innuendos—naive about the obstacles blocking reason's march; nor are they oblivious to the ambiguities hidden in reason's successes.[7] Quite the opposite: these eighteenth century men of letters had all too much firsthand experience with everything which made rational life at once so impossible and so necessary—the repressive policies of despotic government; the oppressive intolerance of ecclesiastical authorities; the strange otherness of non-European cultures; the exciting but unsettling novelty of scientific discovery; and even the tumultuous controversies among intellectuals of different stripes. Indeed, it is precisely their grand—even optimistic—quest for enlightened discourse that brought them into critical contact with the various forces blocking the advent of rational life. Their dream of enlightened rationality, therefore, had to be carved out through persistent and arduous discourse with the irrational.

In this regard, the various artisans of enlightenment culture were deeply committed to dialogue—but always in two senses. On the bright side, its proponents envisioned, as Peter Gay put it,

> a world united by its celebration of diversity, a cosmopolitan harmony orchestrated in free individuality; an open world, not of absolutes or of persecution, but of pacific and continuous dialogue.[8]

It is no wonder, then, that "conversation" became such "an indispensable part of the enlightenment's way of life."[9] Its practitioners hungered for such dialogue. On the French scene, the venue for these exchanges, characteristically, was among kindred spirits, as in the gatherings at Madame Geoffrin's salon or at Baron D'Holbach's house at Grandval, or through the critical debates on art and culture in Melchior Grimm's *Correspondance littéraire*. On the darker side, however, discourse was frequently controversial and regularly filled with personal or professional danger, as in the repeated collisions with official censors, or through the polemical exchanges with the Jesuits who harassed the encyclopedists in the *Journal de Trévoux*. While dialogue represented a beloved ideal, it often proved an arduous necessity. On both scores, this was an era of intellectual ferment, a time of transformation and encounter with the other—a time, therefore, ripe for adventurous and energetic dialogue.

Consequently, this investment in conversation found a natural and efficient outlet in the genre of dialogue. Leading enlightenment figures—Christoph Wieland and Gotthold Lessing in Germany, David Hume in England, and Fontenelle and Voltaire in France—seized upon the genre and transformed it to suit their philosophic ends.[10] Dialogue made it possible to create unusual (or even outrageous) worlds of discourse in order to test the limits of criticism, to explore unmapped venues for dialogue, or to experiment with scientific and cultural novelties. It likewise provided a critically pointed, yet relatively safe vehicle for critical interaction with the world of religion. Dialogue was to serve superbly in the criticism of religion and the promotion of enlightened rationality. As Gay notes, "the mood of the Enlightenment was favorable to dialogue, and dialogue was favorable to the Enlightenment."[11]

Nowhere is this spirit of dialogue more clearly evident than in the work of Denis Diderot, the editor of the *Encyclopedia*, and, as such, the preeminent figure of what came to be known as the French enlightenment. As will become evident in the body of this chapter, Diderot's entire philosophical project—including his critical engagement with religion—is essentially and strategically committed to dialogical forms of thinking. This commitment, in turn, finds an appropriate and powerful literary vehicle in the written dialogue.

Having said this, however, it must not be forgotten that exactly the same thing was true of Anselm—as we saw in the previous chapter. Diderot shares with Anselm the perception that rational inquiry into religious topics is most naturally and most productively carried on through the give and take of conversation; and they are at one in choosing to communicate such inquiry through the literary dialogue. But while they share the genre, they direct it to different (indeed, opposing) ends. Dialogue provides Anselm with a vehicle for showing a relatively small circle of like-thinking readers how to explore the hidden depths of Christian faith, taking them to the mystical limits of religious language, while still stating, by means of the confident, even paternalistic profile, that faith seeking understanding assuredly leads to the confirmation of orthodox belief. Dialogue allows Diderot, in contrast, to demonstrate to an ever-widening circle of readers the practice of criticizing religious superstition and barbarity, prompting them to the very limits of skeptical analysis, while nonetheless stating, by means of the abiding civility and good humor inscribed in the contour of the dialogue form, that serious criticism need not nullify understanding and virtue. The dialogues of Anselm and Diderot, therefore, not only tell us about the conflict of orthodoxy and atheism; they also, and more profoundly, yield dramatic glimpses of their authors' fundamentally different perceptions of what discourse on religion should and will become when faith meets reason in and through dialogue.

My aim in this chapter is to fill in the second side of this contrast by taking a good hard look at Diderot's art of dialogue. In the first section I want briefly to examine some of the personal, philosophical, and cultural reasons that lie behind Diderot's option for the dialogue. This discussion will help to establish the kind of context within which Diderot's dialogues were created and dispersed. The second section takes an initial look at some of the major characteristics of Diderot's deployment of the dialogue genre. To this end, a reading of "D'Alembert's Dream"—a dialogue which Arthur Wilson calls "Diderot's greatest work of all"[12]—will show how far we have come from the world of Anselm's monastic dialogue. For Diderot, rational discourse fuses the eclectic and dialectical fiber of Socratic inquiry with the unfettered and adventuresome spirit of scientific experimentation, even as it is tempered by caution and civility. I will devote the third section to exploring the impact this form of critical rationality has on religion. Two relatively brief dialogues—"Le Prosélyte répondant par lui-même" and "Conversation of a Philosopher with the Maréchale de ***"—reveal the kind of critical discourse Diderot entertained with religious positions. The final section examines Diderot's most mature and profound experiment with the possibilities and limits of critical discourse in his masterpiece, *Rameau's Nephew,* a dialogue in which he plunges headlong into the uncharted horizons of rational criticism. Following the lead of Hans Robert Jauss and Julia Kristeva, we will see just how boldly—yet cautiously and charmingly—Diderot pursues the limits of rational criticism and experimental conjecture. In contrast to Anselm, for whom grammatical criticism leads to glimpses of that which is most real, Diderot's critical discourse openly (and precariously) engages that which is monstrous and anarchic.

(1) "One Giant Conversation"

Denis Diderot shared with all the *philosophes* a deep and energetic faith in progressive enlightenment. For him it was primarily the *Encyclopedia*—what Arthur Wilson calls that "supreme exemplar of the Enlightenment"[13]—which would give form and motion to the construction of a rational culture. Taking more than sixteen years to complete, the *Encyclopedia* was to be more than a repository "of all the knowledge that now lies scattered over the face of the earth."[14] Indeed, its editors—Diderot and the mathematician Jean le Rond d'Alembert—sought nothing less than to "change men's common way of thinking."[15] In this their aims were at once humanistic and revolutionary. Confronting readers with a myriad of practical information from the world of craftsmen, countless speculations on social or technological improvements, critical notes on the meaning or meaninglessness of key words in theology or politics, extensive material on the superstitious practices of non-Christian religions designed to make similar Christian practices look ridiculous, a consistently anti-clerical polemic, plus eulogies for noble and progressive examples of human behavior, they sought to "inspire in men a taste for science, an abhorrence of lies, a hatred of vice and a love of virtue. . . ."[16] Such grand designs brought Diderot and his scholarly compatriots into discursive contact with a score of other voices—friends whose conversation they relished, experts whose knowledge they reported, enemies whose vices they attacked, and readers whose attention they claimed.

Nothing, in fact, is more basic to Diderot's character than his zest for dialogue. Diderot simply thrived on conversation, and, as Wilson points out, "it was by conversation as much as it was by what he published that he spread his influence and made his leadership felt."[17] He was, in the apt phrase from P. N. Furbank's recent biography of Diderot, an "unquenchable talker."[18] The favored contexts for conversation were Baron d'Holbach's country estate located just outside Paris (called Le Grandval) or the country retreat of Madame d'Epinay (La Chevrette, where Rousseau had found refuge before his falling-out with Diderot and company). While in Paris, conversation often centered around one dinner table or another. In these settings we find Diderot feasting on the company of friends at suppers, over card-games, or during country walks. The main course—without failure—was conversation, filled with story-telling, humor, a good deal of gossip, a bit of filth, and "endless discussions" (as Diderot put it) of a philosophical nature. In Diderot's words, "we talked of art, of poetry, of philosophy, and of love; of the greatness and vanity of our undertakings; of the bittersweet thoughts of immortality; of men, of gods, and of kings; of space and time; of death and life."[19] Many praised his talents for dialogue; one "respectable but freethinking Jesuit" (Furbank's epithet) described his manner in discussion as being "vivid, supremely honest, subtle without being obscure, varied in its forms, speaking with imagination, fecund in ideas and stimulating ideas in others. . . ."[20] Occasionally his intensity and exuberance earned him rebuke, but this seems to have been rare. Diderot lived for conversation. It was both the substance and the method of his philosophical project.

Just how much dialogue was a part of his nature is marvelously captured in Louis Carmontelle's painting of Diderot animated in conversation with his friend Grimm.[21] But it is even more clearly exhibited in Diderot's personal and philosophical identification with Socrates, persecuted man of dialogue. Socrates was for Diderot the classical equivalent of the *philosophes*, and as such, a worthy model for philosophic activity. In his *Encyclopedia* entry on "Socratic philosophy," for instance, Diderot pinpoints the specific methodological and rhetorical qualities he revered so highly in Socrates:

> He [Socrates] made astonishing use of irony and induction: his irony revealed without any effort the ridiculous nature of certain opinions, while his inductive procedure dealt with questions remote from a subject in such a manner as to lead people imperceptibly to acknowledge the very thing they had denied. Add to this the charms of a sure, simple, fluent, and lively manner of speaking, . . . a surprising modesty and a scrupulous consideration not to offend, degrade, humiliate, or grieve people.[22]

Critical irony, dialectical arguments rooted in the complexities of experience, and a vibrant but civil rhetoric—these traits constitute the Socratic legacy Diderot seeks to replicate in his own philosophical labors. When, moreover, he felt threatened or persecuted for daring to speak honestly and critically of religious beliefs and institutions, Diderot was quick to compare himself to Socrates. Those who condemn the *philosophes* will surely look as foolish as the persecutors of Socrates appeared to later generations.[23] Emblematic of his devotion, Diderot sealed his correspondence with a ring bearing the portrait of Socrates. As Wilson remarks, this ring was a "symbol of Diderot's values, a trademark of his secret self."[24] It signified, in short, his deep and abiding commitment to conversation of the Socratic variety.

These biographical notes on Diderot's character go a long way to explaining why he so often chose to incorporate dialogical structures in his writing. There is, as Carol Sherman points out, an "essential and particular presence of dialogism in all degrees and at all levels of his writings."[25] At times he would simply graft his remarks onto selected passages from another author, thereby transforming the original into a dialogue of text and response.[26] But without doubt, Diderot's penchant for dialogical communication finds its "most natural and effective art form" in the literary dialogue.[27] He turned to the genre some twenty times over the years, four of which I will discuss in this chapter. Moreover, in works that, strictly speaking, are not dialogues, Diderot frequently slips into explicit dialogue form. This happens, for example, in "Letter on the Blind for the Use of Those Who See," an early work devoted (not without irony) to exploring the experience of people born without the sense of sight. There, in the midst of his discussion, Diderot inserts an imaginary dialogue between the blind mathematician Nicholas Saunderson and a clergyman who seeks to convince the dying Saunderson of God's providence, basing his arguments on the marvelous design evident in the natural world—none of which prove credible to the dying man, who has never seen the natural world.[28] Intermittent dialogues appear again and again in Diderot's works, in the course of letters, in the middle of historical essays, and within fictional narratives.[29] Diderot clearly relishes these "nested dialogic structures," but he could also do the reverse, as when he frames *The Natural Son* (a play for which he was ridiculed for plagiarism) with a dialogue in which—ironically—Diderot engages an imagined author of the play in an extended conversation concerning good theatrical composition and performance.[30] In addition to these techniques, Diderot does not hesitate to turn a narrator (or himself) directly toward the reader in dialogue, as he does repeatedly (among other places) in *Jacques the Fatalist*, itself a hodgepodge of narrative and dialogue.[31]

The choice of dialogical genre—and more importantly, the particular twists given to the dialogue in Diderot's hands—reveals a very definite, philosophical perception about what constitutes rational communication. For Diderot, rational life is essentially social and dialogical, rather than solitary or systematic. He liked to think of himself as a "citizen" belonging to a "society of men of letters and of skilled workmen"; and he was perplexed and disturbed by the solitary existence of someone like Jacques Rousseau. Indeed, Diderot likely was thinking of Rousseau when he has a character in *The Natural Son* proclaim that "the good man lives in society, and only the bad man lives alone."[32] Diderot, similarly, stood against the grand designs of the "systematic spirit," which "builds plans, and forms systems, of the universe to which it consequently desires to adjust phenomena willy-nilly."[33] For Diderot, what produces insight and understanding is not the solitary musings of a Rousseau or the pretentious ventures of theological system-builders, but the open and unfettered life of dialogue. The examined life is open—through the critical exchanges carried on through dialogue—to the view of others, and hence is viewed from varying perspectives. Diderot aspires to this ideal in the extended conversation that made up his life; and he seeks to replicate (indeed, to participate in) this dialogical process of interaction in almost every work.

This is true even of the *Encyclopedia*, which, at first sight, surely does not appear to be dialogical in form. Although this mammoth work is structured systematically (modeled on the tree of knowledge from Francis Bacon's *The Advancement of Learning*) and organized alphabetically (like a dictionary), its system of cross-references makes it read like an extended conversation. Following an article, the reader is sent off to other entries which either confirm or disturb the information of the first article. As Diderot himself declares, articles confirm each other by indicating "close connections with other subjects" or by putting "added stress on elements of internal consistency within groups of facts"; but the references also serve a "contrasting purpose"—inasmuch as they "confront one theory with others, they will attack, undermine and secretly overthrow certain ridiculous opinions which no one would dare to oppose openly." A "national prejudice," for instance, might be treated with full respect, only to be juxtaposed with dissenting articles which scatter the former like an "idle heap of dust."[34] Articles are counterposed to articles, and the reader who is swept up in this dialectical reference system cannot help but notice that the message (frequently ironic) lies more in the juxtapositions and contrasts than in individual entries themselves. The *Encyclopedia* is, in Wilda Anderson's words, "one giant conversation,"[35] concocted from the myriad voices of its contributors, orchestrated by the silent but effective cross-referencing of its editor, and ceaselessly open to readers who are willing to participate in the intricate web of its conversation. This, in essence, is Diderot's philosophic agenda.[36]

Diderot's "giant conversation"—whether through the *Encyclopedia* or in his proclivity for dialogical forms of writing—however, is not fully explained by pointing either to his extensive habits of personal conversation or to the Socratic cast of his philosophic orientation. There are, after all, external or contextual factors which come into play in Diderot's deployment of literary genres. We must, therefore, round out this analysis of Diderot's option for dialogue by turning and paying close attention to the various social and literary forces which prompted and facilitated Diderot's philosophical communication through dialogue. As Sherman argues very persuasively, Diderot's turn to the dialogue stems from two distinct, but complementary societal factors. In a nutshell, Diderot's choice dialogue was both a strategic decision mandated by the tenuous (even dangerous) social position for a writer of his ilk *and* it was made possible by the cultural forces of the enlightenment in which he lived and breathed. The two factors—as we will see presently—are intimately linked.

To begin with, critical authors in eighteenth century France faced frequent harassment from official censors, as well as the far more ominous threat of arrest and incarceration. Diderot himself was arrested in July 1749 and imprisoned at Vincennes for his early writings, and his position as co-editor of the *Encyclopedia* brought continual, searing opposition from opponents with powerful connections—including both Jansenist and Jesuit.[37] Opposition to the *Encyclopedia* was fierce, to say the least: in 1752 it was suppressed as destructive of royal authority and corruptive of moral and religious life; in January of 1759 the Attorney General of France charged those at work on these volumes with conspiracy to "propagate materialism, to destroy Religion, to inspire a spirit of independence, and to nourish the corruption of morals"; less than three months later, the *Encyclopedia* was condemned by royal decree and all publication suspended.[38] These kinds of pressures have prompted many authors to write under the protective (if not altogether foolproof) cover of the dialogue form—who, after all, can prosecute an author for the position of a particular character?[39] Such obfuscation, however, does not seem to have been Diderot's root motive for turning to the dialogue. In any case, the extent to which he obscured his voice in the dialogic sections of his early writings had not blunted the impact of the prosecutor's indictments. The need for self-protection, it seems, is only a first, circumstantial step in Diderot's choice to write in dialogue form.

In response to these dangers, Diderot severely restricted the publicity of his writings. After his imprisonment at Vincennes, he published only non-controversial works—mainly plays (for example, *A Father and His Family*), pieces on art (*The History and Secret of Painting in Wax*, for instance), and scientific works (like *On the Interpretation of Nature*, which appeared anonymously).[40] Somewhat surprisingly, work continued on the *Encyclopedia* even during the years it was banned, but on this project Diderot shared the protective company of many others (including D'Alembert, contributors, publishers, and a host of pre-paid subscribers), and he could enjoy the goodwill and measured judgment of Lamoignnon de Malesherbes (ironically, the man in charge of regulating the book trade).[41] But even his work on the *Encyclopedia* had to be conducted in utter privacy— behind bolted doors, as he puts it.[42] All other writings—and most importantly, everything provocative—were withheld from public view. A few pieces received clandestine circulation among friends, while others (like *Rameau's Nephew*) did not appear at all during his lifetime. Diderot had gone underground.

For the more daring of his imaginative works and for the more provocative of his philosophical pieces, Diderot clearly needed a broader but secure outlet. He found one in Grimm's *Correspondance littéraire*, an intellectual bulletin destined for foreign royalty who wanted to keep up on the progressive currents of French intellectual culture.[43] This was, to be sure, an ironic situation: clandestine by necessity, Diderot found literary access to some of the most powerful and influential people in all of Europe. This is hardly what one would expect of an underground publication. Though he sometimes complained to Sophie Volland about the amount of work he was putting into Grimm's periodical, it provided him with precisely what he so desperately needed—a relatively safe vehicle for "ideas considered inimical by the government and the church," and consequently, a public stage on which to speak without inhibition and with persuasive effect. As Sherman puts it, Grimm's periodical thereafter became the "vehicle for Diderot's private and audacious philosophical propaganda."[44] It allowed him a public voice.

Diderot's turn to Grimm's intellectual newsletter also proved fortuitous with respect to Diderot's option for dialogical genre, since its elite subscribers called for precisely the kind of dialogical talents so basic to Diderot's character and philosophical orientation. Here, we come to the heart of Sherman's analysis of the public forces that helped bring Diderot to the dialogue form. As she argues, in directing his work to this particular audience, Diderot was able to partake of the new (and growing) literary preferences of this elite readership for critical combat and life-like representation. They preferred, as she puts it, "imaginative, open forms . . . to declamation in the literature of ideas"; they fancied, the "low mimetic modes."[45] Dialogues fit the bill exactly: by "their verisimilitude, their aptitude for combat, and their apparent objectivity," dialogues responded perfectly to this "new literary preferences for living forms."[46] The informed and intelligent readership that subscribed to Grimm's periodical permitted Diderot an "increased possibility of vivacity and allusiveness" in his writing.[47] In other words, they invited and supported the writing of lively and dialectically charged philosophical dialogues.

Sherman's analysis is especially helpful in forcing the reader to look beyond the privacy of Diderot's character to the public forces which gave literary shape to his philosophical imagination. Diderot's dialogues, then, can be seen as a response to the opportunity offered by a very specific audience. His art of dialogue, from that angle, bears a decidedly public cast. Yet many of Diderot's literary creations do not seem intended for public consumption. In fact, many of his dialogues have the tone of private musings fitting only for a small circle of friends. We as readers are left with texts which are—in different senses, but at the same time—both public and private. Peter France puts it well when he says that Diderot's stance typically . . . is half-public, half-private, his voice that of a man talking in a room where are both friends and strangers; sometimes he will talk eloquently to the whole company, but from time to time he will drop his voice and say something private, ironically, and self-deprecating to his friends.[48]

France's comments are right on target: Diderot's dialogical rhetoric always involves a complex mix of private conversation and public address. The two levels of discourse are ineluctably linked and intertwined; as we will see in the following sections, keeping this in mind is crucial for full and appropriate readings of Diderot's dialogues.

Any effort to sidestep the tension between the private and public in Diderot's works will miss the rich complexity of his literary practice. Indeed, what appears to be public frequently winds up being private, and what sounds private often ends up being public. Certainly much of Diderot's philosophical program bears a public purpose—to awaken sleeping souls to rational and virtuous life. Because of this, he abhorred the "private scholar" who restricted the access of other researchers to scientific experimentation.[49] Along the same lines, Diderot carried on a lengthy debate with the sculptor Etienne-Maurice Falconet over the value of posterity as a source of wise judgment and appreciation. For Diderot there could be no more significant and more credible public measure than the verdict of posterity.[50] And when it comes to his imaginative works, especially those dialogues which satirically toy with contemporary people and positions, Diderot clearly packs a potent public punch. In so many different ways, Diderot seeks a public voice and wishes for public judgment.

Yet, as we have seen, Diderot remained very private in his philosophical communications—partly for safety's sake and partly because he did not expect broad support.[51] Indeed, the glaring fact remains that many of the writings for which Diderot is now justly famous were completely unknown (or nearly so) to his contemporaries, including the dialogues treated in the following sections. Diderot's conversational circle was, as we have seen, remarkably private and intimate in nature. For example, in one often quoted passage, Diderot seems to picture an audience of only two readers: he writes with Grimm in mind and it is Sophie whom he wishes to please. What could be more private than this? Yet, once again, it would be missing the deeply humanistic trajectory of Diderot's philosophical labors to downplay the breadth of readers intended by Diderot. In the sentence immediately preceding the reference to Grimm and Sophie, in fact, Diderot insists in a far broader vein that "virtue and virtuous men must always be kept in mind when one writes."[52] Diderot's private audience (Grimm and Sophie) would seem merely to be concrete and available instances of the kind of reading public he thinks good writers should intend. His private circle—what he calls a "beautiful trio of souls"—thereby becomes a living (but safe and trusted) conduit to a much larger public.[53]

The trick to interpreting Diderot's dialogues appropriately, therefore, is to bear in mind the different senses in which his texts are both private and public. To recapitulate, five points must be kept in mind. (a) Diderot is private by necessity. Facing the dangers of repressive government, he encloses himself, bolts his doors, and works in secrecy. (b) Consequently, he also is private by practice; he will converse within the security of an intimate circle of friends.[54] (c) But, as Sherman shows us, Diderot goes public by opportunity. Given a safe but significant vehicle for communicating his philosophical and critical thoughts to an intelligent and appreciative audience, Diderot's forced privacy (a and b) breaks forth into an uninhibited publicity. The relative privacy (security) of Grimm's periodical makes it possible to speak publicly—that is, to actually engage others with a text. (d) Given this opportunity, Diderot proceeds publicly by imagination. Freed from public threats to his welfare, he seizes the opportunity to engage a reading public by imaginatively supposing what others would say—whether the "other" is a blind man, a Tahitian native, a devout theist, a woman, or a die-hard nihilist. Indeed, what is so characteristic of the dialogues, and hence so important for rightly interpreting them, is their far-reaching imaginative scope. When read, the dialogues reveal almost unlimited worlds of discourse. (e) In crafting such imaginative conversations, Diderot takes a public stand before posterity, by critically appealing to the well-measured judgment of all potentially rational people. In the texts and by means of the texts, Diderot's engaging imagination remains open-ended, and thereby challenges later generations.

Each of these factors is crucial for understanding Diderot's dialogues—why he chose to write them, what he meant by them, what they were as texts in their time of composition, what they have come to be (as philosophical literature) for later readers, and what they mean for us as readers (who are, actually, Diderot's posterity). Diderot took up the dialogue in fear of public censorship; as an artistic expression of his penchant for conversation among friends; on the basis of a promising opportunity for publication; in the Socratic spirit of imaginative and critical engagement with others; and in order to address and appeal to posterity. In turn, when we as readers take up Diderot's dialogues, great care must be given to these shifting senses and levels of meaning. Indeed, Diderot's dialogues call for the same kind of hermeneutical dexterity that was required (in the last chapter) to read Anselm's dialogues. Both authors, as will become apparent, talked and wrote in the interstice between private and public worlds. Diderot's critical rationality, therefore, is no more unequivocally public than Anselm's theological quest is purely private or intramural. Both portray discourse over religion as dialogical, but they travel in opposite directions, and they inscribe their differing perceptions and agenda in the fabric of their interlocutors' conversation. Dialogues allow Anselm to entertain the questions of a broader public for the purpose of understanding and confirming the orthodox beliefs of a private, monastic community;

they allow Diderot to emerge from his secure base, even as he simulates the intimacy of friends' conversation, for the sake of engaging a broader audience with relentless and open-ended criticism and imaginative experimentation. Their respective dialogues, as we will see, represent matching sides of the dialectical discourse of faith and reason.

Having seen what brought Diderot *to* the dialogue, it is now time to take the next step by examining *how* he uses the genre to advance his philosophic aims. In the next section, I want to take a close look at one particular dialogue, "D'Alembert's Dream," in order to bring into focus some of the major facets of Diderot's use of the dialogue form.

(2) Diderot's Dialogical Dream

In the summer of 1769, Diderot writes to Sophie Volland that he has just completed two dialogues—one a conversation between D'Alembert and himself, and a second one (titled "D'Alembert's Dream") "which is much longer and serves to explain the first one more fully." Filled with self-satisfaction, Diderot revels in his achievement. "It is the height of extravagance," he tells Sophie, "but at the same time it is most profound philosophy." Despite the "dryness and obscurity of the subject," the characters manage to converse "quite gaily, and quite clearly too."[55] In a subsequent letter, he tells Sophie that he has composed a sequel to the first two dialogues. This piece is far too racy for her eyes—it "would make my sweetheart's hair stand on end"—but it is a grand accomplishment nonetheless. Speaking of the three dialogues as a whole, he once again exults over his literary feat: "You can't imagine anything more profound and more crazy."[56] What Diderot clearly relishes here is the fusion of serious philosophical issues with a style of dialogue which is at once clear, entertaining, and daring. Literary genre and philosophical content have merged in marvelously provocative fashion.[57] For that very reason, this text makes a perfect venue for observing and reflecting upon how Diderot wields the dialogue form.

"D'Alembert's Dream" (now designating the entire triptych of dialogues) ostensibly aims to overturn any view which would explain the genesis of things by appealing to some "outside agency" or extra-natural cause (whether that be a divine being, Cartesian mind, Platonic essences, or "abstract ideas"), in order to promote a thoroughgoing materialistic philosophy of nature built around the concept of "sensibility" and supported by a Lockean epistemology.[58] To this end, the four characters (D'Alembert, Julie de l'Espinasse, Dr. Bordeu, and Diderot) pursue a series of questions having to do with the origin of consciousness and the maintenance of personal identity, as well as the ethical implications which spring from the atheistic and materialistic answers arrived at over the course of their exchange. In the first dialogue, Diderot lays out his materialistic thesis to the attentive but reluctant D'Alembert. All things (conscious beings, great mathematicians, even living planets), he argues, are merely the result of a "certain organization of matter"; hence, there is no need to resort to "theologico-metaphysical fiddle-faddle" to explain why things are as they are. The second dialogue is more extravagant. Diderot has departed and D'Alembert sleeps, though his dreams are so infected with his discourse with Diderot that he continues to talk in his sleep. In their stead, Julie de L'Espinasse converses with Doctor Bordeu whom she has beckoned out of concern for D'Alembert's agitated state. Together they discuss and explore the meaning of D'Alembert's strange murmurings, which Julie has faithfully recorded on paper. In the third dialogue, finally, Julie and Bordeu examine some of the implications of Bordeu's materialism for sexual ethics.

What makes this dialogue so interesting and so useful for my purposes, however, is not simply the propositional content (which could, presumably, be formulated without recourse to dialogue), but the decidedly self-reflexive manner in which Diderot deploys the dialogue form. With great sophistication and subtlety, Diderot speaks through the literary form itself, imaginatively performing an entire philosophy of discursive activity and dramatically initiating his readers in the habits of (what he takes to be) enlightened conversation. Rarely, it should be noted, does he directly *tell* his reader how they can and should think and speak; instead he invites (even prods) them into attending to the forms of communication which transpire within the dialogue, and by that means, he *shows* them how to practice the art of enlightened discourse. In what follows I have isolated seven elements which appear again and again in Diderot's art of dialogue, in each case using "D'Alembert's Dream" for illustration.

(a) Perhaps the most noticeable mark of Diderot's dialogues is the degree to which they succeed in realistically imitating natural conversation. Though authors of dialogues universally aim for such similitude, few achieve it with the liveliness of Diderot. "D'Alembert's Dream," for instance, portrays a conversation between widely recognized figures on the French intellectual scene: Diderot and D'Alembert were co-editors of the *Encyclopedia*, Mlle. Julie de l'Espinasse was the hostess of a Parisian *salon* and intimate friend of D'Alembert, and Dr. Théophile de Bordeu was a medical author and physician. Gone is the anonymous "student" (as we found in Anselm) or the classical Greek names so often used in dialogues (a technique Diderot rejected); in their place Diderot takes speakers directly from everyday life.[59] Such realistic characterization certainly facilitates recognition on the reader's part; but it also sets the parameters of personality within which Diderot will work to make his points, for, as Sherman acutely observes, dialogues provide a "way of arriving at truth" which takes into account the "special ignorance" of their interlocutors. In the case of "D'Alembert's Dream," Diderot's persuasive intent must wind its way in and through Bordeu's intellectual bent, past Julie's latent curiosity and attraction to the doctor, and by D'Alembert's anxiety over Diderot's materialism. He seeks, thereby, to allow the dialogue to transpire with as much of the richness and complexity of everyday life as possible.[60]

Consequently, "D'Alembert's Dream," like so many of his dialogues, quite naturally captures the undisciplined—even disorderly—flow typical of living conversation, including all kinds of stops and starts. Even in the fairly smooth first dialogue, D'Alembert calls Diderot to task for having "stopped short in the middle of our inquiry" into the generation of thinking beings; Diderot had drifted off "a few thousand years into the future" to ponder the conditions necessary for recreating a dead planet.[61] Discussion frequently gets interrupted, as when the sleeping D'Alembert's dreamy muttering intrudes throughout the second dialogue upon Bordeu and Julie, or again when Julie turns to speak with a servant she suspects has shown Bordeu her notes of D'Alembert's dream. Or, to cite just one more example, Julie and the doctor leap wildly from topic to topic; their discourse ranges from the organization of bee hives and of human polyps to the physiological constitution of different personalities, to any number of bizarre stories of abnormal human development. It is difficult at times to discern where their discussion is going. And this is Diderot's point: real conversations are approximations, and they rarely develop in an orderly manner.

> Nearly all conversations are like reckonings that have been drawn up. . . . Where the devil did I put my cane? . . . One seldom has an idea clearly in mind. . . . And now, my hat. . . . And for the simple reason that no man is exactly like any other, we never understand one another exactly; there is always an element of more or less; our language always overshoots or falls short of the actual sensation. We are very well aware of how much judgments differ, and there are a thousand times more differences than we are aware of—which, fortunately, it is impossible to be aware of. . . . Well, I'll be on my way. Good-by.[62]

Such is the nature of human conversation, as Bordeu observes (even as he performs the point) at the end of the second dialogue.

On top of all this, Diderot spices their discourse with all sorts of personal responses of a non-intellectual nature. There is playful bantering—when Bordeu knows what Julie is thinking, she quips that his guess just means that he has "a splendid talent for nonsense." And there is flattery and flirtation—Bordeu praises Julie's aptitude for dialogue and the two confirm a theory concerning how one knows the location of a sensation with a brief kiss.[63] All this is topped off with sexual innuendo—if, as Bordeu claims, "the original shape of a creature changes and develops in response to necessity and habitual usage," what (Julie muses) would issue from "unrestrained amorousness."[64] When D'Alembert later protests that Bordeu is mixing smut with science, he is not far off the mark. The entirety of the third dialogue, after all, is taken up with a moral defense of masturbation and bestiality. Diderot makes no effort to neaten the flow of the discussion; nor does he try to clean it up. When Bordeu complains, in general, that he and Julie have only been able to "skim the surface of a lot of things without getting deeply into any of them," Julie retorts (clearly reflecting Diderot's own understanding of the genre) that no harm has been done, for "we are only having a conversation, not writing a treatise on the subject."[65] All these factors give the dialogue a vivid sense of dramatic activity, and a thoroughly down-to-earth quality.

(b) The reader of Diderot's dialogues, however, should not be fooled by the life-like mode of their presentation—for Diderot is ever-present, shaping the contour of discourse, and working to affect his readers. It is true that, for Diderot, the construction of dialogue must follow the natural path of human discourse.[66] Good dialogues, as he argues in defense of Abbé Galiani's dialogues on the grain trade, must reflect the life-stations and habits of real interlocutors.[67] And yet, as Diderot remarks about aesthetic creations in general, no art is purely imitative, nor should it be. Some room must be left for the author's expression; and, as we will see, something must be left to the reader's imagination and responsibility.[68] The point of a dialogue, for Diderot, is not simply to depict living conversation in a realistic manner, but to depict it in a way that will allow an author to communicate through the choice and arrangement of the interlocutors' words, *and*, simultaneously, will conceal the author's hand from the reader's view. Realistic imitation, therefore, serves the cause of persuasive communication (by lending plausibility to the dialogue's discourse), but it does so by sidestepping the bluntness of direct address (something Diderot and his readers found distasteful). In the crafting of his dialogues, consequently, Diderot goes to great lengths to conceal his presence— what Rosalina De La Carrera calls the "author-function"—and he manages this by "subverting it from within" through the very mimetic techniques which make his texts attractive and interesting.[69] In "D'Alembert's Dream," for example, he effaces himself by leaving after the first round of dialogue; it is as if the author has left the text altogether! So successful is Diderot at this, that the dialogue takes on the appearance of not really being a book at all, or at least, not a book by Diderot.[70] But, of course, it is a book, and Diderot is its author, and the dialogue's verisimilitude remains a vehicle for Diderot's efforts at persuasion.

In the pursuit of his rhetorical aims, Diderot frequently takes great liberties with other people and their work. At times he simply commandeers someone else's work—adding a "supplement" to the original, but redirecting it to his own purposes; in other places he boldly dismembers another author's treatise to construct his own dialogue of quotation and response; and most often, as is the case in "D'Alembert's Dream," he playfully (but presumptuously) seizes the personae and voices of others to serve the discourse of his own literary creation.[71] Furbank aptly calls this Diderot's "suppositious or foisting method," and it is something which appears in one guise or another throughout his corpus.[72] As Furbank writes,

By a feat of dramatic manipulation, not exactly ventriloquism, and something more than the conventional "imaginary conversation," he "takes over" a real-life personage, projecting him into some situation that uniquely enables him to see and utter certain truths.[73]

To a certain extent, of course, every author of dialogue puts words in someone else's mouth—as Anselm does with Boso, for instance. But Diderot goes much, much further than this.

When, in the course of his efforts to show D'Alembert that the generation of conscious life requires "nothing but physical agencies," Diderot, again playful but presumptuous, takes the illegitimate birth of his interlocutor as his evidence. All it takes to create "one of the greatest mathematicians of Europe," he tells D'Alembert, about whom he is speaking, is the illicit sexual encounter of his unwed parents, the "beautiful and naughty canoness Tencin" and the "soldier La Touche." But this daring disclosure of D'Alembert's illegitimacy is nothing compared to what happens in the second dialogue, where Diderot (the author) actually puts D'Alembert to sleep, in which state he begins to practice Diderot's experimental method of conjecture, which, as Furbank points out, D'Alembert held in disfavor. As Furbank puts it, Diderot not only plays a "beautiful joke" on his colleague, but "intrudes himself into the very recesses of his friend's sleeping consciousness, compelling him to re-enact one of his own 'conjectures' or 'dreams'."[74] D'Alembert's wild dreams (or should I say Diderot's) concern alternative forms of human reproduction—imagine a planet populated by human polyps where "males split up to make a new batch of males, and similarly with the females"; or "who knows," perhaps the entire world evolves endlessly through the spontaneous regeneration of minuscule parts of former individuals.[75] All this is outrageously capped off with D'Alembert's masturbatory ejaculation! Which is more audacious on Diderot's part—publicizing D'Alembert's illegitimacy, foisting the method of conjecture onto his colleague, or giving him a wet dream? Diderot's handling of Dr. Bordeu and Julie de L'Espinasse is similarly bold. Bordeu, as it turns out, was not only not D'Alembert's doctor but the adversary of his real physician; and Julie de L'Espinasse was at best an acquaintance, despite the familiarity Diderot shows (and takes) with her in his dialogue.[76] Everyone of these imaginative manipulations remains subtle—submerged, as it were, in the natural, lively, and charming flow of dialogue. But they underscore the seriousness with which Diderot is working to affect his readers and move them to his point of view. Diderot may conceal his face in the flow of natural conversation, but the power of his authorial voice is ever present.

(c) At some point, consequently, readers cannot help but wonder what is real and what is fictional in Diderot's dialogues. Who is speaking when D'Alembert dreams? Whose voice is it that we hear when Diderot (and D'Alembert, for that matter) have left the stage to other characters? What is the reader to think? What is to be believed? Such questions, of course, would never arise in Anselm's dialogues, for there the abbot (and hence, the author) is always in command. But the confusion caused by Diderot's dialogues is no accident. It is, rather, a carefully designed and deliberately intended feature of his literary conversation with readers.

Diderot's dialogues are crafted so as to facilitate *and* simultaneously to disrupt the reader's entry into the text.

On the one side, the dialogue's dramatic realism "makes [the] reader's identification easier," as Sherman puts it.[77] The amicable chatter and playful banter in "D'Alembert's Dream," for instance, provide ready entry points for the reader's imagination. The reader easily slides into the dialogue's world of discourse, thereby becoming an "implicit interlocutor" with the characters in the text, and likewise, also with Diderot.[78] But all this is seductive, for, from another angle, Diderot has no intention of allowing the reader to become too comfortable. He works, instead, to unsettle his readers, trying—consistently and through a variety of means—to prompt and elicit thoughtful response on the reader's part. Diderot's deliberate self-concealment, along with all the outrageous fantasies and startling reversals which fill the pages of a dialogue like "D'Alembert's Dream" creates an initial uneasiness in the reader, thereby increasing the reader's responsibility for what will be taken away from the dialogue. Readers are treated, therein, to what Furbank calls an array of "cosmic vistas and dizzying revisions of scale," as when Diderot vaults from considering the creation of human consciousness to the genesis of "a whole new world," and then to the regeneration of a stalled conversation.[79] They are confronted, similarly, by sudden (and frequent) leaps through a whole series of analogies for the constitution of personal identity: the relation of the center of human consciousness is to the many impressions in different organs and limbs first as a clavichord is to its many strings; then as a cluster of bees is to its "general bond of sympathy"; then as a spider is to its web; and finally as a monastery is to its monks.[80] And if that isn't enough, interpreters of Diderot are faced with a counterpoint arrangement of serious scientific issues (Bordeu bemoans the poverty of our knowledge of foetal development) with a host of outrageous (and seemingly farcical) stories dealing with genetic abnormalities (Siamese twins who live and die in turn) and surgical oddities (the priest undergoing an operation without an anaesthetic).[81] In each of these instances, Diderot puts very strenuous demands on the readers' attention. They are forced—in following the path of the interlocutors' discourse—to adjust to these twists and turns, to maintain their critical balance, and, ultimately, to participate in the kind of experimental and critical thought-processes recorded in the text. What Diderot provides, in sum, is guided disorientation; with an inviting and attractive tone, he forces his readers to the point of intellectual responsibility, as he initiates them in the kind of critical and experimental thinking required for rational life.

(d) The first three features of Diderot's art of dialogue have to do with the shape and purpose of the text—its representative powers, its authorial purpose, and its effects on readers. The fourth element typical of Diderot's dialogues, however, lies directly at the heart of his philosophical project. Diderot's dialogues are exercises in what he calls "experimental eclecticism." The term comes from the

Encyclopedia entry called "Eclecticism," and though it is not, to be sure, a definitive and comprehensive caption for Diderot's philosophical activity, it can serve as a suitable counterpart to the role that "faith seeking understanding" plays in Anselm's theology. In Diderot's words,

> The eclectic is a philosopher who, by riding roughshod over prejudice, tradition, antiquity, universal consent, authority, in a word, everything that subjugates the mass of minds, dares to think for himself, goes back to the most clear and general principles, examines and discusses them, while admitting only what can be proven by experience and reason. After having analyzed all philosophical systems without any deference or partiality, he constructs a personal and domestic one that belongs to him.[82]

There are two key parts to the eclectic's work. The first involves an aggressive criticism directed at anything and everything which restricts independent and free thinking; the second entails a thorough-going but tentative openness to entertain many and different possibilities, what Diderot calls "cultivating the experimental method." Calling eclecticism "the most reasonable of philosophies," he exhorts would-be philosophers to rigorous criticism and experimentation: "I urge philosophers to be distrustful; if they are prudent, they will make up their minds to become disciples in many fields before wanting to be the masters; they will venture a few conjectures before laying down the principles."[83] It is this philosophical spirit—at once critical and conjectural—which informs Diderot's dialogues.

The opening exchanges in "D'Alembert's Dream" illustrate one of three kinds of criticism Diderot has in mind. From the very start, Diderot confronts the reader with a rejection of the idea of God; but what is startling about this is not that Diderot abjures belief in God, but how he conveys it through the dialogue form—that is, as an accomplished fact about which no real debate is needed. D'Alembert opens the dialogue with a declaration of agreement with Diderot that "it's very hard to believe in the reality of a Being that is said to exist somewhere, yet occupies no single point in space; . . . that moves matter and follows the movements of matter, yet does not move. . . ." Such a being, D'Alembert concedes, "seems utterly contradictory."[84] Since the dialogue is written as if it joins Diderot and D'Alembert's discussion in midstream, the reader does not get to hear Diderot's actual criticism of the idea of God. That happened before the text opens, thereby, suggesting that the idea of God does not deserve serious consideration. The really difficult questions, and those which Diderot finds more interesting and more worthy of space in his dialogue, concern the alternative, materialist explanation for the genesis of things. Diderot's criticism of the idea of God, therefore, is delivered through the indirect and extremely confident means of omission. The notion does not even deserve overt debate.

A similarly confident, yet far more blunt, form of criticism is aimed at the idea of the soul. In this case, Diderot feels secure in handling belief in the soul with defiance and ridicule, largely because he has laid down the constructive planks of his materialist world-view already through a series of analogies and arguments. As he tells D'Alembert, it takes nothing but an egg and germ to explain the genesis of living beings: "With it all the schools of theology can be overthrown, as well as the temples of religion on earth."[85] All it takes is heat, motion, and time for an insensitive matter like an egg to "pass over into another form of organization, into sensitivity—into life." "Watch carefully," Diderot urges D'Alembert, what happens in nature. The genesis and maturation of a bird, for instance, allows no room for the idea of some "undetectable element"—about which we can know absolutely nothing—to function as the cause of the bird's animation. To cap off his rejection of the soul, Diderot peppers D'Alembert with a series of questions: "what could such an element be? Did it occupy space, or did it not? How did it get in, or out, without moving? . . . Did it exist earlier? Was it looking for a home?" "Just listen to yourself talk," Diderot warns, "and you will feel sorry for yourself." Anything other than the simple materialist explanation means "a renunciation of common sense and a headlong plunge into an abyss of mysteries, contradictions and absurdities." Religious talk of the soul is "theologico-metaphysical fiddle-faddle!"[86] Throughout all of this, D'Alembert remains relatively passive, while Diderot confidently forwards his criticism by subversion and ridicule. In these cases, Diderot wants nothing else but to "ride roughshod" over the antiquated and superstitious metaphysics of religion.

A far more subtle form of criticism appears in the discourse between Julie and Bordeu in the second and third dialogues. At this point we move from brazen criticism by omission and ridicule to more dialectical forms of reasoning that Diderot retrieves from the classical Socratic practice of *elenchus*. The Greek term literally means examination and refutation. But as Kenneth Seeskin argues in his recent work on Socratic method, *elenchus* involves far more than the logical analysis of propositions. As Seeskin puts it, "*elenchus*. . . has as much to do with honesty, reasonableness, and courage as it does with logical acumen: the honesty to say what one really thinks, the reasonableness to admit what one does not know, and the courage to continue the investigation."[87] Full-blown Socratic *elenchus*, in other words, connotes the kind of examination of a belief or position which forces and facilitates intellectual and moral discovery. But since discovery is "something which must be prepared for, something which the soul must learn" through the give and take of open and thorough-going conversation, *elenchus* requires the nerve, the grit and the stamina to submit long-cherished beliefs and comfortable habits of mind to critical scrutiny.[88] This, of course, is never easy, as any number of Socrates' interlocutors could attest. But for those who risk the conversation, the pay-off can be immense: critical examination by dialogue can unsettle what has appeared certain and expose what long has been hidden; and, consequently, it can turn up fresh insights and yield unexpected reversals of intellectual fortune.

Such is the life of critical inquiry Diderot inscribes in the discourse of his dialogues.

In the exchange between Julie and Bordeu, the process of *elenchus* transpires on two discrete yet overlapping levels. In the first place, and most obviously, it is Julie who undergoes the critical examination by the careful and confident direction of Bordeu. Initially she is confused by D'Alembert's sleepy discourse, while Bordeu finds it quite sensible; she suggests, in fact, that Bordeu may be the one dreaming; and several times, she becomes impatient with what she calls Bordeu's "nonsensical hodge-podge."[89] Before long, and with Bordeu's critical guidance, Julie begins to transcend her intellectual naivete; soon she puts forth her own conjectures about human development, she finds her own stylistic tastes (interestingly, for Fontenelle's dialogues), and she discovers the value of her own ideas—all of which earn her Bordeu's praise.[90] Julie has been delivered from her naivete under Bordeu's critical scrutiny. There is, however, a turning-point in the dialogue at which the critical tide subtly turns toward Bordeu. Though she still regards herself as intellectually malleable, Julie gradually begins to come into her own: *she* begins to ask the leading questions, *she* is the one who is able to explain D'Alembert's fanciful images and later to summarize the whole dialogue, it is *her* intellectual eagerness which propels the inquiry into the many "stories of unusual happenings," and it is *Julie* who rescues Bordeu from his forgetfulness.[91]

On this second level, something clearly has changed. Now Julie controls the flow of discourse, now she knows what *he* is thinking, now she flatters *him*, and so on.[92] Julie has become the agent and Bordeu the recipient of the dialogue's critical edge. Indeed, as De La Carrera points out, Julie gradually is seducing Bordeu: she briefly exposes her thigh, she invites him to sit closer to her, there is a brief kiss, after which she tells Bordeu that he may do anything he likes with her—"so long as I learn something."[93] Bordeu remains completely oblivious to this turn of events; and Diderot does very little to call it to the reader's attention. Julie's grip on Bordeu, however, gradually comes to the surface: their discourse becomes interlocked and fused.[94] When he tries to leave, she begs him to stay and talk longer, and of course, he cannot resist; when he does depart, she has more than enough hold on him to secure a return visit. Their final exchange, fittingly, takes place over a tasty malaga and addresses truly spicy topics. Now Julie is playfully, but more apparently, seductive: she implores him to leave a few things unrevealed, but promises not to draw back no matter how risque the discussion gets. And now when she wraps herself in women's weakness, it is only to impel Bordeu to respond as a man, which he does: "All right for you! I'll have to treat you like a woman in that case. . . ." When, therefore, Bordeu mentions (quite in the spirit of his intellectual inquiry) that he has secured a "nanny goat" with which he will produce a new race of "excellent domestic servants," it pleases Julie's fancy "enormously."[95] Despite her profession of love, Bordeu leaves hurriedly—perhaps indicating, as De La Carrera suggests, his belated recognition and uneasiness with Julie's moves.

These two critical dialectics place Diderot squarely in the Socratic tradition. If anything, Diderot extends the dialectics of criticism latent in Socratic *elenchus* by having the apparently Socratic figure (Bordeu) himself undergo critical exposure. Julie, it turns out, is *the* (or, rather, a *second*) Socratic figure. Like Socrates, she uses her incomprehension "strategically" to get her way with Bordeu, and Bordeu is slow in realizing what actually is transpiring. Contrary to all appearances, *he* has been the one who did not know, and *he* is the one who is moved to new insight. It was *his* naively intellectual approach to conversation that was scrutinized. He thought their discourse was purely intellectual and without consequence, and only slowly does he come to realize that he didn't know what was going on. He comes, in short, to the Socratic realization of his own ignorance. It is as if Socrates himself is critically undone ("seduced") by one of his young male interlocutors!

Diderot fully extends the Socratic tradition of *elenchus* in the decidedly experimental cast he gives to his philosophical project. And though he is willing, even here, to acknowledge a debt to Socrates, the adventurous and probing quality of Diderot's work is his own contribution to the tradition of philosophical eclecticism. As he tells us in *Pensées sur l'interprétation de la nature*, an early work on scientific method, critical inquiry requires the kind of "intuition (*pressentiment*) that is akin to [the] inspiration" possessed by the experienced laborer. It is not established "procedures and results" that are central, but "that spirit of divination by means of which it is possible to smell out (*subodore*), so to speak, methods that are still to be discovered, new experiments, unknown results."[96] In place of syllogistic and mathematical reasoning, therefore, Diderot inserts a roaming and expansive sense of conjecture by which new truths may be sniffed out and put to the test. Drawing on experience and observation, the experimental minded philosopher will explore the nature of things by imaginatively juxtaposing unusual oppositions and drawing unexpected analogies. As if he is anticipating his own dream (called "D'Alembert's Dream") Diderot acknowledges that the spirit of conjecture easily can produce ideas which are nothing short of "extravagant"— "for what other name can be given to that interconnection of conjectures which are based on contrasts or resemblances so remote, so imperceptible, that the dream of a sick man would not seem either more bizarre or more disjointed?"[97] No matter how wild they may seem, the philosopher should proceed forthrightly with new, varied, and ever more far-fetched thought-experiments or "dreams." What this produces is a "tentative and non-dogmatic," yet unfettered and productive approach to philosophical inquiry.[98] Everything can and should be tested, for who knows what fruit experimentation may yield?

This adventuresome spirit of conjecture fills the pages of "D'Alembert's Dream." Indeed, it is what makes the dialogue so fascinating and so dazzling. The text as a whole, of course, is Diderot's own dream; but what we as readers face is a constellation of overlapping conjectures (*rêves*). There is, first off, Diderot's various materialist conjectures about the genesis of human existence; *that* waking dream then becomes internalized in "D'Alembert's Dream," which, in turn, is unraveled by Bordeu and Julie's round of thought-experiments. Every twist and turn of their dialogue is driven by the act of conjecture: perhaps, they imagine, the human brain and nervous system are like a spider with its web—since the spider (like the brain) feels impulses throughout its body (web), though these impulses "get weaker in proportion to the distance from their point of origin."[99] At another point, Bordeu challenges Julie to think of the very processes by which she came into existence. Though she wants to conceive of her beginning as simply reduced in size, Bordeu challenges her with a molecular hypothesis: "In the beginning, you were an imperceptibly small dot made up of still smaller molecules." At the other extreme, the two dream about what it would be like to experience an ever-expanding body, or conversely, to feel one's body getting "smaller and smaller." Still later, when the two wonder about the genesis of sexual identity, Julie proffers the following conjecture: who knows, she muses, "perhaps men are nothing but a freakish variety of women, or women only a freakish variety of men." Or, to take one more example, Bordeu speculates (much to Julie's horror) about the superiority of "cold, serene people" over more "sensitive creatures."[100] Each of these thought-experiments, taken individually, appear "ill-assorted, incoherent, or confused" (Bordeu's description of the dreaming consciousness); taken together, however, they also appear completely "unified, consistent, and well-ordered" (like the person awake).[101] Though given to "the sense of disorder that is characteristic of dreams," experimental inquiry (like dialogue itself) "may be very logically connected on occasions"—thereby displaying "no greater rationality, no greater imagination and no greater eloquence" than could be achieved through more logical and technical forms of reasoning.

(e) The art of conjecture frequently takes Diderot's dialogues to the outer limits of rationality. Whereas some enlightenment figures (Kant, for instance) investigate the limits of reason in order to fix a region within which knowledge can be confirmed as rational, Diderot is more intent on exploring the limits themselves, and, frequently, in tasting what lies beyond these limits. It is as if he is asking: How far can critical experimentation and dialogical examination go? What is the range of conjecture? How deep can subversion cut? How much can be thrown up in the air through experiment? Such questions are, for Diderot, the very stuff of philosophical inquiry. So too with poetry, which, Diderot tells us, "demands a certain something of the enormous, the barbarous and the wild."[102] And as we saw above, scientific investigation itself is not to pull back from exploring the most extravagant hypotheses. Even the *Encyclopedia* is a "sort of monstrosity".[103] What is so striking here is the style and tone of Diderot's attraction to limits. His approach is by no means nihilistic (there is nothing morbid or anguished in Diderot's critical experimentation); nor is his interest mystical (there is nothing of the religious depths evident, for instance, in Anselm). His is, rather, a charming and adventurous anarchism, inviting and alluring as it is dauntless and inventive. It is this limit-language which Diderot inscribes in the discourse of his dialogues.

"D'Alembert's Dream," once again, provides a vivid illustration. Indeed, Julie and Bordeu revel in the extravagant and the monstrous. Bordeu, in particular, is fascinated by cases of genetic abnormality—like the person born with only one eye ("A Cyclops").[104] And both Bordeu and Julie revel in odd medical stories which illustrate how the center of conscious sensitivity relates (or fails to relate) to the various sensible functions extending through human limbs. There is the case of the amputee who still feels sensations in his missing limb; there are stories of people falsely imagining the size of their bodies, of siamese twins who live and die in turn, of the woman suffering "fits of melancholy," of the priest who undergoes surgery without flinching, or, finally, of the philosopher who overcomes an earache by immersing himself in "some problems of metaphysics or geometry."[105] These examples are fantastic, to be sure, even far-fetched; but they are meant by Bordeu to illuminate the range of a materialist theory of consciousness. When Julie protests that Bordeu has "reduced everything to mere sensitivity, memory and organic functions," she is entirely correct; for Bordeu holds nothing back from his exploration of pure, unlimited materialism. All that is needed is the imagination to "perform in thought an operation that nature often performs."[106] Let conjecture follow nature and see what monsters can be dreamed up. There appears to be no end to the matter, as Julie shows when she wonders about the limits of what can be dreamed. "Can you tell me," she asks Bordeu, "what dream it is that no one has ever had or ever will have?"[107] And finally, in the third dialogue, even moral limits are breached. Nothing is more fantastic (Julie calls it "monstrous") than Bordeu's farcical story of the "infamous rabbit who did the rooster's duty for a score of shameless hens who seemed to be enjoying it."[108] Bordeu (or, rather, Diderot) is having great fun experimenting with nature, and facing the monsters he discovers therein.

(f) Despite the willful and energetic indulgence Diderot takes with intellectual and moral limits, his dialogues characteristically (and somewhat surprisingly) retain an undeniable caution and civility. They hold back (or pull back) from the limits. We need not consider again whether Diderot's reserve stems from fear of official reprisals or from a natural civility; the two clearly are intertwined. But what is evident in a dialogue like "D'Alembert's Dream" is the graceful avoidance of anything too shocking for readers. This dialogue is charming through and through, even as it entertains the outrageous and engages monsters. Even in the third dialogue, Diderot carefully inserts expressions of reserve and humor around the more outrageous talk of masturbation and bestiality. As Sherman notes,

Diderot gives his dialogues an "aire of scandal," yet simultaneously, and sincerely, tries to "render the discussion acceptable to the reader."[109] It also must be recalled that this text (like so many of Diderot's dialogues) remained unread (except by a few friends in 1769 and by the subscribers to Grimm's *Correspondance Littéraire* in 1782) and unpublished (until 1830). Indeed, if the story is to be believed, Diderot acceded to D'Alembert's demand that he destroy the manuscript; apparently Julie de L'Espinasse (who heard of her part in the dialogue) had complained to D'Alembert that it had presumptuously put inappropriate words in her mouth.[110] Both in the text and with it, Diderot steps back from the edges of reason and morality, even as he flirts with what lies on the other side.

(g) One last feature of Diderot's art of dialogue demands attention, for it is—in many ways—precisely the element which gives these texts their critical power and literary merit. Diderot's own philosophical statement, what he wants to convey to readers, is buried in and expressed through the genre, not simply through the content overtly expressed by specific characters.[111] It is true, of course, that any author who takes up the dialogue genre makes a statement by the way in which the form is deployed. Anselm, for instance, did not have to say explicitly that theological discourse is guided from beginning to end by the intramural standard of the abbot's authority and orthodox truth; this much was evident purely through the manner in which the interlocutors engaged and interacted with each other. But Diderot goes much further in speaking through the literary form. For him, the dialogue serves a performative function, in the sense that the characters' discourse frequently mirrors (and indeed, participates in) the very things about which they speak. The reader of Diderot's dialogues, consequently, must learn to listen extra carefully—not only to what is said, but also to how things are said, and, even more so, to the link between the two.

In "D'Alembert's Dream," for instance, Diderot strikes up parallels between human "communication and the functioning of biological systems."[112] As Wilda Anderson puts it, "the literary format stages an experiment in which the characters perform an unwitting demonstration and elaboration of the idea they are discussing."[113] And *what* they are discussing is the generative processes of nature, by which some inactive thing becomes active through contact with something else. Two good examples are at hand already in the first dialogue. All that is needed to generate a living being from a marble statue, Diderot tells D'Alembert, is natural processing: pulverize the marble, compost it, feed the humus to plants, eat the plants, and presto—you have a living being. A similar process explains the birth of a thinking person (Diderot's example, once again, is D'Alembert himself): start with certain molecules in the "delicate young bodies of his future parents," bring the man and woman together in sexual intercourse, from which follows the germination of the egg and the growth of a fetus, then birth and lactation, and in a matter of years, a thinking human being is created. In both cases the recipe is much the same: "eat, digest, distill in a closed vessel, and you have the whole art of making a man."[114] All that is required is, in De La Carrera's words, a "nature that communicates," that is, a biological system driven by interaction, assimilation and reproduction.[115]

But the reverse is also true. If natural generation is communicative, then communication is naturally generated: bring speakers together in dialogue, allow for the assimilation of ideas, and watch the generation of new thoughts. The recipe is the same. Diderot's image of the clavichord that produces music (the new product) when plucked (affected) by the musician's hand (a sensible agent) is not only (for him) a useful analogy for human existence ("We humans are," he says, "instruments gifted with sensation and memory"), it is also precisely what Diderot does with D'Alembert through their conversation. As Diderot puts it, "all human intercourse consists merely of making noises and doing things," and this holds equally for the genesis of life, of music, and of ideas.[116] So too with the analogy of the hive that Diderot uses to describe material existence generally; his characters (including the dreaming D'Alembert) perform the analogy of forming an interlocking whole in their discourse. Notice the performative coincidence of form (their talk) and content (the bees):

> **Bordeu** (narrating D'Alembert's notes as taken by Julie): . . . the bunch [of bees] now forms a whole, a single animal, one and the same, whereas formerly it was only a collection of animals. . . . All our organs—"
> **Mlle. De L'Espinasse**: Did you say, "all our organs"?
> **Bordeu**: Yes. For anyone who has practiced medicine and made a few observations—
> **Mlle. De L'Espinasse**: Why, that's just the language he used! No tell me what comes after that.
> **Bordeu**: After that? ". . . are only distinct animals [i.e., like bees] held together by the law of continuity in a general bond of sympathy, unity, or identity."[117]

Dialogue too is simply a "certain organization of matter."[118] As De La Carrera puts it, all the metamorphoses of nature—"of the creation of sounds from impressions, of a bee swarm from individual bees, and of flesh from marble"—"are a product of the communication through contact that sensibility makes possible."[119] And should there be a break in such processes—whether in a solar system whose sun gets snuffed out or in a conversation that is interrupted—there is no need (and no way) to rescue it by some supernatural agency. What Diderot calls sensibility ("communicative contact") takes the place of God as the source of biological *and* dialogical life. The recipe remains constant.

The really important thing to note about Diderot's performative deployment of the dialogue genre—and ultimately, therefore, about his materialistic or biological rhetoric as it is presented in "D'Alembert's Dream"—is what it means for the kind of "experimental eclecticism" at the heart of his philosophical project. What is crucial is to see how the transformations effected by means of critical dialogue and experimental thinking are themselves natural metamorphoses. And this is precisely what occurs through performance in "D'Alembert's Dream," as De La Carrera argues very persuasively. D'Alembert ingests Diderot's materialism, then digests it while he sleeps, only to wake with a new perspective on things; at first Julie considers D'Alembert's ravings mere noise, but over time (through conversation with Bordeu and by her own conjectural dreams), they become intelligible; and finally, though Bordeu approaches Julie's naive sensibilities as the confident and active source of explanations, he gradually—through contact and a good bit of flirting—begins to be moved (aroused?) by Julie, only to leave the scene when Julie's "effective seduction" becomes too direct.[120] The "circuit of communication,"[121] as De La Carrera puts it, remains open in the end, as a tacit invitation to readers to enter the natural processes of criticism and dialogue. And this, after all, is Diderot's own rhetorical point: through the performative display of critical and experimental dialogue, he hopes to include readers in the natural loop of his material *elenchus*, and thereby to initiate them (that is, us) in the art of enlightened discourse. To one extent or another, this remains a constant mark of Diderot's dialogues.

In sum, Diderot's use of the dialogue form bears certain characteristic marks. With great consistency, they are crafted so as to imitate living conversation, which allows their author to makes his persuasive points while simultaneously concealing his own presence. This combination of dramatic realism and authorial self-effacement has the odd effect on readers of both facilitating their entry into the text, while disrupting any uncritical accommodation. At the heart of his dialogues stands the unsettling but liberative practice of Socratic *elenchus*, matched with an adventuresome and highly imaginative interest in conjecture. At times, as we have seen, Diderot's penchant for criticism and experimentation takes discourse to the limits of rationality, leaving his readers face to face with the fantastic and the monstrous; but more often than not, he pulls back from the edge, partly from caution and partly from civility. Finally, Diderot's dialogues play a performative function—what he has to say to readers, particularly about the kind of rational discourse he hopes they will practice—is *shown* rather than *said* in the dialogue. With these elements in mind, we now are in a position to take a close look at the impact of Diderot's critical and experimental rationality on dialogue over religious issues.

(3) Two Dialogues over Religion

The eighteenth century enlightenment unleashed a torrent of criticism toward organized religion. "*Écrasez l'infame*," cried Voltaire, taking aim at the seductive superstitions, vicious factionalism, and violent dogmatism linked to the Christian religion. Religion induces enthusiasm, Voltaire argues, and "enthusiasm is exactly like wine; it can excite so much tumult in the blood vessels, and violent vibrations in the nerves, that the reason is completely overthrown by it."[122]

But while the enthusiast may be annoying, it is the fanatic who causes Voltaire alarm: "the man visited by ecstasies and visions, who takes dreams for realities and his fancies for prophecies, is an enthusiast; the man who supports his madness with murder is a fanatic." And religion had all too many fanatics! It was an "almost incurable" disease, he wrote with an eye on the fanatical persecution of the Calas family or the massacre at Saint Bartholomew in 1752.[123] Voltaire concluded that "every sensible man, every honorable man, must hold the Christian sect in horror."[124] As ferocious as his criticism of religion was, Voltaire was not interested in destroying what he perceived to be religion's rational and moral core. For him, "the worship of a supreme Being, and the submission of one's heart to his eternal commands" is still quite reasonable; everything which goes beyond that is superstition and must be criticized and expunged.[125] Like many of the English deists and German *Aufklärer*, Voltaire upholds a stripped-down religion comprised of metaphysical belief and an imperative to tolerance and justice.

Diderot's attitudes toward religion, however, were considerably more radical. He had no interest in saving religion from its excesses (as Kant and so many other Christian rationalists apparently wanted); nor did he find worth in the humanist compromise between classical learning and Christian piety practiced by the Jesuits. Although there are faint suggestions that Diderot once contemplated an ecclesiastical career—he claims to have "hesitated between the Sorbonne and the Comédie," surely a jest on the ubiquity of acting—his very first works brought him into conflict with official censors.[126] The Parlement of Paris, for instance, branded his deistic *Philosophical Thoughts* as "scandalous, and contrary to Religion and Morals."[127] From that point forward—including his imprisonment, the suppression of the *Encyclopedia*, the persistent "jeopardy of arrest and punishment" for his work,[128] and the constant wrangling with polemical attacks on the *philosophes*—Diderot faced what he called a "multitude of moral obstacles."[129] Certainly it is understandable to find Diderot striking out at religion in the 1762 *Addition to the Philosophical Thoughts*: in a caustic tone, he wonders how anyone could find the heavenly father of Christians to be good; and anticipating Nietzsche, he imagines the origin of religion to lie in the bitter resentment of a persecuted misanthrope.[130] In a more personal vein, Diderot encountered the stultifying and unnatural power of religion in the person of his clerical brother, and he responds with sarcastic reproach: "Woe to the family that has a saint in it."[131] Both publicly and personally, therefore, Diderot experienced the dark and repressive side of religion; and he responded with sharp and unremitting criticism.

Still, there is a good dose of civility in Diderot's discourse on religious matters. He was not, as many have noted, a proselytizer for atheism; nor did he engage in public invective against his ecclesiastical adversaries. Instead, he was more likely to assume a distantly ironic stance. Standing back with amazement, he could laugh at the follies perpetrated in the name of religion, and jab critically at what he took to be ridiculous or offensive. To take but one example, Diderot took great pleasure laughing at the antagonism and mutual destruction of the Jesuits and the Jansenists in France. With these religious enemies, he writes to Sophie, it is as if "two roof-beams which propped one another up had a quarrel. The master of the house, growing impatient with their wrangling, knocked one of them down, and down fell the other."[132] Though he clearly enjoyed laughing critically at the absurdities of these religious groups, Diderot nonetheless could be quite respectful of religious individuals—as he is when he meets one of those rare people who appear to be both religious and rational. He clearly is pleased, for instance, with the open-minded monk who is able to accept criticism of celibacy without taking offence; and he is most delighted upon meeting two apparently free-thinking and atheistic monks. The latter, he tells Sophie, truly were "witty, gay, decent and knowledgeable men"—fitting company, in short, for respect and for dinner.[133] The critical edge in Diderot's discourse with religion, therefore, comes tempered with caution and civility; and in so doing, it repeats the same kind of dialogical posture and strategies we found at work in "D'Alembert's Dream."

The *Encyclopedia* provides a well-rounded picture of Diderot's attitudes and methods toward religion. When necessary, Diderot (and his contributors) could speak directly against the religious world: when speaking of Christian intolerance, for instance, Diderot bluntly challenges his readers to face the contradiction between Christian precepts and intolerance of others.[134] More often than not, however, Diderot's criticisms of religion are indirect—partly for caution's sake and partly for ironic effect. (It must have rankled the theologians of the Sorbonne, for instance, that religious matters received so little coverage in comparison with the mundane world of ordinary craftsmen.[135]) And when religion is addressed, Diderot radically expands the horizons of consideration by placing orthodoxy against the background of countless heresies and variations in belief. Or again, the encyclopedists loved to lampoon non-Christian traditions clearly parallel to Christian beliefs. In both cases, plurality serves to relativize Christian self-understanding. At other times an article might offer rationalistic explanations for apparent irrationalities in scripture; but here the critical blow was struck not through the strength of their explanations, but obliquely through the author's intentionally weak or confusing ponderings. Whether dealing with Old Testament accounts of creation or certainty regarding miracles, the *Encyclopedia* articles frequently created more doubts than they allayed.[136] And, of course, the system of cross-references sowed seeds of doubt and confusion through the unsettling juxtaposition of articles: the entry on "God," for instance, addresses Pierre Bayle's skeptical rejection of proofs for the existence of God, after which readers are sent to the article on "atheism" (where they discover more reasons for not believing in God) and to the entry on "creation" (which takes up the difficulties surrounding the very idea of divine creation). By all these indirect means, the *Encyclopedia* provoked critical uncertainty and questioning of religious tenets.

It is precisely this rhetoric—at once critically unsettling and measured and civil—which Diderot embedded in the imaginary conversation of two little dialogues on religions. Though these texts are by no means Diderot's most celebrated, and though they certainly are not his most sophisticated deployment of the genre, they nonetheless provide good examples of Diderot's critical dialogue with the world of religion. In them we see, once again, (a) the personal and philosophical commitment to Socratic criticism and experimental inquiry, as well as the peculiar blend of private conversation and public address, which marks Diderot's creative philosophical production in a repressive cultural context. And we again face (b) the various traits common to Diderot's art of dialogue— representative realism; the "suppositious or foisting method" practiced by the author; a seductive but unsettling effect on readers; an "experimental eclecticism" advanced through the interlocutors' discourse; a proclivity for the limits of rationality, tempered by both caution and civility; and, finally, a knack for mirroring precisely what is being said in the dialogue.

The first of Diderot's dialogues I will consider—"Le Prosélyte répondant par lui-même"—was written in 1763 as a response to a dialogue written by a Christian theologian who dared to satirize the *philosophes*. Naigeon, Diderot's friend and the editor of some his papers, refers to the author of this satirical dialogue as "an ignorant controversialist," and tells us that Diderot found in it "only miserable commonplaces which to the embarrassment of human reason, the different schools of theology have been repeating for nearly twenty centuries. . . ."[137] In fact, this parody of Diderot and his friends—titled "Introduction aux grand principes, ou réception d'un philosophe"—is a witty and effectively direct spoof which probably angered Diderot precisely because it succeeded in touching the intended raw nerve. In any case, it proved sufficiently irksome to precipitate a response in kind; and, apparently, a response that made its way to the author of the satirical piece.

The satirical dialogue stages an initiation rite for *philosophes*, replete with an examination of the proselyte's beliefs modeled on a catechetical review for confirmation in the church. As the dialogue opens we find a godfather addressing the wise man, informing him that a young man wishes to become a "*philosophe*."[138] When interrogated about his principles, the young initiate answers in brief, seemingly memorized formulas. Believing nothing that is not firmly demonstrated, his views on religion are decidedly unorthodox. A deist, he believes in God only if the word "God" refers to "nature, universal life, general motion" and a "supreme intelligence" that does not interfere in the workings of the world. Most everything

else about religion he rejects: revelation is a device invented by priests for dominating people; ritual life is not useful; the soul is (in Lockean terms) nothing but
"the result of sensation"; and immortality is but an hypothesis.[139] On ethical questions the proselyte rejects all external standards: born "free and independent,"
human beings are subject only to conventional standards of justice. The notion of
eternal punishment is simply a "political invention for containing the masses."[140]
Having given these correct answers, the wise man declares the applicant to be
"enlightened." In rapid form the proselyte gives assent to the creed of the *philosophes*: he believes that faith is nothing but a superstition made for the ignorant; he renounces the "fanaticism of continence," humility, and poverty; and he
promises to recognize reason as the "sovereign arbiter of all that the supreme
Being could or had to do," the "infallibility of the senses," and the "voice of
nature and the passions."[141] Having successfully passed the exam, the wise man
pronounces him "unbaptized" in the name of Rousseau, Montesquieu, and Voltaire. He is, finally, commissioned to "pull up, destroy, overturn, stomp on religion," and to incite people to revolution. All this he is to confirm with "miracles": "to blind those who see, to render deaf those who hear, and to make limp
those who walk straight."[142]

In his dialogue, Diderot answers the challenge of this parody by working within the same imaginary setting and circumstances, only now giving fuller,
more accurate, and more persuasive voice to the would-be *philosophe*. Immediately the reader encounters the shift. Instead of demanding wisdom, now the
proselyte searches for truth, and instead of answering the wise man's questions
with formulaic replies and dogmatic self-assurance, he now echoes Socratic ignorance and humility. When asked about the soul, for instance, he curtly replies that
he doesn't talk about what he cannot know.[143] In general, Diderot's proselyte gives
more thoughtful and convincing replies: he rejects all "positive religions" (those
which rely on "historical proofs") in favor of one written in the human heart. This
universal religion was the guide of Socrates and will continue with humanity
forever. Historically founded religions, on the other hand, are simply "schools for
illusion."[144] Of their worship, God has no need. Besides, the proselyte contends,
the many revelations put forth by the world's religions all contradict each other
and they all contradict reason.[145] It is better, he repeats, to tend to the religion
engraved in the hearts of all mankind.

> A religion founded on these simple notions would find no unbelievers; it would
> make a single people of all men; it would not cover the earth with blood in times of
> ignorance, and it would not be a despised phantom in enlightened times. But it is not
> the *philosophes* who make religions; they are the work of ignorant enthusiasts, or of
> ambitious egoists.[146]

Here, the proselyte gives full voice to the *philosophe*'s critique of religion.

On ethical questions, the proselyte's responses are once again more complete and more powerfully articulated. When asked about the origin of evil, he asserts that it is a "necessary consequence of the general laws of nature." It is impossible to imagine a world without evil.[147] Asked what he believes about justice and injustice, the proselyte responds that justice consists in faithfulness to established conventions, something that holds across cultures though the specifics are culturally variant. Our primary duty in human life is to "become happy" and to "promote the happiness of others" by being virtuous.[148] He does not say what virtue is, but he is considerably more emphatic when rejecting the duties of continence (which he distinguishes from chastity), penance for sins, and mortification. He renounces these evils with all his heart. The call to humility is similarly rejected, since self-love is necessary, while forgiveness of others is a good which antedates Christianity. An enlightened existence must listen carefully to the voice of reason when it speaks "the language of virtue."[149]

In itself this dialogue is simply a concise summary of Diderot's views on various religious questions. As a dialogue, it is wholly expository, and hence lacks the dialectical movement characteristic of Diderot's more famous dialogues. As Carol Sherman says of this type of dialogue, the second interlocutor (the wise man) "incarnates no point of view and poses no serious objections" to the lead character who represents Diderot.[150] It lacks, therefore, the intricate layering of critical examination that criss-crosses the discourse in "D'Alembert's Dream." The dialogue becomes more dialectical, and hence more interesting, when read as a dialogue *with* another dialogue. Then the shifts introduced by Diderot into the wise man and the proselyte's conversation take on considerable importance. Seen in this light, as a dialogue with another dialogue, Diderot's text transcends mere exposition by forcing readers of both dialogues to examine critically the veracity of the satirical rendition of critical discourse.

To begin with, Diderot not only makes the proselyte a more faithful and articulate spokesman for the *philosophes* (saying what a real *philosophe* would say), but he also (and more significantly) recasts the discursive interaction between the wise man and the proselyte. In the satirical piece the wise man appears as a *philosophe*, one who truly possesses wisdom, while the proselyte simply spouts the correct replies. In Diderot's dialogue, conversely, the conversation is reversed: when, for instance, the wise man asks the proselyte whether he believes in "the testimony of God," Diderot has him respond not with a simple, formulaic answer but with counter-questions. He cannot imagine how God could speak except through natural agents ("through flies as well as by elephants"); but "has God ever spoken otherwise?" Now the tables have turned, and the wise man must come up with answers. When he does so—claiming that God speaks through his favorites—the proselyte blasts him out of the water with questions, counter-positions, and a brusque dismissal: to whom does God speak? To Zoraster? Noah?

Moses? Mohammed? These are all impostors. "Why do you seek to seduce me," he asks, "what have I to do with your would-be revelations?"[151] For his part, the proselyte listens to God only through the voice of his conscience, not through the wise man's "false doctrines."

> Do you think that if God wanted to teach me something more than what he himself has written in my soul, he would use you? Isn't he the one who makes me breathe, who makes me think? Does he need spokesmen to make me know his will? Get away from me, and fear lest this God, of whom you dare to say you are the interpreter, punishes you for having borrowed his name in order to deceive me.[152]

The wise man ignores the pointedness of these questions, and consequently misses their point. Returning to the format where *he* asks the questions, the would-be wise man queries whether the proselyte believes in God—truly a strange question to ask considering the critical subversion of revelation just asserted by the proselyte.

How deep this reversal of roles goes becomes clear only by comparing the endings of the two dialogues. While in the satirical piece the wise man ceremoniously "unbaptizes" the proselyte, Diderot's dialogue closes without any initiation. It is, in the end, the proselyte who expounds to the wise man on reason and virtue. Given the catechetical format inherited by Diderot, this is very strange: what was the purpose of the examination if not initiation? For that matter, why is the proselyte depicted as such if not to formalize a conversion? And how wise *is* the wise man if he is to receive instruction from a prospective convert? These questions underscore Diderot's message, which comes to the fore only by looking at this text as a dialogue with another dialogue. While seeming to imitate the satirical dialogue, Diderot transforms the original. Indeed, practicing what Furbank calls his "foisting" method, Diderot takes over the conversation and changes it completely. It is not just the content that is changed, but the entire quality of the discourse. In Diderot's hands, the discussion is *not* an examination for the sake of initiation into a system of correctly held dogmas, but a critical examination (*elenchus*) of false certainties and superstitions. Discourse shifts, in other words, from catechesis to *elenchus*—from confident spouting of what is known (dealing in answers) to critical searching (dealing in questions).

As a result, Diderot flip-flops the location of wisdom and ignorance. Real wisdom lies in the kind of discursive criticism practiced by Diderot's proselyte, while real ignorance lies in the uncritical arrogance of the so-called wise man. The proselyte, clearly, is Diderot's protagonist; he is a Socratic figure who professes not to have wisdom but to be in search of it. Like Socrates, it is the proselyte's questioning—Socratic *elenchus*—which examines and unsettles the so-called wise man. In the end the wise man is not wise at all; certainly, he is not qualified to initiate the proselyte. In fact, it is the wise man who is initiated in the wisdom of criticism practiced by the proselyte through the process of dialogue—only he is too thick-headed to glean the point.

This reversal—something which Diderot shows performatively through the conversation of the two dialogues rather than by any explicit statement—is what Diderot hopes to drive home to the reader. He hopes to show his readers who participate in the dialogue between the dialogues that true enlightenment lies neither in religious doctrine nor in dogmatic (really, doctrinaire) skepticism, but in searching and questioning dialogue. The *philosophe* is the one who stands against the superstitions and illusions fabricated under the guise of religion; but he also refuses to indulge in dogmatic rejections of religion. This is a remarkable point to be made by someone like Diderot, who had completely renounced religious belief (including the deism of the proselyte) by the time this dialogue was written; it shows, I take it, how dedicated Diderot was to the critical practices embodied by Socratic dialogue. In the end, Diderot leaves his readers in the liminal space of the two dialogues' controversy: the critical loop remains open for the reader to decide not only which view to hold on this or that topic, but also how to comport oneself in discourse over religious questions.[153]

In 1774, while passing through Holland on return from his visit to Catherine II of Russia, Diderot wrote another little dialogue on religious questions. Bearing the title "Conversation of a Philosopher with the Maréchale de ***," the piece was published in 1777 under the name of Thomas Crudeli (the Italian poet and author who had died in 1745), although it had appeared earlier in the *Correspondance littéraire* in 1775.[154] Unlike so many of Diderot's dialogues, this work did find its way into the public eye, although—for caution's sake—it could not bear Diderot's own name.

Like much of the "Proselyte," this dialogue concentrates on the relationship of religion and the moral life. When the dialogue opens, for instance, Madame la Maréchale (a partially disguised name for the Duchesse de Broglie with whom Diderot had enjoyed conversations) immediately turns to this topic:

Maréchale: Are you not M. Crudeli?
Crudeli: Yes.
Maréchale: The man who believes in nothing?
Crudeli: I am.
Maréchale: But your morals are the same as a believer's.
Crudeli: Why not, if that believer is an honest man?
Maréchale: And you put that morality into practice?
Crudeli: As well as I can.
Maréchale: What! you do not steal, or kill, or pillage?
Crudeli: Very rarely.[155]

With this comic opening the opposition is set: the Maréchale believes that the moral life depends on and is enhanced by religion, while Crudeli doubts that religion contributes anything positive and is convinced that it may do a great deal of harm to morality.

The most striking thing about this dialogue is its juxtaposition of devastating criticism of religion with a "gentle and gracious" manner.[156] As Sherman notes, the dialogue's "apparent frivolity" is "proportionate to the seriousness and audacity of its attack on organized religion."[157] Crudeli (read Diderot) assures the Maréchale, for instance, that he did not set out to persuade her of anything. He has not got the "proselytizing mania"—"not in the least."[158] It is the Maréchale, in fact, who presses the conversation forward, insisting that Crudeli put off going to see her husband for just a few more minutes of talk. The light and unaffected atmosphere is maintained throughout by repeated jumps and starts in the conversation which we have come to see as commonplaces in Diderot's dialogues. It is also sustained by the repeated references to the imminent arrival of the Maréchal. This genteel tone is not an incidental or cosmetic addition to the dialogue; with it, Diderot "reassures the reader by giving a jocular turn to what might otherwise seem unrelentingly heretical."[159] And, more importantly, he brings criticism of religion down to earth and installs it in a thoroughly natural setting.

The whole dialogue bears a decidedly Socratic flavor. Through Crudeli's questions and test-cases, the Maréchale's unexamined and inconsistent confidence that religious belief promotes morality is progressively dismantled. With each step in the discussion he becomes bolder and she distances herself further and further from her original position. She admits, to begin with, that nonbelievers behave every bit as morally as believers, and with no more inconsistency.[160] When she proposes that religion is an inducement to good behavior—what could be wrong with another reason for being moral?—Crudeli counters by citing the "terrible ravages religion has caused in the past and will cause in the future":

> it has created and now perpetuates the most violent national hatred. No Mussulman but believes he is doing an action agreeable to God and the holy prophet in exterminating every Christian. And the Christians on their side are scarcely more tolerant. Think how it has created and still perpetuates in the same country divisions rarely suppressed without the shedding of blood. . . . Think how it has created and still perpetuates, in society between citizens, and the family between relatives, the most violent and most lasting of hatreds.[161]

The Maréchale protests that these are abuses, not the essentials of religion. Even this defense will not hold, however, for she must agree with Crudeli that no more dangerous idea could be invented than "belief in an incomprehensible being about whom men should never agree and to whom they should attach more importance than to their own lives." "That is an idea which might well be disastrous, if lunatics got hold of it," she admits.[162]

Once the Maréchale begins to make concessions, Crudeli becomes progressively sharper in his criticism, bolder with his skepticism, and more audacious in his speculations. He wonders, for instance, whether there really are any Christians in the world. Even an ordinary person—a woman he knows who is remarkably like the Madame Maréchale, for instance—quickly sets the moral precepts of the Gospels aside when it suits her vanity.[163] In fact, he suggests, it is best that religion has so little influence on morals. Think of the disastrous consequences "if twenty thousand Parisians took it into their heads to base their conduct strictly on the Sermon on the Mount. . . ."[164] What chaos would result! It is best to live without the superstitions of religion. If there be a God, it certainly would forgive people their doubts while chastising their immoralities.[165] By the time Crudeli is finished, the Madame is spinning: "It is [she says] enough to make one's head go round, is it not?"[166] The Maréchale has been undone.

Without question, this dialogue is not a conversation between equals. The Madame Maréchale is a pious woman—at times overly confident in her beliefs, at times silly and flustered, but like many (indeed, most) Christians, her religion is filled with unexamined inconsistencies. More positively, however, she is strikingly honest and (at times) very open-minded. Throughout the dialogue, for instance, she readily admits the strength of Crudeli's points when they strike her as true. Occasionally she joins forces with him (in a manner reminiscent of Julie De L'Espinasse in "D'Alembert's Dream") to add examples of religious hypocrisy drawn from her own experience. And she is, as Sherman notes, "remarkably eager to participate in a discussion which is critical of her religion."[167] Crudeli, on the other hand, is a confident but tolerant skeptic. As he puts it, "I allow everyone to think as he pleases, provided I am allowed to think as I please."[168] In Sherman's words, Crudeli is Diderot's picture of the ideal atheist: "kind, good-humored, understanding, tolerant." He criticizes Christian intolerance, "without being, for all that, intolerant himself."[169] And most importantly, while the inconsistencies between Christian belief and moral action are exposed and criticized, Crudeli never attacks the Madame. Indeed, when his critical boldness once offends her, he quickly assures her he was thinking of "one of my neighbors, who is as honest and pious as you: who thinks herself a Christian in all sincerity just as you do."[170] Crudeli's critical discourse is consistently suggestive and provocative, but it is up to the Maréchale (and hence to the reader) to draw the lesson herself.

The dialogue ends—unexpectedly—with Crudeli admitting that he would gladly submit to religious belief and practice if his safety were threatened. The Maréchale asks him:

> **Maréchale**: By the way, if you had to state your principles to the magistrates, would you make a clean breast of them?
> **Crudeli**: I should do my best to hinder the magistrates performing a brutal act.
> **Maréchale**: Oh, you coward! And if you were at the point of death, would you submit to the ceremonies of the Church?
> **Crudeli**: I should not fail to do so.
> **Maréchale**: Oh, you wretched hypocrite![171]

With this ending, the reader comes to share the Maréchale's experience of having her head spin, for what appeared to be a completed conversation now turns out to be unfinished. By this means, Diderot throws these opposites—man and woman, skeptic and believer—back into the same fold in two ways. Despite their opposition about religion, they share "the fundamental moral identity of human beings."[172] Religion may well be an unnecessary addition to the moral life—as Diderot argues by way of Crudeli's critical discourse. But with this curious ending, he adds a self-critical point as well: the believer and the skeptic share the common human fault of inconsistency. And with this admission, Diderot throws the dialogue open to his readers who must face these issues for themselves. The dialectic of criticism, consequently, remains open-ended; and the burden of responsibility, as happens so often in Diderot's dialogues, rests with the reader.

While neither of these little dialogues ranks among Diderot's most celebrated works, they do provide sufficiently vivid and accomplished literary examples of the kind of critical discourse Diderot imagined (or, at least, wished to entertain) with religious voices. If we take a glance back to compare these dialogues with those of Anselm discussed in chapter two, it quickly becomes apparent both how much and how little these two masters of dialogue share in their perceptions of the place and purpose of critical discourse over religious matters. They share, most obviously, the sense that rational discussion of religious topics is best pursued through the give and take of conversation; and they agree that conversation about religious issues is naturally and effectively expressed through the literary dialogue. Within this shared horizon, however, the differences are striking—and, therefore, very instructive.

Both Anselm and Diderot worked within restricted and enclosed environments, but Anselm craves the insulated privacy of the monastery (accepting intrusions from the larger public world only reluctantly and only to serve the intellectual needs of his monks), while Diderot yearns for publicity (the "Proselyte" was sent to his theological opponent and the "Conversation" actually was published) even as he seeks protective cover from repressive public authorities (neither dialogue carried Diderot's name as author). Given their different social locations, each crafts his dialogues to satisfy distinct literary demands. Anselm's dialogues, recall, require no more realism than is needed to reflect the paternalistic relationship between abbot and monk, while Diderot couches his two dialogues on religion with as much dramatic realism as he can muster. The "Conversation," certainly, is more successful in imitating what Peter France calls the "relaxed and urbane tone of polite conversation," but the "Proselyte" is at least fairly successful in reflecting the living flavor of controversial discourse.[173] Both authors are, as one might expect, altogether confident in pursuing their rhetorical agenda. Anselm exudes a magisterial confidence grounded in the conviction of the unshakable truth of orthodox church teaching, while Diderot either wields his sword of criticism with abandon—at times (as in the "Proselyte") confident that he can "ride rough-shod" over the absurdities of religion, and at other times (in the "Conversation," for instance) relaxing in the conviction that religious beliefs fundamentally are sense-less and vapid.

Anselm and Diderot share the conviction that reason has an important place in religious discourse, but they travel in opposite directions—as it were—in the dialectical encounter of faith and reason. Anselm's dialogues depict the uses of reason in the life of faith in several ways: as abbot, Anselm stands invariably open to any and all questions that his monks might bring to him; and he consistently meets these questions with arguments, frequently appealing to their shared sense of what is "fitting" and sometimes building a more formidable case with so-called "necessary reasons." Though Anselm's openness to conversation truly does lead to profound discoveries regarding the nature and existence of God, the paramount interest in all of his discourse is to confirm the verity of church teaching, and, hence, to settle the anxieties and doubts plaguing his monks. Reasoned conversa-tion, for Anselm, is to serve faith's self-understanding by alleviating uncertainty and confirming belief. Diderot's dialogues on religion, to say the least, paint a very different picture of reason's critical dialogue with religion. Reason, for Diderot, plays a subversive and liberative role; depending on the complexion of the religious interlocutor, its criticism can be either aggressive and hostile (as in the "Proselyte") or charming and emancipatory (as in the "Conversation"). The proselyte, for instance, greets the religious wise man with defiance, ridicule, and a barrage of lethal counter-questions; he seeks, above all, to expose the ignorant folly of religious beliefs, and hence to undercut his religious interlocutor's uncriti-cal arrogance. The "Conversation," alternatively, shows a gentler approach (and one more typical of Diderot's dialogues), where the rational skeptic Crudeli tact-fully presses the Maréchale to examine her religious assumptions, thereby helping her to rise above her superstitious view of life. Rational criticism of religion plays a crucial part in both Anselm and Diderot, but it cuts in diametrically opposed directions. In Anselm's dialogues, the discursive practice of criticism shores up religious belief, while in Diderot's it topples them.

For both Anselm and Diderot, dialogue about religion leads to the limits of intelligible language and rational communication. These are, however, altogether different limits. Anselm conducts faith's critical inquiry to the outer edges of con-ceivability, leaving his interlocutors (and thus, himself and his readers) face to face with the mysterious (and finally inconceivable) quality of God's mercy— that love than which none greater can be conceived. Diderot, for his part, follows critical discourse to the limits of Socratic irony and skepticism. In the "Proselyte" everything is stood on its head (the wise man turns out to be ignorant, and the initiate ends up being the wise man); while in the "Conversation" Crudeli exposes both the errors and the dangers of religious life, leaving his religious interlocutor with her head spinning, and most likely on the verge of feeling insulted. Interestingly, both Anselm and Diderot step back from these limits. They are simply too dangerous. Mystical discovery, for Anselm, cannot (and should not) contravene orthodox authority; and skepticism, for Diderot, has its practical limits in the power of the magistrate.

In the end, both bequeath to their readers what they think rational criticism through dialogue can contribute to the world of religion, but it is a vastly different inheritance. Anselm's dialogues model (what he takes to be) the correct process of faith seeking understanding; he invites his readers to identify with the searching questions raised by his monks, and thereby to be led back, satisfied by Anselm's explanations, to the self-same beliefs with which they began. In Diderot's dialogues, conversely, the characters graphically perform the kind of critical and conjectural discourse which (he feels) will free them from religion and initiate them to a more rational life. But Diderot will do no more (nor can he) than lead readers to the point of decision, hoping against hope that his readers—like the good eclectic—will now "dare think for themselves," and thus, through critical dialogue, learn to construct their own "personal and domestic" view of life.[174] It is with this goal in mind that Diderot strategically leaves his readers in a lurch at the end of both dialogues—the "Proselyte" ends without resolving the cognitive gap between the wise man and the proselyte; and the "Conversation" closes with an unexpected and even self-critical note.

The final section of this chapter follows the trajectory of Diderot's art of dialogue one more—very significant—step beyond what we have seen thus far, offering a reading of *Rameau's Nephew*, truly Diderot's masterpiece in the dialogue genre, and the point at which he experiments most boldly with the outer limits of critical and conjectural discourse. It is here that we face the ultimate contrast between Anselm and Diderot's practice of criticism through dialogue.

(4) Diderot's Mimetic Monster

Rameau's Nephew is Diderot's most celebrated and yet most enigmatic work in dialogue form. All of his talents for composing charming and realistic dialogues packed with philosophical provocation and unsettling irony combine here to form what Wilson rightly calls "an absorbingly intricate and complex work."[175] For that very reason, this text continues centuries later to command the attention of readers, even while it resists any settled consensus of interpretation. It is in *Rameau's Nephew* that we find Diderot taking his readers by means of dialogue to the far reaches of critical discourse—where critical experimentation and Socratic examination hover near (or considerably beyond) the borders of rationality and civility. This dialogue provides us with Diderot's most highly developed version of the kind of reasoned criticism through dialogue that Diderot deployed elsewhere against religion; and thus with an excellent counterpoint to Anselm's limit-breaching, meditative criticism of the grammar of belief.

The dialogue opens with a narrator telling us of his habit of taking solitary strolls, during which he lets his thoughts "wander in complete abandon," "accosting" any and every idea but "sticking to none." On this particular day, while taking refuge from the rain in the Café de Régence, the narrator is himself accosted by Rameau, the nephew of the famed composer of the same name.[176] While Diderot presents the narrator (called "Mr. Philosopher" by Rameau) as a man of reason and integrity, Rameau is described by the narrator as "one of the weirdest characters in this land of ours where God has not been sparing of them." "Blessed with a strong constitution, a singularly fervid imagination, and lung-power quite out of the ordinary," Rameau the nephew is said to be unfailingly variable (ragged one day, a gentleman the next, for instance), all to play the genial but cynical jester who leaches off the rich by entertaining them with his foolish antics.[177] The narrator's portrait of Rameau, it should be noted, is not far removed from the nephew's self-image; he boasts that he is as impudent as Diogenes and—true to his unabashed hedonism—he is "fond of consorting" with the likes of Phryne.[178]

Only recently, it turns out, Rameau has been evicted from a rich man's house for daring to show "a bit of common sense for once." Rameau, it seems, has infuriated his wealthy host by comparing himself (who managed to be seated between the host and the *abbé*) to a giant prick between two nuts (*"un maestoso cazzo fra duoi coglioni"*). His error is not the coarse joke (which the guests accept like so many other entertaining pieces of folly from Rameau), but the sudden sense of his own importance, which keeps him from apologizing (even insincerely) to Monsieur. Taking his "exceedingly rare" gift for "foolery" seriously for a moment, Rameau ends up on the street for committing "an incomparable piece of folly"— that is, for having the stupidity of showing "a bit of taste, intelligence and reason."[179] His new found situation, then, serves as the jumping off point for the dialogue between Rameau (now designated "He") and the narrator (now strangely objectified with the first person "I").

The conversation to follow bears all the marks characteristic of Diderot's art of dialogue. Most noticeably, Diderot's knack for capturing the sound of living voices in conversation is evident once again. Every twist and turn of the dialogue—from Rameau's wavering assessment of genius, through his defense of sophistical education and his unflinching apology for "the art of dodging disgrace, dishonor and the law," to his scandalous and abusive treatment of his wife—displays what Wilson rightly calls, "a disarming air of casualness and off-handedness."[180] Every step of the dialogue is natural and life-like. The semblance of living conversation arises in part, as it did in "D'Alembert's Dream," from the spontaneous zigzagging with which the dialogue moves from topic to topic. As Peter France puts it, the dialogue moves "sinuously and spasmodically," reflecting thereby the chaotic order so typical of everyday conversation.[181] Diderot's dialogue also gains a realistic guise from the many references to known figures of eighteenth century France sprinkled over the course of the conversation—though, oddly, the readers for whom these references would naturally convey a recognizable reality never saw this dialogue in print. Diderot's flair for recreating living conversation extends even to the odd and unusual, as when the nephew mimes the playing of an allegro of Locatelli; or, even more bizarrely, when he launches into a frenzied pantomime of "a whole orchestra, a complete opera-house" with "an enthusiasm so near to madness that it was uncertain whether he would ever get over it. . . ."[182] In this dialogue, even the weird appears life-like!

And yet, as we have seen before, the realism of Diderot's dialogues belies his active presence as author working to move an audience to understanding and insight. Diderot artfully crafts the lively voices of *Rameau's Nephew*, all the while lurking in the background, concealing his identity, resisting easy identification with either character, but subtly manipulating the flow of conversation, and ironically foisting all kinds of things on public personae. All of these things we have seen before in Diderot's dialogues, though now the artful dodging and maneuvering is extended to new lengths. It is not clear, for instance, who speaks for Diderot; some have identified him with "I," others see him in "He," while more and more interpreters accept the confusion and recognize his presence in the dialectical play of both characters.[183] Nor is it at all evident just what the dialogue is about, since this text truly is, as Peter France puts it, a catalogue (or perhaps an encyclopedia) of Diderotian concerns. If there is a unifying theme to the dialogue, it is the relationship between art in general (and music in particular) and the good life ("of what is the right way to live"[184]); but such connections only rarely rise to view, and they quickly fade behind the text's complexity and disorder. Readers, lastly, are left wondering what is real and what is made up; when is the text to be believed and when is it to be read with suspicion? Readers must be especially alert, for instance, as Diderot lets Rameau comment on current musical debates, or when he heaps praise on figures notorious for their criticism of the *Encyclopedia*; or again when Diderot usurps the real nephew's persona for his own philosophical purposes.[185] Each of these moves—the author's self-effacement, the scrambled order of discourse, the resulting lack of topical focus, and the adroit manipulation of known personae—attract and entice readers, even as they challenge and unsettle. And that, clearly, is Diderot's point. As Julie Kristeva says, *Rameau's Nephew* "does not want to settle down"; nor, it is clear, does Diderot want his readers to become too settled or comfortable.[186] Such is the intended effect of Diderot's critical and experimental agenda.

As the reader immediately perceives, it is the nephew who causes the most disquiet. He is the protagonist of Diderot's fondness for Socratic criticism and the agent of his imaginative experimentation. In the first place, Rameau is given an explicitly Socratic role. Characters like this, the narrator tells us, are

> the speck of yeast that leavens the whole and restores to each of us a portion of his natural individuality. He stirs people up and gives them a shaking, makes them take sides, brings out the truth, shows who are really good and unmasks the villains.[187]

Reminiscent of the Socrates of the early Platonic dialogues, the nephew gives the narrator an intellectual shake-down by subjecting his self-certainty to critical examination (a kind of Socratic *elenchus*); and he "brings out the truth" (the maieutic function of the Socratic midwife) by delivering the narrator from the confidence of his assumptions and exposing him to the naked truth. Also like Socrates, the nephew touts the importance of self-knowledge. Rameau presents himself as the one person honest enough to face (and accept) his own ignorance. He knows absolutely nothing![188] In the second place, Rameau advances Diderot's penchant for conjecture and experimentation. As we saw in "D'Alembert's Dream," Diderot loves to proceed by what Peter France calls "the fruitful disorder of dreams, madness, and casual conversation, where the writer or speaker is led on by analogies to unexpected new ideas."[189] Nowhere is this more true and more advanced than in *Rameau's Nephew*: who can guess where and how the nephew will turn, as he playfully experiments with different forms of ass-kissing (some literal, some not), with the various "idioms" of his professional mooching, with the hundred or more ways of seducing a young girl, or, finally, with the universal art of devising and deploying masks.[190] There appear to be no restraints whatsoever on the nephew's free-flowing conjectural musings.

But something is amiss here. Something has changed from the Socratically-inspired experimental eclecticism seen in Diderot's other dialogues, and this brings us to the heart of the matter. In a word, Rameau is more cynical than Socratic; and his wild conjectures are more maniacal than experimental. The nephew's criticisms, first of all, are not exactly Socratic. There is no disciplined *elenchus*, in which premises latent in an interlocutor's stance are shown to lead to contradictions with that stance.[191] The nephew's critical examination proceeds by counterpoint, not by question and answer; it is his manifold strangeness, rather than searching and questioning, that elicits truth. Thus, even though Rameau takes up the "Socratic position of maieutically directing the conversation," as Jauss puts it, "only the function is Socratic, not the method of the maieutic."[192] Nor is the outcome recognizably Socratic: not only is there no buried or latent truth there to be discovered (as in Plato's middle dialogues), but the self-knowledge at the heart of Socrates' philosophical life is twisted and perverted. When, for instance, Rameau claims self-knowledge, it is (strangely) to brag about his ignominious character: "I am an ignoramus, a fool, a lunatic, rude, lazy and what we in

Burgundy call an out and out shirker, a rogue, a gormandizer." "Nobody knows me better than I do myself," he adds.[193] These qualities, he remarks, make him a good teacher; unlike most educators (who think they know something, but really don't), Rameau knows he knows nothing—and that makes him better for his students, since they will not have to unlearn anything later on. We have, clearly, moved beyond Socrates.

In the second place, the nephew's conjectures and playful thought-experiments move far beyond the experiments of "D'Alembert's Dream." Gone are the innocent conjectures about genetic manipulation and gone are the slightly scandalous musings about Doctor Bordeu and his goat. In their place are the anarchic ravings of a lunatic and the abusive schemes of an immoralist. The nephew's frenzied exercises in pantomime illustrate the former. When, for instance, "I" suggests that he seek readmittance to the table of the rich by begging the Madame's pardon, Rameau launches into animated pantomime of such a scene.

> He flung himself down with his face pressed to the ground, he seemed to be holding the point of a slipper between his hands, and he wept and sobbed, saying: "Yes, my little queen, yes, I promise, never in my life, in my life." Then suddenly rising to his feet he went on in a serious and thoughtful tone: Yes, you are right. I think that is best. She is kind hearted. Monsieur Vieillard says she is so kind! I know myself that she is. And yet to have to go and eat humble pie in front of the bitch![194]

The nephew's musical pantomimes exemplify the same mercurial spirit of conjecture.

> With cheeks puffed out and a hoarse, dark tone he did the horns and bassoons, a bright, nasal tone for the oboes, quickening his voice with incredible agility for the stringed instruments to which he tried to get the closest approximation; he whistled the recorders and cooed the flutes, shouting, singing and throwing himself about like a mad thing; a one-man show featuring dancers, male and female, singers of both sexes, a whole orchestra, a complete opera-house, dividing himself into twenty different stage parts, tearing up and down, stopping, like one possessed, with flashing eyes and foaming mouth.[195]

Though entertaining (everyone is amazed), Rameau's imaginative performances are deranged. With "flashing eyes and foaming mouth," Rameau takes Diderot's experimental imagination to the edges of madness.

Similar moves occur in the moral sphere, though the effect now is more disturbing than bizarre. What were playful ventures about sexual ethics in "D'Alembert's Dream" become vicious exercises in self-serving abuse and intrigue in *Rameau's Nephew*. Rameau, it seems, studies the world's moral literature, not to become morally enlightened, but in order to learn what vices are and how not to sound like you have them![196] And, unfortunately, he is (in his own words) "a much better moralist" than musician.[197] Thus we find him reveling in the brilliant treachery perpetrated by the "renegade of Avignon": this man, it seems, conned a Jewish man out of his wealth by preying on the man's fear of the Inquisition, only to turn the man who trusted him ("his good friend the Israelite") in to the authorities, who proceeded to turn him into a "fine bonfire."[198] What courage! What "highly skillful duplicity," Rameau exclaims in delight! As "I" perceives (in horror), the nephew imagines this "execrable crime. . . like a connoisseur of painting or poetry examining the beauties of a work of art." Such is the range of his moral imagination. He wants to be classed among the "great blackguards" of all time.[199] And judging from the heartless and brutal treatment of his wife—he only married her to gain a fortune from prostituting her—he already stands in that class.[200] Rameau never stops experimenting with new ways to practice his self-absorption, to feed his hedonism, and to polish his skills at deception.

Recent interpreters of *Rameau's Nephew* have focused on these kinds of moves as efforts to push beyond a Socratic model of critical discourse. Jauss, for one, argues that Diderot is struggling with "how to accept the openness of Socratic dialogue literally," that is, fully and unequivocally, without the Platonic assumption that dialogue leads inevitably to predetermined Truth.[201] Diderot's ironic task, in Jauss' view, is the "renewal of Platonic dialogue in its open Socratic form for the purpose of summoning it against philosophical dogmatism and, in particular, against the Platonic unity of the Good and the Beautiful." The dialogue represents "an extension of Platonic dialogue after the cessation of its idealistic premises."[202] To accomplish this, Diderot must transfer the Socratic role to the anti-philosopher—that is, to someone like Rameau's nephew; and such an audacious philosophical adjustment requires a genre shift, a transformation of Socratic dialogue into something sufficiently open and unrestrained to test the "final truths" by listening to the strange voices of alien speech. That genre, Jauss argues, is "Menippean satire," the "genre of final questions," something classically represented in texts like Petronius' *Satyricon* or Lucian's dialogues.[203] In the nephew's pantomime of the human condition, Diderot "transcends the dialogical form of the renewed Socratic dialogue to the polyphony of Menippean Satire," in order to examine and criticize fully, radically, and openly, the manifold forms of human folly.[204]

Kristeva echoes much the same approach to *Rameau's Nephew*, though she more pointedly shows Diderot's connections to the genre of classical Cynicism. In her view, Diderot's dialogue yields a character (the nephew) who is much closer to the Cynic Diogenes of Sinope (412–323 B.C.E.) than to Socrates. The "eccentric dogman," Diogenes was known for his "rancorous and scornful" behavior, not only toward Alexander, but in "mockery of vices and social conventions" generally.[205] Holding up the natural, simple, and unfettered life as ethical ideal, this "Socrates gone mad" wielded irony and sarcasm at the pretense and hypocrisy of human culture.[206] "Eccentric, if not insane," Kristeva writes, "the cynic displays the *other* of reason; foreign to social conventions, he discredits himself in order to have us face our shameful otherness."[207] But as Kristeva notes, Diderot's "strategy of strangeness" outstrips even Diogenes; for when "I" points out to the nephew that the Cynics were "the Carmelites and Cordeliers of Athens" (signifying an austere lifestyle), he quickly distances himself from the classical Cynic.[208] In response to which, Kristeva concludes:

> ... the Nephew counterfeits Diogenes: his cynicism is an "effrontery," a sham that scoffs at the philosophical loftiness eventually chosen by Diogenes. He replaces the cynic virtue of the Ancients with infatuation, flattery, glibness, and material ease. The Nephew is the cynic's cynic: he experiences its rhetoric and carries it to its peak, remaining up to the end foreign to ethical identity, even that of the cynic.[209]

Stripped of its ethical rigor, the Nephew's pantomime is "faithful only to Menippus' rhetoric, not to Diogenes' virtues."[210] In saying this, Kristeva links up with Jauss' reading of *Rameau's Nephew*.

Jauss and Kristeva help in focusing attention on Diderot's move beyond his much beloved Socratic paradigm; and they highlight the way in which he incarnates the strange, critical rhetoric of the Cynics. But, accurate as these readings are in unraveling the point of *Rameau's Nephew*, they do not tell the whole story. What they tend to elide is the way in which Diderot looks back to Socratic discourse, even as he transcends it in substance and in genre. He "looks back," so to speak, for two reasons: (a) because the new, more exotic form is an extension (really, a natural and historic outgrowth) *of* the Socratic genre; and more significantly, (b) because the new approach is devised for the purposes of critically and experimentally testing its root form. Diderot's art of dialogue in *Rameau's Nephew* is connected to the Socratic in the first sense in as much as the classical Cynics were the most logical and among the most prominent successors to Socrates. Antisthenes and his student Diogenes, for example, hung on to the ethical focus of Socratic maieutic without the metaphysical trappings devised by Plato; and they furthered (even as they transformed) the rigorous examination and criticism of individual lives.[211] To pick up Menippean forms, therefore, is to participate in the historic evolution of the Socratic life of criticism. Such participation, however, links up Diderot's dialogue with its Socratic paradigm in the second sense, for in repeating experimentally the historic development of the Socratic to the Cynic, Diderot tacitly tests the trajectory of Socratic criticism. It is, after all, the same critical agenda only intensified, heightened, and exaggerated with fresh method and genre; and to experiment with the newly cast form is, for Diderot, to examine and test the limits of Socratic criticism itself. To make this last point stick, granted, requires a bit more discussion of Diderot's text.

The important thing is not the identification of *Rameau's Nephew* with a particular figure or genre.[212] What is important is to note the underlying impetus of Diderot's dialogue, and then to follow the trajectory his imaginative experiment gives to this original force. Like so much of his work, *Rameau's Nephew* gives initial hints (as we have seen) that its lead character bears a Socratic function. But, soon after, this critical impetus undergoes mutation, transforming itself into the Cynicism of Diogenes. By the dialogue's end, however, Rameau leaves Diogenes behind, preserving—as both Jauss and Kristeva argue—only the Cynic rhetoric of Menippean satire. Even at that point, the trajectory of Diderot's dialogue goes further yet, for in some significant ways Diderot carries his readers beyond Menippean satire as well. The latter genre, as we will see in chapter five, blends comic perspective with serious moral judgment for the sake of ironic criticism. But Rameau simply is not Menippus; he lacks the simple but cutting humor found in Menippean figures (like Lucian's Menippus), he lacks the inherent moral sensitivity which drives Menippean humor, and he lacks the subtlety required for irony. Rameau is crude, despicable, and blunt; and as such, he supersedes not only Socrates and Diogenes but Menippus as well. How bold and far-reaching is the trajectory of Diderot's project in this dialogue. It represents what France calls "Diderot's furthest advance into the realm of disorder";[213] it is his most advanced, most radical exercise in experimental eclecticism—the impetus for which Diderot owes a debt to Socrates.

What Diderot discovers at the limits of critical reason is a monstrosity, and Rameau is that monster. In the first place, Rameau is a monster musically. Consider the frenzy and distemper of one bit of musical performance thrown into the middle of the conversation:

> He began to warm up and sang, at first softly, then, as he grew more impassioned, he raised his voice and there followed gestures, grimaces and bodily contortions. . . . He sang thirty tunes on top of each other and all mixed up: Italian, French, tragic, comic, of all sorts and descriptions, sometimes in a bass voice going down to the infernal regions, and sometimes bursting himself in a falsetto voice he would split the heavens asunder, taking off the walk, deportment and gestures of the different singing parts: in turn raging, pacified, imperious, scornful. Here we have a young girl weeping, and he mimes her simpering ways, there a priest, king, tyrant, threatening, commanding, flying into a rage, or a slave obeying. He relents, wails, complains, laughs, never losing sight of tone, proportion, meaning of words and character of music.

Needless to say, "all the chess-players [in the café] had left their boards and gathered round him" to watch, and for good reason.[214] A musical monster lurked in their midst.

But Rameau is also a monster morally—though this may not be apparent to every modern reader. Above all, he insists, it is important to avoid being virtuous.

Virtues are unnatural, and though people laud them, they do not fit very well. Consequently, virtue makes people "ill-tempered" and "miserable"; or more graphically, it "freeze[s] you to death, and in this world you have to keep your feet warm."[215] In place of the virtuous life, the nephew advocates unadulterated hedonism: "good table, good company, good wines, pretty women, pleasures of all descriptions, amusements of every kind"—those are goods worth pursuing.[216] There simply is no reason to do anything that does not serve oneself. In the end, therefore, the only really important thing in life is to "evacuate the bowels easily, freely, pleasantly and copiously every evening."[217] Hence it is important to cultivate the "social talents"—those skills necessary to survive and flourish in a culture given over to "debauchery and luxuriousness." And those are precisely the things the nephew has tried to pass on to his son, especially the centrality of money: "Money, money. Money is all, and the rest, without money, is nothing."[218] Fortunately, the proud father beams, he is already "greedy, smooth, a thief, a waster and a liar."[219] Clearly, Rameau is as morally despicable as he is musically bizarre.

The question, at this point, shifts back to Diderot. What is the point of creating such a character? Why undertake this limit-breaching venture? The answer, I think, lies in specifying just what kind of monster is facing us in this dialogue. In a word, Rameau is a *mimetic monster*. He is a pure mirror. All he does is imitate; and he practices this art of reflection as thoroughly and consistently as can be imagined. Consider first his view of music. For Rameau "a tune is an imitation, by means of the sounds of a scale . . . either by the voice or by an instrument, of the physical sounds or accents of passion."[220] Taking a jab at the old fuddy-duddies (e.g., Rebel and Francoeur) who fear the advances of Italian music in France, the nephew confidently predicts the triumph of the Italian style: "We shall become inured to the imitation of the accents of passion and of the phenomena of nature by melody or voice or instrument, for that is the whole extent and object of music."[221] Music is imitation. When, therefore, Rameau launches into his pantomime of an opera, the whole point is to mime every conceivable passion.[222] Something similar happens in an earlier display of musical pantomime:

> His voice went like the wind and his fingers flew over the keys, sometimes abandoning the top part so as to do the bass, sometimes leaving the accompaniment to take up the top part again. One passion after another flitted across his face—you could see tenderness, anger, pleasure, grief and feel the *pianos* and *fortes*.[223]

And that, Rameau contends, is the point of music. It also is at the heart of his dramatic, excessive, even monstrous mimetic existence.

But, second, Rameau's morality (if it can be called that) also is purely imitative. Since there is "no such thing as the absolutely, essentially, universally true or false" when it comes to human behavior, one must do "what self-interest dictates"—whether that be good or bad, wise or foolish, serious or ridiculous," and so on.[224] The secret to a successful life, Rameau contends, is to cultivate the art of appearances (what he calls the "moral idioms" of a trade); one must reflect back what people expect and manage how one is perceived. There need be, he admits, "no intrinsic value" involved, for "value [is] conferred by public opinion." Image is everything. The trick is to "conform" to expectations, to feed people's vanities, and to play the needed role. And this is precisely what Rameau does as a music teacher. Having a good name as a music teacher is won by giving (and sustaining) the impression of being highly demanded for lessons. No knowledge of music is needed. The lesson starts with casual comments about the weather, followed by impressive sounding gossip about opera, spiced with a few obscure comments about leading intellectuals (Voltaire). After a spell, the young girl finds her (chewed up) music book, she plays a bit, he complements her work but chastises her mother for not making her practice, he corrects her hand position ("I had to do something"), he insists she play a "G" (though he cannot see the keyboard), there is plenty of flattery and diversion, "the hour was going by," and then the time is up, the fee is paid, and "that is what is called a lesson in accompaniment."[225] No music has been learned and everyone is happy!

Roughly the same thing occurs when Rameau mooches off the rich. His role at their table, and what they expect of him, is to play the jester. He entertains them with his playful antics, groundless gossip, crude jokes, and brazen insults; in turn, they feed him with fine fare. It is, in Rameau's words, a "tacit agreement"; "the chap . . . treats us to his hospitality in exchange for such flattering deceptions."[226] Besides, he adds, if they live "with folk like us," they should expect "all sorts of dirty tricks" and gossip.[227] The essence of this contract lies in the jester's ability to reflect the folly of his hosts back at them. There is nothing to Rameau but "the sentiment and opinion of the whole of society."[228] And whatever the venue, Rameau's counsel for success remains the same: "butter people up, good God, butter them up, watch the great, study their tastes, fall in with their whims, pander to their vices, approve of their injustices."[229] Such a policy will bring plenty of praise and pleasure. When "I" criticizes this lifestyle, Rameau counters with a mimetic answer: he is no worse than those he serves—how could he be, since there is nothing to him that is not reflected from his hosts? His life is "identical with theirs." The rich won their wealth by stealing, so he is "helping them to make restitution."[230] In the end, therefore, "Rameau must be what he is—a thief happy to be among wealthy thieves. . . ."[231] At all of this, "I" cannot help but be impressed: "You have taken the talent for making fools of people and bootlicking as far as it will go."[232] Indeed, he has taken (im)moral imitation as far as it will go.

From beginning to end, imitation is the key to Rameau's bizarre and depraved character. What is crucial to see at this juncture is how Rameau's limit-breaching mimetic treatment of music and morality is repeated more fundamentally in his criticisms of life and culture generally. Criticism, in Rameau's voice, proves mimetic as well; and it is, naturally, an especially frightful and hideous form of imitation. That is why it is so important for him to distinguish his critical function from the likes of Menippus; he does not humorously observe the various "pantomimes of the human species" from a heavenly perch, like Menippus does in Lucian's "Icaromenippus."

> No, no, I tell you. I am too heavy to soar so high. I leave such misty realms to the cranes. I am of the earth, earthy. I look about me and take up my positions or find fun in watching the positions taken up by others. I am an excellent mimic. . . .[233]

Rameau is of the earth (or perhaps the gutter); and he plays his critical function—forcing the examination of life and drawing out the truth of people's lives—by using the same masks and moves as "flatterers, courtiers, flunkeys and beggars."[234] And though he (and his type) may "look jovial," he is as dangerous as a monster.

> we are all foul-tempered and voracious of appetite. Wolves are not more famished, tigers no more cruel. We devour like wolves when the earth has been long under snow, like tigers we tear to pieces anything successful.[235]

In all this, oddly and monstrously, Rameau echoes the revelatory principle of Socratic-Menippean criticism: he "stirs people up and gives them a shaking," he "makes them take sides, [and] brings out the truth. . . ."[236] The nephew's methods of criticism, however, are no longer Socratic and well beyond Menippus.

Diderot has created a character whose discourse allows him to experiment with the limits of Socratic-Menippean criticism. As in "D'Alembert's Dream," here, too, Diderot performs his experiment by means of the imitative function of the dialogue form. In this regard, interestingly, he too is a mime. Through the artful performance of a literary dialogue, Diderot mirrors the trajectory by which critical discourse reaches its limits. It is, as Kristeva puts it, an "extraordinary flight of polyphonic fancy":[237] by creating and representing the nephew's outrageous positions, his scandalous proposals, and his mad mimetic displays which push the envelope of normalcy, order, and reason, Diderot examines Socratic examination and experiments with Menippean criticism not by testing its premises for the sake of exposing latent contradictions, and not by humorous satire, but by practicing these very forms of discourse to the hilt, driving them (as Jauss puts it) "aporetically to the extreme."[238] As a dialogue, it turns the reader's attention inward to examine the inherent limits of pure criticism. It critically performs, thereby, the limit-breaching madness of pure, unadulterated cynical criticism. In musical terms, *Rameau's Nephew* is Diderot's performance of "La Folia," the popular air (meaning "mad" or "empty headed") subsumed in compositions by major seventeenth and eighteenth century composers.[239] As a piece of moral criticism, it is his "Praise of Folly," though without Erasmus' Christian conclusions. As a dialogue, it stands unrivaled for its thorough-going criticism of criticism and its bold experimentation with the madness of pure cynicism.

But Diderot does not leave his readers perched at this precarious point. As we saw earlier in "D'Alembert's Dream," Diderot gracefully pulls back from the boundary between civility and scandal. In the ending of "Conversation of a Philosopher with the Maréchale de ***," Diderot similarly steps back from scandal by leaving (quite unexpectedly) the dialogue between believer and skeptic open-ended. The same reserve appears regarding *Rameau's Nephew*, and for good reason. In the first place, the nephew's professional mimicry is exposed as being unproductive. He is, in this regard, identical with Socrates, who admits to Theaetetus:

> I am so far like the midwife, that I cannot myself give birth to wisdom; and the common reproach is true, that, though I question others, I can myself bring nothing to light because there is no wisdom in me. The reason is this: heaven constrains me to serve as a midwife, but has debarred me from giving birth.[240]

When, similarly, "I" asks Rameau why—with all his passion, memory and enthusiasm for music—he has "never done anything worth while" himself, he can answer (typically) only in a flurry of pantomime depicting his aberrant birth as a conglomerate of images. When pressed again, "why haven't you ever tried producing a work of art?," he mimes his own barren mimicry, and then says:

> That's about it, I think. It's coming. It shows you what it means to find an *accoucheur* who knows how to stimulate and induce labour pains and deliver the baby. Left to myself I take up my pen to write. I bite my nails and rub my forehead. Nothing doing. Good night.[241]

And with that, the nephew's imitative criticism reaches its limits. This mutant Socrates is barren; his path cannot lead anywhere fruitful.

In the second place, Diderot sprinkles his text with tacit doubts about the tenability of Rameau's life and stance. The nephew is caught, as Furbank notes, in the vicious, self-consuming circle of his own unbridled cynicism. What happens, Furbank asks,

> if you take cynicism literally, as a serious philosophy, and actually try to live by it? The answer is quite unexpected. There *is* no rock bottom. It is impossible to take your stand on cynical certainties, for they shift and give way under your feet, and you find yourself not standing on a rock but pursuing an ever-retreating, ever-changing, shadow.[242]

Such is Rameau's predicament when he claims to be completely honest about his dishonesty (what kind of honesty could that be?); or again, when he vaunts his perfect consistency ("Isn't it true that I am always the same?"), which means, of course, being consistently variable; or again, finally, when he espouses his hatred for geniuses, though he aspires to be a genius at mocking geniuses. In the end, the nephew is caught (and devoured) in his own critical web. By dedicating himself to mirroring a society of mask wearers, it becomes literally true (as the narrator puts it) that "nothing is less like him than himself," since he is only "like" what he mirrors.[243] There is nothing else to him! He destroys himself, therefore, as the narrator hinted early in the dialogue, by criticizing the "order of things" that (literally) gives him his life.[244] *That* is how dependent the pure mirror is on that which it mirrors; and *that*, of course, is why Rameau's momentary lapse into common sense is so disturbing—for it reveals to the light of day the vacuous and jaded quality of unmitigated cynicism. *That*, as Furbank concludes, is an "alarming discovery"[245]—which, in the end, is Diderot's point in this dialogue.

Finally, Diderot pulls back from the edge by keeping his "alarming discovery" to himself. Indeed, as Furbank notes, Diderot "never once refers to this, his masterpiece, and, at least so far as we know, never showed it to anyone."[246] This is truly an astonishing fact given Diderot's tack of publishing his work surreptitiously through vehicles like Grimm's literary review. His daring experiment in dialogue only found readers decades later, first in a translation by Goethe published in 1805, second in a French translation of Goethe's German text in 1821, and then third in the publication of original manuscripts in 1891.[247] Like those of Socrates and like the nephew, Diderot's revival and experiment with the trajectory of Socratic criticism ends without giving birth—at least knowingly. We can only surmise his reasons for this discretion, but it seems evident that the extra degree of caution quite suitably matches the extra measure of imaginative license he took in crafting this dialogue. Perhaps Diderot has the magistrate in the back of his mind, once more. Whatever his reasons for not going "public" (even among friends), Diderot's deliberately private handling of his text helps to confirm that *Rameau's Nephew* was not intended as a celebration of shallowness, depravity, and moral anarchy, as suggested by some commentators. Quite the opposite. If anything, this dialogue is a testimony to the unspeakable and unlivable limits of Socratic criticism, where even Diogenes seems tame. It represents, therefore, a self-critical warning about the outer limits of critical and experimental reason.

Diderot never unleashed the likes of Rameau's nephew on religion. Nor did he publicly unleash such unmitigated criticism on anything at all. But the critical discourse practiced by the nephew in *Rameau's Nephew* is, as this chapter makes evident, the natural extension of the "experimental eclecticism" Diderot directed against theism (in "D'Alembert's Dream") and against religion generally (in the "Proselyte" and the "Conversation"). In *Rameau's Nephew*, however, Diderot takes this critical discourse as far as it will go, just as Anselm does in "Why God Became a Man." The dialogues of Anselm and Diderot must appear, at first glance, an odd match. And, indeed, their contexts, purposes, and methods are worlds apart.

At one crucial point, however, their projects converge. They both venture to the outer limits of critical reason, they both risk a conception of what lies beyond the threshold of language, and, interestingly, they both step back from the edges they have discovered. Anselm, we have seen in chapter two, conducts his dialogue by meditative intensification of the grammar of belief to the outer edges of conceivability, leaving his readers face to face with the mystery of God's mercy—that love than which no greater can be conceived. Diderot, as we have seen in this chapter, conducts his dialogue by Socratic criticism and experimental conjecture to the threshold of pure cynicism, leaving his readers face to face with a human monster—that fool than which no greater can be imagined. In both cases, critical discourse through dialogue functions as a mirror: in Anselm's case, grammatical analysis allows (with the grace of God) human words to mirror—briefly, but significantly—the fullness of divine love; while for Diderot, critical experimentation yields another pure mirror (Rameau) whose words reflect the emptiness of unadulterated cynicism. These are, granted, very different limit-cases; and they are reached by vastly different discursive practices. Placing them side by side, however, points up the polar extremes of insight lying at the limits of critical discourse over religion—whether in the service of faith's self-understanding or for the sake of exposing the errors and follies of religious life.

But the dialogues also reveal—as Anselm and Diderot independently discovered—the dangers lurking at those limits, and the need for caution. Anselm's formula of perfection and Diderot's pure mirror cannot be conceived and cannot be spoken—at least not for long and not in public. The splendor is too great for Anselm; the chaos is too unsettling for Diderot. Readers, therefore, are to be warned. Discourse will collapse if either strategy of criticism is followed to the edges. Thus we find reasoned argument giving way to the passion of prayer in Anselm, and verbal exchange yielding to the wild gestures of pantomime in Diderot. In either case, readers are advised to step back from the limits. Readers of Anselm are to step back in obedient praise and reverent awe, finding certainty in the house of orthodoxy, while readers of Diderot are to hold back with Socratic bafflement and ironic laughter, while maintaining a certain reserve and civility. Of course, neither master of dialogue wishes to put an end to discourse over religion. Quite the opposite: through their different deployments of the dialogue genre, they invite readers to take up critical discourse about religion, they arm their followers with certain strategies and practices for engaging successfully in that discourse, and, finally, they caution their audience about the limits facing such discursive practices. Both Anselm and Diderot know—though from different sides—about the enticing possibilities and the overwhelming limits of discourse over religion. It is these tensions, finally, which come to life in their literary dialogues.

Notes

¹ Denis Diderot, *Letters to Sophie Volland*, trans. Peter France (London: Oxford University, 1972) 85.

² Immanuel Kant, *Critique of Pure Reason*, trans. Norman Kemp Smith (New York: St. Martin's, 1929) 9. Diderot proclaimed similarly: "All things must be examined, debated, investigated without exception and without regard for anyone's feelings. . . . We must ride roughshod over all these ancient puerilities, overturn the barriers that reason never erected. . . ." Denis Diderot, *The Encyclopedia; Selections*, trans. Stephen Gendzier (New York: Harper, 1967) 93.

³ Immanuel Kant, "What is Enlightenment?," *On History*, ed. by Lewis White Beck (Indianapolis: Bobbs-Merrill, 1963) 3. See Horace, "Epistles," Book I, epistle 2, line 40. Voltaire had earlier taken up the same shibboleth. Voltaire, *Philosophical Dictionary*, "Freedom of Thought," 356.

⁴ Immanuel Kant, *The Conflict of the Faculties; Der Streit der Fakultäten*, trans. Mary J. Gregor (New York: Abaris, 1979), the first part dealing with the conflict between the philosophical and theological faculties. See Jacques Derrida, "Mocholos; or, The Conflict of the Faculties," *Logomachia: The Conflict of the Faculties*, trans. by Richard Rand and Amy Wygant (Lincoln: University of Nebraska, 1992) 3–34.

⁵ Johann Gottfried von Herder, *Reflections on the Philosophy of the History of Mankind*, ed. Frank E. Manuel (Chicago: University of Chicago, 1968) 116. See also 79–118.

⁶ Denis Diderot, from the "Letter of the author to M. * * *," published as the preface to Nicholas-Antoine Boulanger, *Récherches sur l'origine du despotisme oriental*. I take the passage from Arthur Wilson, *Diderot* (New York: Oxford University, 1972) 437.

⁷ A must-read for all post-modern critics of the enlightenment, see Peter Gay, *The Enlightenment; An Interpretation. Vol. 2, The Science of Freedom* (New York: Norton, 1969) 101–108. Gay splendidly documents the reservations and qualifications affixed to the *philosophe*'s "geography of hope." On Kant's caution (even skepticism) regarding moral and political progress, see *The Conflict of the Faculties*. Herder likewise concedes that progress is anything but smooth, subject as it is to the myriad environmental factors native to specific cultures. Hume is more blunt in his skepticism: "No advantages in this world are pure and unmixed." "When the arts and sciences come to perfection in any state," therefore, "from that moment they naturally, or rather necessarily decline, and seldom or never revive in that nation, where they formerly flourished." David Hume, "Of the Rise and Progress of the Arts and Sciences," in *Essays: Moral, Political, and Literary*, ed. Eugene F. Miller, revised edition (Indianapolis: Liberty Classics, 1987) 130 and 135. Hume says much the same thing about political progress. See "Idea of a Perfect Commonwealth," *Essays*, 528–529. Diderot, in kind, clearly distinguishes scientific from moral progress: "We are more enlightened. Are we better? That is another question." Wilson, *Diderot*, 576. Similarly Voltaire: "What does a dog owe to a dog, and a horse to a horse? Nothing. No animal depends on his kind; but since man has received the gleam of divinity called *reason*, what is the result? He becomes a slave almost everywhere in the world." Voltaire, "Equality," *Philosophical Dictionary*, trans. Peter Gay (New York: Harcourt, Brace and

World, 1962) 245. For a discussion of the various responses to the limits of reason, see Giorgio Tonelli, "The 'Weakness' of Reason in the Age of Enlightenment," *Diderot Studies*, vol. 14, ed. Otis Fellows and Diana Guiragossian (Geneva: Droz, 1971) 217–244.

[8] Peter Gay, *The Enlightenment; an Interpretation. Vol. 1, The Rise of Modern Paganism* (New York: Norton, 1966) 171.

[9] Gay, *The Enlightenment; an Interpretation. The Rise of Modern Paganism*, 178.

[10] See, for instance, Christoph Martin Wieland, "Göttergespräche" and "Gespräche im Elysium," *Sämmtliche Werke* 25 Bd. (Leipzig: Georg Joachim Göschen, 1796); Gotthold Ephraim Lessing, *Lessing's Masonic Dialogues (Ernst und Falk)*, trans. Rev. A. Cohen (London: Baskerville, 1927); Lessing, *Nathan the Wise*, trans. Walter Frank Charles Ade (Woodbury, N.Y.: Barron's, 1972); David Hume, "A Dialogue," *An Inquiry Concerning the Principles of Morals*, ed. Charles W. Hendel (Indianapolis: Bobbs-Merrill, 1957) 141–158; Hume, *Dialogues Concerning Natural Religion*, ed. Norman Kemp Smith (Indianapolis: Bobbs-Merrill, 1947); Fontenelle, *Dialogues of Fontenelle*, trans. Ezra Pound (London: Egoist, 1917); Voltaire, *Dialogues et anecdotes philosophiques* (Paris: Garnier, 1966); and Voltaire, *The Works of Voltaire* vol. 4 (Paris and London: E. R. DuMont). D. J. Adams' *Bibliographie d'ouvrages français en forme de dialogue; 1700–1750* (Oxford: Oxford University, 1992) gives more than ample evidence of how widespread the use of dialogue was in eighteenth century France.

[11] Gay, *The Enlightenment; An Interpretation. The Rise of Modern Paganism*, 172.

[12] Wilson, *Diderot*, 559.

[13] Wilson, *Diderot*, 470.

[14] Denis Diderot, "The Encyclopedia," *Diderot; Rameau's Nephew and Other Works*, trans. Jacques Barzun and Ralph H. Bowen (Indianapolis: Bobbs-Merrill, 1964) 277.

[15] Diderot, "The Encyclopedia," 296. In a letter to Sophie Volland dated September 26, 1762, Diderot similarly claims that the *Encyclopedia* will "cause a revolution in the minds of men," although he harbors no fantasies that his accomplishment will win him any rewards—"We shall have served the human race; but we shall have been reduced to cold unfeeling dust, long before anyone is grateful to us." *Diderot's Letters to Sophie Volland*, trans. Peter France (London: Oxford University, 1972) 125. For D'Alembert's views on the *Encyclopedia*, see Jean Le Rond D'Alembert, *Preliminary Discourse to the Encyclopedia of Diderot*, trans. Richard N. Schwab (Indianapolis: Bobbs-Merrill, 1963).

[16] Diderot, "The Encyclopedia," *Diderot; Rameau's Nephew and Other Works*, 294.

[17] Wilson, *Diderot*, 174 and 173.

[18] P. N. Furbank, *Diderot; A Critical Biography* (New York: Alfred A. Knopf, 1992) 98.

[19] Diderot, *Letters to Sophie Volland*, 16, the letter dated May 11, 1759.

[20] Furbank, *Diderot*, 100.

[21] See Carmontelle's work in Wilson, *Diderot*, among the plates between 364–365.

[22] Denis Diderot, *The Encyclopedia; Selections*, trans. Stephen J. Gendzier (New York: Harper and Row, 1967) 233.

[23] Diderot, *The Encyclopedia; Selections*, 234–35. Ironically, this section was deleted by Diderot's publisher Le Breton as too provocative. See also Wilson, *Diderot*, 446 and 702. Diderot purportedly translated Plato's *Apology* from memory while captive in Vincennes. See "Apologie de Socrate traduite de mémoire au château de Vincennes," *Oeuvre Complètes* (Paris: Hermann, 1975) 245–281. See Wilson, *Diderot*, 109.

[24] Wilson, *Diderot*, 446. See also Katharine Carson, "Socrates Observed: Three Eighteenth-Century Views", *Diderot Studies*, vol. 14, ed. Otis Fellows and Diana Guiragossian (Geneva: Droz, 1971) 273–281.

[25] Carol Sherman, *Diderot and the Art of Dialogue* (Geneva: Droz, 1976) 11.

[26] See, for instance, Denis Diderot, "Apologie de L'Abbé Galiani," *Oeuvres politiques* (Paris: Garnier, 1963) 61–124; or again, Diderot's "Réponse de Diderot a l'examen du prosélyte par lui-Même," *Oeuvres Complètes de Diderot*, ed. J. Assézat (Paris: Garnier, 1875), vol. 2, 94–99. The latter is a sequel to an exchange of dialogues on religion; see the third section of this chapter. See also Diderot, *Réfutation suivie de l'ouvrage d'Helvétius intitulé l'homme* in *Oeuvres Complètes de Diderot*, vol. 2, 275–456, a text constructed dialogically out of quotations from Helvétius and Diderot's responses, which slips into overt dialogue form. See 306–308 and 356–367 for examples. One of Diderot's first works follows this same format: in *Principes de la Philosophie Morale, ou Essai sur le Mérite et la Vertu*, Diderot translates passages from Schaftebury followed by extensive notes of his own, thereby creating an inter-textual dialogue. See *Oeuvres Complètes de Diderot*, 17–121, but especially 17–41. See D. J. Adams, *Diderot, Dialogue and Debate* (Liverpool: Francis Cairns, 1986) 19–35 on this text. Where possible, references to works of Diderot not translated into English come from the Assézat edition; given the presently uneven state of Diderot publications, however, recourse will be made—where necessary—to the more recent (yet incomplete) *Oeuvres Complètes*, edited by Herbert Dieckmann, Jacques Proust, Jean Varloot, et al. (Paris: Hermann, 1975), and to *Oeuvres politiques* cited above.

[27] Wilson, *Diderot*, 444. In defense of dialogue, Diderot wrote: "Nothing conforms more to the search and persuasion of the truth; to the search, because by doubting one becomes sure of everything; to persuasion, because it allays the fears of people's passions. . . . Dialogue is the true instructive way; because what do the master and the disciple do? They dialogue unceasingly." Diderot, "Apologie de L'Abbé Galiani," *Oeuvres politiques*, 112.

[28] Denis Diderot, "Letter on the Blind," *Diderot's Early Philosophical Works*, trans. Margaret Jourdain (Chicago and London: Open Court, 1916) 108–114. See Furbank, *Diderot*, 62–64.

[29] In correspondence, see Denis Diderot, *Letters to Sophie Volland*, 41–48. For dialogues inserted in the midst of historical work, see Denis Diderot, "Essai sur les règnes de Claude

et de Néron," in *Oeuvres Complètes de Diderot*, vol. 3, 15–407. See, for instance, 107–108, 226–237, 285–286, and 356–357. For a helpful discussion of the use of dialogues in Diderot's historical method, see Rosalina De La Carrera, *Success in Circuit Lies: Diderot's Communicational Practice* (Stanford: Stanford University, 1991) 83–123. For dialogues in fictional works, see Denis Diderot, "This Is Not a Story" in *This Is Not a Story; and Other Stories*, trans. P.N. Furbank (Oxford: Oxford University, 1993) 17–36.

[30] The phrase comes from Sherman, *Diderot and the Art of Dialogue*, 13. See Denis Diderot, "Entretiens sur le fils naturel," *Oeuvres Complètes de Diderot*, vol. 7, 85–168. See the discussion in Furbank, *Diderot*, 139–147.

[31] Denis Diderot, *Jacques the Fatalist*, trans. Michael Henry (New York: Penguin, 1986).

[32] Diderot, "Le Fils Naturel; Comédie," *Oeuvres Complètes de Diderot*, Act IV, Scene iii, 66. Translation from Wilson, *Diderot*, 255. Rousseau took offense at this remark. See Wilson, *Diderot*, 254–59. Voltaire had written much the same thing a year earlier in the first edition of his *Philosophical Dictionary*. The solitary person may be saintly, Voltaire grants, but he should be called "virtuous only when he performs some act of virtue from which other men benefit." Voltaire, *Philosophical Dictionary*, trans. Peter Gay (New York: Harcourt, Brace and World, 1962) 495.

[33] From the *Encyclopedia* article titled "Philosophie" in *Oeuvres Complètes de Diderot*, vol. 16, 291. Translation from Wilson, *Diderot*, 191. (There is question whether Diderot penned this article; but the point clearly met with his editorial approval.) On the dialectical play of systematic thinking and creative interpretation in Diderot's thought, see Herbert Dieckmann, *Cinq Leçons sur Diderot* (Geneva: Droz, 1959) 41–68. Such a combination, Dieckmann rightly notes, has won Diderot many critics who crave more systematic order in their philosophy.

[34] Diderot, "The Encyclopedia," *Diderot; Rameau's Nephew and Other Works*, 295–296.

[35] Wilda Anderson, *Diderot's Dream* (Baltimore and London: Johns Hopkins University, 1990) 105. On the dialogical nature of Diderot's cross references, see also Sherman, *Diderot and the Art of Dialogue*, 12 and 39; and Wilson, *Diderot*, 243.

[36] Stephen Werner adds an intriguing connection between the *Encyclopedia* and Socratic criticism and dialogical genre: the *Encyclopedia* is a "Socratic drama," which, by its "theatrical" discourse, revises long-established categories of knowledge and undermines common assumptions. "Theatrical writing," Werner writes, "endorses a style of dialogue and confrontation meant to clash with scholarly exposition and sober analysis. Above all, it problematizes genre. An encyclopedia can no longer be taken as an established or fixed form. It must be seen as open and variable." As he argues, it is the plates (and the technical-scientific articles which attend them) which function as the Socratic "agents of change": "their presence opens up the closed world of encyclopedia writing (and that of classical discourse) to the shock of the new." See Stephen Werner, *Blueprint: A Study of Diderot and the Encyclopédie Plates* (Birmingham, Alabama: Summa, 1993) 88–96. For the plates, see *L'Encyclopédie, ou Dictionnaire raisonné des sciences des arts et des Métiers*, vol. 4, titled *Recueil de Planches, sur les sciences, les arts libéraux, et les art Méchaniques, avec leur explication* (Paris: Pergamon reprint).

[37] See, for instance, Wilson, *Diderot*, 103–116, on Diderot's imprisonment.

[38] Wilson, *Diderot*, 150–160 and 332–342. Shortly thereafter, the Catholic church added its two cents: laity were threatened with excommunication and priests with suspension if they did not hand over their copies of the *Encyclopedia* for destruction by fire. See Wilson, *Diderot*, 359.

[39] Diderot appeals to the distinction between an author's voice and that of an interlocutor in his "Apologie de L'Abbé Galiani," *Oeuvres politiques*, 80.

[40] See Furbank's "Chronology of Diderot's Writings" in *Diderot*, 476–483; and Sherman, *Diderot and the Art of Dialogue*, 34.

[41] See Sherman, *Diderot and the Art of Dialogue*, 37. See the references to the remarkable efforts of Malesherbe on behalf of the *philosophes* in Wilson, *Diderot*.

[42] See Wilson, *Diderot*, 337.

[43] See Furbank, *Diderot*, 117.

[44] Sherman, *Diderot and the Art of Dialogue*, 41. For Diderot's complaints about his workload, see Diderot, *Letters to Sophie Volland*, 192–193, the letters dated August 23 and August 31, 1769.

[45] Sherman, *Diderot and the Art of Dialogue*, 29–30.

[46] Sherman, *Diderot and the Art of Dialogue*, 41 and 47. In her words, "the passage to the dialogue as his instrument of philosophic expression corresponds to the (forced) limitation of his audience." See 43.

[47] Sherman, *Diderot and the Art of Dialogue*, 34 and 43.

[48] Peter France, *Rhetoric and Truth in France: Descartes to Diderot* (Oxford: Clarendon, 1972) 203. On Diderot's real, intended, and imagined readers, see Dieckmann, *Cinq Leçons sur Diderot*, 15–39.

[49] See, for instance, Diderot's criticism of René-Antoine de Ferchaut Réaumur for refusing the request to observe a cataract operation on a girl blind from birth. "Letter on the Blind for the Use of Those Who See," trans. Margaret Jourdain, *Diderot's Early Philosophical Writings* (Chicago and London: Open Court, 1916) 68–19. On this conflict, see Wilson, *Diderot*, 97–99; and Furbank, *Diderot*, 56–57.

[50] Diderot, "Lettres à Falconet," *Oeuvres Complètes de Diderot*, vol. 18, 79–336. See Wilson, *Diderot*, 507–512; and Gay, *The Enlightenment; An Interpretation. The Science of Freedom,* 90–91. Posterity, however, can be a frustrating audience: it is difficult to live on the "incense of posterity" alone, he tells Sophie. Diderot, *Letters to Sophie Volland*, 97.

[51] Though an early work, the opening lines of "Philosophical Thoughts" aptly describe Diderot's sense of audience: "I write of God; I count on a very few readers; and do not

hope to find many in agreement with me. If these thoughts please nobody, they are certainly bad, but I should count them sorry stuff if they were to everybody's taste." See *Diderot's Early Philosophical Works*, 27.

[52] Denis Diderot, "Discours sur la poésie dramatique," trans. John Hope Mason, *The Irresistible Diderot* (London: Quartet, 1982) 141. The text is addressed to Grimm.

[53] Diderot's phrase comes from his *Letters to Sophie Volland*, 19. On the public function of Diderot's privately intended audience (Grimm and Sophie), see Dieckmann, *Cinq Leçons sur Diderot*, 32–33.

[54] Diderot's world of conversation was relatively small and safe—made up of trusted friends like Melchior Grimm and Madame d'Epinay, the Baron and Madame d'Holbach, Abbé Galiani, and Father Hoop (so called "because he is so wrinkled and dried-up and old-looking"), though it always remained open to a steady influx of visitors (Helvétius, the painter Louis-Michel Vanloo, and David Hume, to mention just a sampling); and, through correspondence and travel, it extended across Europe to Switzerland (Voltaire), Russia (Falconet and Catherine the Great), and England (Hume again).

[55] Denis Diderot, *Letters to Sophie Volland*, 194. The letter is dated August 31, 1769.

[56] Diderot, *Letters to Sophie Volland*, 199. The letter is dated early September, 1769.

[57] Twentieth century critics concur. Thus Wilson notes, "D'Alembert's Dream" is a "remarkably successful example of this union of literature and philosophy." Wilson, *Diderot*, 570. Diderot's enjoyment of a literary genre which is at once profound and crazy does not satisfy the genre standards of much professional philosophy. See Dieckmann, *Cinq Leçons sur Diderot*, 67. See also Herbert Dieckmann, *Die künstlerische Form des Rêve de D'Alembert* (Köln: Westdeutscher, 1966).

[58] For a discussion of Diderot's concept of "sensibility" in "D'Alembert's Dream," see B. Lynne Dixon, *Diderot, Philosopher of Energy: The Development of his Concept of Physical Energy, 1745–1769* (Oxford: Oxford University, 1988) 133–187.

[59] Diderot, *Letters to Sophie Volland*, 194. Diderot entertained the idea of naming his characters "Democritus, Hippocrates, and Leucippe." See letter 38, dated August 31, 1769.

[60] A good discussion of "Diderot's gift for creating the feeling of living conversation" in his philosophical "theatre of the mind" (or dialogues) is to be found in Peter France, "Public Theatre and Private Theatre in the Writings of Diderot," *The Modern Language Review* 64 (July 1969) 522–528.

[61] Denis Diderot, "D'Alembert's Dream," in *Rameau's Nephew and Other Works*, trans. Jacques Barzun and Ralph H. Bowen (Indianapolis: Bobbs-Merrill, 1964) 98.

[62] Diderot, "D'Alembert's Dream,"165–166. Compare Diderot, *Letters to Sophie Volland*, 119: "There is no logic in conversation and it seems that the jolting of a carriage, the various things you see as you go along, and the increasingly frequent silences all contribute to make it still more disjointed."

63 Diderot, "D'Alembert's Dream,"128–132.

64 Diderot, "D'Alembert's Dream,"123.

65 Diderot, "D'Alembert's Dream,"150.

66 Denis Diderot, "De la Poésie Dramatique," *Oeuvres Complètes de Diderot*, vol. 7, 319–322, section seven titled "Du Plan et du Dialogue."

67 Denis Diderot, "Apologie de L'Abbé Galiani," *Oeuvres politiques*, 80 and 82–83.

68 Diderot writes in the *Salon* of 1767: "When one writes, must one write everything? When one paints, must one paint everything? Please, let my imagination supply something." I take this passage from Gay, *The Enlightenment; An Interpretation. The Science of Freedom*, 276.

69 De La Carrera, *Success in Circuit Lies*, 33.

70 France, *Rhetoric and Truth in France*, 221.

71 There is no better example of Diderot "supplementing" another's work than "Supplement to Bougainville's 'Voyage'," *Diderot: Rameau's Nephew and Other Works*, 179–228.

72 See Furbank, *Diderot*, 62. Perhaps the most daring of suppositions occurs where Diderot presumes to speak for his readers. See, for instance, the opening paragraph of "This is Not a Story," where Diderot warns his readers that he has "introduced a personage" who will speak for them. See Denis Diderot, *This is Not a Story, and Other Stories*, 17.

73 Furbank, *Diderot*, 62.

74 Furbank, *Diderot*, 324.

75 Diderot, "D'Alembert's Dream," 115–117.

76 See Furbank, *Diderot*, 325–326.

77 Sherman, *Diderot and the Art of Dialogue*, 48.

78 Sherman, *Diderot and the Art of Dialogue*, 80.

79 Furbank, *Diderot*, 331–332. See Diderot, "D'Alembert's Dream," 92–99.

80 Diderot, "D'Alembert's Dream," 101, 111–113, 126–127, and 145.

81 Diderot, "D'Alembert's Dream," 141–142 and 151.

82 Diderot, *The Encyclopedia; Selections*, 86.

83 Diderot, *The Encyclopedia; Selections*, 86–91.

[84] Diderot, "D'Alembert's Dream," 92.

[85] Diderot, "D'Alembert's Dream,"101.

[86] Diderot, "D'Alembert's Dream," 101–103.

[87] Kenneth Seeskin, *Dialogue and Discovery: A Study in Socratic Method* (Albany, N.Y.: State University of New York, 1987) 3.

[88] Seeskin, *Dialogue and Discovery*, 3.

[89] Diderot, "D'Alembert's Dream,"120 and 113.

[90] Note these developments in Diderot, "D'Alembert's Dream," 118–130.

[91] For this transformation, see 130–163 of Diderot, "D'Alembert's Dream."

[92] See, for instance, Diderot, "D'Alembert's Dream," 171 and 165.

[93] De La Carrera, *Success in Circuit Lies*, 153–160. For these moves by Julie, see Diderot, "D'Alembert's Dream," 122, 125, and 132 respectively.

[94] See, for instance, Diderot, "D'Alembert's Dream," 128 and 139.

[95] See Diderot, "D'Alembert's Dream," 167–174.

[96] Denis Diderot, *The Irresistible Diderot*, ed. John Hope Mason (London: Quartet, 1982) 66.

[97] Diderot, *The Irresistible Diderot*, 66–67.

[98] Wilson, *Diderot*, 531. See also Furbank, *Diderot*, 109–13, on "conjecture." Dieckmann similarly notes Diderot's option for a literary form which will give proper place to "conjecture, analogy, intuition and imagination" in the context of scientific inquiry. See Dieckmann, *Die künstlerische Form des Rêve de D'Alembert*, 7–34.

[99] Diderot, "D'Alembert's Dream,"126–127.

[100] See Diderot, "D'Alembert's Dream," 129, 139, 135, and 157 respectively.

[101] Diderot, "D'Alembert's Dream," 157.

[102] See Diderot, "De la poésie dramatique," *Oeuvres Complètes de Diderot*, vol. 7, 371. Translation from Wilson, *Diderot*, 529.

[103] Furbank, *Diderot*, 130. Diderot writes of the *Encyclopedia*: "Here we are swollen and exorbitant, there meagre, small, paltry, dry and emaciated. . . . We are alternately dwarfs

and giants, colossi and pygmies, straight and well-proportioned, and crooked, hump-backed, limping and deformed. Add to these oddities a style of discourse sometimes abstract, obscure or *recherché*, more often careless, long-winded and slack, and you have to compare the entire work to the *monster* in poetic theory, or something even more hideous." Quotation taken from Furbank, *Diderot*, 130–131.

[104] Diderot, "D'Alembert's Dream," 132–133.

[105] For these examples, see Diderot, "D'Alembert's Dream," 138, 139–140, 141–142, 150, 151, and 152 respectively.

[106] Diderot, "D'Alembert's Dream," 162 and 132.

[107] Diderot, "D'Alembert's Dream," 159.

[108] Diderot, "D'Alembert's Dream," 173.

[109] Sherman, *Diderot and the Art of Dialogue*, 87.

[110] See the preface to "D'Alembert's Dream," in *Diderot: Rameau's Nephew and Other Works*, 89–90.

[111] Leo Spitzer calls attention to this confluence of message and style. For Spitzer, Diderot's "perpetual desire to transcend the rationally graspable" is sewn into the style of his writing: "in this writer, nervous system, philosophical system, and 'stylisic system' are exceptionally well-attuned." See Leo Spitzer, *Linguistics and Literary History; Essays in Stylistics* (Princeton: Princeton University, 1948) 135.

[112] De La Carrera, *Success in Circuit Lies*, 128.

[113] Anderson, *Diderot's Dream*, 63.

[114] Diderot, "D'Alembert's Dream," 94–96.

[115] De La Carrera, *Success in Circuit Lies*, 140.

[116] Diderot, "D'Alembert's Dream," 105.

[117] Diderot, "D'Alembert's Dream," 113.

[118] Diderot, "D'Alembert's Dream," 99.

[119] De La Carrera, *Success in Circuit Lies*, 135.

[120] See De La Carrera, *Success in Circuit Lies*, 141–160.

[121] De La Carrera, *Success in Circuit Lies*, 162.

[122] Voltaire, *Philosophical Dictionary*, trans. Peter Gay (New York: Harcourt, Brace and World, Inc., 1962), "Enthusiasm," 252.

123 Voltaire, *Philosophical Dictionary*, "Fanaticism," 267.

124 Quotation taken from Peter Gay, *The Enlightenment; An Interpretation. The Rise of Modern Paganism,* 391.

125 Voltaire, *Philosophical Dictionary*, "Superstition," 473.

126 From Wilson, *Diderot*, 30. See also 30–38.

127 From Wilson, *Diderot*, 55.

128 See Wilson, *Diderot*, 338 and following.

129 From Wilson, *Diderot*, 198.

130 See Wilson, *Diderot*, 445. On the development of Diderot's stance toward religion, see Aram Vartanian, "From Deist to Atheist: Diderot's Philosophical Orientation," *Diderot Studies*, vol. 1, ed. Otis E. Fellows and Norman L. Torrey (Syracuse: Syracuse University, 1949) 46–63. See also Peter France, *Diderot* (Oxford: Oxford University, 1983) 29–37.

131 Quotation taken from Wilson, *Diderot*, 433.

132 Diderot, *Letters to Sophie Volland*, 109.

133 Diderot, *Letters to Sophie Volland*, 139–142 and 195.

134 Diderot, *The Encyclopedia; Selections*, "Intolerance," 152–156.

135 See Wilson, *Diderot*, 133.

136 See Wilson, *Diderot*, 203.

137 "Advertissement de Naigeon," in *Oeuvres Complètes de Diderot,* vol. 2, 73–74.

138 Diderot, "Introduction aux grand principes, ou réception d'un philosophe," in *Oeuvres Complètes de Diderot,* vol. 2, 76.

139 Diderot, "Introduction aux grand principes, ou réception d'un philosophe," 77.

140 Diderot, "Introduction aux grand principes, ou réception d'un philosophe," 78.

141 Diderot, "Introduction aux grand principes, ou réception d'un philosophe," 78–79.

142 Diderot, "Introduction aux grand principes, ou réception d'un philosophe," 79.

143 Diderot, "Le Prosélyte répondant par lui-même," *Oeuvres Complètes de Diderot,* 80 and 84.

144 Diderot, "Le Prosélyte répondant par lui-même," 81.

[145] Diderot, "Le Prosélyte répondant par lui-même," 83.

[146] Diderot, "Le Prosélyte répondant par lui-même," 84.

[147] Diderot, "Le Prosélyte répondant par lui-même," 85.

[148] Diderot, "Le Prosélyte répondant par lui-même," 85.

[149] Diderot, "Le Prosélyte répondant par lui-même," 88.

[150] Sherman, *Diderot and the Art of Dialogue*, 55.

[151] Diderot, "Le Prosélyte répondant par lui-même," 82.

[152] Diderot, "Le Prosélyte répondant par lui-même," 82.

[153] Diderot continued the dialogue with the satirist, but through a different genre. See the satirist's "Examen du prosélyte; Répondant par lui-même," followed by Diderot's "Réponse de Diderot a l'examen du prosélyte répondant par lui-même". Diderot constructs his response—typically—as a dialogue of quotations and rejoinders. See *Oeuvres Complètes de Diderot*, vol. 2, 89–99.

[154] See Furbank, *Diderot*, 482; and ed. J. Assézat, *Oeuvres Complètes de Diderot*, 505–506.

[155] Denis Diderot, "Conversation of a Philosopher with the Maréchale de ***," *Dialogues*, trans. Francis Birrell (New York: Capricorn, 1969) 167.

[156] Wilson, *Diderot*, 653.

[157] Sherman, *Diderot and the Art of Dialogue*, 90.

[158] Diderot, "Conversation of a Philosopher with the Maréchale de ***," 177.

[159] Sherman, *Diderot and the Art of Dialogue*, 97.

[160] Diderot, "Conversation of a Philosopher with the Maréchale de ***," 168–169.

[161] Diderot, "Conversation of a Philosopher with the Maréchale de ***," 171.

[162] Diderot, "Conversation of a Philosopher with the Maréchale de ***," 172.

[163] Diderot, "Conversation of a Philosopher with the Maréchale de ***," 173–175.

[164] Diderot, "Conversation of a Philosopher with the Maréchale de ***," 175.

[165] Diderot, "Conversation of a Philosopher with the Maréchale de ***," 181–183.

[166] Diderot, "Conversation of a Philosopher with the Maréchale de ***," 184.

[167] Sherman, *Diderot and the Art of Dialogue*, 97.

[168] Diderot, "Conversation of a Philosopher with the Maréchale de ***," 177.

[169] Sherman, *Diderot and the Art of Dialogue*, 97.

[170] Diderot, "Conversation of a Philosopher with the Maréchale de ***," 173.

[171] Diderot, "Conversation of a Philosopher with the Maréchale de ***," 184.

[172] Sherman, *Diderot and the Art of Dialogue*, 98.

[173] Peter France, *Rhetoric and Truth in France*, 218.

[174] See, once again, Diderot's description of "eclecticism" from *Encyclopedia; Selections*, 86.

[175] Wilson, *Diderot*, 422. On Diderot's effective use of the dialogue form to experiment with the confrontation of order and disorder, see Lester G. Crocker, *Diderot's Chaotic Order; Approach to Synthesis* (Princeton: Princeton University, 1974) 91–92.

[176] Jean-Philippe Rameau (1683–1764) wrote numerous works for solo harpsichord, though he became famous more for his operas, including "Les Indes galantes," the overture of which the "nephew" sings a bit in Diderot's dialogue. The elder Rameau also composed a set of trio sonatas (titled "Pièces de clavecin en concerts"), the fifth of which is important—as will be shown—for understanding Diderot's dialogue. The relationship between Rameau and Diderot was checkered at best. Early on the two were on friendly working terms, with Diderot apparently assisting (or as Wilson puts it, "ghost-writing") Rameau's thoughts on harmony in a clearer manner than the composer could manage on his own. See Wilson, *Diderot*, 89. Diderot also speaks in very flattering terms of Rameau's music in *The Indiscreet Jewels*. See Denis Diderot, *The Indiscreet Jewels*, trans. Sophie Hawkes (New York: Marsilio, 1993), 41–43. The relationship cooled, when, after refusing to write the articles on music for the *Encyclopedia*, Rameau publically criticized Rousseau's *Encyclopedia* essays on music. Still, Diderot and the encyclopedists did not attack Rameau in the "quarrel of the buffoons," an extended conflict over the relative merits of French and Italian music for opera. Wilson suggests that they did not want to stir up Rameau, who was regarded as "the greatest living practitioner" of the French style, even though the encyclopedists favored the melody and naturalness of the Italian style. It may also be the case that Rameau's music was more complex and nuanced than the terms of the debate allowed. In *Rameau's Nephew* the narrator speaks disparagingly of Rameau's character, but gives a more nuanced assessment of his music. Though he will be surpassed by the Italians, he is far more interesting and worthy than the traditional plainsong associated with Lully. See Diderot, *Rameau's Nephew*, 35–36.

[177] For these early descriptions of the nephew, see Diderot, *Rameau's Nephew*, 33–34.

[178] Denis Diderot, *Rameau's Nephew and D'Alembert's Dream*, trans. L. W. Tancock (Middlesex: Penguin, 1966), 37. Diogenes of Sinope (412–323 B.C.E.) was a Greek Cynic philosopher; Phryne was a courtesan of great renown in the fourth century B.C.E.

[179] Diderot, *Rameau's Nephew*, 86–87 and 46.

[180] Wilson, *Diderot*, 418.

[181] France, *Rhetoric and Truth in France*, 230. Jean-Pierre Barricelli argues that the work's "life-like spontaneity and music-like fluidity" arises from Diderot's decision to give his work an "overall architecture" based on "musical analogy." The dialogue progresses, he argues, "musically by relations, that is, by oblique and affinitive communications". In this case, the mimetic art of dialogue becomes more sensitive to the currents of everyday life by adapting the imitative qualities of music to dialogue form. Given the central role given to music in the dialogue, there is much to be said for Barricelli's reading. See Jean-Pierre Barricelli, "Music and the Structure of Diderot's *Le Neveu de Rameau*," *Criticism*, Spring 1963, 5 (2): 95–111. For another, far more philosophically laden reading of *Rameau's Nephew* based on musical analogy, see Julia Kristeva, "La Musique parlée ou remarques sur la subjectivité dans la fiction à propos du 'Neveu de Rameau'," *Langue et Langages de Leibniz à l'Encyclopedie*, ed. Michèle Duchet and Michèle Jalley (Paris: Union, 1977) 163–224. See also Stephen Werner, *Socratic Satire; An Essay on Diderot and Le Neveu de Rameau* (Birmingham, Alabama: Summa, 1987). Werner highlights the connection between Italian opera (itself a "Socratic art form" for Diderot) and Socratic irony in *Rameau's Nephew*.

[182] Diderot, *Rameau's Nephew*, 53 and 102–104. Perhaps Diderot had in mind the frenzied capricios of Locatelli's "The Art of the Violin," especially that titled "Il Laberinto Armonico" contained in Concerto No. 12. Locatelli, *The Art of the Violin*, vol. 2, Susanne Lautenbacher (violin) and Mainz Camber Orchestra (Vox, 1991).

[183] For helpful summaries of the various lines of interpretation concerning Diderot's identity, see Hans Robert Jauss: *The Dialogical and the Dialectical Neveu de Rameau: How Diderot Adopted Socrates and Hegel Adopted Diderot* (Berkeley: Center for Hermeneutical Studies, 1983) 6–8; and Herbert Josephs, *Diderot's Dialogue of Gesture and Language: Le Neveu de Rameau* (Columbus: Ohio State University, 1969) 107–113.

[184] Wilson, *Diderot*, 418.

[185] On the historical nephew of Rameau (Jean-François Rameau), see Milton F. Seides, "Jean-François Rameau and Diderot's Neveu," in *Diderot Studies*, vol. 1, 143–191. For primary sources see André Magnan, *Rameau le Neveu; Textes et Documents* (Paris: Université de Saint-Étienne, 1993). See also Furbank, *Diderot*, 242–242.

[186] Julia Kristeva, *Strangers to Ourselves*, trans. Leon S. Roudiez (New York: Columbia University, 1991) 135.

[187] Diderot, *Rameau's Nephew*, 35. See Jauss, *The Dialogical and the Dialectical Neveu de Rameau*, 10–11; and Stephen Werner, *Socratic Satire; An Essay on Diderot and Le Neveu de Rameau* (Birmingham, Alabama: Summa, 1987) 56–59.

[188] See Diderot, *Rameau's Nephew*, 45 and 58.

[189] Peter France, *Rhetoric and Truth in France*, 198.

[190] Diderot, *Rameau's Nephew*, 49, 62, 76, and 73–76.

[191] See Gregory Vlastos, *Socratic Studies* (Cambridge: Cambridge University, 1994) 4.

[192] Jauss, *The Dialogical and the Dialectical Neveu de Rameau*, 10–12.

[193] Diderot, *Rameau's Nephew*, 45.

[194] Diderot, *Rameau's Nephew*, 48.

[195] Diderot, *Rameau's Nephew*, 103.

[196] Diderot, *Rameau's Nephew*, 82.

[197] Diderot, *Rameau's Nephew*, 112.

[198] Diderot, *Rameau's Nephew*, 95–96.

[199] Diderot, *Rameau's Nephew*, 95–97.

[200] Diderot, *Rameau's Nephew*, 123–125.

[201] Jauss, *The Dialogical and the Dialectical Neveu de Rameau*, 2.

[202] Jauss, *The Dialogical and the Dialectical Neveu de Rameau*, 8 and 13.

[203] Jauss, *The Dialogical and the Dialectical Neveu de Rameau*, 2–4.

[204] Jauss, *The Dialogical and the Dialectical Neveu de Rameau*, 12.

[205] Kristeva, *Strangers to Ourselves*, 137.

[206] Eduard Zeller, *Outlines of the History of Greek Philosophy*, trans. L. R. Palmer (London: Routledge and Kegan Paul, 1955) 111.

[207] Kristeva, *Strangers to Ourselves*, 137.

[208] "He" finds Diogenes' difficult lifestyle repugnant: unlike the "dog," the nephew "must have a good bed, good food, warm clothes in the winter and cool ones in summer, leisure, money and lots of other things, and I would rather owe them to charity than have to work for them." Diderot, *Rameau's Nephew*, 122–123.

[209] Kristeva, *Strangers to Ourselves*, 137–138.

[210] Kristeva, *Strangers to Ourselves*, 138.

[211] See Eduard Zeller, *Outlines of the History of Greek Philosophy*, 108–112.

[212] As Stephen Werner rightly notes, *Rameau's Nephew* is "a work of literature which refuses genre"—that is, it resists and shatters all "definitive framing statements" about its form and purpose, including the label of Menippean. Werner counsels readers to remain

"faithful to the pluralities" of the Socratic irony at work in Diderot's text. See Werner, *Socratic Satire*, 64–65 and 73.

213 France, *Rhetoric and Truth in France*, 233.

214 Diderot, *Rameau's Nephew*, 102. Ironically, Diderot may well have taken his thematic cue for the creation of this musical monster from Rameau the uncle. The fourth trio sonata of Jean-Philippe Rameau's "Pièces de clavecin en concerts" contains three movements, titled respectively "La Pantomime," "L'Indiscrete," and "La Rameau." See Jean-Philippe Rameau, "Pièces de clavecin en concerts," (Frans Brüggen, Sigiswald Kuijken, Wieland Kuijken, and Gustav Leonhardt), Das Alte Werke, Warner Music, 1992.

215 Diderot, *Rameau's Nephew*, 68–69.

216 Diderot, *Rameau's Nephew*, 41.

217 Diderot, *Rameau's Nephew*, 52.

218 Diderot, *Rameau's Nephew*, 110.

219 Diderot, *Rameau's Nephew*, 108.

220 Diderot, *Rameau's Nephew*, 98.

221 Diderot, *Rameau's Nephew*, 100. The nephew's judgments on music (and, hence, presumably Diderot's) are limited by the political and cultural baggage associated with perceptions of what counts as "French" or "Italian" music. At times, these extra-musical associations seem to skew musical judgment. Jean-Féry Rebel (1661–1747), for one, was famous for his "imitative" instrumental work, notably "Les Elémens," which mimes the creation of the world from chaos.

222 Diderot, *Rameau's Nephew*, 104.

223 Diderot, *Rameau's Nephew*, 54.

224 Diderot, *Rameau's Nephew*, 83.

225 Diderot, *Rameau's Nephew*, 60–62.

226 Diderot, *Rameau's Nephew*, 78.

227 Diderot, *Rameau's Nephew*, 89.

228 Diderot, *Rameau's Nephew*, 78.

229 Diderot, *Rameau's Nephew*, 65.

230 Diderot, *Rameau's Nephew*, 64 and 63.

[231] Diderot, *Rameau's Nephew*, 70.

[232] Diderot, *Rameau's Nephew*, 74.

[233] Diderot, *Rameau's Nephew*, 120. See Lucian's "Icaromenippus, or the Sky-Man," *Lucian*, vol. 2, trans. A. M. Harmon (Cambridge, Mass.: Harvard University, 1988) 267–323.

[234] Diderot, *Rameau's Nephew*, 121.

[235] Diderot, *Rameau's Nephew*, 80.

[236] Diderot, *Rameau's Nephew*, 35.

[237] Kristeva, *Strangers to Ourselves*, 134.

[238] Jauss, *The Dialogical and Dialectical Neveu de Rameau*, 17.

[239] See, for instance, the "Folia" of composers like Arcangelo Corelli, Marin Marais, Francesco Geminiani, Antonio Vivaldi, and C.P.E. Bach.

[240] See Plato's "Theaetetus," *Plato's Theory of Knowledge (The Theaetetus and the Sophist of Plato)*, trans. Francis M. Cornford (Indianapolis: Bobbs-Merrill, 1957), 150c.

[241] Diderot, *Rameau's Nephew*, 115.

[242] Furbank, *Diderot*, 252.

[243] Diderot, *Rameau's Nephew*, 34.

[244] Diderot, *Rameau's Nephew*, 43.

[245] Furbank, *Diderot*, 258. See also Leo Spitzer, *Linguistics and Literary History*, 166–167.

[246] Furbank, *Diderot*, 242. Diderot wrote the dialogue in 1761, and then worked again on it in 1762, 1766, 1767, and 1775. See Wilson, *Diderot*, 417.

[247] See L. W. Tancock's introduction to Denis Diderot, *Rameau's Nephew and D'Alembert's Dream* (Middlesex: Penguin, 1966) 19–22.

PART TWO

IRONY AND RELIGION

4
Duplicity and Shiftiness in Religious Discourse: A Reading of Hume's *Dialogues*

"Man is a very variable being, and susceptible of many different opinions, principles, and rules of conduct. What may be true, while he adheres to one way of thinking, will be found false, when he has embraced an opposite set of manners and opinions."

—David Hume, "Of Commerce"[1]

"It appears to me, that there are strong symptoms of priestcraft in the whole progress of this affair. . . . Thus, sceptics in one age, dogmatists in another; whichever system best suits the purpose of these reverend gentlemen, in giving them an ascendant over mankind, they are sure to make it their favourite principle, and established tenet."

—David Hume, *Dialogues Concerning Natural Religion*[2]

Talk about religion is notoriously messy. Philosophical rationalists, theological defenders of orthodoxy, and common folk too harried for complications, may demand constancy, uniformity, and certainty in religion, but such aspirations elide the rhetorical slips, slides and shifts which typify living religious discourse. While one might prefer a coherent, forward-moving flow of arguments and counter-arguments composed of terms with single connotations and fueled by consistent and trustworthy motives, one is more likely to encounter strategies of indirection; lateral and crossed movement; shifting perspectives; ironic misalliances; assorted ambiguity; and duplicitous motives. Some such moves are unconscious, but frequently deliberate, and, in any case, many of them appear inevitable. Duplicity and shiftiness are common fare in religious discourse.

David Hume understood this phenomenon well. He knew vividly from personal experience how his skeptical and empiricist challenges to religious belief had landed him amid a confusing, multi-leveled, frequently ironic discourse. He knew, for instance, that his work was received differently by the Conservative clergy ("Highflying Party") who campaigned against his appointments at Edinburgh (1744) and Glasgow (1751) and later sought his excommunication (1755–56), than by the Moderate clergy who intellectually befriended him in his early Edinburgh days and later shielded him from conservative attacks. Similarly, Hume realized that it was possible to converse civilly with tolerant and thinking critics like Robert Wallace or George Campbell (with whom Hume had amicable exchanges), while no discourse at all was possible with the likes of William

Warburton (whose raillery intimidated Hume and his publisher Andrew Millar into suppressing the publication of Hume's "Of Suicide" and "Of the Immortality of the Soul").[3] The voices of religion spoke on distinct levels, their meaning, tone, and purpose shifting wildly, so that if he was to speak at all, Hume would have to shift accordingly.

Moreover, Hume was cognizant of the deep-seated ambiguities and the strange misalliances which affected all who participated in theistic discourse. The defense of God-talk could turn from rationalism (in the manner of Descartes) to empirical evidence (in the hands of Joseph Butler) to unmitigated dogmatism (in the allegations of the conservatives). The interests, strategies, even the grammars of each group shifted while ostensibly talking about the same God. Conversely, he knew that his own skeptical questioning of metaphysical knowledge would resound with vastly different senses and consequences in the ears of Christian fideists or French *philosophes* like d'Alembert, Holbach, and Diderot; each party would applaud Hume's doubts, but be suspicious of his meaning and motives—the fideists of Hume's surreptitious atheism, the *philosophes* of his lingering theism. In a word, Hume saw clearly that discourse with the various protagonists and antagonists was not homologous. It would require of the "man of letters" great adeptness in dealing with the shifting perspectives and frequently duplicitous agendas of the interlocutors. At times, he too would not be able to avoid being shifty and speaking with a mixed voice.

Hume's thoughts on religion take two separate but complementary tracks. First, there is his concern with issues in philosophical theism, particularly the argument based on the design and purpose evident in the natural world for the existence of God.[4] Second, there is the interest he shares with authors like Diderot in criticizing the forces of superstition and enthusiasm that infect popular religion and church theologies.[5] I suggest, however, that a third, rhetorical concern with the shiftiness and duplicity typical of religious discourse undergirds these two substantive points of interest. This comes out most clearly in Hume's *Dialogues Concerning Natural Religion*, which not only replicates argumentation on natural design and God in dialogue form, but also, and more importantly, gives artistic form to the ambiguous and confusing contours of religious language which he encountered in life. Hume understood the irrational forces at work in attempts to talk with others about religion, and this understanding is embedded in the discursive fabric of the *Dialogues*. In this chapter, therefore, I will use Hume's *Dialogues* as a model for reflection on the rhetorical complexities and irrationalities endemic to religious discourse—including discourse within Hume's text; between Hume and his readers; and between Hume's text and its readers.[6]

It is true, of course, that "duplicity" and "shiftiness" are morally loaded terms. Both commonly suggest something which is blameworthy. Duplicity connotes deceit or dissimulation, and shiftiness indicates evasive and tricky behavior. Neither seems praiseworthy; and, indeed, Hume heaps plenty of criticism on both. But, as will become apparent very shortly, the communicative strategies and practices illustrating these terms are more ambiguous. Indeed, there are neutral—even laudable—aspects of each of these forms of rhetorical action: (a) speaking with a double voice may simply be a rhetorical necessity when faced with the challenges of different interlocutors, and using words in two senses at once may be a sign of ironic insight; (b) shifting about, similarly, may connote an astute or resourceful character, just as "crafty" and "tricky" may describe someone who is skilled at difficult rhetorical maneuvers. Not every doubleness and not every shifting conduct, in short, carries this morally negative weight, though, admittedly, the neutral (much less the positive) connotations of "duplicity" and "shifty" are largely foreign to common parlance. The slide between the morally negative and the neutral meanings of these words—confusing though it may be—is central to Hume's *Dialogues*. A great deal of what is at stake here pivots on whether or not, and to what degree, such lateral moves and rhetorical concealments are perceived as innocent or culpable. Where possible, I will use the neutral term (i.e., "doubleness" or "shifting") when a shift is presented as necessary and blameless; I will use the morally charged term (i.e., "duplicitous" or "shifty") when the issue is charged with accusation and recrimination. As will become evident, the difference is not always very clear. What *is* apparent is that everyone who enters into discourse over religious topics becomes involved in this phenomenon—and that includes the characters of the dialogue (both religious and skeptical), Hume as author, as well as readers and critics of Hume's text.

Faithful to my own theme, I too will shift my perspective several times. In the first section, I will collect examples in which speakers in the *Dialogues* shift their meaning or strategy and appear duplicitous either to their interlocutors or to the reader. In the following section, I will offer an interpretation of this phenomenon drawing solely on explanations voiced within the text. Changing vantage for the third section, I will examine the ironic doubleness and shiftiness of Hume's authorial voice. Finally, I will step back and consider the shifting receptions of Hume's *Dialogues* in the history of philosophy. All told, I will advance what I take to be a typically Humean thesis that, while interlocutors on religion may aspire to coherence and constancy, their discourse naturally and inevitably falls short, landing those who wish to speak about religion in an awkward but still liveable morass of shifting meaning and duplicitous interests.

(1) A Sampling of the Dialogues

In the opening section of the *Dialogues*, Philo the skeptic concurs with the pious Demea in stressing "the weakness, blindness, and narrow limits of reason" (I.131). Sensing "some raillery or malice" in Philo's words, Cleanthes takes aim at the skepticism of his interlocutors. His first salvo is a familiar challenge to the skeptic: Philo's profession of skepticism is insincere and "only in jest" (I.132), for it is "impossible . . . to persevere in . . . total skepticism" (I.132). What he says and what he does are "at variance," and hence he is convicted of duplicity by his very conduct (I.137). When Philo responds that a proper methodological adjustment must be made between the study of "trade, or morals, or politics" in comparison with natural theology (I.134–35), Cleanthes levels a second charge. In this regard, the skeptic is guilty of "an unequal conduct" (I.137), i.e., of meticulously weighing evidence in most studies, but then dogmatically refusing to do so when it comes to "the theological and religious" (I.137). Skeptics operate with a double standard, and consequently are nothing but a "sect of jesters and railliers." (I.137) All in all, they live duplicitous lives and they are willfully shifty in their philosophical methods.

Turning his eyes to the more traditionally based Demea, Cleanthes notes that while Patristic and Reformation authors denounce reason, modern Christians since Locke have valued reason in the service of theological reflections. Ironically, this criticism of Demea's religious skepticism triggers a counter-charge of shiftiness and duplicity from Philo. In his words, "there are strong symptoms of priestcraft" in the history of religious thought:

> During ignorant ages, . . . the priests perceived that atheism, deism, or heresy of any kind, could only proceed from the presumptuous questioning of received opinions, and from a belief that human reason was equal to everything. (I.139)

In such periods, reason had to be denounced. We might recall Tertullian castigating reason, or Luther inveighing against the use of philosophy in theology. In more enlightened ages, however,

> [where people] have learned to compare the popular principles of different nations and ages, our sagacious divines have changed their whole system of philosophy, and talk the language of Stoics, Platonists, and Peripatetics, not that of Pyrrhonians and Academics. If we distrust human reason, we have now no other principle to lead us into religion. Thus, skeptics in one age, dogmatists in another; whichever system best suits the purpose of these reverend gentlemen, in giving them an ascendent over mankind, they are sure to make it their favourite principle, and established tenet. (I.139–40)

So Philo responds in kind. If the skeptic's behavior suggests shiftiness and duplicity, then church history gives like evidence of religious shiftiness and duplicity. I will return later to this important passage (and related texts) as the crucial rhetorical key for interpreting the *Dialogues*. For now, however, I simply cite it heuristically, as an entryway into a host of supporting examples—first of Philo's shiftiness, and then that of the two religious speakers.

At numerous junctures, Cleanthes and Demea perceive Philo to be shifty and duplicitous. Frankly, it is hard not to agree with them. Early on, Cleanthes notes that "a man of ingenuity and invention" like Philo can give an "air of probability" to even the most "absurd argument" (III.152). As their conversation proceeds, this observation proves premonitory. After Cleanthes forwards his notion that the natural order of the world reveals the existence of an intelligent designer, analogous to the workings of the human mind, Philo proceeds by rhetorical "invention"[7] to explore the range of analogy possible within Cleanthes' anthropomorphic assumptions. Perhaps, Philo suggests, the world was created by multiple designers (V.167); or "why not become the perfect anthropomorphite" and ascribe sexual reproduction to divine agency? (V.168). Or, perhaps the world (with all its imperfections) is the "first rude essay of some infant Deity" or the "production of old age and dotage in some superannuated Deity" (V.169). Extending his fanciful ruminations even further, Philo suggests that the origin of the world may just as well be ascribed to biological generation or vegetation as to reason or design— perhaps, in other words, the cause of the world is a vegetable (VI.172; VII.176). Finally, Philo wonders whether the world is not generated ectypally (by self-propagation) rather than archetypally (VIII.183–86; and VI.174).

From Philo's point of view, all this invention is "for the sake of variety," for there is "no other advantage" to one view than to another (VII.177). The key word is *perhaps*: perhaps this view, perhaps that, or perhaps "none at all" (V.169). For him, "the matter seems entirely arbitrary" (VII.179). For Cleanthes, on the other hand, Philo's "ingenuity and invention" (III.152) is a cover for his "skeptical play and wantonness" (III.153). Imagining so many contradictory hypotheses is the result of "too luxuriant a fertility" (III.155). Early in the dialogue, he challenges Philo in a way that echoes throughout the text; by daring Philo to "choose . . . your party, . . . without ambiguity or evasion" (III.154). From Cleanthes' point of view, Philo's rhetorical invention serves no legitimate purpose, except to allow Philo irresponsibly to evade taking a clear position for himself. Philo is shifty and cannot be trusted.

Philo also appears duplicitous in his strange alliance with Demea. I say "strange" because it is so unexpected that a self-professed skeptic would find himself arguing on the same side of the fence as a mystically-minded dogmatist. To begin with, it should be noted that their alliance initially is based on a genuine agreement: they agree fundamentally on the severe limits of human knowledge of matters divine (although they quickly construe these limits differently), and they speak in chorus about the depth and breadth of evil and misery in the world (X). Their compact is ratified in two key ways. First, it is confirmed when Cleanthes groups the two together under the common banner of "atheists" (I.140–141) and "mystics" (IV.158). Thus, we find Cleanthes asking, ". . . how do you mystics, who maintain the absolute incomprehensibility of the Deity, differ from skeptics or atheists, who assert that the first cause of All is unknown and unintelligible?" (IV.158). When Philo adopts the label ("our mysticism, as you call it") (VI.172 and X.199), the alliance is established publicly. Second, the alliance between Demea and Philo is confirmed when Philo concurs with Demea that God's existence is "unquestionable and self-evident" (II.142). While Hume scholars have taken this pronouncement to be "coyly ironic" (i.e., duplicitous), it functions within the dialogue to assure Demea of their concord.

There are early signs, evident apparently to Philo and certainly to the perspicacious reader, that this alliance is more limited than Demea might think. At one point, for instance, Philo favors (with Cleanthes) drawing on experience to test the hypothesis that there is a divine designer of the world (II.144). When Demea protests, Philo quickly patches up the rift by assuring Demea that his agreement with Cleanthes is only strategic (II.145); he will think from within Cleanthes' position in order to show the "inconveniences" buried in his assumptions. This satisfies Demea that he and Philo are still working together, but the reader cannot help noticing that Philo's turn to experience is motivated by philosophical interests far different from Demea's. However, there are gradual signs that Demea cannot accept the skeptical agenda of Philo's playful inventiveness: he is horrified at Philo's conjecture of a senile god (V.169); he becomes unsettled when he realizes how useless these speculations are, given the practical demands of popular religion (VI.170); and he is outraged at Philo's talk of God as a cosmic vegetable. Still—and here we see the dialectical, even dramatic, development carefully crafted by Hume—the breakdown of their alliance is postponed when Cleanthes (rather than Philo) takes the critical lead against Demea's *a priori* demonstration for God's existence (IX.188–90), and again when Philo and Demea jointly pose the problem of evil against Cleanthes' theism (X.193–99). The question of Philo's duplicitous accord with Demea is answered only gradually, in glimpses, as Cleanthes and Demea begin to realize the true nature of this strange alliance.

Philo's intentions finally are revealed in part X, when Cleanthes calls Philo to task for his duplicity. "Have you at last," he inquires "smilingly, betrayed your intention, Philo? Your long agreement with Demea did indeed a little surprise me; but I find you were all the while erecting a concealed battery against me" (X.199). For Cleanthes, Philo is really an enemy of religion. The alliance with Demea is but a subtle, strategic act of duplicity. A little slow on the uptake, Demea only gleans what is going on in the following section. Philo is just beginning to suggest that God might be responsible for evil, when Demea cries out,

> Hold! Hold! Whither does your imagination hurry you? I joined in alliance with you, in order to prove the incomprehensible nature of the divine Being, and refute the principles of Cleanthes. . . . But I now find you running into all the topics of the greatest libertines and infidels; and betraying that holy cause which you seemingly espoused. Are you secretly, then, a more dangerous enemy than Cleanthes himself? (XI.212–13)

Rightly so, Cleanthes is amazed that it has taken Demea so long to perceive Philo's shifty intentions. Retrospectively, he adds, "your friend Philo, from the beginning, has been amusing himself at both our expense . . . " (XI.213).

The most glaring (and notorious) example of Philo's shiftiness, however, appears in part XII. After refusing to identify himself with any theistic view or argument, Philo suddenly and repeatedly acknowledges "the inexplicable contrivance and artifice of nature" (XII.214). In his words, "A purpose, an intention, or design strikes everywhere the most careless, the most stupid thinker; and no man can be so hardened in absurd systems, as at all times to reject it" (XII.214; compare 215). He even speaks harshly against those who deny the argument from design: "to what pitch of pertinacious obstinacy must a philosopher in this age have attained, who can now doubt of a supreme intelligence?" (XII.215). Even more astonishing, Philo confesses himself to be a deeply religious man: "no one has a deeper sense of religion impressed on his mind, or pays more profound adoration to the divine Being . . ." (XII.214). "To be a philosophical skeptic," he contends, is "in a man of letters, the first and most essential step towards being a sound, believing Christian" (XII.228). This metamorphosis has generated enormous consternation in Hume scholarship. Surprisingly, Cleanthes is not overly bothered by Philo's apparent reversal, certainly not to the degree that he resents Philo's shifty behavior in the preceding discussions. I will return in the next section to offer an interpretation of how this turnabout should be read; and I will speak in the third section to what Hume might have meant by putting these words into Philo's mouth. Presently it is important to shift gears in order to look through Philo's eyes at the shiftiness of his religious interlocutors.

As the passages cited above from the first part of the *Dialogues* make clear, Philo finds a certain shiftiness and duplicity in the priestly and theological defenders of religion. There are "symptoms of priestcraft" in religion, Philo insists, for when reason threatens religion it is assailed, but when it assists the cause of religion it is embraced (I.139–40). A similar protest occurs in part XII: "when divines are declaiming against the common behavior and conduct of the world," they stress how little influence the notion of eternal rewards and punishments have on people's actions; for this purpose, churchmen "describe almost all human kind as . . . sunk into the deepest lethargy and unconcern about their religious interests" (XII.220–21). When the church is threatened politically, however, these same divines "suppose the motives of religion to be so powerful, that, without them, it were impossible for civil society to subsist; nor are they ashamed of so palpable a contradiction" (XII.221). The last clause underscores Philo's point, since this piece of intentional shiftiness is perfectly palpable.

Indeed, Philo observes, there appears to be "a habit of dissimulation" built into religion, where "fraud and falsehood become the predominant principle" (XII.222): the "superstition or enthusiasm" so common to popular religion covers over and "weakens extremely men's attachment to the natural motives of justice and humanity" (XII.222). This unnatural dissimulation then breeds deeply damaging psychological shifts that are reinforced by grossly contradictory doctrines. Most strikingly, religious people are subject to the psychological shift between joyful, enthusiastic exaltation of the Deity and terror-filled melancholy sustained by the doctrine that "the damned are infinitely superior in number to the elect" (XII.225). In sum, Philo finds religion infested with doctrinal inconsistences, strategies of dissimulation, and widespread experiences of hypocrisy. For him, the protagonists of religion are the ones who are shifty and duplicitous.

Neither Cleanthes nor Demea appears to suffer from these psychological shifts. There are, however, several ways in which the religious speakers in the *Dialogues* do appear shifty—both to Philo and to the careful reader. First, from Philo's vantage, there is a considerable shift *between* the theism of Cleanthes and Demea. More will be said about this presently, but it is already obvious in this context that the duplicitous "priestcraft" mentioned by Philo as standard practice in the defense of religion is at work in the alternating forms of argument used first by Cleanthes and then by Demea. Second, there is a shifting (that is, equivocating) use of key terms by Cleanthes. When he suggests to Demea, in the fourth part, that there is little difference between "you mystics" and atheists (VI.158), Philo can only complain that Cleanthes has turned the meaning of words inside out. How, Philo queries, can idolaters and "Christian theologians" both be atheists? What is an atheist, or for that matter, what is a theist, if "all the sound, orthodox divines" are atheists? Philo, in short, catches Cleanthes shifting the meaning of terms in mid-argument.

Third, in an important and little noticed sense, Cleanthes takes up a shifty tack in his dealings with Philo. Most of the doubleness in Cleanthes' discourse has to do with his shifting appraisal and uses of skepticism. It is Cleanthes, recall, who disparages the entire notion of skepticism. For him skeptics are duplicitous in their lives and in their methods. What is more, and here again note Cleanthes' blurring of terms, "atheists and skeptics are almost synonymous" (139). As the dialogue proceeds, however, it becomes evident that Cleanthes' "experimental theism" has an important stake in the rigorous weighing of evidence typical of skeptical methods. He claims, in fact, to be *the* reasonable skeptic in his testing of the evidence for design, claiming in turn that Philo's skepticism is only "affected" (III.154). What Cleanthes misses, however, is the "suspense or balance" of judgment which Philo calls the "triumph of scepticism" (I.135–36). Cleanthes' "scepticism" wants positive results, not an arbitrary indifference. It is, therefore, a twisted piece of self-indicting irony, when Cleanthes defends his own inability to solve Philo's difficulties by noting that Philo is likewise unable to provide any solutions (VII.181). This is ironic, of course, since this inability to resolve such obscure matters is precisely what Philo has been promoting. Cleanthes has, in short, fallen headlong into a deeper sense of skepticism than he would like. Just how far he has slid is evident in section IX, where he counters Demea's *a priori* demonstration with the same kind of skeptical questioning used by Philo earlier: "why may not the material universe be the necessarily existent Being . . .?" (IX.190). And when Cleanthes ties the possibility of natural religion to human happiness, Philo pointedly warns that doing so will introduce a "total scepticism" (X.200). Cleanthes' shifts are, to be sure, inadvertent. Nonetheless, they do point up the truth of Philo's perception that the defenders of religion will be critically minded (even skeptical) when it is to their advantage, and then back off when it appears deleterious.

One final shift demands mention: namely, the ironic twist of expectations in the closing words of the dialogue. Here the student narrator Pamphilus offers an appraisal of the different arguments, concluding that "Philo's principles are more probable than Demea's; but that those of Cleanthes approach still nearer to the truth" (XII.228). Since to most modern readers it is Philo and not Cleanthes who has the upper-hand, this passage immediately raises questions about Hume's intentions. This question will be taken up in the third section. In the next section, however, I will offer a reading of the examples of shiftiness and duplicity just reviewed, drawing exclusively on those explanations embedded in the course of the dialogue.

(2) Shiftiness and Duplicity

Most interpreters of the *Dialogues* have dealt with the examples of shiftiness and duplicity just reviewed on the authorial level. Philo's unexpected profession of faith, for instance, instantly is read as an expression of Hume's evasiveness or possible disingenuousness. Such a reading, I suggest, is a mistake, and one that skews our understanding of the rhetorical dynamics within the text and may cause a misreading of Hume's philosophical intentions regarding religious questions. What must be attended to are the explanations of Philo's shiftiness and duplicity embedded *within* the conversation with Cleanthes and Demea. That focus will constitute the task of this section.

Philo gives a general account of his shifting rhetoric in part VIII. Cleanthes has just censured him for his overly "fertile" invention; Philo has let his skeptical imagination run rampant through a host of possible analogies for God without showing commitment to any of them. Philo's response reflects the charge back onto his theist interlocutor.

> What you ascribe to the fertility of my invention . . . is entirely owing to the nature of the subject. In subjects, adapted to the narrow compass of human reason, there is commonly but one determination, which carries probability or conviction with it; and to a man of sound judgement, all other suppositions, but that one, appear entirely absurd and chimerical. But in such questions as the present, a hundred con-

tradictory views may preserve a kind of imperfect analogy; and invention has here full scope to exert itself. (VIII.182)

The key point here ascribes Philo's imaginative variation to "the nature of the subject." In such abstruse and speculative matters, where only the lowest probability is licensed, nothing but a skeptical "suspense or balance" of positions is warranted (I.136). In this regard, it is important to note the consistency of Philo's skeptical rhetoric. As he puts it, it is "no more difficult" to conceive an internal cause of the natural world, than to conceive an external one (II.146; compare IV.164, VI.171, XI.212). If "a hundred contradictory views" are all probable, why blame the skeptic for imaginatively wandering among them? The skeptic's shiftiness, Philo argues, arises from the vacuum of certainty and definiteness among the theists.

Philo goes beyond this general account of his rhetoric in three key texts. Together, these texts make the connection explicit between his basic contention that skeptical shiftiness is a natural reaction to the ambiguities of theistic language *and* the immediate opposition he is facing in his conversation with Cleanthes and Demea. The first uses offsetting imagery of conflict and tolerance to explain and promote the skeptic's shiftiness. Toward the end of part VIII, Philo counsels humility and tolerance in theological discussions: since we can never "reasonably expect greater success in any attempts of this nature," the difficulties with any and every theistic perspective "may teach, all of us, sobriety in condemning each other" (VIII.186). With this advice in mind, Philo next grounds the skeptic's posture in the pointless conflicts between theistic systems:

> All religious systems, it is confessed, are subject to great and insuperable difficulties. Each disputant triumphs in his turn; while he carries on an offensive war, and exposes the absurdities, barbarities, and pernicious tenets of his antagonist. But all of them, on the whole, prepare a complete triumph for the sceptic; who tells them, that no system ought ever to be embraced with regard to such subjects: For this plain reason, that no absurdity ought ever to be assented to with regard to any subject. A total suspense of judgement is here our only reasonable resource. (VIII.186–87)

It is the endless, shifting conflicts *between* theistic systems that make the skeptical suspense of judgment so reasonable. The self-canceling disputes of theists, Philo proceeds to say, point toward a more reasonable and peaceful victory for the skeptic.

> And if every attack, as is commonly observed, and no defence, among theologians, is successful; how complete must be *his* victory, who remains always, with all mankind, on the offensive, and has himself no fixed station or abiding city, which he is ever, on any occasion, obliged to defend? (VIII.187)

The skeptic *is* shifty, in other words, but this shiftiness is virtuous, because instead of plaguing people with pointless theological conflicts, it stands tolerantly "with all humanity" by not taking up residence in any theistic system.[8]

In a second text, Cleanthes recognizes how "the injudicious reasoning of our vulgar theology" has given the skeptical Philo "a handle of ridicule," making it possible for him to amuse himself at both his expense and Demea's (XI.213). Cleanthes' reference to "our" vulgar theology is somewhat misleading here, since the rest of the passage makes clear that he is thinking solely of Demea's theology. What Cleanthes has in mind—the "strange topics . . . so fondly cherished by orthodox divines and doctors," as well as by Demea—are "the total infirmity of human reason, the absolute incomprehensibility of the divine nature, the great and universal misery and still greater wickedness of men" (XI.213). He then begins to draw the same chronological contrast struck by Philo in part I, between an ignorant age where theology assails reason and the modern world where reason is accepted in the service of theology.

> **Cleanthes:** In ages of stupidity and ignorance, indeed, these principles may safely be espoused; and perhaps, no views of things are more proper to promote superstition, than such as encourage the blind amazement, the diffidence, and melancholy of mankind. But at present. . . .

Immediately recognizing Cleanthes' shift for what it is worth, Philo interrupts with a crucial rejoinder:

> Blame not so much, interposed **Philo**, the ignorance of these reverend gentlemen. They know how to change their style with the times. Formerly it was a most popular theological topic to maintain, that human life was vanity and misery, and to exaggerate all the ills and pains which are incident to men. But of late years, divines, we find, begin to retract this position, and maintain, though still with some hesitation, that there are more goods than evils, more pleasures than pains, even in this life. When religion stood entirely upon temper and education, it was thought proper to encourage melancholy; as indeed, mankind never have recourse to superior powers so readily as in that position. But as men have now learned to form principles, and to draw consequences, it is necessary to change the batteries, and to make use of such arguments as will endure, at least some scrutiny and examination. This variation is the same (and from the same causes) with that which I formerly remarked with regard to scepticism. (XI.213)

This passage is the most important corollary to Philo's charge quoted from part I, that the defenders of theism are guilty of "priestcraft." Theists are duplicitous, or guilty of "priestcraft," when they turn from denunciation of reason and promotion of melancholy to acclamation of reason and celebration of human possibilities. They simply adjust their views (and their rhetoric) to meet the new winds of the times. The closing sentence of this passage, though not perfectly clear in its reference, strikes up the connection to Philo's earlier statement that theists are skeptical in one age, dogmatists in another (compare I.139–40).

In the above texts the shiftiness and duplicity of theologians or "orthodox divines" are connected to the shifting tacks of Demea and Cleanthes. The "variation" between theological ages is, in other words, enacted in Philo's dialogue with Demea and Cleanthes. It is Cleanthes who identifies Demea with the anti-reason theologies of ignorant ages, and then begins to position himself as the bearer of a more rational theism. What he fails to notice is that his self-aggrandizing contrast to Demea is precisely that same contrast or piece of shiftiness which Philo had detected earlier. The upshot of this connection is crucial for interpreting the entire *Dialogues*, for the opposing argumentative strategies of Demea and Cleanthes are now seen for what they are—not simply separate or independent philosophical positions, but two integral dimensions of religious duplicity. They embody religious duplicity in their shifting voices.

The same point is made again (and carried further) in a third text from part XII. After Demea departs ("on some pretence or other") (XI.213), Philo no longer is faced with double interlocutors who address him from shifting angles; consequently, the discussion with Cleanthes turns to the rhetorical problems encountered in the earlier discussion. Cleanthes notes that it is "absolutely impossible to maintain or defend" a total suspense of judgment, as Philo seemed to be promoting. Philo agrees completely (XII.216). The whole matter of their dialogue appears to have been a mere "dispute of words," "a species of controversy" which ("from the very nature of language") "is involved in perpetual ambiguity" (XII.217). In "controversies concerning the degrees of any quality or circumstance," as for example the degree of Cleopatra's beauty, disputants may "agree in their sense and differ in the terms, or vice versa; yet never be able to define their terms, so as to enter into each other's meaning . . ." (XII.218). Such is the case with disputes about God. Theological quarrels, Philo insists, are "merely verbal, or perhaps, if possible, still more incurably ambiguous. . ." (XII.218). The terms of the dialogue about religion are two-sided (or worse), so that disputants may endorse either side till they drop, but the matter forever will remain unsettled.

To illustrate his point, Philo imagines holding a dialogue with a theist and an atheist. The structure of Philo's imaginary dialogue is crucial, since it shows why the skeptic must shift in order to address the two-sided, ambiguous, and hence shifting dispute concerning theism. Since the debate pivots on whether God is analogous to (like or unlike) a human designer, Philo experiments with both sides of the analogy. He presses the theist to admit "the great and immeasurable, because incomprehensible, difference between the human and the divine mind"; and, turning to the atheist, he queries whether or not there isn't at least "a certain degree of analogy [likeness] among all the operations of nature." Both interlocutors, Philo is confident, must give their assent to the question posed to them.

> Where then, cry I to both these antagonists, is the subject of your dispute? The theist allows, that the original intelligence is very different from human reason: The atheist allows, that the original principle of order bears some remote analogy to it. Will you quarrel, Gentlemen, about the degrees, and enter into a controversy, which admits

not of any precise meaning, nor consequently of any determination? If you should be so obstinate, I should not be surprised to find you insensibly changing sides; while the theist on the one hand exaggerates the dissimilarity between the supreme Being, and frail, imperfect, variable, fleeting, and mortal creatures; and the atheist on the other magnifies the analogy among all the operations of nature, in every period, every situation, and every position. Consider then, where the real point of controversy lies, and if you cannot lay aside your disputes, endeavour, at least, to cure yourselves of your animosity. (XII.218–19)

Philo, once again, plays the mediator, not taking a position for himself, but shifting from side to side of a dispute over an ambiguous subject matter. His shifting argument is mandated by the polarized voices in the dispute, which reflect the inherently ambiguous nature of the subject matter. Echoing the irenic words of part VIII, he hopes by means of this mediation (shifting) to engender a more peaceable discussion.

In this imaginary dialogue with a theist and an atheist, it may not appear that Philo is referring to his discourse with Demea and Cleanthes. There are textual warrants, I suggest, for making this connection once again. The theist's position (which stresses the likeness of God and human mind) and Philo's corresponding advice certainly match his interaction with Cleanthes; and oddly enough, the atheist's view (which stresses the unknowability of God) matches that of Demea. Although Demea is not an "atheist" in the common sense of that word, he twice is identified as an atheist by Cleanthes (II.141 and IV.158); and more importantly, Philo's rejoinder to his imaginary atheist (telling him to admit some likeness between God and world) is exactly what he tells Demea. In fact, Philo had performed this same two-sided shift earlier with Cleanthes and Demea. Thus we find Philo cautioning Demea that not all experience should be excluded as evidence for God, but only that which bears a "very weak analogy"; turning to Cleanthes, on the other side, he points out how striking is the "dissimilitude" between nature and human design (II.144). Since talk about God is ambiguous, always involving "proportional analogy" (likeness) and "proportional difference" (unlikeness) (XII.217), the mediating skeptic must turn and shift in order to bring the two sides beyond their controversies and animosities: theist and atheist; Cleanthes and Demea; likeness and dissimilitude; previous ages and the modern age; and so on.

The point of these examples is clear: the duplicity and shiftiness of the skeptical Philo are methodically grounded in the ambiguity and duplicity built into theistic discourse. Philo's procedures are the natural response to the shifting voices of theism. What is more, Philo's motives are not simply to suspend the possibility of God-talk, but to cure theistic disputes of their animosities and establish a more humble, tolerant basis for discourse. Philo's rhetoric reflects an irenic spirit.

Given this reading of Philo's performance in the *Dialogues*, what are we to make of his acknowledgment of design and his professions of theistic belief? Three factors might account for Philo's apparent turnabout without doing violence to his words and without having recourse to Hume's motives as philosophical author. First, as scandalous as this will sound to orthodox interpreters of Hume, there is no reason *within* the dialogue not to believe Philo's professions of belief. The temptation not to believe Philo arises from importations of Hume's supposed atheism or from an uncritical association between atheism and skepticism. In either case, Philo's professions of belief appear grossly contradictory, perhaps even hypocritical. This forces the interpreter to pick and choose what to believe from Philo. If, however, we are to take Philo at his word, then such professions must not be left as strange exceptions to his skepticism. The key is to discover how Philo's "belief" fits integrally into his skeptical posture; to do so requires a very precise reading of Philo's skepticism. To this end, several factors must be kept in mind.

To begin with, Philo's rhetorical practice consistently aims to establish a "suspense of judgement." This, he declares, is the "triumph of scepticism" (I.136). When, for instance, he taunts Cleanthes with the suggestion that the world may just as likely be "spun from the belly as from the brain" (VII.180–81), he is not endorsing the idea of creation by "natural gestation" any more than he is arguing against creation by divine reason. His rhetorical aim invariably is to suspend judgment from settling on any and all options. Philo's agenda, therefore, is not that of the atheist who takes the position that there is no divinity, but that of the skeptic who wishes to withhold philosophical assent to any metaphysical conclusion, pro or con.

Along the same lines, Philo's strategic posture is unfailingly irenic, not antagonistic. Too little is made in commentaries on the *Dialogues* of Philo's civility. While Philo's skeptical "invention" certainly spells disaster for theistic positions, he gains this effect not by argumentatively assaulting Cleanthes and Demea, but by standing above the theistic fray (defending "no fixed station or abiding city"), shifting back and forth between his rival interlocutors to cure them of their animosities and hostilities. When Philo exhorts his interlocutors to be humble in advocacy and tolerant in argument, this is part and parcel of his skeptical approach to dialogue, not empty preaching (VIII.186). For my purposes, that Philo's method is skeptical (but not atheist) and irenic (and not antagonistic) means that his professions of belief constitute a shift, but not a complete (and possibly disingenuous) reversal. Still, even granting this point, what accounts for Philo's shift from the mediating and irenic skeptic to one who professes belief in God?

The answer is to be found in a third characteristic of Philo's skepticism. For him, skepticism is mitigated by the necessities of life. To this effect, Philo twice agrees with Cleanthes when the latter insists that a comprehensive skepticism is impossible. In Philo's words, the skeptic "must act, I own, and live, and converse like other men; and for this conduct he is not obliged to give any other reason than the absolute necessity he lies under of so doing" (I.134; compare XII.214). No reason can be given because when one stands aside from philosophy, even the skeptic is subject to the impressions and beliefs of purpose, intention, and design in the natural world. Philo's "belief" is just that—a set of lived impressions which "strike everywhere the most careless, the most stupid thinkers" (XII.214). Theistic belief is not here a matter for philosophical argument. It is not, therefore, in competition with philosophical judgment, for Philo's shift to natural belief is a concession to life, not a developed position. He will not try to philosophically specify or justify this belief. Once again, consequently, Philo's professions of belief do not constitute a disingenuous turnabout, but simply a shift proper to anyone who tries to practice philosophy. Philo's "belief," therefore, should not come as a surprise; and because it is so minimal and philosophically empty, it certainly does not spell a reversal of a skepticism interested in suspense (not refutation) and civil discourse (not antagonism).

A second factor contributing to an understanding of Philo's statements in part XII concerns his words on the excesses and dangers of popular religion. Cleanthes raises this new topic by claiming that even "corrupted religion" is "better than no religion at all" (XII.219). Philo cannot agree, and levels a devastating psychological critique of popular religion. For Philo, there is a great distance between Cleanthes' "genuine theism" (which is "the mere product of philosophy") and the religion practiced by people (XII.225). When talking about religion, therefore, "we must treat of [it], as it has commonly been found in the world . . ." (XII.223). The way that religion works in the world is deleterious for both the moral life and the political good of society. For individuals, the superstition and enthusiasm propagated by religion "weakens extremely men's attachment to the natural motives of justice and humanity." In particular, "the steady attention alone to . . . eternal salvation is apt to extinguish the benevolent affections, and beget a narrow, contracted selfishness." And as if superstition and "bigoted credulity" are not bad enough, religion also fosters zealotry. In Philo's words, "no morality can be forcible enough to bind the enthusiastic zealot. The sacredness of the cause sanctifies every measure which can be made use of to promote it" (XII.222). The same superstition and enthusiasm wreaks havoc on the public good too; the many sects vie for dominance, resulting in "endless disputes, quarrels, factions, persecutions, and civil commotions" (XII.223). Behind all this, moreover, stands the priest, who Philo suggests should be "confined within very narrow limits" in both "number and authority" to protect the power and authority of the magistrate.

This critique of religion is important for understanding Philo's apparent duplicity in professing belief in God for several reasons. To begin with, there is a striking difference in rhetorical strategy when Philo turns from considering the argument from design to a psychological treatment of popular religion. Where Philo is the shifting mediator throughout the discussion of philosophical theism, his words on religion are sharply and unqualifiedly critical. He was indirect and shifting earlier; now he is direct and blunt. The reason for this rhetorical shift is two-fold: (a) with Demea absent, the role of shifting mediator between two theistic disputants is no longer necessary; and (b) more significantly, having accomplished the neutralization of theistic controversies, he now can turn to more pressing questions. It is easy, after all, to acknowledge the central tenet of philosophical theism ("that the causes of order in the universe probably bear some remote analogy to human intelligence"), especially if it bears no effect on human life (XII.227). Very little is at stake in such an admission. This is not the case, however, with actual religion. With religion as it is popularly practiced, a great deal is at stake—the moral seduction and subjugation of ordinary people—and this must be addressed and combated.

This contrast in importance, and the consequent contrast in rhetorical strategy and tone, give us more insight into Philo's professions of theistic belief. They tell us, to begin with, that whereas Philo may be a theist (in the most natural and minimal sense), he certainly is not religious. Actual religion constitutes a bastion of superstition and enthusiasm for Philo. There is nothing ambiguous about popular religion; it simply is harmful to human life. With this turn to religion "as it has commonly been found in the world" (XII.223), we are faced with a most pronounced rhetorical shift. Compared with this turn, his renowned professions of belief—which have received so much critical attention—are relatively incidental. The more interesting (and significant) shift in Philo's approach lies not in his concessions to theism, but in his turn to take on the superstitions and enthusiasms of institutional religion. The fact that commentators have spent so much energy on Philo's shift to theism tells us, I suspect, more about the interests (and prejudices) of philosophical commentators than it does about Philo.

A third factor shedding light on Philo's remarks in part XII can be handled briefly. One of the more interesting cues for reading Philo's words arises from the shifting use of names for theistic or non-theistic persons. Early in the discussion, as we have seen already, Philo's skepticism and Demea's mysticism are lumped together as forms of atheism (I and II). Immediately following this, however, Cleanthes also claims to be a skeptic; Philo's skepticism is said to be only an affectation (III.154). Who then is the real skeptic, if both a theist (Cleanthes) and an atheist (either Demea or Philo) are skeptics? In part IV the name-calling starts in earnest, and the meaning of these terms begins to shift wildly. Indeed, Philo challenges Cleanthes on the shifting sense of these names:

> You are honouring with the appellation of atheist all the sound, orthodox divines [who hold positions like Demea's] . . . and you will at last, be, yourself, found, according to your reckoning, the only sound theist in the world. But if idolaters be

atheists, . . . and Christian theologians the same; what becomes of the argument, so much celebrated, derived from the universal consent of mankind? (IV.160)

Here we get a preview of Philo's "suspense of judgement" which appears later in the text. Do these differences, Philo asks, really make a difference? Do they rest on any reasonable evidence? Philo's answer, of course, will be negative. Specifically, if Philo claims to be a theist too, due to the experience of order and design natural to everyday life, can that label carry much weight when theism has already been equated with skepticism, skepticism likened to mysticism, and mysticism compared with atheism? All in all, Philo's so-called reversal in part XII can hardly be considered very startling, since the entire question of what makes anyone anything has been neatly hung in the balance by his skeptical strategy.

(3) Hume's Shiftiness

The various forms of shiftiness and duplicity reviewed in the first section, as well as the clues and explanations provided with the *Dialogues*, manifest Hume's interest in the nature and processes of religious discourse. To use Wittgenstein's famous distinction, Hume's rhetorical focus rarely is said, but it is shown vividly through the evolving dialogue of Philo, Cleanthes, and Demea. That is, Hume presents his claim that the protagonists of theism are shifty and duplicitous (guilty of "priestcraft"), as well as his experience that the skeptic who engages these protagonists will be perceived (and accused) of also being shifty and duplicitous, by showing his readers the convoluted situations and the confusing rhetorical machinations that transpire in such discourse. To say this outright is one thing; to show it by participating in it through dialogue form, however, is something altogether more significant, for by enacting his message through imitation and participation, Hume involves himself in the same doubleness and shiftiness. Let us turn, therefore, to four key instances of Hume's own shiftiness.

(a) *Hume as Writer of Dialogue.* Hume is shifty, first off, in his choice of genre. The dialogue form, in its very structure, results in a doubleness of voice. The author's voice is heard behind and through the characters' voices, always inviting the question of who is speaking, author or character. To be sure, most dialogues (like Anselm's) leave little room for doubt on this matter, since authors of dialogues usually have very definite agenda that shine through their lead character's assertions. Even in such dialogues, however, a slight displacement of voice occurs, since the author deliberately chooses to speak indirectly through the lead character's encounter with opposition. Hume's *Dialogues*, quite differently, have spawned two centuries of debate about which voice speaks for Hume. Clearly this is no accident. As much as any dialogue writer in the history of Western philosophy (including Diderot), David Hume successfully exploits the possibilities for indirection and self-effacement within the dialogue form. The very fact that Hume's identity continues to be debated gives evidence of his success at shifting his voice between and behind his characters.

Hume's choice of the dialogue form is part and parcel of his philosophical method and style of writing; consequently, so is a certain shifting and doubleness of voice. First a word on Hume's method. In "Of the Dignity or Meanness of Human Nature," Hume notes that, in learning about life, people are "commonly more influenced by comparison than by any fixed unalterable standard in the nature of things."[9] People learn by comparing what is different. This pedagogical insight is rooted in human nature, since, for Hume, "Man is a very variable being. . . . What may be true, while he adheres to one way of thinking, will be found false, when he has embraced an opposite set of manners and opinions."[10] Learning depends on comparison, and, because of this, people naturally shift about from view to view. The Humean self is, after all, like the commonwealth; an association of different elements, and the result remains fluid. Faithful to these points, a great deal of Hume's thought develops by careful comparison and composition. Time and time again, he sets out terms of comparison in order to mediate opposites or to pull together disparate elements. Thus we find Hume associating (only to contrast) abstruse with common philosophy at the beginning of the first *Enquiry*; shallow and abstruse thinkers in "On Commerce"; the learned and the conversable in "Of Essay Writing"; and so on.[11] In many other places, including most of his *Essays*, but also *The Natural History of Religion*, Hume pulls together myriad examples from classical, oriental, and modern history in order to make his point by comparison.[12]

As Jerome Christensen has demonstrated in his recent work on Hume's literary career, Hume sought by all these means to execute a strategy of correspondence and composition. He wished to play "the mediator between parties, discourses, [and] epochs,"[13] trying to "compose" what is disparate, since (in Hume's words) with human happiness, as with most phenomena, "no one ingredient can be entirely wanting without destroying, in some measure, the relish of the whole composition."[14] And the one who will perform this composition must play the "ambassador" or middle-man between different realms. Notice the mixing of economic and political metaphors in Hume's self-portrait:

> 'Tis with great Pleasure I observe, That Men of Letters, in this Age, have lost, in a great Measure, that Shyness and Bashfulness of Temper, which kept them at a Distance from Mankind; and, at the same Time, That Men of the World are proud of borrowing from Books their most agreeable Topics of Conversation. 'Tis to be hop'd, that this League betwixt the learned and conversible Worlds, which is so happily begun, will be still farther improv'd to their mutual Advantage; and to that End, I know nothing more advantageous than such *Essays* as these with which I endeavour to entertain the Public. In this View, I cannot but consider myself as a Kind of

Resident or Ambassador from the Dominions of Learning to those of Conversation; and shall think it my constant Duty to promote a good Correspondence betwixt these two States, which have so great a Dependence on each other. I shall give Intelligence to the Learned of whatever passes in Company, and shall endeavour to import into Company whatever Commodities I find in my native Country proper for their Use and Entertainment. The Balance of Trade we need not be jealous of, nor will there be any Difficulty to preserve it on both Sides. The Materials of this Commerce must chiefly be furnish'd by Conversation and common Life: The manufacturing of them alone belongs to Learning.[15]

The man of letters—ambassador and middle-man—is the one who facilitates "this League between" different realms of experience, who composes the correspondence between opposites. In this regard, Hume embodies his commitment to dialogue throughout his career by going "between merchant and prince, learned and conversable, England and France, man and woman. . . ."[16]

Hume's style of writing—though most commonly not in dialogue genre—gives powerful expression to these methodological commitments.[17] As M. A. Box has shown in his study of the development of Hume's style, Hume aspired throughout his career "to make abstruse philosophy less abstruse";[18] or in Hume's own words, to reconcile "profound enquiry with clearness, and truth with novelty."[19] As Box tells it, Hume moved in quest of this ideal from the "peremptory tone" and "epigrammatic paradoxicality" of the *Treatise* to a "more subtle ironic coyness" in mid-career to the "natural novelty" and gentle persuasion of the second *Enquiry*. What emerges in Box' narrative is Hume's life-long quest for a "form and a voice" that would "wed instruction with entertainment," thereby providing an educated audience with philosophical lessons delivered in a lively, natural, and pleasurable style.[20] Here, once again, we see the two-sided, mediating design of Hume's project. In method and style, he aspired to go between; literally, to *be* the go-between; or, put differently, to work rhetorically through the medium of dialogue. To write in this manner mandates a shifting voice.

Unfortunately, Box remains strangely silent about how the dialogue form fits into Hume's stylistic quest; and he considers Hume's treatment of religion to be an exception to, not an example of, his natural and mediating style. I think Box is incorrect on both scores, and that his analysis of Hume's style merits extension to dialogue and to religion. First, as Box readily acknowledges, conversation and dialogue are at the heart of Hume's entire project as a philosopher and man of letters. Indeed, for Hume, "the very habit of conversing together, and contributing to each other's pleasure and entertainment" causes "an encrease in humanity."[21] Conversation is a fundamental human good. And as Christensen astutely observes, Hume not only depicts conversation as "a process of composition," but more importantly, he imitates it "in the process of [his own literary] composition."[22] This literary imitation of the good of amicable conversation appears and develops throughout the *Essays* and both *Enquiries*, but it finds a most natural and fitting expression in the dialogue form. For the dialogue allows Hume the opportunity as author to conduct a conversation that will be natural yet philosophically rich. There should be, Hume tells us, a "tolerable equality maintained among the speakers"; it should not be an occasion for didacticism; and the author should avoid that "vulgar Error . . . of putting nothing but Nonsense into the Mouth of the Adversary."[23] With these standards in hand, Hume composed dialogues which fulfil the very stylistic ideals which Box attributes to Hume; that is, they "combine the strongest arguments with the art of couching them in lively terms, thereby compensating somewhat for the reader's natural resistance to abstruse reasoning."[24]

Second, when it comes to religious questions, Hume continues to play the role of ambassador and middleman, searching for a "form and voice" which will allow him to mediate between people of different stripes. Thus, for instance, we find him writing to Lady Jane Home from Edinburgh in 1755, complaining that "from accusing me of believing nothing, they now charge me with believing every thing. I hope you will be perswaded, that the Truth lyes in the middle betwixt these Accusations."[25] Hume stands in between, ready to "promote a good Correspondence betwixt" the skeptical and the credulous, or between various forms of theism. "Of Superstition and Enthusiasm" provides an example of precisely this double mediation. Speaking fluently to the educated world, Hume contrasts two species of corrupted religion, dispassionately weighing their merits and demerits.[26]

The Natural History of Religion provides a more extended example. From section to section, Hume ranges far and wide, engaging different forms of religious belief or practice. Sounding precisely like Philo in the *Dialogues*, he notes that "the principles of religion have a kind of flux and reflux in the human mind, and that men have a natural tendency to rise from idolatry to theism, and to sink again from theism into idolatry." Caught in the "alternate revolution of human sentiments," people "fluctuate betwixt these opposite sentiments."[27] History exposes the shiftiness of religious sentiments. Indeed, Hume points up, as Philo does in the *Dialogues*, a certain disguise or simulation in religious people: "they make a merit of implicit faith; and disguise to themselves their real infidelity, by the strongest asseverations and most positive bigotry." Faith rests upon hypocrisy, but despite their confessions, the religious mind stands "betwixt disbelief and conviction, but approaching much nearer the former than the latter."[28]

Hume's shifting method is stated only in the closing paragraph: since it is impossible to uphold a "deliberate doubt" with respect to all things religious, the only solution is to

> enlarge our view, and opposing one species of superstition to another, set them a quarrelling; while we ourselves, during their fury and contention, happily make our escape into the calm, though obscure, regions of philosophy."[29]

As Philo shifts between Cleanthes and Demea, so, here, does Hume shift back and forth, orchestrating a mutually nullifying dispute between the hypocritical shiftings of religious life. Hume takes up a position "in between," not for the purpose of espousing a compromise or effecting an easy reconciliation, but to play off the opposite sides of religious hypocrisy, and to deliver thereby a piece of philosophical wisdom to the educated world. Consequently, the "Balance of Trade" (as he calls it) is maintained, for common life provides the material for conversation while the philosopher manufactures the dialogue.

Nowhere are Hume's dialogical method and style more perfectly applied to religious topics than in the *Dialogues*.[30] Hume was quite proud of this text, writing to his friend Adam Smith that "nothing [could] be more cautiously and more artfully written" than his *Dialogues*.[31] His "caution" and "artfulness" should not be dismissed as a sign of disingenuous efforts to protect himself by concealing his real message. Rather, Hume boasts of his method and style, of his success in playing out the role of "Ambassador from the Dominions of Learning to those of Conversation." Indeed, he points up the importance of the dialogue form in the preface of the *Dialogues*, and then again in later passages that echo what is said in the preface. The statements on dialogue come from the mouth of Pamphilus, the student narrator whom critics usually dismiss as a dim-witted prop or a wimpy Platonist. John Valdimir Price, for instance, characterizes him as "a weak and (to Hume) philosophically ignominious character."[32] Like other Hume scholars, Price is led to this view by Pamphilus' misguided assessment of the arguments at the end of the *Dialogues* (XII.228). Mossner goes further, dismissing Pamphilus' initial remarks as fundamentally misguided.[33] I suggest, in contrast, that Pamphilus' remarks are consistent expressions of Hume's commitment to a dialogical method and style.

What Pamphilus says about dialogue is this: instruction in the form of dialogue has fallen on hard times in recent days, because the genre has difficulty living up to the rigorous expectations of current "philosophical enquirers." The "freer air" and grace of dialogue appears to be an "unnatural" vehicle to "deliver a System"; and it tends to sacrifice the "order, brevity, and precision" demanded by philosophical readers (Preface. 127). Still, he adds, dialogue bears a two-fold value: (i) Its "novelty of manner," "vivacity of conversation," and "variety of lights" (voices) are perfect for topics that are "so obvious" that discussion may seem unnecessary yet "so important" that they cannot be too frequently rehearsed. Religious doctrines like "the being of God" meet both criteria. (ii) The dialogue form is perfectly suited for those questions of philosophy that are "so obscure and uncertain" that they outstrip the reaches of human reason, yet "so interesting" that "we cannot restrain our restless enquiry regarding them." When faced with inherently dialectical questions, where "reasonable men may be allowed to differ, [and] where no one can reasonably be positive," the open and indeterminate nature of the dialogue is most appropriate. At the same time, this genre creates a "company" of conversation, which, by including the reader, "unites the two greatest and purest pleasures of human life, study and society" (Preface.127–28). Philosophical questions, like those concerning the "nature of God," meet both of these criteria.

There is good reason, I think, to credit these words on dialogue not simply to the mouthpiece of Pamphilus, but directly to Hume. First, Pamphilus' remarks match Hume's life-long interest in wedding philosophical rigor to a natural style. With their novelty, vivacity, and diversity, dialogues blend "study and society" (the "Learned" and "company")—and this marriage is a well suited context for those encounters over religious and philosophical questions in which interlocutors come to the conversation with sharply different expectations. Two perspectives (one doctrinal and one philosophical) come together over apparently common questions, and their fusion through conversation generates instant rhetorical tensions. The first pole of each perspective stands in sharp conflict: what is to the theist "so obvious, so certain" is very obscure and uncertain to the skeptically-inclined philosopher. Everything is already fixed for the former, while the latter finds everything up in the air. If we read this opposition dialogically, regarding it as the rhetorical condition for discourse on questions about God, then the stage is set for opposition. The second pole of each perspective may appear less opposed, but this is deceiving. Being important and being interesting are both positive features, but they stand nonetheless at cross purposes. For the religious, talk about God is important (since it "cannot be too often inculcated"); for the philosopher, such talk is truly interesting as an object of "restless inquiry." While the former expects confirmation of belief, the latter expects "nothing but doubt, uncertainty, and contradiction" (Preface.127–28). The dialogue form is so appropriate, therefore, because it enacts discourse under these sometimes sharp, sometimes curious rhetorical conditions. Pamphilus' description of the dialogue form suits it perfectly to the conditions faced by Philo and his theistic interlocutors.

Two pieces of evidence from within the *Dialogues* illustrate that Hume is using these key terms from the preface to frame the conditions and contours for discourse. He first re-introduces these same couplings in part X, but they are now in Philo's hands, as the latter admonishes Cleanthes for not seeing that misery and suffering in human life are "most obvious, certain and important" (X.200). Ironically, Philo uses only the coupling held by Pamphilus to describe the religious appropriateness of dialogue, showing thereby the reversal that has transpired. Then in part XII, Philo repeats these terms (albeit in a more veiled way): the probability that the cause of world order bears "some remote analogy to human intelligence" is said to be obvious and astonishing (interesting), yet obscure, uncertain, and ill-defined (XII.227). By means of these couplings, varied to characterize the developed status of the conversation, Hume frames the entire *Dialogues* with signals marking the rhetorical parameters for what will transpire (or has transpired) in discourse between a skeptic like Philo and two very different theists. Pamphilus describes the general conditions for such discourse. Philo labels the end result. And, by this means, Hume makes a philosophical point about the complex and convoluted conditions for religious discourse.

To think within the parameters of dialogue, and to write within those rhetorical limits, mandates that Hume take up more than one voice. In this regard, a certain doubleness and shiftiness is unavoidable for the dialogical thinker. Indeed, Hume shifts his voice repeatedly to achieve his purposes. He speaks (i) through the text as a whole, since the entire composition constitutes Hume's vehicle for dialogue with his readers; (ii) through each one of the characters, since even the words articulating positions which Hume finds philosophically repugnant must be imagined and spoken by him; and (iii) especially through Philo, who pursues Hume's skeptical, ironic, and irenic aims. The first level of speech is most often overlooked by philosophical critics interested only in identifying Hume with a fixed position. Only by acknowledging Hume's voice as the creator of the entire composition, however, can we begin to see Hume as being interested in the play of rhetorical forces, which constitutes religious discourse. The second level supplements the first: to write in dialogue form is already an act of imaginative understanding, one that involves the author in every word of the text. In the most obvious sense, an author of a dialogue must imaginatively construct the voice of the other, whether it be friend or adversary. In most cases, to be sure, authors fail to make their adversary anything more than "straw men," so that this second level of speech bears little significance. Hume, on the contrary, goes to great lengths in order to let his others speak plausibly and intelligently.[34] In this sense, Hume speaks through each of the characters not only when they express what he espouses, but also when they do not. On both of these two levels, Hume cannot help but shift about, giving voice not only to his own opinions but to the opposition's as well.

As most contemporary critics now agree, Hume speaks primarily through Philo.[35] It is Philo who functions as the instrument of Hume's dialogical method and style, who allows him to move about the shifting and duplicitous voices of religion. Philo enacts Hume's stance "in between" the shifting voices of theism. Philo is the middle-man, crafting the correspondence between the skeptical and the theistic; exposing the "flux and reflux" of the religious mind; setting the ambiguities of religion "quarrelling" with each other; and pointing toward the "calm, though obscure, regions of philosophy," where judgments on religious questions are held in suspense. Philo is the voice of Hume's dialogue. This identification of Hume's dialogical commitments and Philo's voice appears in three key ways, each being another instance of Hume's shifting voice: it is Philo who personifies Hume's mitigated skepticism, who maintains his ironic vantage, and who embodies his commitment to civil and irenic discourse.

(b) *Hume as Skeptic*. As Hume makes clear in *An Enquiry Concerning Human Understanding*, his skepticism is not total and absolute, but is mitigated by the exigencies of life. Certainly, for Hume, a small dose of undiluted skepticism concerning the range of human knowledge (what he calls "Pyrrhonism") is healthy, since it can humble those who claim to know too much. "There is," he writes, "a degree of doubt, and caution, and modesty, which, in all kinds of scrutiny and decision, ought forever to accompany a just reasoner."[36] Still, unbridled doubt is unlivable, for "no durable good can ever result from it; while it remains in its full force and vigor." In words which come to be a constant refrain in Hume's philosophy, "Nature is always too strong for principle,"[37] including the skeptical principles of academical philosophy. In a passage that adds a gloss to the ending of *The Natural History of Religion* quoted earlier, Hume derides the abstraction and impracticalities of philosophical thinking, even those of the skeptic:

> The reflections of philosophy are too subtle and distant to take place in common life, or eradicate any affection. The air is too fine to breathe in, where it is above the winds and clouds of the atmosphere.[38]

Hume may wish to stand above the fray of antagonists, orchestrating their dialogue to the point at which judgments are suspended; but, at the same time, he insists on involvement in and even concessions to the complexities and irrationalities of human life. Human beings, after all, are guided by taste and sentiment, not by "general maxims."[39]

Hume's mitigated skepticism results in a shifting approach to philosophical questions as he moves back and forth between suspicion and life. This holds equally true of his treatment of religion. On one hand, not only is Hume not religious, he is actively suspicious of organized religion and resolutely opposed to the clergymen who wield power in religious institutions. Sounding exactly like Philo in part XII of the *Dialogues*, Hume sharply criticizes the dehumanizing superstitions and foolish enthusiasms perpetrated in the name of religion. His most virulent thrusts, however, are reserved for the clergy. Consider, for instance, Hume's indictment of clerical duplicity and dissimulation. Unlike most people, he tells us,

> clergymen, being drawn from the common mass of mankind, as people are to other employments, by the views of profit . . . will find it necessary, on particular occasions, to feign more devotion than they are, at that time, possessed of, and to maintain the appearance of fervor and seriousness, even when jaded with the exercises of their religion. . . . They must not, like the rest of the world, give scope to their natural movements and sentiments: They must guard over their looks and words and actions: And in order to support the veneration paid them by the multitude, they must not only keep up a remarkable reserve, but must promote the spirit of superstition, by a continued grimace and hypocrisy. This dissimulation often de-

stroys the candor and ingenuity of their temper, and makes an irreparable breach in their character.[40]

Mossner surmises that Hume would have softened these remarks had he already known his moderate clergy friends in Edinburgh.[41] Though Mossner may be correct, Hume's indictment of clerical duplicity is too central a part of his philosophy to be dismissed altogether. The origin of priests, Hume tells us, is "the invention of a timorous and abject superstition, which, ever diffident of itself, dares not offer up its own devotions, but ignorantly thinks to recommend itself to the Divinity, by the mediation of his supposed friends and servants."[42] Given this psychological explanation for the genesis of priests, it is only natural that this caste would be found avidly "promoting ignorance and superstition and implicit faith and pious frauds."[43] The clergy, after all, have an interest in fostering the fears that guarantee their existence. But priests are even more dangerous for society and government: they spawn a "mutual hatred and antipathy among their followers," thereby engendering "a spirit of persecution, which has been the poison of human society. . . ."[44] All "wise governments," Hume warns, will be on guard against those in this profession, who "will for ever be actuated by ambition, pride, revenge, and a persecuting spirit."[45] When Philo complains of the "priestcraft" of divines, he is simply voicing Hume's well-established indictment of religious (in this case, clerical) shiftiness and duplicity.

On the other hand, Hume's approach to religion consistently is not atheistic. Though skeptical of religious life and practice, Hume repeatedly affirms the reasonableness of belief in some sort of God. Thus, for instance, we find him in *The Natural History of Religion* insisting that "the whole frame of nature bespeaks an intelligent author," a judgment repeated several times.[46] The same affirmation is repeated by Philo, as we have seen, in the *Dialogues*. When the latter text is read against the background of Hume's other works, there seem to be no grounds for disbelieving his theistic affirmations. While many Hume scholars dismiss these affirmations, there are some who trust the text enough to acknowledge some limited degree of theistic belief. Kemp Smith, for one, points up the minimal quality of Hume's belief in God: Hume's belief is "so neutral and colourless," it is nothing but a "beggarly minimum."[47] J. C. A. Gaskin, I think, most accurately describes the level of Hume's belief; for him, Hume stands in the middle "between deism and atheism." Hume's position amounts to

a highly attenuated deism which is not positively advocated. It is the religion of a "citizen of the world" who has, after due consideration, rejected the beliefs of all particular sects in favour of a true religion whose sole credo is a diffidently held belief in an intelligent origin of natural order and whose sole observance is the morality which would anyway have been followed for other reasons "were there no god in the universe."[48]

A "citizen of the world," Hume resides in the middle between the protagonists and antagonists of religion. Like Philo in the *Dialogues*, who defends "no fixed station or abiding city," Hume moves freely without positive religious commitments, seeking skeptically through dialogue to suspend judgments (either theistic or atheistic) for which there is not sufficient experience or reason. Hume's skepticism, mitigated by the habits of life, therefore constitutes another source of his shifting rhetoric, for it leaves him standing between the theist and the atheist, as he shifts back and forth between skeptical criticism and religious affirmation.

(c) *Hume as Ironist*. A great deal of Hume's shiftiness and doubleness of meaning issues from his aptitude for irony. Indeed, Hume is a master of irony, and the *Dialogues* prove no exception to his knack for sensing life's double meanings and ambiguities. To understand the rhyme and reason of Hume's shifting voice requires clarification of his uses of irony.

Hume's skepticism and irony go hand in hand as he pursues his dialogical aims. As Price notes, the skeptic is always "quicker to see the disparity between men's deeds and men's actions. . . ."[49] Skepticism serves irony by casting doubt on the "superficial level" of meaning. As Price puts it, referring to Hume, "the level of meaning which best represents the author's feelings is, in other words, skeptical about the surface meaning of the words simply interpreted."[50] It is the skeptical vantage point, therefore, that allows Hume to shift from level to level, playing ironically with the doubleness endemic to human life.

There is also an intimate connection between Hume's irony and his attitudes toward religion. In Price's words, "irony in religion . . . brings out the best in artistry, the best in scholarship, and the best in philosophy from David Hume." Religious fervor, dogmatic arguments, and "pretensions to intelligence by religionists" were favorite targets for his "ironic thrusts" and parodies. The *Dialogues* are, in this regard, a "book full of irony."[51] In Price's reading of Hume, as in so many critics, the shifts and unexpected surprises in the *Dialogues* (e.g., Philo's alliance with Demea, Philo's professions of belief, Pamphilus' verdict in favor of Cleanthes) are expressions of Hume's satirical assault on religion and of his crafty, even disingenuous desire to conceal his real intent from the targets of his satire. The *Dialogues* are, for Price, a "systematic attack on the argument from design and its related concepts," and to pull off this assault, Hume must shift his meaning so that it is "recognized by the perspicacious few and unperceived by the multitude."[52]

Consider a few examples from Price's analysis. First, Philo's "ostensible professions of piety" are "strategically ironic and should not be taken seriously."[53] Through Philo's shiftiness, Hume "deceived those who were stupid enough to be deceived."[54] When, therefore, Hume has Philo criticize the skeptic at the beginning of part XII, this is not "hypocritical self-criticism"; Hume simply "is not saying what he means . . ." and, thus, should not be believed. Philo's professions of belief in God are "qualified in a way calculated to hide . . . irony from the faithful. . . ."[55] The same analysis holds, for Price, concerning the ending of the *Dialogues*. From Price's perspective, for Hume to allow Pamphilus to declare Cleanthes the victor is "nothing more than a condescending sop to the rigidly righteous, who, if they thought about the person speaking and about the superiority of Philo's reasoning, would realize the insult."[56] These examples illustrate Price's Hume: a satirically aggressive author, camouflaging his real message with irony. A strong note of elitism and condescension mark this portrait of Hume.

There is much to be said for Price's reading. First, it underscores the critical and pedagogical function of Hume's irony. In Price's words, "the ultimate function of Humean irony in dealing with religious concepts [is] to change, in some desirable manner, men's ways of thinking about the world."[57] Hume criticizes in order to instruct; he wished "to call the attention of other intelligent human beings to the ironic doubleness in human life."[58] More precisely, Hume wished to expose those places in life in which conflict exists "between appearance and reality, between words and deeds, [and] between promise and performance."[59] Given the extent of hypocrisy and dissimulation in religious life and practice, religious shiftiness and duplicity become prime objects of Hume's criticism and instruction. Second, it is certainly true that Hume (like Diderot) was sensitive throughout his career to the dangers of publication on religious issues, causing him to withdraw and withhold publishing on several occasions.[60] To speak indirectly, to write ambiguously, and to be ironic afford one personal and professional safety; this profile fits Hume's temperament as individual and as citizen, and would have allowed him to catch his opponents off-guard. On all counts, then, ironic doubleness and shiftiness would have served his purposes well.

Still, there is something missing in this interpretation of Hume's *Dialogues*. Too much emphasis gets placed on the aggressive, satirical character of Hume's irony. On one hand, Price acknowledges that "most irony in Hume's writings is good-natured, not venomous."[61] The ironic Hume can "enjoy the foibles of human nature and the doubleness of men's actions" because he has coordinated "the serious and the playful in his ironic mode of life."[62] On the other hand, when it comes to Hume on religion, Price tends to construe Hume's irony satirically rather than comically. Thus we hear of "condescending sop[s] to the rigidly righteous," and of the *Dialogues*' "systematic attacks on the argument from design."[63] Price certainly is not alone. Indeed, most philosophical critics interpret Hume as being satirical, and the evidence lies in their choice of violent, even military, verbs. Kemp Smith, for instance, insists that Hume is "consciously, and deliberately, attacking 'the religious hypothesis'. . . ."[64] Even Richard White, who rightly picks up on the comical character of the *Dialogues*, speaks of Hume's "malice" and his "assault" on religion.[65] In such negative readings of Hume, Philo's professions of piety are taken as "strategically ironic and [consequently] should not be taken seriously." In order to be "discreet," Hume "deceived those who were stupid enough to be deceived."[66]

What these critics miss is the way in which Hume's ironic voice expresses his commitment to a dialogical method and his interest in a mediating style. When Hume speaks ironically in the *Dialogues*, he is neither attacking nor deceiving. Rather, he stands playfully between religious opposites, coyly orchestrating their encounter and marveling at the duplicity and shiftiness rampant between them. Hume is a subtle and benevolent ironist, not a satirist intent on concealing his invective behind thinly disguised character deployments. Through Philo's lead, he makes no claims to knowledge of God for himself, but artfully and skeptically suspends the possibility of anyone else making such claims as well. Hume's irony mimes theistic discourse, and what emerges from the reflection are some unexpectedly shifting and duplicitous weaknesses that lie therein. To this end, there is no reason for Hume to level assaults or to hide his real views. Hume's mimesis exposes the fact that religious discourse is already bankrupt, while he simply has no rationally defensible view on the subject. Those who choose to see attacks and concealment in Hume's work, I suspect, are importing their own more strident alienation from religion into Hume's text.

A good example of the two approaches to Humean irony concerns two passages characterizing Philo's skepticism, the first in the Preface where Pamphilus refers to Philo as a "careless sceptic," the second at the end of the *Dialogues* where Philo suggests that even "the most careless, the most stupid thinker" (including himself) admits a design to the world (XII.214). According to Price, Hume is not engaging in "hypocritical self-criticism." He is, rather, "saying the opposite of what he means. . . ." For Price, it is impossible that a philosopher would call his own views careless or stupid without "loading the concession with ambiguity."[67] What marks Price's reading of Hume is his conclusion not to take Hume's text seriously. The first problem with this reading of these passages is that it needlessly and unimaginatively restricts Hume's intentions: either his words are direct and to be taken literally, or they are indirect and to be read in their opposite sense. But another, more subtle level of irony is at work in Hume's words. What makes Hume's irony so interesting, in fact, is that he is not being crudely evasive or dishonest; rather, he playfully—but intentionally—conjoins both positive and negative meanings in the same words.

This more subtle use of irony in the *Dialogues* finds support in two pieces of evidence. First, as Robert Hurlbutt discovered through careful perusal of Hume's corpus, Hume frequently uses the word "careless" in a positive, affirmative way to describe the inevitable and natural return of the philosopher from the rigors of skepticism to the everyday forces of belief and habit. As Hurlbutt puts it, "there is no deception here with regard to Hume's position. To call a philosopher a careless skeptic is not to belittle him, rather it is to reflect sympathy with the necessities of life, shared by the *truly* philosophical as well as the vulgar."[68] In other words, Hume is perfectly serious when he acknowledges his own "carelessness"; it is a light-hearted, but perfectly serious, confession of the doubleness of mitigated skepticism. As Box puts it, Hume was profoundly aware of his own "nagging doubt and compulsive, naive belief." He saw in himself, and he enacts through Philo, "his own double nature as a willfully critical intellect and a causally determined psychological phenomenon. He recognizes that he is simultaneously a philosopher and one of the vulgar."[69] Hume admits his own duplicity, but doing so amounts to no more than a simple confession of being human, and for the skeptic this is worth an ironic smile.

Second, the fact that Hume felt warranted in using a word like "careless" in this ironic manner receives some philological explanation in a comparison of eighteenth and twentieth century usage. Samuel Johnson's *A Dictionary of the English Language*, for instance, reveals an interesting combination of positive and negative meanings current in Hume's day. Careless could mean: (i) "without care, without solicitude, unconcerned, negligent, inattentive, heedless, regardless, thoughtless"; (ii) "cheerful, undisturbed"; (iii) "unheeded, thoughtless, unconsidered"; or (iv) "unmoved by, unconcerned at."[70] The first and third definitions are pejorative (to be careless is to be thoughtless); while the second and fourth are positive (to be careless is to be carefree). Contemporary usage retains echoes of the latter meaning, but it now seems more natural linguistically to take up the negative sense. Doing so, however, leads to a certain carelessness about the word's historical range, and thus to a misunderstanding of Hume's meaning. In the passages quoted above, Hume intentionally splices together all four meanings. The positive connotations suggest sufficient ambiguity to warrant application of the term to Philo's character: he cheerfully stands between rival positions, defending no "fixed station or abiding city" (VIII.187). As a man of letters, he is free from the cares of one domain as opposed to another. With this connotation in mind, the apparently negative sense of "careless" is softened and given nuance: Philo is thoughtless and inattentive to the rigorous demands of absolute skepticism, and thus carelessly turns away from skeptical doubt to the natural beliefs of everyday life. But, as Hurlbutt's analysis shows, this is a concession Hume is more than happy to make, for the mitigated skeptic realizes the impossibility and undesirability of unrelenting doubt. Even the skeptic is human, and that makes for a certain negligence Hume is not afraid to admit.

The full dialectic of Humean irony with respect to religion, therefore, traverses the following steps: there is, first, a perception of the duplicity and shiftiness of life. Next, Hume exposes these forms of shiftiness by engaging them dialogically and skeptically for the purposes of critical education. This leads, characteristically, to the nullification of opposite positions. The resulting suspense of judgment thereby allows the skeptic to escape from the fray into the calm air of philosophy.

But it is impossible, finally, to reside in those heights for very long; the philosopher is human too, and must "carelessly" remain in the midst of the doubleness and shiftiness of ordinary life. The key to Hume's irony is that he speaks from all of these levels. Each has its own integrity, but the larger picture remains incomplete unless each level is kept in dialectical tension with its opposite. When, therefore, Philo shifts about and appears duplicitous in the *Dialogues*, Hume is not being disingenuous and satirical; rather, he is—ironically—enacting and displaying the shiftiness and doubleness built into the fibers of human existence. Hume is shifty, consequently, because human nature is shifty.

(d) *Hume as Irenicist*. A central dimension of Hume's method and style is his desire to bring about "a good Correspondence" between different states of experience. A crucial feature of this commitment to dialogue is a mediating, even irenic spirit. Indeed, there is no shortage of biographical evidence showing Hume's disdain for controversy and rancor, and his commitment to civil and polite conversation. When John Stewart, Professor of Natural Philosophy at Edinburgh, insulted Henry Home and belittled Hume, the latter responded as a "Lover of Peace":

> When I am abus'd by such a Fellow as Warburton, whom I neither know nor care for, I can laugh at him: But if Dr. Stewart approaches any way towards the same Style of writing, I own it vexes me: Because I conclude, that some unguarded Circumstance of my Conduct, tho' contrary to my Intention, had given Occasion to it. . . . All Raillery ought to be avoided in philosophical Argument both because it is unphilosophical, and because it cannot but be offensive, let it be ever so gentle.[71]

Then there is Hume's letter to George Campbell, thanking him for the "civil and obliging" manner in which Campbell had criticized Hume's essay "Of Miracles."[72] And there is Hume's response to an anonymous critic of the same essay, calling for friendship and conversation:

> When I write to you, I know not to whom I am addressing myself; I only know he is one who has done me a great deal of honour, and to whose civilities I am obliged. If we be strangers, I beg we may be acquainted as soon as you think proper to discover yourself; if we be acquainted, I beg we may be friends; if friends, I beg we may be more so. Our connection with each other, as men of letters, is greater than our difference as adhering to different sects or systems. Let us revive the happy times, when Atticus and Cassius the Epicureans, Cicero the Academic, and Brutus the Stoic, could, all of them, live in unreserved friendship together, and were insensible to all those distinctions, except as they furnished agreeable matter to discourse and conversation.[73]

Passages like the two quoted are characteristic of Hume, not anomalous; civility is a trait documented throughout Mossner's biography.

Plenty of evidence in Hume's writings suggests that he considered his dialogical role as man of letters to include an irenic duty and function. One example, taken from "The Rise of the Arts and Sciences" will suffice. In this text, Hume portrays the virtues necessary for the "arts of conversation," noting (in opposition to the previous quotation) that the ancients tended to lack "that polite deference and respect, which civility obliges us either to express or counterfeit towards the persons with whom we converse."[74]

> Among the arts of conversation, no one pleases more than mutual deference and civility, which leads us to resign our own inclinations to those of our companion, and to curb and conceal that presumption and arrogance, so natural to the human mind. A good-natured man, who is well educated, practices this civility to every mortal, without premeditation or interests.[75]

To be the "Ambassador" between realms, even for skeptical and comical ends, requires respect and civility. Such a personal posture—so regularly overlooked in philosophical studies of Hume—resounds throughout his corpus.[76]

Beneath these examples and texts lies an anthropological insight that stands at the heart of Hume's philosophy. While Hume steadfastly pursued his dialogical agenda as man of letters, he understood all too well the human propensity for dispute and hostility. Thus we find him writing in "Of Parties in General":

> Two men travelling on the highway, the one east, the other west, can easily pass each other, if the way be broad enough: But two men, reasoning upon opposite principles of religion, cannot so easily pass, without shocking; though one should think, that the way were also, in that case, sufficiently broad, and that each might proceed, without interruption, in his own course. But such is the nature of the human mind, that it always lays hold on every mind that approaches it; and as it is wonderfully fortified by an unanimity of sentiments, so is it shocked and disturbed by any contrariety. Hence the eagerness, which most people discover in a dispute; and hence their impatience of opposition, even in the most speculative and indifferent opinions.[77]

An anthropological insight here is wedded to an ethical imperative. Hume exhorts his readers along a path of tolerance and mutual respect, but he realistically expects the irrational forces of human nature to override his ideal. Or, as Price put it, there is "an inclination in Hume's thought to argue that much can be done to improve mankind, but won't be."[78] As an author, however, Hume opts for civility rather than despair.

There are, to be sure, limits to Hume's irenicism. The unfortunate business with Rousseau, for example, shows Hume susceptible to the same impulse toward controversy he saw generally in human nature. Nonetheless, even where critics see Hume on the attack—when treating religious questions, for instance—the irenic spirit in his commitment to dialogue shows itself. In "Of Superstition and Enthusiasm," an essay dealing with the two faces of religion Hume found most dangerous to human welfare, his style and tone remain tempered and civil. His aim is not to irritate, but to instruct by conversing naturally with his readers about dangerous tendencies in religion. In calling Hume irenic, I do not suggest that he promotes compromises with religion or even between religious forces; nor am I denying the existence of sharply critical, even hostile remarks about religion (e.g., the clergy) in his correspondence. Rather, Hume consistently seeks to address his readers with civility and respect, going so far as to treat subjects he disdains (e.g., enthusiasms of all sorts) in a measured and open manner. This holds equally for the *Dialogues*, where Hume's agenda is not "consciously, and deliberately, [to] attack 'the religious hypothesis',"[79] as Kemp Smith has it, but to shift back and forth between the ambiguous voices of theism in order to suspend unreasonable judgments and lead his readers naturally and civilly to a more rational perspective on the world. Hume's shiftiness in the *Dialogues*, therefore, is an example of (not an exception to) the irenic impulses at work in his dialogical agenda.

(4) Reading the *Dialogues*

One more form of shiftiness and duplicity is connected with Hume and his *Dialogues;* that being the multiple and shifting receptions given to this text in later centuries. Indeed, duplicity and shiftiness abound in the reading of Hume.

As Roland Hall, Hume's twentieth century bibliographer, put it, "The most striking feature of Hume scholarship is the extent of disagreement."[80] This range of interpretation given to Hume extends throughout his philosophical writings. Michael Morrisroe, Jr., for instance, points up the diffusion of interpretation regarding Hume's ethics. In his words, philosophical schools today rely on Hume, even as they "proclaim their adversary relationships to one another."[81]

Hume's views on religion also have given rise to antithetical interpretations. This began even while Hume lived. The conservative, "Highflying" clergy were convinced that Hume represented a threat to the true faith. In their eyes, he was the great infidel, worthy to be accused of "Heresy, Deism, Scepticism, Atheism, etc."[82] Contrarily, the moderate clergy appreciated and tolerated Hume as a friend and intellectual. The French *philosophes*, ironically, remained suspicious that Hume was not entirely free of religious sentiments. So Mossner writes:

> The *philosophes* simply could not understand Hume's skeptical or agnostic position and were inclined to think that he had not entirely thrown off the shackles of bigotry. "So that poor Hume," wrote Sir James Macdonald from Paris to an English correspondent, "who on your side of the water was thought to have too little religion is here thought to have too much."[83]

Whether for this reason, or due to Hume's affable and benevolent character, Voltaire could still canonize his English friend as "Saint David."[84] But what irritated these free-thinking Frenchmen became something of an obsession for James

Boswell, who badgered the dying Hume with interviews, seeking to reconcile the fact that Hume led a good, moral life despite his renunciation of the Christian religion. In a far different sense from Voltaire, Boswell solved the matter by dreaming that he had discovered Hume's diary, "from which it appeared that though his vanity made him publish treatises of skepticism and infidelity, he was in reality a Christian and a very pious Man."[85] What an amazing shift from Voltaire to Boswell!

The *Dialogues* are not exempt from this remarkable diversity of interpretation. Hume scholars have shifted dramatically, for instance, in their ideas of which character speaks for Hume. In the past, many saw Cleanthes as Hume's mouthpiece. Thus B. M. Laing confidently asserts that "there is no difficulty in deciding, for the *Dialogues* illustrate clearly the relation of Hume to scepticism. Cleanthes is Hume."[86] Others have identified Pamphilus as Hume. So writes C. W. Hendel: "We can identify the author only with 'Pamphilus'. . . . It is this Pamphilus who passes the final judgment, after making significant comments from time to time throughout the course of the discussion."[87] In opposition to these views, Kemp Smith argues that "Philo, from start to finish, represents Hume"; he adds an important twist to this point of view, however, by stressing that Hume's teaching "is developed in and through the argument as a whole."[88] Breaking lines with the normal course of debate, James Noxon finds Hume so deeply agnostic as to make it impossible to identify with any position.[89] John Laird is a bit more decisive in his skepticism: for him, none of the speakers conclusively speak for Hume.[90] Clearly the interpretation of Hume's *Dialogues* has shifted around considerably. A similar shift appears on the question of whether or not Hume was religious, with most critics seeing him as anti-religious, some as agnostic, and a few suggesting he was at least more religious than most interpreters have been willing to grant.[91]

What are we to make of this conflict of interpretations? Why does it arise and why does it persist? There is, I suggest, a single cause with two sides which explains the shifting tides of interpretation given to the *Dialogues*. On the one hand, the variety of readings given to this text is attributable to Hume's own shifts and ironic doubleness. As I argued in the last section, the *Dialogues* enact Hume's project of being a skeptical yet irenic ironist working and writing in a dialogical manner. Precisely these four traits of Hume's method and style make him difficult to pin down to any specific position: (a) as a dialogical thinker Hume plays the ambassador *between* opposing worlds, seeking "to promote a good Correspondence betwixt" opposites; (b) as a skeptic he assigns himself "no fixed station or abiding city, which he is ever, on any occasion, obliged to defend," thereby dwelling *between* the shifting voices of theism; (c) as an ironist he coyly mimes the hypocrisy and duplicity of religious life, standing in the balance *between* philosophy and life, seeking thereby to speak in such a way that the ambiguities and nuances of religious language will refract simple or direct understanding; and

(d) as irenicist he seeks to expunge "all Raillery" from "philosophical argument," intent instead on cultivating the habit of "mutual deference and civility" *between* opposing factions. Because he stands in between, Hume finally cannot be pinned down to any set position. His philosophy rests on movement—a shifting back and forth—and the *Dialogues* enact this alteration. A partial explanation why the interpretation of this text has varied so much is that, historically, readings have been insensitive to this aspect of Hume's dialogical method and style.

On the other hand, Hume understood his audience very well. He recognized, in particular, that the shiftiness and duplicity in the religious world around him would condemn his own words to an ever-shifting reception. In this regard, the duplicity and shiftiness he portrayed in the *Dialogues* would reverberate with his readers. Duplicity and shiftiness would persist, with the *Dialogues* standing *in between*. By means of this text, Hume has not only reflected mimetically the shiftiness and duplicity inherent in theistic discourse, embedding this phenomenon in the rhetoric of the interlocutors' dialogue, he has also, and more importantly, cast this shiftiness and duplicity forward into the reception of this text. The text imitates it, and those who partake of it through interpretation repeat what the text imitates. Thereby, Hume's audience participates in the very phenomenon Hume sought to expose through the writing of the *Dialogues*. In accomplishing this, Hume shows not only literary craftsmanship, but a far-ranging sense of humor. He knew that faithfully intersecting theistic voices with the voice of a mitigated skeptic guaranteed that his text would be read in the same confusing (indeed, shifting and duplicitous) manner that took place in the discourse he experienced in life and used as his model for the *Dialogues*. His text reflects its all too human sources in the confusions of religious discourse, and simultaneously anticipates later readers' participation in these same realities. Perhaps this helps to explain the dying Hume's insistence and anxiety that his *Dialogues* be published—he understood (and must have relished) the powerful legacy his work would enjoy.

What Hume achieved through the *Dialogues Concerning Natural Religion*, therefore, has broad implications for understanding the workings of religious discourse. Through dialogue with Hume's *Dialogues*, those who choose to engage in discourse on religious questions come face to face with the ways in which their own efforts to speak about religion participate in the shifting and double-minded discourse which Hume imitated in the writing of his text. What they will see are all the rhetorical entanglements and discursive slides which make so much of religious discourse irrational. From the nature of the subject, talk about religion suffers the ambiguities of language, the shifting agenda and strategies taken up by representatives of different camps, and the duplicitous motives which characterize religious adherents. In such situations, understanding is precarious at best. Efforts to speak reasonably, to argue consistently, to understand clearly, or to know with certainty, though noble in themselves, break apart against the all too human propensity for ambiguity, indirection, dissimulation, hypocrisy, and dogmatism. Even one who makes these defects the focus of discussion will be affected. There seems to be no escape. Those who find themselves engaged in conversation with others on religious topics, whether by choice or from necessity, had best be mindful of the rhetorical entanglements they will encounter and the irrationalities that will come to color even their best efforts.

And yet there is a brighter side to dialogue with Hume's *Dialogues*. In particular, those engaged in discourse on religion might take a lesson from Hume's skeptical commitment to check religious shiftiness and duplicity in a manner both playfully ironic *and* gently irenic. On one hand, Hume shares with Diderot a critical agenda aimed at philosophical theism, popular superstition, and organized religion. The whole business of religion, Hume tells us, is "a riddle, an aenigma, an inexplicable mystery," which, when critically scrutinized, leads only to doubt and uncertainty. Like Diderot, Hume presents readers with a criticism of religion performed through the genre of dialogue. But in place of Diderot's experimental eclecticism stands Hume's ironic skepticism. Since even the critical voice will be caught up in the shiftiness and duplicity of religious discourse, it is necessary, as Hume counsels, to step back from the fray, marveling at the "fury and contention" carried on between the opposed "species of superstition," while making a quiet "escape into the calm, though obscure, regions of philosophy."[92] What Hume proposes, therefore is a different—"radically ironic"[93]—kind of shift: this alone provides a workable escape, even if it cannot cure human nature (and hence, most people) of the habits of superstitious belief. Irony is, as Hume shows us through his masterful deployment of the dialogue genre, the best antidote available for the ubiquitous duplicity and shiftiness in religious discourse.

On the other hand, Hume's critical irony points up the desirability of civil and irenic discourse about religion, something we will see more vividly in the dialogues of Erasmus. Hume shows his readers the value of skeptically challenging the pretensions and hypocrisies that infest religious life, but doing so with benevolent irony and respectful civility. "Mutual deference and civility," Hume counsels, are the keys to amiable and enlightened conversation.[94] Hume's skeptical irony strives to be civil, even as it rigorously examines and criticizes religious positions. Humean irony, consequently, has less bite to it than Diderot's Socratically-inspired satire. This is, to be sure, an aspect of Hume's philosophy of religion that has received far too little notice; it is also a dimension of discourse deserving more widespread imitation and practice. Certainly, when it comes to talk about religion, we might go a long way toward making religious discourse as peaceable and reasonable as possible if we followed Hume's admonition: "All Raillery ought to be avoided . . . in philosophical Argument, both because it is unphilosophical, and because it cannot but be offensive, let it be ever so gentle."[95]

Notes

[1] David Hume, "Of Commerce," *Essays; Moral, Political, and Literary*, ed. Eugene F. Miller (Indianapolis: Liberty Classics, 1985) 255–256.

[2] David Hume, *Dialogues Concerning Natural Religion*, ed. Norman Kemp Smith (Indianapolis: Bobbs-Merrill, 1947) I. 139. All references to Hume's *Dialogues* will give the section and page numbers from Kemp Smith's edition; because of their large number, I will embed these references in the flow of my text.

[3] A telling example of Warburton's hostility and raillery, he calls Hume "a puny Dialectician from the North . . . who came to the attack with a beggarly troop of routed sophisms." Ernest Campbell Mossner, *The Life of David Hume*, second edition (Oxford: Clarendon Press, 1980) 326.

[4] This is the concern, for instance, of *An Enquiry Concerning Human Understanding* (Chicago: Henry Regnery, 1965), section XI; as well as Hume's *Dialogues Concerning Natural Religion*, ed. by Norman Kemp Smith (Indianapolis: Bobbs-Merrill, 1947), parts I–XI.

[5] Hume pursues this interest in part XII of the *Dialogues*, and in essays like "Of Superstition and Enthusiasm," from David Hume, *Essays*, 73–79. See James Dye, "Hume on Curing Superstition," in *Hume Studies* 12/2 (November 1986) 122–140.

[6] A number of essays have called attention to the rhetorical patterns and interests in Hume's *Dialogues*. See, for instance, Michael Morrisroe, Jr., "Linguistic Analysis as Rhetorical Pattern in David Hume," W. B. Todd, ed., *Hume and the Enlightenment: Essays Presented to Ernest Campbell Mossner* (Edinburgh and Austin, 1974) 72–82. See also: Gary Shapiro, "The Man of Letters and the Author of Nature: Hume on Philosophical Discourse," *The Eighteenth Century* 26 (1985); Terrence W. Tilley: "Hume on God and Evil: *Dialogues* X and XI as Dramatic Conversation," *Journal of the American Academy of Religion* 55 (Winter 1988) 703–726; and more recently, William Lad Sessions, "A Dialogic Interpretation of Hume's *Dialogues*," *Hume Studies* 17 (April 1991) 15–39.

[7] What becomes a term of criticism for Cleanthes is simply a rhetorical method for Philo. On "invention" as rhetorical device, see Richard McKeon, "The Method of Rhetoric and Philosophy: Invention and Judgment," from McKeon, *Rhetoric: Essays in Invention and Discovery*, ed. by Mark Backman (Woodbridge, CN: Ox Bow Press, 1987) 56–65. In McKeon's words, "invention" is "the art of discovering new arguments and uncovering new things by argument. . . ." McKeon, *Rhetoric*, 59.

[8] Norman Kemp Smith suggests that Hume "presumably" meant to write "against all humanity" instead of "with all humanity." Hume, *Dialogues*, 187. He cites the ending to Hume's *The Natural History of Religion*, which speaks of escaping the "fury and contention" of religious views "into the calm, though obscure regions of philosophy." David Hume, *The Natural History of Religion*, (Standford: Standford University, 1957) 76. Apparently, Kemp Smith reads this escape as taking a stand against humanity. As I will argue in the third section of this paper, Kemp Smith's view overlooks the deeply humanistic tenor of Hume's skeptical aloofness, as well as the necessity he consistently acknowledges of re-

turning to the "beliefs" natural to human life. Hume's "offensive" is against superstitious systems, while his skeptical aloofness intends to facilitate a tolerant existence "with all mankind."

⁹ David Hume, "Of the Dignity or Meanness of Human Nature," *Essays*, 81.

¹⁰ Hume, "Of the Dignity or Meanness of Human Nature," *Essays*, 55–56.

¹¹ These two essays are to be found in Hume, *Essays*, 253–267 and 533–537 respectively.

¹² As David Tracy argues, Hume's venture in *The Natural History of Religion* "can be interpreted as an early comparativist analysis of the possible 'origins' of religion in human nature. . . . Hume fashioned, in this fascinating text, a kind of philosophically construed philosophical anthropology." Tracy, "On the Origins of Philosophy of Religion: The Need for a New Narrative of Its Founding," ed. Frank Reynolds and David Tracy, *Myth and Philosophy* (Albany: State University of New York, 1990) 18.

¹³ Jerome Christensen, *Practicing Enlightenment; Hume and the Formation of a Literary Career* (Madison: University of Wisconsin, 1987) 18.

¹⁴ David Hume, "Of Refinement in the Arts," *Essays*, 270.

¹⁵ David Hume, "Of Essay-Writing," *Essays*, 535.

¹⁶ Christensen, *Practicing Enlightenment*, 169.

¹⁷ Hume wrote two dialogues: *Dialogues Concerning Natural Religion*; and "A Dialogue," appended to David Hume, *An Inquiry Concerning the Principles of Morals*, ed. Charles W. Hendel (Indianapolis: Bobbs-Merrill, 1957) 141–158. Section XI of *An Enquiry Concerning Human Understanding*, published as "Of a Particular Providence and of a Future State" but originally titled "Of the Practical Consequences of Natural Theology," also is written in conversational form. See Kemp Smith's commentary in *Dialogues*, 51, footnote 1. Frequently, like Diderot, Hume also inserts small dialogues within other texts, as he does in the middle of *The Natural History of Religion*, between a Catholic "Sorbonnist" and a "priest of Sais"; and again, in the imaginary conversation with a theist and an atheist in *Dialogues* XII. 218.

¹⁸ M. A. Box, *The Suasive Art of David Hume* (Princeton: Princeton University, 1990) 51.

¹⁹ Hume, *An Enquiry Concerning Human Understanding*, 13.

²⁰ M. A. Box, *The Suasive Art of David Hume*, 52.

²¹ Hume, "On Refinement in the Arts," *Essays*, 271.

²² Christensen, *Practicing Enlightenment*, 25.

²³ All three passages from Hume are taken from Ernest C. Mossner, "Hume and the Legacy of the *Dialogues*," ed. G. P. Morice, *David Hume; Bicentenary Papers* (Edinburgh: Edinburgh University, 1977) 3–4.

²⁴ Box, *Suasive Art*, 61.

²⁵ David Hume, *New Letters of David Hume*, ed. Raymond Klibansky and Ernest C. Mossner (New York: Garland, 1983) 231.

²⁶ Hume, *Essays*, 73–79.

²⁷ Hume, *Natural History of Religion*, 46–48.

²⁸ Hume, *Natural History of Religion*, 60.

²⁹ Hume, *Natural History of Religion*, 76. Philo speaks in the same manner when he characterizes the happy state with respect to religious questions as "the calm and equable." (XII.226)

³⁰ As David Tracy puts it, "In Hume's ironic hands, the dialogue form is not an extended monologue nor a single argument but rather a sustained and implicitly *comparativist conversation* among genuine others." See David Tracy, "On the Origin of Philosophy of Religion: The Need for a New Narrative of its Founding," 17. In this regard Hume faithfully follows his classic source in Cicero's *The Nature of the Gods* (New York: Penguin, 1972). Cicero also collects and contrasts the rival philosophies (Epicurean, Stoic, and Academic) in dialogue form. See John Valdimir Price, "Sceptics in Cicero and Hume," *Journal of the History of Ideas* 25 (1964) 94–106. For a good discussion of Hume's use of the dialogue form, see Robert H. Hurlbutt, III, "The *Dialogues* as a Work of Art," in Hurlbutt, *Hume, Newton, and the Design Argument*, revised edition (Lincoln: University of Nebraska, 1985) 213–243.

³¹ David Hume, *The Letters of David Hume*, vol. 2, ed. J. Y. T. Greig (Oxford: Clarendon, 1932) 334.

³² John Valdimir Price, *The Ironic Hume* (Austin: University of Texas, 1965) 132.

³³ Mossner, *The Life of David Hume*, 6: "The sole function for Pamphilus is to provide cover for dissimulation." This includes, for Mossner, Pamphilus' statements on dialogue.

³⁴ Hume writes to Sir Gilbert Elliot, for instance, requesting help in strengthening the voice of Cleanthes. See Hume, *The Letters of David Hume*, 153–54; or the relevant passages amply quoted in Kemp Smith, *Dialogues*, 87–88. Hume's commitment to lending plausibility to his opponents receives sufficient evidence from the *Dialogues* themselves.

³⁵ See, for instance, William A. Parent, "An Interpretation of Hume's *Dialogues*," *Review of Metaphysics* 30 (Sept. 1976) 96–114.

³⁶ Hume, *An Enquiry Concerning Human Understanding*, 169.

³⁷ Hume, *An Enquiry Concerning Human Understanding*, 167; compare 40. Thus Hume says of the skeptic: "While others play, he wonders at their keenness and ardour; but he no sooner puts in his own stake, than he is commonly transported with the same passions, that

he had so much condemned, while he remained a simple spectator." See Hume, "The Sceptic," *Essays*, 176.

[38] David Hume, "The Sceptic," *Essays*, 172.

[39] Hume, "The Sceptic," *Essays*, 169.

[40] David Hume, "Of National Character," *Essays*, 199–200, footnote 3.

[41] Mossner, *The Life of David Hume*, 274. J. C. A. Gaskin calls Hume's note on the clergy "astonishingly tactless." See Gaskin, *Hume's Philosophy of Religion*, second edition (Atlantic Highlands, N.J.: Humanities Press International, 1988) 5. In Hume's defense, two points should be noticed: (a) Hume's criticism of the clergy is aimed at the profession not the person. Thus he acknowledges already in "Of National Characters" that "several individuals escape the contagion" linked with clerical life. See 201. (b) Hume's anti-clericalism is not something incidental. Rather, it echoes the long-standing suspicion of priests in English "free-thinking" literature. See J. A. I. Champion, *The Pillars of Priestcraft Shaken; The Church of England and its Enemies, 1660–1730* (Cambridge: Cambridge University, 1992).

[42] Hume, "Of Superstition and Enthusiasm," *Essays*, 75.

[43] Hume, "Of National Character," *Essays*, 200.

[44] David Hume, "Of Parties in General," *Essays*, 63 and 62. So too in "Of Superstition and Enthusiasm," Hume writes of the disastrous effects of priestly ambition: "Till at last the priest, having firmly established his authority, becomes the tyrant and disturber of human society, by his endless contentions, persecutions, and religious wars." See 78.

[45] Hume, "Of National Character," in *Essays*, 201. These same sentiments recur throughout Hume's *The History of England: From the Invasion of Julius Caesar to the Revolution of 1688* (Indianapolis: Liberty Classics, 1983–1985). For an excellent discussion touching upon Hume's critique of priestcraft in the history of England, see Donald T. Siebert, *The Moral Animus of David Hume* (Newark: University of Delaware, 1990) 62–135.

[46] Hume, *Natural History of Religion*, 21. See also 30, 35, 45, 92 and 94.

[47] Kemp Smith, ed., *Dialogues*, 25.

[48] Gaskin, *Hume's Philosophy of Religion*, 229.

[49] Price, *Ironic Hume*, 58.

[50] Price, *Ironic Hume*, 7.

[51] Price, *Ironic Hume*, 127, 146, and 127 respectively.

[52] Price, *Ironic Hume*, 130–31 and 26 respectively.

[53] Price, *Ironic Hume*, 139 and 140.

[54] Price, *Ironic Hume*, 141.

[55] Price, *Ironic Hume*, 131.

[56] Price, *Ironic Hume*, 130.

[57] Price, *Ironic Hume*, 31.

[58] Price, *Ironic Hume*, 146.

[59] Price, *Ironic Hume*, 145.

[60] See Mossner's *The Life of David Hume* for information on Hume's withholding of publications, especially chapter 10 on *A Treatise on Human Nature*; chapter 24 on Hume's "Four Dissertations"; and chapter 39 concerning the *Dialogues*. See also Kemp Smith, ed., *Dialogues*, 87–96, for the evidence on Hume's attitudes and reviews of the *Dialogues*. Numerous reasons are cited to explain Hume's willingness not to publish the *Dialogues* during his lifetime, including his desire to avoid persecution from religious enthusiasts, and his inclination by temperament not to incite the vulgar to controversy. Box also suggests that Hume's indirect style and restraint in publication stemmed from his fear that directness and publication might do harm to the fragile liberty of the press at the time. Box, *Suasive Art*, 210. On top of these reasons, Christensen points to "Hume's temporizing for the sake of sales." See Christensen, *Practicing Enlightenment*, 178.

[61] Price, *Ironic Hume*, 29.

[62] Price, *Ironic Hume*, 159 and 152 respectively.

[63] Price, *Ironic Hume*, 130–31.

[64] Kemp Smith, ed., *Dialogues*, vi.

[65] Richard White, "Hume's *Dialogues* and the Comedy of Religion," *Hume Studies* 14 (November 1988) 390–407.

[66] Price, *Ironic Hume*, 140 and 141.

[67] Price, *Ironic Hume*, 138 and 139 respectively.

[68] Robert H. Hurlbutt, III, "The Careless Skeptic—The 'Pamphilian' Ironies in Hume's *Dialogues*," *Hume Studies* 14 (November 1988) 231. Thus, Hume can speak of "an innocent dissimulation, or rather simulation, without which it is impossible to pass through the world." *The Letters of David Hume*, 440.

[69] Box, *Suasive Art*, 196.

70 Samuel Johnson, *A Dictionary of the English Language*, vol. 1 (Beirut: Librairie du Libon, 1978) 272–73. The same kind of analysis could apply to "stupid," where it does not refer to an ability level (idiotic or moronic), but to the state of stupefaction or thoughtlessness typical of everyday life.

71 Quotation taken from Mossner, *The Life of David Hume*, 259.

72 See Mossner, *The Life of David Hume*, 292–94.

73 Quotation taken from Mossner, *The Life of David Hume*, 295–96.

74 David Hume, "Of the Rise and Progress of the Arts and Sciences," *Essays*, 128.

75 David Hume, "Of the Rise and Progress of the Arts and Sciences," *Essays*, 126.

76 See, for instance, Hume's discussion of "the qualities agreeable to others" in *An Inquiry Concerning the Principle of Morals*, ed. Charles W. Hendel (Indianapolis: Bobbs-Merrill, 1957) 83–89. Here, as elsewhere, Hume emphasizes the importance of civility and mutual deference—qualities that allow "an easy stream of conversation [to be] maintained, without vehemence, without interruption, without eagerness for victory, and without any airs of superiority." See 84.

77 Hume, "Of Parties in General," *Essays*, 60–1.

78 Price, *Ironic Hume*, 66.

79 Kemp Smith, ed., *Dialogues*, vi.

80 Roland Hall, *Fifty Years of Hume Scholarship* (Edinburgh: Edinburgh University, 1978) 3.

81 Michael Morrisroe, Jr., "Linguistic Analysis," 72.

82 Hume, *The Letters of David Hume*, vol I, 57. See Gaskin, *Hume's Philosophy of Religion*, 244–245; note 14 for similar passages.

83 Quotation taken from Mossner, *The Life of David Hume*, 485.

84 Quotation taken from Mossner, *The Life of David Hume*, 566.

85 Quotation taken from Mossner, *The Life of David Hume*, 606.

86 B. M. Laing, *David Hume* (New York: Russell and Russell, 1968) 179.

87 C. W. Hendel, *Studies in the Philosophy of David Hume* (New York: Garland, 1983) 269–70. Still, Hendel gives nuance to his views by acknowledging that both Cleanthes and Philo "express his [Hume's] own thinking." See 271.

[88] Kemp Smith, ed., *Dialogues*, 59 and 58 respectively.

[89] James Noxon, "Hume's Agnosticism," ed. V. C. Chappell, *Hume; A Collection of Critical Essays* (Notre Dame: University of Notre Dame, 1966) 361–383.

[90] John Laird, *Hume's Philosophy of Human Nature* (Archon, 1932) 297. So also Terrence W. Tilley, "Hume on God and Evil," 719.

[91] The majority see Hume as anti-religious; James Noxon reads the Hume of the *Dialogues* as agnostic; while T. E. Jessop argues that Hume is misunderstood unless we acknowledge the real, albeit minimal, senses in which he continued to participate in the cultural life of religion. See T. E. Jessop, "The Misunderstood Hume," ed. William B. Todd, *Hume and the Enlightenment; Essays Presented to Ernest Campbell Mossner* (Edinburgh: University Press, 1974) 1–13.

[92] David Hume, *The Natural History of Religion*, 76.

[93] Tracy, "Origins of Philosophy of Religion," 17.

[94] Hume, "On the Rise and Progress of the Arts and Sciences," *Essays*, 126.

[95] Quotation taken from Mossner, *Life of David Hume*, 259.

5

When the Dead Speak: Lucian's Serio-Comic Dialogue and the Elision of Irony

"Dialogue and comedy were not entirely friendly and compatible from the beginning. Dialogue used to sit at home by himself. . . . Comedy gave herself to Dionysus and joined him in the theatre, had fun with him, jested and joked, sometimes stepping in time to the pipe and generally riding on anapaests. Dialogue's companions she mocked as 'Heavy-thinkers,' 'High-talkers,' and suchlike. . . . Dialogue however took his conversations very seriously, philosophising about nature and virtues. So, in musical terms, there were two octaves between them, from highest to lowest. Nevertheless I have dared to combine them as they are into a harmony, though they are not in the least docile and do not easily tolerate partnership."

Lucian in "To One Who Said 'You're a Prometheus in Words'"[1]

Toward the end of Plato's *Apology*, Socrates ponders the nature of death: is dying annihilation or is it a migration to another realm, where the dead from previous ages reside? He finds both possibilities attractive, but the latter especially captures his imagination. How marvelous it would be, he muses, to converse with the poets and sages of the past, or to encounter "heroes of the old days who met their death through an unfair trial, and to compare my fortunes with theirs—it would be rather amusing, I think." Amusing perhaps, but full of possibilities for intriguing conversation. Socrates, to the end, and beyond, would like nothing more than to spend his time "there, as here, in examining and searching peoples minds, to find out who is really wise among them, and who only thinks that he is." With an eye on his own imminent death, he adds whimsically: "At any rate I presume that they do not put one to death there for such conduct, because apart from the other happiness in which their world surpasses ours, they are now immortal for the rest of time, if what we are told is true."[2]

As it turns out, it makes no difference whether "what we are told" is true or not, for a genre of fictional writing—the dialogue of the dead—has made such otherworldly conversations possible.[3] Although Plato never followed up on this Socratic fantasy by casting his mentor in a dialogue among the dead, Socrates himself appears again and again in underworld conversations: his reputation for rigorous questioning is sometimes intact, while at other times the paradigmatic mocker of all pretensions to knowledge becomes the recipient of biting derision. Lucian, for instance, eulogizes Socrates by portraying him still wandering about "cross-questioning everyone" despite having swollen legs from drinking the hemlock; but in another Lucianic text, Socrates is exposed as a fraud, kicking and screaming as he resists death and the journey to the underworld.[4] In this genre, authors soon become characters for later authors: so we find Lucian conversing with Erasmus at the pen of Voltaire,[5] then all three gather again in an imaginary conversation constructed by Peter Gay.[6] Indeed, in the realm of the dead, the most unlikely speakers interact: philosophers of different stripes and from different ages meet; the powerful and the rich meet the forgotten and the poor of their own day; military leaders from different empires meet to compare reputations, as do famous prostitutes. The possibilities are limitless. Discourse is freed to roam where it will, far beyond the strictures of the living.

Socrates is correct: dialogues among the dead[7] are amusing. But they are also deadly serious, for they give expression to some extremely powerful and profound criticism. As a genre of dialogue, classical dialogues among the shades fashion a world of "serio-comic" discourse: that is, they create a fictional venue for serious laughing, where all sorts of human pretensions, vices and follies are leveled through ironic and comical critique. The Greek word "*spoudogeloios*" translates literally to mean "serious jester" or "serious laughter." In Mikhail Bakhtin's language, "serio-comic" characterizes those genre of literature in which "there is a weakening of . . . one-sided rhetorical seriousness, . . . rationality, [and] dogmatism," and at the same time, an "atmosphere of joyful relativity" (as in a carnival) where free-form imagination is not afraid to challenge reigning orthodoxies or to turn the familiar on its head to see what comes of it. Serio-comic figures (Socrates or Cynics like Menippus or Diogenes) and serio-comic texts (including dialogues of the dead) confront the realities with which we live in an adventurously dialectical manner, but they do so playfully and with a keen sense of irony. Serious matters become the object of dialectical critique, but the satirical blow is indirect, ironic, softened with a laugh. In this regard, serio-comic texts fully endorse Plato's statement that the one who is going to be prudent "can't learn the serious things without learning the laughable, or, for that matter, anything without its opposite."[8]

This chapter aims to tender a rhetoric of serio-comic discourse. To get a handle on the serio-comic and the part it plays in religious discourse, I will turn initially to the dialogues of the dead classically drafted by Lucian of Samasota in the second century, and then secondarily to later imitators of Lucian's dialogues. Through a reading of Lucian and his successors, I wish to advance three main points. First, these dialogues embody the voice of a dissident, even subversive reason, one ironically sensitive to the folly and baseness so common to human traditions, but also comically suspicious of the ways these vices receive legitimacy. What is important to see is the way that Lucian's art of dialogue is bound up with an ironic criticism of human existence. As will be shown, the venue for these dialogues (pitching conversation in a world marked by the finality of death) and the formal structures they enact (resulting in the blending of the serious and the comic) provide unique possibilities for exposing and criticizing human depravity and arrogance. A fresh, usually ironic understanding about the course of human life is thereby communicated to readers—but this can only be achieved by shifting discourse to the limits of normality and shattering conventional expectations. Fantasticality and comedy consequently promote wisdom through criticism. The first two sections will treat Lucian's serio-comic voice.

Lucian's serio-comic dialogues reveal an immediate connection to Hume's art of dialogue. Most significantly, Hume and Lucian share an ironic vantage on human affairs, which allows them to direct penetrating criticism at various forms of pretense and arrogance. Indeed, Lucian's dialogues—including the dialogues of the dead—provided Hume with a classic model for ironic criticism in dialogue form. Though he never composed dialogues of the dead, their importance for him clearly is signaled in the report by Adam Smith shortly before Hume's death. As Smith tells it, Hume manifested a "great cheerfulness" in the face of death, even to the point of imagining himself as a character in one of Lucian's dialogues. Having just read these dialogues, he tells Smith, he can think of no excuse to give Charon for not entering his boat destined for the underworld: "he had no house to finish, he had no daughter to provide for, he had no enemies upon whom he wished revenge," and so on. Nevertheless, in the spirit of Lucian, he proceeded to invent "several jocular excuses he supposed he might make to Charon, and with imagining the very surly answers which it might suit the character of Charon to return to them."

> I thought I might say to him, Good Charon, I have been correcting my works for a new edition. Allow me a little time, that I may see how the Public receives the alterations." But Charon would answer, "When you have seen the effect of these, you will be for making other alterations. There will be no end of such excuses; so, honest friend, please step into the boat." But I might still urge, "Have a little patience, good Charon, I have been endeavouring to open the eyes of the Public. If I live a few years longer, I may have the satisfaction of seeing the downfall of some of the prevailing systems of superstition." But Charon would then lose all temper and decency. "You loitering rogue, that will not happen these many hundred years. Do you fancy I will grant you a lease for so long a term? Get into the boat this instant, you lazy loitering rogue.[9]

As this story suggests, Hume recognized his debt to Lucian. He shared with Lucian a bent for ironically exposing the folly of human behavior (even his own), and he appreciated the light-hearted and outrageous format Lucian crafted for communicating such criticism, even though he tended away from the satiric tone that frequently appears in Lucian's dialogues. Just as Hume sought to stand above the fray of controversy to offer his skeptical observations, so too Lucian casts his serio-comic criticism in a world apart.

Second, though religious institutions and their functionaries would have us believe that religious matters are deadly serious, the comical—in particular, an ironical posture that fuses the comic with the serious—constitutes an important and widely recurring fiber of religious experience. Indeed, the ironist sensibilities embodied in a serio-comic genre like the classical dialogue of the dead enact dialectical patterns which typically recur in religious understandings of human life; consequently, there is reason to consider the irony of classical serio-comedy as a crucial possibility for religious discourse. Though religious institutions proceed in a largely serious vein, religious classics from various traditions (including Lucian's dissident Cynicism) offer their followers a rare but powerful blend of critical acuity and humorous civility. There are good reasons, therefore, to explore those genre of religious writing that sustain a serio-comic angle on life. This will be the focus of section three.

Third, later dialogues of the dead show a development away from the full-blown menippean tradition of serio-comedy. The serio-comic balance of humor and gravity proves too precarious and too demanding to maintain, and consequently unravels of its own weight. As the final section will show, some later dialogues of the dead pursue speculative questions, others have didactic purposes, and many thrive on invective. Although the genre remains the same in its basic outline, its serio-comic structures are eroded and ironist aims forgotten: menippean fantasy becomes serious; comic satire becomes invective; and indirection becomes direct and blunt. The history of the genre suggests a certain inevitability in these developments; in its very dialectical structure, it is vulnerable to and ultimately succumbs to more sober agenda. Because of the intimate connection of serio-comic genre and religion, the same elision of irony affects religious discourse. Though religious discourse perennially holds open the possibility of serio-comic perception, other interests that inhabit the religious world work to wrench religious eyes to more simple, less dialectical, views of life. The sedimentation of serio-comic criticism, I suggest, spells the demise of an important possibility for religious discourse.

(1) Serio-Comic Patterns

Before turning to examples of Lucian's dialogues, it might prove helpful to make an initial, formal sketch of the rhetorical dialectics of classical dialogues of the dead, trying thereby to isolate the conditions necessary for serio-comic perception. In the next section, I will examine the textual source for these rhetorical traits in Lucian's dialogues among the dead.

(a) As a genre, dialogues of the dead participate in the sentiments typical of Socratic dialogue. The most important aspect of Socratic texts for my purpose is their ability to combine irony with serious inquiry. In Mikhail Bakhtin's words, the dialogues of Socrates provide us with "laughter, Socratic irony, the entire system of Socratic degradations combined with a serious, lofty and for the first time truly free investigation of the world, of man and of human thought."[10] This blending of laughter and serious inquiry is no accident, for as Bakhtin makes clear, it is typical of Socratic dialogue to bring interlocutors (as well as the reader) into "a zone of direct and even crude contact," where anyone's claim to knowledge may be investigated "fearlessly and freely."[11] Discourse is brought low and close to the ordinary. On this level, no piety or certainty can escape the "comical operation of dismemberment" effected through Socratic interrogation.[12]

(b) Classical dialogues of the dead operate on the same plane, yet they are not purely Socratic. They also bear the distinguishing traits of "menippean satire," a genre of literature named for Menippus of Gadara, a Cynic of the third century B.C. Characterizing classic works like Petronius' *Satyricon*, the *Apocolocyntosis* of Seneca, several of Horace's satires, as well as most of Lucian's corpus, menippean satire combines what would appear to be "absolutely heterogeneous and incompatible elements: philosophical dialogue, adventure, fantasticality, slum naturalism, utopia, and so forth."[13] Frequently written in eclectic and mixed genre (e.g., "a potpourri of tales, songs, dialogues, orations, letters, lists"[14]), menippea deal with "naked ultimate questions" (usually of an ethical nature) not through extensive argumentation, but by provoking and testing such questions through fantastic adventures (e.g., ascent to heaven or descent to the nether world), extraordinary situations (e.g., travels through strange lands), or collisions with "worldly evil, depravity, baseness, and vulgarity in their most extreme expression."[15] The favorite concern of menippea is with sharp contrasts (luxury and poverty), "oxymoronic combinations" (the "virtuous hetaera"), and "abrupt transitions and shifts, ups and downs, rises and falls, unexpected comings together of distant and disunited things, mesalliances of all sorts."[16] Dialogues among the dead partake in all these menippean features, and as satires in this genre, they provide an important vehicle for the tradition of serio-comedy.

(c) An ironic posture fashions the serio-comic worlds typical of classical dialogues among the dead. This ironic stance depends upon two things held in dialectical tension. On one hand, discourse passes quite naturally. Characters from different centuries and from different places are brought together in a shared moment of conversation without affectation. In Bakhtin's words, they are "'contemporized': . . . brought low, represented on a plane equal with contemporary life, in an everyday environment, in the low language of contemporaneity."[17] On the other hand, of course, the nether world is clearly not "on a plane equal with contemporary life." They are not among the living. Their contemporaneity is fantastic. Discourse may be natural and unpretentious, but it nonetheless has been relocated to an ethereal plane of existence. The world of the dead is a different time and a different place. Geographic and generational boundaries are nullified and there is no return to the living, thereby creating a detached, distanced venue for conversation. This utopian relocation of discourse, counterposed with the ordinary and the natural tenor of the dialogue, sets the stage for an open and frank evaluation of the ways of the living—hence the importance of the judgment scene in these dialogues. In taking a critical look at human life, the ironist is detached and involved at the same time.

(d) The ironic method of serio-comic dialogue depends upon indirection. In dialogues among the dead, a living author speaks to living readers by way of the conversation of the dead. Such indirectness is key to the irony of these dialogues, for by couching criticism in a fantastic scene, contemporary reference is suggested, but still left in question—the author remains masked and the reader unsure how directly the comic blow was intended. Indirection thus serves to protect authors from violent repercussions, while sustaining the reader's uncertainty. To be sure, dialogues among the dead make critical statements, yet indirection (in varying degrees) keeps them from invective.

(e) Just as essential to serio-comic technique is the practice of dissimulation. In dialogues among the dead, authors willfully dissimulate: they dabble with famous persona and they rearrange customary appearances. The dead, after all, are highly malleable. Socrates can be *made* to say most anything and Thomas More can turn out to be quite other than he seems. From subtle shifts to complete reversals, dialogues of the dead entertain a playful experiment with appearances and realities. Such dissimulation pays rich dividends. Above all, it compels the reader to question appearances: are people who they say they are? are things as they seem? Dissimulation, therefore, can be revelatory insofar as its playful experimentation with appearances discloses something heretofore unnoticed. Yet there is a price for dissimulation; as Aristotle remarks, even the ironist with elegant manners (like Socrates) is a dissembler, and hence is potentially dangerous.[18]

(f) The most prominent outcome of classical dialogues among the dead involves the dialectic of the *alazon* and the *eiron*. The former is the proud one (who pretends to be more than he is), while the latter is the ironist (who pretends to be less than he is). In fine menippean fashion, dialogues of the dead work to undermine the self-serious, the arrogant, and the wealthy. At its most basic, the ironist exposes the *alazon*'s pretense to knowledge or moral self-righteousness through questioning (as in Socratic *elenchus*) or by letting the *alazon* incriminate himself through his own speech. In full dialectical form, however, there is a complete inversion of status (the master falls into servitude and the slave rises to prominence) or a reversal of fortunes (the rich become poor, and the destitute wealthy). In the ironic world of serio-comedy, realities belie appearances, certainties crumble into ambiguities, and standard hierarchies suffer inversion. Such dialectical inversions were the aim of classical Cynic discourse, and they are the main agenda of menippean dialogues of the dead.

With these tactics and structures in mind, I turn now to their classic expression in the dialogues of Lucian of Samasota.

(2) Cynicism and Menippean Humor

The dialogues of Lucian represent the classical locus for dialogues of the dead. A Syrian by birth, Lucian worked as a professional orator, and perhaps as a sophist, in Greece, Asia Minor, and Gaul during the reign of Hadrian, Antonius Pius, and the early years of Marcus Aurelius.[19] Though very little is known of Lucian's public career, his literary corpus manifests a witty and ironic mind at work, reflecting his affiliations with Cynic thought and his commitment to menippean genre. As he ranges through the traditions of the Roman world, he imitates while ironically twisting and comically experimenting with these very same traditions. His dialogues, in particular, abound with parody, burlesque, and satire, even as they treat serious topics and venerable traditions. It was this spirit and its rhetorical execution that made him so important throughout the centuries.[20]

Lucian is a master of the serio-comic. Indeed, he shows his methodological self-consciousness in this regard when he boasts that he is the first to combine serious dialogue with comedy. In "The Double Indictment," for instance, Lucian stages his own trial before the gods. Oratory accuses Lucian of maltreatment in their marriage, abandoning her for Dialogue; and Dialogue indicts him for blending such a dignified genre with "Jest and Satire and Cynicism. . . . At last he even dug up and thrust in upon me Menippus, a prehistoric dog, . . . a really dreadful dog who bites unexpectedly because he grins when he bites."[21] Lucian is acquitted of Oratory's charges, since Oratory has become a courtesan, courting the attention of the rabble. And he wins the case against Dialogue by pointing out how much he did for the genre.

> When I took him in hand, he was still dour, as most people thought, and had been reduced to a skeleton through continual questions. In that guise he seemed awe-inspiring, to be sure, but not in any way attractive or agreeable to the public. So first of all I got him into the way of walking on the ground like a human being; afterwards by washing off all his accumulated grime and forcing him to smile, I made him more agreeable to those who saw him: and on top of all that, I paired him with Comedy, and in this way too procured him great favour from his hearers, who formerly feared his prickles and avoided taking hold of him as if he were a sea-urchin.[22]

Throughout his dialogues, even the so-called "Platonic dialogues" (e.g., "Zeus Catechized"), Lucian trims the wings of classical dialogue, insisting that serious inquiry and comical laughter walk hand in hand.

As the deceased are escorted by Hermes to the underworld, they are met by Charon, the ferryman of the river Styx. Together, Hermes and Charon strip the dead of all they have, so as not to sink Charon's ferry. Menippus readily throws away his only possessions, and consequently is given the seat of honor. Others are not so lucky: a great beauty loses her lips, hair, skin, and cheeks; a tyrant loses his wealth, vanity, pride, diadem, and mantel; an athlete is stripped of his strong body; and the armor and prizes of a general are peeled away. A philosopher, it seems, has the most to take off: he loses not only his clothes but also his "ignorance, contentiousness, vanity, unanswerable puzzles, thorny argumentation, . . . idle talk, splitting of hairs," plus a host of vices. Comments Hermes: "If you came on board with all these, not even a battleship would be big enough for you."[23] The effect of this disrobing is humiliating, for each shade loses that which defined its existence in life. As Menippus puts it, "after stripping off all their quondam splendour—wealth, I mean, and lineage and sovereignty—they stood there naked, with hanging heads, reviewing, point by point, their happy life among us as if it had been a dream."[24]

The scene for Lucian's dialogues of the dead is the underworld of classical Greek mythology. Among the sites of Hades, the place of punishment is the most striking. It is also the most gruesome: "The sound of scourges could be heard, and therewithal the wails of the roasting on the fire; there were racks and pillories and wheels; Chimera tore and Cerberus ravened."[25] What Lucian seeks to stress, however, time and time again, is the complete equality of shades in this place of existence. When Menippus enters the Ascherusian Plain, he finds it difficult to tell the shades apart, "for all, without exception, become precisely alike when their bones are bare." The dead are indistinguishable, since "their bones [are] all alike, undefined, unlabelled, and unable ever again to be distinguished by anyone."[26] Even the great figures of Homer "lie unrecognizable and ugly, all so much dust and rubbish."[27] All are equal in this fantastic realm. The rich are indistinguishable from common people (except for their groans) and the beautiful are on a par with everyone else.[28] Only the poor cobbler willingly enters, for he knows that there "the tables are turned, for we paupers laugh while the rich are distressed and lament."[29]

Lucian's dialogues of the dead abound with searing but humorous lampoons. His targets include: (a) the wealthy and the greedy; (b) the powerful (especially generals and tyrants); (c) the physically beautiful; and (d) philosophers. Each shade is leveled with biting irony as it transits from life to death.

(a) Menippus taunts the wealthy as they lament the loss of their money and property. They foolishly hang on to their fame and fortune, building great monuments for their corpses, when in the end, the rich man too is "flung in a cubbyhole, inconspicuous among the rest of the plebeian dead, deriving only this much satisfaction from his monument, that he was heavy laden with such a great weight resting upon him."[30] Worse yet, the souls of the rich, "who plunder and oppress and in every way humiliate the poor," are condemned to be reincarnated in donkeys for two hundred and fifty thousand years, "transmigrating from donkey to donkey, bearing burdens, and being driven by the poor. . . ."[31] The greedy too, especially those who scheme to inherit a rich old man's wealth, are trapped in

Lucian's irony: the "would-be heir" dies before the rich man (an "amusing fate for the rascals to suffer"), or, better yet, the young man conniving for the old man's money dies first and the old man becomes his heir ("the fawn's caught the lion").[32]

(b) Generals and tyrants also are satirized in Lucian's dialogues of the dead. In "The Downward Journey," Cyniscus prosecutes the tyrant Megapenthes for practicing "every sort of savagery and high-handedness upon his miserable fellow-citizens." For his punishment, he alone does not drink the "water of Lethe," and is thereby condemned to suffer in his memories.[33] More generally, the gods of the afterlife condemn the folly of war. So Charon says, "How silly are the ways of unhappy mankind, with their kings, golden ingots, funeral rites and battles—but never a thought for Charon."[34] Special attention is given to the deification of Alexander. To such claims, Diogenes questions: "Aren't you ashamed, Alexander? Won't you learn to forget your pride, and know yourself, and realize you're now dead?"[35]

(c) In one dialogue of the dead, Menippus asks Hermes to show him the beautiful people of both sexes. When Hermes points out a few beauties from the past, Menippus complains: "I can only see bones and bare skulls, most of them looking the same." When shown Helen, he finds only a skull! Was it for this that the Greeks went to war? They clearly were unaware of the short-lived value of physical beauty.

(d) Singular attention is devoted to the ignorance and hypocrisy of philosophers. In "Philosophies for Sale," Lucian has staged an auction of philosophers, humiliating each with a low selling price for the so-called wisdom each has to offer. In a sequel, the dead philosophers of old come back to life to retaliate against him for such abuses. They accuse him of making a mockery of all that is most serious, and more importantly, of having "suborned Dialogue, our serving-man, employing him against us as a helper and a spokesman." Lucian (here called "Frankness, son of Truthful, son of Renowned Investigator") defends himself before Philosophy who acts as judge: he admits to being "a bluff-hater, cheat-hater, liar-hater, [and] vanity-hater," but also claims (surely with a smile) to be "a truth-lover," the devotee of true philosophy. Those who call themselves philosophers are impostors and hypocrites; they are more interested in money and fame than in truth and knowledge. After being acquitted of the charges, Lucian demonstrates his point by "fishing" for "philosophers," snagging his catch with fame and pleasure as his bait.[36]

Throughout these lampoons, Lucian exposes the folly and ignorance of human life. Death levels pretenses and topples the arrogant. Behind the satire, however, stands a sketch of the authentic life, usually embodied in one of Lucian's Cynic spokesmen. What Lucian's heroes do most is laugh. Menippus and Diogenes are "always laughing and generally mocking" the dead, tormenting them with songs ("a string of 'Know-Thyself's'"), and jeering at their lamentations.[37] Unlike most people, they face death nobly, "without having to be forced or pushed, but of [their] own accord, laughing and cursing at everyone."[38] When entering the after-life, it is Menippus alone who gets to keep his virtues, "independence, plain speaking, cheerfulness, noble bearing, and laughter."[39] These heroes are at once detached and forthcoming. They strive, above all, "to put the present to good use and to hasten on [their] way, laughing a great deal and taking nothing seriously."[40] Classically, these markings fit the Cynic (at least, Lucian's version of them); in my terms, they characterize the ironist. These figures generate the comic effect necessary for Lucian's serio-comedy.

Throughout the ages, Lucian's allies and enemies alike have interpreted his dialogues as satirically directed at his own contemporaries. More recent Lucianic scholarship is less certain. In a major work on Lucian, J. Bompaire sees Lucian as a stylist exclusively working with the literary traditions of the classical world. This interpretation has met with blistering criticism, especially from Barry Baldwin, who insists that Lucian be read with reference to topical issues of his own day.[41] As R. Bracht Branham points out, however, the choice between these two views of Lucian is a false one. A more likely reading acknowledges both Lucian's classicism and his concern with issues of interest to second century audiences. What makes Lucian interesting, in fact, is how he holds the two together, speaking *about* the gods and other figures of the past, but *to* contemporary listeners in a topical way. In "Menippus," for instance, Lucian speaks through the traditional commonplace of a philosophical quest, but by this means he offers "an ironic commentary on the contemporary thirst for metaphysical certainties." In Christopher Robinson's words, "tradition supplies the matter of dialogue, but contemporary reference provides its literary cohesion."[42] What is at stake in this conflict of interpretations is the nature of Lucianic serio-comedy, for only the mediating position allows for the delicate balancing of indirection and direct reference necessary to serio-comic irony. Without the classical casting, Lucian's dialogues become direct satire, possibly invective; but without contemporary reference, Lucian's comic play with tradition says nothing serious to an audience.

(3) Serio-Comedy and Religious Discourse

Dialogues of the dead treat an enormous range of subjects. Included in this scope are religious questions concerning the gods and the ends of human life. So too, many dialogues of the dead portray discourse directed satirically at religious beliefs or practices. However, whether or not these dialogues explicitly address religious topics, they frequently enact and embody recognizably religious sensibilities. As we have seen, serio-comedy transports the interlocutors (and hence the readers) to the limits of the expected and the ordinary, so that questions of common gravity can be examined wryly, with a comic twist. This move beyond the ordinary (literally, an act of transcendence) and the consequent ironic delight in ambiguity and inversion give the serio-comic a recognizably religious dimension. First, the imaginative transfer catapults discourse to the limits of ordinary expectations and assumptions, giving the interlocutors a taste of the gods' vantage on life. And second, this transfer proves revelatory, for the new perspective ironically uncovers the truth of things: from the limits of life, the characters see the futility of their presumptions, the shallowness of their certainties, and the injustice of their hierarchies. A serio-comic genre like the dialogue of the dead, therefore, achieves dialectically what is typically religious—an act of transcendence or encounter with final limits and a breakthrough from blindness to a new way of seeing worldly life. In method and message, the serio-comic bears a religious dimension.

This is not, however, to suggest that everything religious is serio-comic, since a great deal of religion strives to be solemn and grave; nor does it undermine the fact that many serio-comic pieces self-consciously take satiric aim at (serious) religious institutions and their practitioners. Much religion has no taste for serio-comic irony; and many ironists have no fondness for religion. Nevertheless, the dialectical achievement and the serio-comic message of classical dialogues of the dead do strike notes which typically recur in the history of religions. Indeed, there is no shortage of examples from the history of religions in which we are invited into a world of irony and encouraged to laugh about serious matters.

The "zany wit" of Zen Buddhism, for instance, insists on ironic humor and laughter as an instrument to break through the intellectual barriers that blind us from *satori*.[43] In a kindred spirit with Lucian, Zen stories take satirical aim at the most enlightened persons from the perspective of death:

> The usual posture for Zen monks to die in is sitting, that is, doing zazen, but the Third Patriarch, Seng Ts'an, died (in 606) standing with clasped hands. Chihhsien of Huanchi'i, died 905 A.D., asked his attendants, 'Who dies sitting?' They answered, 'A monk.' He said, 'Who dies standing?' They said, 'Enlightened monks.' He then walked around seven steps with his hand hanging down, and died. When Teng Yin-feng was about to die in front of the Diamond Cave at Wutai, he said to the people around him, 'I have seen monks die sitting and lying, but have any died standing?' 'Yes, some,' they replied. 'How about upside down?' 'Never seen such a thing!' It was decided to carry him to the burning-ground, but he still stood there without moving. People from afar and near gazed with astonishment at the scene. His younger sister, a nun, happened to be there, and grumbled at him, saying, 'When you were alive you took no notice of laws and customs, and even now you're dead you are making a nuisance of yourself!' She then prodded her brother with her finger and he fell down with a bang. Then they went off to the crematorium.[44]

Even the reputation of the enlightened ones, it seems, are toppled comically with death. It all amounts to a bang!

In a different vein, medieval Hindu myths characterizing the creative but blinding power of Visnu's *maya* comically undermine the pretensions to power of gods like Indra. One such tale portrays the mighty Indra, puffed up with his own sense of grandeur, demanding that an even more magnificent palace be built to fit his greatness. Indra's pride, however, is undercut by a small brahmin boy (alias Visnu), who notes that no other Indra has ever succeeded in building such an extensive residence. Indra is stunned: he is not the only Indra? The boy nods calmly: "Yes, indeed, many have I seen. . . ."

> Who will number the passing ages of the world, as they follow each other endlessly? . . . Who will count the Indras in them all—those Indras side by side, who reign at once in all the innumerable worlds; those others who passed away before them; or even the Indras who succeed each other in any given line, ascending to godly kingship, one by one, and, one by one, passing away? King of Gods, there are among your servants certain who maintain that it may be possible to number the grains of sand on earth and the drops of rain that fall from the sky, but no one will ever number all those Indras.[45]

When an army of ants passes, the boy identifies them as yet more Indras: "This army is an army of former Indras." To say the least, Indra (and his ego) are flattened. The boy can only laugh, as does the reader, to see such a mighty one brought low by the wisdom of the diminutive god.

A similar stripping of false pretension occurs in a Sufi story. When a certain student fails to understand the master's words, the master seizes the student's headdress, wraps it around his neck, and proceeds to half-strangle him. After the student is released, he stands shaken and confused, embarrassed without his proper headdress, red-hot with anger, yet not wanting to offend his master. The master only laughs, and in this moment the student discovers how great is his fear of humiliation. His own sense of propriety and self-respect have governed his life, and only an outrageous and comical gesture by the master can break through his self-seriousness. Here again, we see the *alazon-eiron* dialectic at work in a serio-comic manner.[46]

In the most ancient of Christian traditions, there are similarly strong currents of serio-comical composition. As Bakhtin points out, the "classical Christian dialogic syncrises" (dyads) of the tempted and the tempter, the believer and the nonbeliever, the righteous and the sinner, the beggar and the rich man, etc., as well as the "corresponding anacrises" ("provocations through discourse or plot situation") are familiar to literature developed "within the orbit of menippea." In Bakhtin's words,

> As in the menippea, rulers, rich men, thieves, beggars, hetaerae come together here on equal terms on a single, fundamentally dialogized plane. Here, as in the menippea, considerable importance is given to dream visions, insanity, obsessions of all

sorts. And finally, Christian narrative literature also absorbed into itself kindred genre: the symposium (the gospel meals), the soliloquy.[47]

Bakhtin does not point out, although it certainly would corroborate his suggestion, the centrality of ironic reversals of fortune in the various Jesus traditions, especially in the parables. Bakhtin is suggesting, therefore, that the traditions comprising Christian Scriptures were developed in the same cultural and literary orbit as menippean satire.

Some recent biblical scholarship lends support to Bakhtin's intriguing suggestion. An early work of Hans Dieter Betz, for instance, charts the astonishing number of formal and substantive parallels between Lucian and the New Testament.[48] More recent work on the social level of early Christianity, notably by Abraham Malherbe, suggests "a certain level of literary culture" among New Testament writers who would certainly be informed by the collections of sayings and proverbs from Greek and Roman literature.[49] As Malherbe points out, this cultural education of biblical authors would include some familiarity with the Cynics, "those philosophical street preachers who sought the moral reformation of the masses."[50] It is the Cynic, as Lucian reminds us, who carries the serio-comic.

In *A Myth of Innocence: Mark and Christian Origins*, Burton L. Mack corroborates Malherbe's proposals. For Mack, the social history of New Testament literature allows us to see Jesus more as a Cynic than as an eschatological prophet. In Mack's words,

> Jesus' use of parables, aphorisms, and clever rejoinders is very similar to the Cynic's way with words. Many of his themes are familiar Cynic themes. And his style of social criticism, diffident and vague, also agrees with the typical Cynic stance. . . . Jesus' wisdom was neither a Greek philosophical ethic nor a Jewish proverbial instruction, though flavoring from each is evident as one might expect at the end of the Hellenistic age. Jesus' wisdom incorporated the pungent invitation to insight and the daring to be different that characterized the Cynic approach to life.[51]

Mack supports this thesis with evidence from both the substance of Jesus' teaching (especially its moral purposes) and the form in which Jesus' pronouncements were recorded in the earliest biblical sources (especially the *chreia* or anecdote typical of Cynic teaching).[52]

For my purposes, these lines of biblical research are important because they alert us to the presence of serio-comic structures in some of the earliest strands of Christian tradition. At the very least, this research mandates that we take seriously the serio-comic dimension in the roots of the Christian religion. The comic parables, for instance, quintessentially embody the ironist perspective, the playfulness of the menippean spirit, and the serio-comic inversions so common in Hellenistic culture. The single dialogue among the dead in the canonical Gospels (The Parable of Lazarus and the Rich Man, *Luke 16:19–31*) has been muted by several redactions. Nonetheless, without the addition of verses 27–31, which use the dialogue to underscore the sufficiency of Mosaic and prophetic tradition and to point forward to the resurrection of Jesus, the original story and dialogue comically play with the beggar and the rich man's reversal of fortune. Thus says Abraham to the rich man's request for water: "Remember, my child, that you received your blessings during your life, while Lazarus had only misfortunes. Now he is comforted here, and you are in great pain." (vs. 25) Here, in rudimentary form, we see the *alazon-eiron* dialectic so common to menippean and Cynic traditions.

Christian serio-comedy endures through the centuries, although it most often is submerged beneath mainstream currents. The work of Erasmus of Rotterdam represents a classic expression of this spirit, particularly *The Praise of Folly*, and also his dialogues among the dead. In these dialogues, Erasmus not only makes a call for peace in the Europe of his day but turns to challenge those who cause and legitimate warfare. In "Charon," for instance, Erasmus calls attention to the "new epidemic, born of difference of opinion. It has so corrupted everybody's mind that sincere friendship exists nowhere. . . ."[53] No one trusts or listens to anyone else. Faction and discord abound. And to make matters worse, church leaders give religious legitimation to these hostilities:

> **Alastor:** They proclaim in their evangelical sermons that war is just, holy, and right. And—to make you marvel more at the audacity of the fellows—they proclaim the very same thing on both sides. To the French they preach that God is on the French side: he who has God to protect him cannot be conquered! To the English and Spanish they declare this war is not the Emperor's but God's: only let them show themselves valiant men and victory is certain! But if anyone *does* get killed, he doesn't perish utterly but flies straight up to heaven, armed just as he was.
>
> **Charon:** And people believe these fellows?
>
> **Alastor:** What can a pretense of religion not achieve? Youth, inexperience, thirst for glory, anger, and natural human inclination swallow this whole. People are easily imposed upon. And it's not hard to upset a cart that's ready to collapse of its own accord.[54]

In this little exchange we see an essential step in Erasmus' discourse on war: to expose and question the mechanisms of legitimation which serve to make war seem morally acceptable. Only rarely does an Erasmian speaker acknowledge the possibility that it might be "righteous to fight for wife and children, parents and friends, and for civil peace."[55] More often than not, however, Erasmus rejects religiously grounded attempts to justify war morally, as he does, for instance, in "Military Affairs": such explanations from the pulpit can never justify what really happens in war—"burning houses, looting churches, violating nuns, robbing poor people, murdering harmless ones."[56]

In "Julius Excluded from Heaven," to take a second example, Erasmus lampoons the recently deceased Pope Julius II, the so-called warrior pope. Blustering and arrogant, Julius appears at the gates of heaven, demanding of St. Peter that he be admitted immediately.

> **Julius:** Stop this nonsense, if you know what's good for you; for your information, I am Julius, the famous Ligurian; and, unless you've completely forgotten your alphabet, I'm sure you recognize these two letters, P.M.
> **Peter:** I suppose they stand for Pestis Maxima.
> **Genius:** Ha ha ha! Our soothsayer has hit the nail on the head!
> **Julius:** Of course not! Pontifex Maximus.
> **Peter:** Well you could be thrice Maximus and even greater than Mercuries Trismegistus [thrice-great Mercury], but can't come in here unless you're Optimus, and by that I mean holy.[57]

At the liminal point between life and death, this pompous pontiff is stood on his head and leveled though simple questioning. Julius is exposed as a fraud.

> **Peter:** . . . Were you eminent in theology?
> **Julius:** Certainly not: I hadn't time, I was too busy with my wars. But there are plenty of monks occupied with it, if that's any good to you.
> **Peter:** Well, did you win many souls for Christ by the saintliness of your life?
> **Genius:** He sent a good many to Tartarus.
> **Peter:** Were you famous for your miracles?
> **Julius:** This is all old-fashioned stuff.
> **Peter:** Did you pray simply and regularly?
> **Julius:** What's he jabbering about? Lot of nonsense![58]

And so it goes! The comic effect of Erasmus' piece pivots on the ironic contrast of a spiritual leader thoroughly involved in the most corrupt and vicious of earthly enterprises, and the ultimate irony of a pope excluded from heaven. Erasmus comes dangerously close to invective in this dialogue, but the comic indirection of its setting and Julius' ironic self-incrimination maintains a comic tone throughout. Comic though it may be, however, Erasmus here offers his readers a powerful (and serious) critique of the papacy of his day.[59]

At the very least, these few examples show the presence of serio-comic perceptions in the history of religions. They also suggest, more importantly, that serio-comic irony is vital to the religious sensibilities of these various traditions. This is the main point: religion is not purely serious. At crucial points in the various traditions, the religious imagination seeks mythically (even outrageously) to look at things from a fantastically transcendent perspective, from which to relish and laugh at the ambiguities, the self-deceptions, and the inversions of human life. In each of these traditions, an ironic sense of humor about the most serious of questions proves central to authentic experience of the world. In these various worlds, religion is not purely serious. Something essential would be lost to Zen Buddhism without the topsy-turvy humor aimed even at the most enlightened monk; the Hindu sense of *maya* and the power of Visnu would be diminished without that ironic blend of cosmic gravity and simple humor with which Indra is leveled; and the Sufi celebration of law and discipline would be misinterpreted aside from the risque (even Zen-like) humor hurled at the self-serious student. Similarly, something essential to Christianity is lacking when the simple reversals from Jesus' parables or the humorous barbs of Erasmus' colloquies give way to dogmatic or legal seriousness. At the very least, religionists should be cognizant of the necessary place filled by serio-comic perceptions. Indeed, the absence of serio-comedy in some traditions is not an argument against this point, but simply a sign that the dialectics required for serio-comic irony have given way or been submerged by non-ironic agenda. The final section of this chapter turns to this occurrence.

(4) The Elision of Irony

The history of this dialogical genre after Lucian is rich and varied, but it also illustrates the form's fragility and vulnerability. Though there are notable examples of the survival of the Lucianic spirit and serio-comic structures, most later dialogues among the dead turn away from the Lucianic tradition. The outward form of the genre persists, but it is transformed in four key ways: (a) the balance of the serious and the comical tilts toward the serious; (b) the satiric indirection of serio-comic dialogues becomes increasingly direct; (c) the setting for down to earth conversation becomes less and less fantastic; and (d) the ironist dialectic of the *alazon* and the *eiron* gradually disappears. These same developments affect dialogues among the dead which deal with religious issues. Speculation, didacticism, and invective turn this genre away from the classically serio-comical commitments embodied in so many religious traditions. In the process, the fantastic is played down to accommodate immediate practical concerns; the serio-comical balance becomes more reflective and ardent; and the indirection so integral to irony is replaced by direct statement. In this section I will look at these three lines of development in the dialogue of the dead, in each case highlighting the ways in which the form's four, key dialectic structures are transformed.

(a) *The Speculative Turn.* In many ways, those authors who use the dialogue among the dead to pursue serious philosophical issues continue to maintain its serio-comic structures. George Santayana's *Dialogues in Limbo*, for instance, has all the markings of serious Platonic inquiry, yet the dialogues are laced with humor, as when four classical interlocutors seriously argue whether philosophies carry distinctive scents.[60] The dialogues of Bernard Le Bovier de Fontenelle, the seventeenth century French master of dialogue, also bear a serio-comic touch. In his dialogue between Charles V and Erasmus, for instance, we find Erasmus questioning Charles' claim to greatness, since Charles' glory is the result of chance and inheritance, not personal merit. With a Lucianic flavor, however, Charles proceeds to turn the tables. Erasmus' pride in his knowledge is shown to be vain, since his intelligence is also the result of luck: "is there less luck in being born with a respectable cerebrum than being born son to a king?"[61] And, in another Fontenelle dialogue, Descartes lambasts the third false Demetrius for his ridiculous attempt to become Czar, when two such previous attempts have failed. Descartes' pride in his philosophical achievement, however, is subverted when the false Demetrius points out how many philosophical pretenders to wisdom preceded Descartes. "I was but the third in my kind, . . . but you were more than a thousand deep in the list of those who understood to practice upon the faith of mankind."[62] These dialogues focus on the odd juxtaposition of characters in order to draw out a speculative point about luck and vanity. But in doing so, they also capitalize on the comic effect of the *alazon-eiron* dialectic.

Already in Fontenelle, however, a speculative interest comes to the fore. At times this amounts to nothing more than pursuing a moral lesson, usually stated outright at the end. In many dialogues, however, Fontenelle takes a serious interest in the dialectics of serio-comedy itself. The dialogue between Strato (an Aristotelian philosopher and tutor to the king of Egypt) and Raphael of Urbino (representing the practical artist) illustrates this well. While Strato sensibly defends the rule of reason, Raphael argues most persuasively for the importance of prejudices. "These prejudices are reason's supplement. All that is lacking on one side can be got out of the other."[63] Through this ironic complementarity of reason and prejudice, Fontenelle forwards a serious philosophical point, and his point is not simply a defense of prejudice but an observation on the larger truth born of the dialectic of reason and prejudice. In comically juxtaposing reason and prejudice, and in maintaining their tension against "reasonable" expectations that reason would prevail, Fontenelle transcends serio-comic critique of rationalism and makes a more profound (and serious) point about the serio-comic relation of reason and prejudice. In a word, Fontenelle here becomes serious about the serio-comic.

Fontenelle is a master of juxtaposition and dialectic. Known for his early contribution to the battle of the ancients and the moderns, he alternatively experiments with criticism of each. In a dialogue between the shades of two physicians (Erasistratus the ancient and Harvey the modern), Fontenelle calls into question the self-aggrandizing posture of modern physicians.[64] Then again, in his most famous dialogue, a cross-cultural conversation between Cortez and Montezuma,[65] he has Cortez boast of European superiority and blast the primitive superstitions of the Indians; Montezuma counters by noting that the much heralded Athenians were even more superstitious. In Montezuma's eyes, it is a shame the Indians lacked ocean-going ships, for then they could have exercised their right to conquer the Europeans instead of being conquered. The dialogue ends in a draw, but the effect is to foil the self-importance of modern Europeans. Fontenelle, however, checks both moderns *and* ancients in the dialogue between Socrates and Montaigne. Socrates is confident that people became wiser in later centuries; Montaigne laments the fact that they are "madder and more corrupt than ever before."[66] But Fontenelle holds each assertion in check; neither ancient nor modern is superior. There is at best an "imperceptible inequality" of reason in different ages. Here again, in these three dialogues, we see Fontenelle seriously speculating over serio-comic dialectics. His concern is not the superiority of either party, but the dialectic of expected modern superiority (the serious) and the unexpected worth of the ancients (the comic). For Fontenelle, the serio-comic dialectic is a serious, speculative issue.[67]

Matthew Prior, the eighteenth century British poet, provides a good example of the speculative turn in dialogues of the dead dealing with religious issues. The dialogue opens with the Vicar of Bray greeting his former patron, the recently martyred Thomas More. With Lucianic flavor, the vicar tells More: "I saw you Executed. Oh! that ugly seam, Sir, that remains still about your Neck. Oh Sir a head sewed on again never sits well. I pittyed You, Sir, I prayed for you."[68] The vicar, it turns out, is fully unprincipled (having continued in his Catholic vicarage though obeying Parliament's rejection of popery), while More is the paragon of principle, even after death. In their vastly different styles (the vicar vulgar but full of life, and More decorous and formal but quite stiff), they proceed to examine each other's choices in life. The Vicar defends his actions for survival: "We were not all Born to be Martyrs any more than Lord Mayors." A simple man, he finds it "very strange that with all [More's] Law and Learning you should not have had wit enough to keep your head upon your shoulders."[69] At first More is self-confident in his superiority, but as the dialogue proceeds, it is the wise More who begins to look foolish! More possessed great principles, but he lacked the practical vices which belong to the "great Majority of Mankind."[70] In the end, More becomes dogmatic and angry with the Vicar. His principles (and hence his death) prove irrelevant to the ordinary person like the Vicar.

What we see in this dialogue is the classic dialectic of the *alazon* and the *eiron*, replete with comic reversal. However, as Frederick Keener points out, "neither the vicar nor More is Prior's hero," for More in the end seems "as much a victim of his scrupulous conscience as the vicar was the pawn of his own passion for survival."[71] Indeed, as Fontenelle did in his speculative dialogues of the dead, Prior too leaves us with a tense but comic juxtaposition, in this case between a principled and an unprincipled life. Like Fontenelle, Prior confronts his readers with a serious observation about a serio-comic tension endemic to human life. Prior, too, becomes serious about the serio-comic.

(b) *The Urge to Educate.* To some degree all dialogues among the dead seek to teach an audience. Many times, however, didactic agenda reign, and, consequently, the genre is transformed. The dialogues of George Lyttleton, written in the 1760's, illustrate this unquestionably non-Lucianic use of the dialogue of the dead. In the words of Lyttleton's biographer, these dialogues are "rather too grave to be quite Lucianic, too polite to be merry, and too wise to be entertaining."[72] For the most part, Lyttleton's dialogues lose any semblance of the serio-comic. In Dialogue III, for instance, Plato and Fenelon (an earlier, French writer of didactic dialogues of the dead) flatter each other's wisdom and literary style. Showing his distaste for the serio-comic, Lyttleton has Plato say of Fenelon's dialogues: "Your Dialogues breathe the spirit of Virtue, of unaffected Good Sense, of just Criticism, of fine Taste. They are in general as superior to your Countryman Fontenelle's, as Reason is to False Wit, or Truth to Affection." For Fenelon (and hence for Lyttleton), it is the truth of "Common-place Morals" which matters, and for pedagogical reasons, its delivery must be simple, direct, and understandable. The two interlocutors conclude that it is better to rely on "cool Reason and sober Truth" than on sentiment.[73] Didacticism cannot tolerate too much sentiment, too much play, or too much humor.

Lyttleton's use of the dialogue of the dead is serious and conservative. In Dialogue XXII, for instance, Lucian and Rabelais meet and appraise each other's work. Throughout the dialogue, they praise each other's noble use of ridicule to undercut errors and pretensions. But in the end, Lyttleton can only go so far with these two great menippeans. Thus he has Lucian lament the fact that he and Rabelais did not also use their wit to "combat the Flippancy and Pertness of Those, who argue only by Jest against Reason and Evidence, in Points of the highest and most serious Concern."[74] If they had put their wit and humor to defend truly serious matters, then they would have truly received the acclamation of all ages. The comic, it seems, has its place, but only within the pale of the serious. In a similar vein, Lyttleton devotes most of his dialogues to culturally and politically conservative ends. For such purposes, the setting among the dead serves not to heighten irony and question the proud or self-serious, but to put a stamp of finality on the lessons taught. The finality of death becomes the finality of the truth taught, and most often this is a lesson of virtue, patriotism, and reasonableness. In Lyttleton's hands, therefore, the dialogue of the dead has shifted from a vehicle for serio-comic questioning to an amusing means to teach moral or political lessons.[75]

Religious dialogues among the dead also become didactic. Usually this means taking up apologetic strategies to correct errant thinking and to educate readers in the ways of orthodoxy. A contemporary piece, *Between Heaven and Hell; a Dialog Somewhere Beyond Death,*[76] illustrates this apologetic use of the dialogue among the dead. In this dialogue, the shades of C. S. Lewis (the reasonable, orthodox Christian) discusses the divinity of Christ with John F. Kennedy (the modernist, humanist) and Aldous Huxley (the radical, interreligious ecumenist). The discussion proceeds in a civilized and friendly tone, with C. S. Lewis pursuing rational "proof" of Jesus' divinity against these two adversaries. Though

Kennedy and Huxley are characters of strength, they cannot stand up to the force of Lewis' arguments. Huxley's "gnostic Jesus" who is a great teacher among many others and Kennedy's human Jesus fade in the face of Lewis' orthodox Christ. The dialogue ends in a blend of rationalism and dramatic mysticism. Huxley concludes that "we must follow the argument in order to follow the truth, and we must follow the truth in order to follow the light." All then agree in their "love of the light," when suddenly Kennedy exclaims:

> "Look! The light! It is coming!
> **Huxley:** "We must follow it. . . . Oh! It's too bright. I never realized how hard it is to follow it. It's like the rising sun."
> **Kennedy:** "No, it's . . . it's . . ."
> **Lewis:** "It's the Rising Son. He is coming!
> **The Light:** "Are you coming?"

With this spectacular ending, Lewis' labored argument is confirmed with a mystical flurry. Though this entire dialogue is comical (or rather, farcical), it nonetheless is deadly serious. The spectacular ending serves to ensure the entire dialogue's agenda, namely, to teach the likes of Kennedy and Huxley the truth about the orthodox Christ—and that is serious business.

(c) *The Lure of Invective.* This genre carries with it great potential for criticism. Frequently, however, the comical lampoons typical of Lucian give way to invective. At its extreme, such rhetoric bristles with scorn and ridicule. The dialogue of the dead can be taken in this direction, where the intention is to commit an opponent (deceased or living!) to hellfire. It makes all the difference, of course, whether the victim is living or dead, and for polemical purposes it clearly is tempting to use the convenient setting of Hades to fry a living adversary.[77] The same polemical ends are more frequently expressed in blistering diatribe. As the place of final judgment, the dialogue of the dead offers a unique opportunity for final, negative judgment. Such rhetoric abounds in pamphlet dialogues of the seventeenth and eighteenth century.

At its best, however, the power of invective remains satirical. As David Worcester points out, invective satire "pulls the punch" through techniques of indirection. In Worcester's words, "gross invective, or abuse, is distinguished from satiric invective by direct, intense sincerity of expression. Satiric invective shows detachment, indirection, and complexity in the author's mind."[78] The needed indirection is oftentimes supplied by the outrageous quality of the language used. As Worcester puts it, "The virulence lessens in proportion as the language grows bombastic, exotic, or sesquipedalian."[79] The same effect results from the fantastic quality of the setting. Thus, for example, in "A Dialogue between Moses, Diogenes and Mr. Loke," by Lytton Strachey (but falsely attributed to Voltaire),[80]

Moses is assaulted by Diogenes and Locke for deceit and lies, yet the verbal attack is humorous precisely because of its extravagant rhetoric; the fact that the interlocutors are Diogenes and Locke also takes away the sting. And yet satiric invective does not want too much indirection. It seeks, in fact, to flatten a target as much with attack as with laughter. Thus we find Nicolas Boileau-Despreaux parading romantic novelists of his day across the stage of scrutiny, one after the other being interrogated and humiliated.[81] This text is reminiscent of Lucian's "Philosophers for Sale," but whereas Lucian is chopping at stock types, Boileau aims at specific people. Lucian's aim is comical; Boileau's is polemical. The difference is crucial, for whereas dialogues of invective satire can be funny, their business is serious and their methods decidedly direct. There is little room for serio-comic irony when this genre is turned to the ends of invective.

So too, this genre can be put to the ends of religious invective. "News from Heaven: A Dialogue between S. Peter and the Five Jesuits Last Hang'd" is a perfect example.[82] This little pamphlet was written to denigrate the memory of five Jesuit priests executed for their involvement in the "popish plot" of seventeenth century England. As with Erasmus' dialogue at the gates of heaven, so too here, the five Jesuits recently hung and quartered show up for admittance to heaven and are interrogated by St. Peter. When they produce their "recommendations" from the "Vicar of Christ, thy successor at Rome," St. Peter denies having given any authority to such men: "Y'are a company of Lying Rascals, and deserve to have your Ears cut off. . ." (2). St. Peter rejects altogether their appeal to papal authority: "I tell ye once again, I have no such Vicar as you talk of; and he has deceived both himself and you too" (2). Neither is there any evidence of Loyola, Francis, or Dominic on the register of saints. When the Jesuits complain that all these men were canonized through elaborate ceremony in Rome, St. Peter can only exclaim: "Lord! how the Affairs of the Church are alter'd since I liv'd upon the Earth: there was no such thing in my time" (3). In desperation, one of the Jesuits once again cites the authority of recent popes. St. Peter vaguely remembers some of these men, "but not one that I could think worthy of Admittance never since Constantine's time" (4). A famous bishop came for admission once, but the good souls he persecuted "kick'd him with his heels upward into Hell, where he fell with his Head between Lucifer's Thighs, to the great amazement of the old Gentleman" (4). Having had enough of this exchange, St. Peter tells them to be off, "else I must be forc'd to call for Martin Luther, and then ye know what will become of you" (4). After Peter retires, Radamanthus (the judge of the classical underworld, now in charge of Purgatory) whips them into Purgatory, ordering the Executioner to lash them and "then to shut them up in a smoaky hole for sixty millions of Platonic Years" (4). A text like this has but one purpose, to castigate its opponents with fire and scorn. The fact that this dialogue occurs among the dead adds to the direct invective, for now these men can be tried, condemned, executed, and punished a second time, no more than a month after their real execution!

In sum, the history of this genre shows an unmistakable drift away from the serio-comic spirit embedded in Lucianic dialogue. In its later development, the dialogue among the dead becomes more serious, more direct, more mundane, and less ironic. Why is this?

I suggest that the dialectics which comprise the serio-comic or ironist stance are inherently tense and fragile; and that, consequently, the delicate balance they require for success is difficult, even impossible, to maintain with any kind of permanence. It is a rare, tenuous, and short-lived form of discourse. As a result, writers of dialogues among the dead are attracted to certain features that the genre has to offer: the philosopher, to the dialectic itself; the educator, to the conservative finality of the genre; and the polemicist, to the genre's power of criticism. When one of these interests is pursued, the serio-comic unravels. While the genre may remain the same, it is only its outer shell, for the full dialectical constitution of the serio-comic has been diverted toward new ends.

Serio-comic criticism also is dangerous. It invites its listeners to live at the limits of the ordinary; it stands accepted customs and sacred traditions on their head; it revels in dissimulation, indirection and laughter; and it challenges every serious convention or standard that makes life stable and dependable. In all of these ways it is subversive and anarchic. Even the polemicist (or the prophet in Jewish and Christian traditions) will be frustrated by serio-comic discourse, for it typically pulls the punch, trusting the power of laughter over that of invective. It claims, in all of this, a measure of independence too demanding for the ordinary person and too threatening to institutions. The simple exposure of the *alazon*'s pretensions to greatness—whether in Jesus' parables or Lucian's dialogues–exerts an immediate and compelling claim to attention, but it is another matter altogether to take up such discourse personally. Laughing at the folly of the powerful takes courage, as does the readiness to laugh at our own hypocrisy. How many have the nerve to laugh at a tyrant? Which of us is so free as to laugh at our own follies? More gravely, who has the stomach to pitch discourse gleefully among the dead? And on the institutional level, what organization or government consistently can tolerate the ironic dissonance typical of menippean criticism? History is replete with cases of such intolerance; it is deemed safer to marginalize serio-comic critique, whether through censure or execution. Religious institutions commonly do both.

In doing so, however, something essential to religious discourse is lost. If religion loses its sense for the fantastic, if it domesticates its ironic perspective on the ambiguities and follies which typify human life, if it abdicates its sense of humorous critique, then it has squandered one of its classic possibilities. Since religious traditions regularly *do* abjure this form of discourse, they becomes sources of convention and order. There, religious language proves conservative and comforting, and the classic voices of serio-comic irony remain buried. Their recovery remains a permanent imperative, but a formidable challenge, and necessarily a tenuous achievement. Such a retrieval requires an imaginative leap from the security of custom to the dangerous, classic genre of serio-comic criticism. One way to make this leap would be to listen more attentively when the dead speak.

Notes

[1] Lucian, "To One Who Said, 'You're a Prometheus in Words,'" *Lucian*, vol. 6, trans. K. Kilburn (Cambridge, Massachusetts: Harvard, 1959) 425–427.

[2] Plato, "Apology," 40c–41c. *The Collected Dialogues of Plato*, ed. Edith Hamilton and Huntington Cairns (Princeton: Princeton University, 1961).

[3] An anonymous eighteenth century dialogue of the dead plays ironically with the truth-value of these fictional conversations. An atheist criticizes Charon (ferryman to the underworld) for working so hard and fretting over his task, when "all the while thou art doing nothing; for there is no such thing" as an immortal soul. *Dialogues of the Living and the Dead: in Imitation of Lucian and the French* (London, 1701) 24. The irony, of course, is that the truth of the atheist's point is quite sufficient whether or not there is a soul.

[4] Lucian, "Menippus," *Lucian*, vol. 4, trans. A. M. Harmon (London: William Heinemann, 1969) 103; and Lucian, "Dialogues of the Dead," *Lucian*, vol. 7, trans. M. D. Macleod (Cambridge: Harvard University, 1961) number 4, 19–21.

[5] Voltaire, "Conversation of Lucian, Erasmus and Rabelais," *Candide and Other Writings*, ed. Haskell M. Block (New York: Modern Library, 1956) 465–69.

[6] Peter Gay, *The Bridge of Criticism; Dialogues among Lucian, Erasmus, and Voltaire on the Enlightenment* (New York: Harper and Row, 1970).

[7] I say "dialogue among the dead," rather than the more conventional "dialogue of the dead," because I wish to include dialogues between living and dead speakers, as well as dialogues between the gods of the underworld, the living, and the dead. Though technically not "dialogues of the dead," these closely related forms share the same structures and achieve the same ends.

[8] Plato, *Laws*, 7: 816 d–e. *The Laws of Plato*, trans. Thomas L. Pangle (Chicago: University of Chicago, 1980) 208.

[9] "Letter from Adam Smith, LL.D. to William Strahan, Esq.," David Hume, *Essays; Moral, Political, and Literary* (Indianapolis: Liberty, 1985) xlv–xlvi.

[10] M. M. Bakhtin, *The Dialogic Imagination* (Austin: University of Texas, 1981) 25.

[11] Bakhtin, *The Dialogic Imagination*, 22–23 and 25.

[12] Bakhtin, *The Dialogic Imagination*, 24. For Bakhtin's theory of the "carnivalistic base of Socratic dialogue," see Mikhail Bakhtin, *Problems of Dostoevsky's Poetics*, ed. and trans. Caryl Emerson (Minneapolis: University of Minnesota, 1984) 109–133.

[13] Bakhtin, *Dostoevsky's Poetics*, 134. For an annotated compendium of menippean works and critical studies of menippea up to 1660, see Eugene P. Kirk, *Menippean Satire; An Annotated Catalogue of Texts and Criticism* (New York: Garland Publishing, 1980).

[14] Kirk, *Menippean Satire*, xi.

[15] Bakhtin, *Dostoevsky's Poetics*, 114–115.

[16] Bakhtin, *Dostoevsky's Poetics*, 118. Bakhtin's larger thesis regards menippea (as well as Socratic dialogue) as expressing a "carnivalistic" spirit: "the clamping principle that bound all these heterogeneous elements into the organic whole of a genre, a principle of extraordinary strength and tenacity, was carnival and carnival sense of the world." See Bakhtin, *Dostoevsky's Poetics*, 122–134.

[17] Bakhtin, *The Dialogic Imagination*, 21.

[18] Aristotle, *Nicomachean Ethics*, 4: 7. *The Basic Works of Aristotle*, ed. Richard McKeon (New York: Random House, 1941).

[19] On Lucian's life, see Christopher Robinson, *Lucian and His Influence in Europe* (London: Duckworth, 1979); on the question of whether or not Lucian was a "sophist," see Barry Baldwin, *Studies in Lucian* (Toronto: Hakkert, 1973) 18 and following.

[20] On Lucian's influence, see Christopher Robinson, *Lucian and His Influence in Europe* (London: Duckworth, 1979).

[21] Lucian, "The Double Indictment," *Lucian*, vol. 3, trans. A.M. Harmon (Cambridge, Mass.: Harvard University, 1921) 147

[22] Lucian, "The Double Indictment," *Lucian*, vol. 3, 149. See also "To the One who said 'You're a Prometheus in Words,'" 425–427, where Lucian defends his innovative mating of dialogue and comedy.

[23] Lucian, "Dialogues of the Dead," *Lucian*, vol. 7, number 20, 111.

[24] Lucian, "Menippus," *Lucian*, vol. 4, 93.

[25] Lucian, "Menippus," *Lucian*, vol. 4, 95.

[26] Lucian, "Menippus," *Lucian*, vol. 4, 97–99.

[27] Lucian, "Dialogues of the Dead," *Lucian*, vol. 7, number 6, 27.

[28] Lucian, "Dialogues of the Dead," *Lucian*, vol. 7, number 1; number 3 on the rich; on the beautiful, see "Dialogues of the Dead," *Lucian*, vol. 7, numbers 5 and 30.

[29] Lucian, "Downward Journey," *Lucian*, vol. 2, trans. A. M. Harmon (Cambridge, Mass.: Harvard University, 1988) 33.

[30] Lucian, "Menippus," *Lucian*, vol. 4, 101–103.

[31] Lucian, "Menippus," *Lucian*, vol. 4, 107.

[32] Lucian, "Dialogues of the Dead," *Lucian*, vol. 7, numbers 16 and 18 respectively. See numbers 15–19 for variations on this theme.

[33] Lucian, "The Downward Journey," *Lucian*, vol. 2, 49–57.

[34] Lucian, "Charon, or the Inspectors," *Lucian*, vol. 2, 447. In a famous dialogue, imitated later by Erasmus in "Charon," Charon ironically laments the peace among the living, since the absence of war means no business for Charon. See "Dialogues of the Dead," *Lucian*, vol. 7, number 14, 73–77.

[35] Lucian, "Dialogues of the Dead," *Lucian*, vol. 7, number 12, 61–67. See also number 13 on the same topic.

[36] Lucian, "The Dead Come to Life, or the Fisherman," *Lucian*, vol. 3, 9–81.

[37] See Lucian, "Dialogues of the Dead," *Lucian*, vol. 7, numbers 1–3; and "Menippus, or the Descent into Hades," *Lucian*, vol. 4, 105. The underworld is a perfect place for Menippus and Diogenes, for there one can "laugh endlessly without any doubts." "Dialogues of the Dead," *Lucian*, vol. 7, number 1, 3.

[38] Lucian, "Dialogues of the Dead," *Lucian*, vol. 7, number 4, 21. See also number 20, 119: Menippus is not fearful of the upcoming judgment, for "the life of each of us will be revealed." See also number 22.

[39] Lucian, "Dialogues of the Dead," *Lucian*, vol. 7, number 20, 113.

[40] Lucian, "Menippus, or the Descent into Hades," *Lucian*, vol. 4,109.

[41] J. Bompaire, *Lucien écrivain: Imitation ét creation* (Paris, 1958); Barry Baldwin, *Studies in Lucian* (Toronto: Hakkert, 1973) 104.

[42] Christopher Robinson, *Lucian and his Influence in Europe* (London: Duckworth, 1979) 52.

[43] Nancy Wilson Ross, *The World of Zen; An East-West Anthology* (New York: Random House, 1960) 183–184.

[44] Ross, *The World of Zen*, 188.

[45] Heinrich Zimmer, *Myths and Symbols in Indian Art and Civilization* (New York: Harper and Row, 1946) 3–11.

[46] The Shaikh Al-'Arabi Ad-Darqawi, *Letters of a Sufi Master* (London: Perennial Books, 1969) 33–34.

[47] Bakhtin, *Dostoevsky's Poetics*, 135.

[48] Hans Dieter Betz, *Lukian von Samosota und das Neue Testament* (Berlin: Akademie, 1961).

[49] Abraham J. Malherbe, *Social Aspects of Early Christianity* (Baton Rouge: Louisiana State University, 1977); see also Malherbe, *Moral Exhortation, a Greco-Roman Sourcebook* (Philadelphia: Westminster, 1986).

[50] Malherbe, *Social Aspects of Early Christianity*, 19.

[51] Burton L. Mack, *A Myth of Innocence; Mark and Christian Origins* (Philadelphia: Fortress, 1988) 68–69.

[52] Mack, *A Myth of Innocence*, ch. 7, "The Pronouncement Stories."

[53] Erasmus, "Charon," *The Colloquies of Erasmus*, trans. Craig R. Thompson (Chicago and London: University of Chicago, 1965) 391.

[54] Erasmus, "Charon," 391–392.

[55] Erasmus, "The Soldier and the Carthusian," *The Colloquies of Erasmus*, 131.

[56] Erasmus, "Military Affairs," *The Colloquies of Erasmus*, 14.

[57] Erasmus, "Julius Excluded from Heaven: A Dialogue," ed. A. H. T. Levi, *Collected Works of Erasmus*, vol. 27 (Toronto: University of Toronto, 1986) 169. For related dialogues among the dead, see "Charon" and "The Apotheosis of that Incomparable Worthy, John Reuchlin" in *The Colloquies of Erasmus*.

[58] Erasmus, "Julius Excluded from Heaven," 171.

[59] For a similar dialogue among the dead, cast in the Erasmian style, see Alfonso de Valdes, *Dialogue of Mercury and Charon*, trans. Joseph V. Ricapito (Bloomington: Indiana University, 1986).

[60] George Santayana, *Dialogues in Limbo* (Ann Arbor: University of Michigan, 1957).

[61] Fontenelle, "Charles V, Erasmus," *Dialogues of Fontenelle*, trans. Ezra Pound (London: Egoist, 1917) 28.

[62] Bernard Le Bovier de Fontenelle, *Nouveaux Dialogues des Morts*, ed. Donald Schier (Chapel Hill: University of North Carolina, 1965) 177. See John W. Consentini, *Fontenelle's Art of Dialogue* (New York: Columbia University, 1952) 49–51 and 69. Compare also Fontenelle's dialogue between Anacreon and Aristotle, *Dialogues of Fontenelle*, 15–18.

[63] Fontenelle, "Strato, Raphael of Urbino," *Dialogues of Fontenelle*, 49. In other dialogues, Fontenelle experiments with the dialectics of reason and the passions, and reason and deception. See Fontenelle, "Herostrate, Demetrius de Phalere" and "Callirhee, Pauline," *Nouveaux Dialogues*, 109–115.

[64] Fontenelle, "Erasistrate, Herve," *Nouveaux Dialogues*, 74–76.

[65] Fontenelle, "Fernand Cortez, Montezume," *Nouveaux Dialogues*, 183–186. See Consentini, *Fontenelle's Art of Dialogue*, 52–53.

[66] Fontenelle, "Socrates, Montaigne," *Dialogues of Fontenelle*, 22.

[67] As if to confirm this reading, Fontenelle expressly defends the importance of comedy over purely serious reflection, but in doing so he forwards a serious point about the balance of comedy and reason in our lives. See Fontenelle, "Bombastes Paracelsus and Moliere," *Dialogues of Fontenelle*, 50–54. On this dialogue, see Consentini, *Fontenelle's Art of Dialogue*, 48–49 and 71.

[68] Matthew Prior, *Dialogues of the Dead, and Other Works in Prose and Verse* (Cambridge: Cambridge University, 1907) 247. On Prior's dialogues of the dead, see Nicolas H. Nelson: "Dramatic Texture and Philosophical Debate in Prior's *Dialogues of the Dead,*" *Studies in English Literature, 1500–1900,* 28 (Summer 1988) 427–441.

[69] Prior, *Dialogues of the Dead*, 248.

[70] Prior, *Dialogues of the Dead*, 255 and 257.

[71] Frederick Keener, *English Dialogues of the Dead; A Critical History, an Anthology, a Check List* (New York: Columbia University, 1973) 63 and 62 respectively.

[72] Johan S. Egilsrud, *Le "Dialogue des Morts" dans les Littératures Française, Allemande et Anglaise, 1644–1789* (Paris: L'entente, 1934) 162, 168.

[73] George Lyttleton, *Dialogues of the Dead* (New York: Garland, 1970) 16–22. In Dialogue XXIV, a similar defense of reason is sounded, this time against the disease of Pierre Bayle's skepticism. Reason and order here replace the serio-comic.

[74] Lyttleton, *Dialogues of the Dead*, 240.

[75] At the extremes of didacticism, the dialogue of the dead is reduced to a conduit for mere information, as happened in the journalistic, obituary dialogues of David Fassman. See John Rutledge, *The Dialogue of the Dead in Eighteenth-Century Germany* (Bern: Herbert Lang, 1974) ch. 3. At that point, the serio-comic is dead.

[76] Peter Kreeft, *Between Heaven and Hell; A Dialog Somewhere Beyond Death with John F. Kennedy, C. S. Lewis and Aldous Huxley* (Downers Grove, IL: Intervarsity Press, 1982).

[77] On polemical dialogues of the dead involving not yet deceased speakers, see Keener, *English Dialogues of the Dead*, 69–72.

[78] David Worcester, *The Art of Satire* (New York: Russell and Russell, 1940).

[79] Worcester, *The Art of Satire*, 24.

[80] Lytton Strachey, "A Dialogue between Moses, Diogenes, and Mr. Loke," *Books and Characters, French and English* (New York: Harcourt, Brace, and Company, 1922) 142–144. See Keener, *English Dialogues of the Dead*, 137–138 on Strachey's authorship.

[81] Nicholas Boileau-Despreaux, *Dialogues, Reflexions critiques, Oevres diverses*, ed. Charles H. Boudhors (Paris: Société les Belles Lettres, 1960) 7–54.

[82] Anonymous pamphlet entitled "News from Heaven: A Dialogue between S. Peter and the Five Jesuits Last Hang'd," without publication information. University of Notre Dame library.

PART THREE

AN ETHIC OF DISCOURSE

6
The Praise of Peace:
Erasmus' Ethic of Discourse

"Concord binds in a sweet bond, discord disrupts even those who are joined by blood. The one builds cities, the other demolishes; the one creates wealth, the other dissipates. Discord turns men into beasts. Concord unites souls after death with God. I do not exhort you, I do not pray you, I implore you, seek peace."

—Erasmus, "Oration on Peace and Discord"[1]

The ancient masters of rhetoric commonly held that the power of speech lifts human beings above the realm of brute animals. Isocrates contends, for instance, that "the power to persuade each other"—rather than reliance on sheer physical strength—allows human beings to escape "the life of wild beasts" by forming institutions of cooperation and civility. Without these institutions and the laws that regulate them, Isocrates notes, "we should not be able to live with one another."[2] Cicero echoes much the same sentiment when he imagines the mythical day on which a "great and wise" man transformed brutish humanity "from wild savages into a kind and gentle folk" through the rational and eloquent power of persuasive speech. Certainly, Cicero adds, "only a speech at the same time powerful and entrancing could have induced the one who had great physical strength to submit to justice without violence. . . ."[3] At the same time, however, both authors well knew the disastrous effects on public life when "the power of eloquence [is] unaccompanied by any consideration of moral duty." In ancient days, Cicero tells us, men of "low cunning supported by [oratorical] talent grew accustomed to corrupt cities and undermine the lives of men";[4] and when these "rash and audacious men had taken the helm of the ship of state great and disastrous wrecks occurred."[5] Good people must study eloquence, therefore, "in order that evil men may not obtain great powers to the detriment of good citizens and the common disaster of the community."[6] Isocrates likewise exhorts the young king Nicocles of Cyprus to be diligent in pursuit of moral wisdom and virtue[7]—that is, if the power of his language is to be turned to goodness and justice. Underlying the hortatory tone of these two defenses of rhetoric, of course, is recognition of the suasive art's moral ambiguity.

A scholar and devotee of these classics, Erasmus of Rotterdam puts forth a similar, rhetoric-based portrait of human life. For Erasmus, too, humans are the only creatures bearing "the gift of speech, the chief promoter of friendly relations."[8] But like his classic exemplars, Erasmus also recognizes the equivocal character of human speech. "In human society," he tells us, "nothing is more destructive than an evil tongue, and yet nothing is more healing if a man use it rightly." The human tongue, in short, is both a "deadly poison and a life-giving remedy."[9] On the down side, Erasmus knew firsthand "the reckless frenzy of men's tongues" all too often breeds tumult and devastation.[10] How easily human beings revert to the savagery of animal life! Indeed, one Erasmian character notes,

> The majority of people . . . bark like dogs, whinny like horses, grunt like pigs, moo like cows, yelp like foxes, crackle like grasshoppers, blather like camels, trumpet like elephants, growl like boars, roar like leopards, groan like bears, bray like donkeys, bleat like sheep, honk like geese, squawk like woodpeckers, caw like crows, croak like ravens, rustle like storks, hiss like geese, and in short remind you of every sort of animal rather than speak in a human and humane manner.[11]

This litany of animal noises, all of which describes the brutish speech of human beings, is found (with typical Erasmian irony) on the civil tongue of a lion in conversation with a bear. But though Erasmus is fond of depicting poor or acrimonious speech in animal terms—Carmelites are called camels and Franciscans squid, for instance—he also observes how easily humans sink below the level of animals: the latter live together "peacefully and harmoniously according to their different species," while human beings, "for whom concord was so fitting and who have the greatest need of it, are not reconciled to each other by Nature," but "fight, brawl, and rage against each other in perpetual discord, strife and war."[12] When speech fails, people fare worse than animals.

In "The Tongue," a late work written in Basel during the more turbulent days of reformation activities, Erasmus shifts his metaphor for the failure of human speech. Drawing as is his custom on both biblical and non-scriptural classical sources, he warns readers that human civilization is at risk from a hazardous and all too infectious disease affecting the human tongue. Worse even than that "disease of unknown origin" (variously called "the French" or the "Spanish pox") is the "affliction of an unbridled tongue." With an eye on his own European culture, Erasmus notes that

> this deadly sickness of a malicious tongue has infected the whole world with its awful venom, pervading the courts of princes, the homes of commoners, theological schools, monastic brotherhoods, colleges of priests, regiments of soldiers, and the cottages of peasants. So great is the force of the onslaught that it threatens the total ruin and destruction of the liberal arts, good morals, civic harmony, and the authority of the leaders of the church and the princes of the realm alike.[13]

There is no escape from this contagion: infection and destruction loom on the horizon. And the Christian world, most certainly, is not immune! Indeed, Erasmus laments, among those who have "put on Christ" in baptism, the "old tongue" appears to be flourishing. The symptoms include "indiscreet chattering, head-long lying, [and] bitter quarreling," not to mention speech that is "abusive, slan-derous, reviling, immodest, forswearing, beguiling, impious and blasphemous."[14] These "sins of the tongue" threaten human welfare—both between people and before God.

What makes Erasmus so interesting and so compelling, however, is not his diagnosis of the sins of human speech but his life-long effort to point up and se-cure a more noble and virtuous practice of discursive activity. Having confronted his readers with a graphic account of depraved speech, he holds up the ideal of discourse that is humane, peaceful, clear-thinking, and charged with the recon-ciling energy of love. Though Christian peoples make a practice of "battling to the death with so many conflicting dogmas," they are called (in principle) to imi-tate "Christ's tongue"—and "this is a modest tongue, a healing tongue, mild and reconciling all things that are in heaven and earth."[15] Putting an ironic gloss on the famous prayer attributed to St. Francis, Erasmus outlines the irenic quality of dis-course which should lie at the heart of Christian life:

> Instead of the venom of slander, let our tongue offer brotherly rebuke, instead of insults, consolation, instead of curses, prayers to God, instead of denigration, a mild and honest reproof, instead of a hotbed of conflicts, conciliatory speech, instead of the poison of ulceration, sound doctrine, instead of muttering, psalms and hymns, in-stead of quarrelling, spiritual chants, instead of silly tales, the speech of knowledge, instead of accusation against our neighbour, the confession of our own evils, instead of the most bitter persecution of other mens' failures, the desire to give healing.[16]

Though it remains an apt expression of the authentic Christian ideal of a gentle and irenic tongue, true to the spirit of Francis' prayer for peace, this passage must have rankled Franciscans of the day, who elsewhere in "The Tongue" receive prominent attention for their calumny, deceit, and hypocrisy.[17]

It is this dimension of Erasmus' work—an ethic of discourse crafted from both classical and scriptural resources, centered on irenic dialogue, and modeled on the healing love of God in Christ—that constitutes the focus of this chapter. I turn to Erasmus at this juncture because (like Isocrates and Cicero) he was acutely aware of the role of speech in the human project of building and sustaining civi-lized communities. He also was cognizant of the moral weakness and depravity that beset human discourse, and of the fragility of human civilization. Yet he was hopeful—at times even optimistic—that human speech could be turned to the co-operative and constructive ends of peace and concord. Finally, he was convinced that the ethical choice between quarrelsome and irenic forms of discourse in-volves a coincident theological option between the "living words of God" and the "dead words" that arise from the "tomb" of an impious mouth.[18] Something fun-damental and all important is at stake in the way we wield our powers of speech.

For Erasmus, in sum, it is speech that makes us human. The failure of human discourse makes us barbaric (or worse). Speech (God's *"sermo"* of love in Christ) can reconcile us to God, and good speech (irenic conversation) can heal the burdened soul and reconcile human relationships.[19] It is this ethic of discourse—at the heart of what Erasmus calls the "philosophy of Christ"–that shines through the massive body of writings produced by Erasmus.

And shines through it does—quite literally—by way of the varied and "highly original genres"[20] which Erasmus either creates himself or borrows from others for his writings. Indeed, Erasmus was intensely and consistently genre-conscious, and for good reason. Since the manner in which speech is exercised matters ethically, as we have seen above, it was only natural (and necessary) that Erasmus place a concomitant emphasis on his own discursive performance. His ethical ideals for discourse, after all, were not simply something to be described second-hand; they had also to be enacted in his own literary discourse. And for this purpose, clearly, the form counts for a great deal. Erasmus' keen awareness of this fact is written into the extremely deliberate, diversified, and creative manner in which he chooses and deploys literary genre.

There is, first, his massive personal correspondence; those "quasi-public documents" by which Erasmus formed contact with "all the world" and by which he built and nurtured a treasured complex of friendships.[21] Secondly, the *Adages*—that ever-growing compilation of reflections and essays tacked onto classical proverbs, totaling in the end some 4251 pieces, through which Erasmus bridged the contemporary life of readers with the wisdom of the classical past, while simultaneously revealing unexpected continuities between pre-Christian and Christian thought.[22] Then, third, there is Erasmus' creative transmutation of the false encomium in the much celebrated *Praise of Folly*—a work that saw thirty-six editions from twenty-one presses in Erasmus' lifetime, and one in which he blends comical invitation to self-knowledge, satirical criticism of abusive behavior, and spirited exhortation to authentic Christian life. But there are also lesser known genre, like his *Paraphrases* in which he undertakes a subtle but highly suggestive hermeneutical exercise by "re-writing" biblical texts in what he hopes will be clearer and more accurate language.[23] And last, but certainly not least, there is the dialogue—a genre to which Erasmus makes a singularly creative contribution by fusing the Socratic interest to draw out the truth with the eclectic, down to earth, and leisurely style of Ciceronian conversation, topped off with the wit and bite of Lucianic irony.

Everything about Erasmus speaks through these genres: his dedication to classical learning, his love of language (especially good Latin, but also words and rhetoric generally), his interest in effective pedagogy, his commitment to friendship and concern for reputation, his Christ-centered and scripture-based piety, his insistence that non-Christian wisdom can and will enhance Christian faith, his persistent effort to reform church policy and practice, his controversies (repeatedly with orthodox theologians, and later with reformers), his sharp wit and playful sense of irony, his repeated pleas for peace and concord in human relations, his willingness (frequently misunderstood) to mediate disputes so as to reconcile opposition, and his ethical optimism (tempered but never destroyed by the frustration of his later years). While it may be unfounded to claim any one of these items as *the* material centerpiece of Erasmus' work, there is good warrant for accenting how, in each case, these concerns and projects converge in his choice and use of genre. Erasmus is precisely the kind of author who wields literary style such that, as Martha Nussbaum puts it, the "style itself makes claims, [and] expresses its own sense of what matters."[24] Erasmus makes the identical point in his oft repeated praise of linguistic and literary "style." Though his emphasis on good style (and Latin) may seem antiquated to twentieth century readers, it is much more than a symptom of Renaissance erudition. Indeed, for Erasmus, the style of anyone's speaking and writing constitutes "the appearance of the mind," for better or for worse. For Christian authors, as well, the style of communication is the "surest proof" of life in Christ—or the lack of it.[25] What appears through Erasmus' own style is his root encomium of peaceful and humane discourse between people. Erasmus self-consciously crafts his literary communications through genre and style expressly to feature, encourage, and defend irenic standards for human discourse. It is Erasmus' ethic of discourse, in sum, which speaks through his deployment of genre.

This chapter will show how this ethic appears and works in and through Erasmus' literary dialogues that deal with religious questions and topics. Indeed, as will become increasingly evident, religion was, for Erasmus, both an especially intense source of distorted and malicious speech and the supreme fountain of authentic and reconciling discourse. One of his most basic agenda regarding the religious world is the need to open up discursive space for learned and critical thinking about religion. In the first section of this chapter, I will look at two extended dialogues in which Erasmus works, against the prejudices of various anti-intellectuals and against the pretensions of assorted pseudo-intellectuals, to bring classical learning and Christian faith together into a complementary but critical harmony. The next section will take a second look at the playful and ironic twist Erasmus gives to criticism of miscellaneous forms of religious folly—including superstition, deceit, graft, and aggression. It is here that Erasmus shows himself to be the successor of Lucian by crafting criticism of religion in a serio-comic fashion. The hallmark of Erasmian dialogue lies in the ideal of irenic mediation of disputes; and even where Erasmus is not able to sustain these high standards in his own discourse, his dialogues continue to put forth literary expressions of this ethic. In the third section, I will look at dialogues in which Erasmus not only exhorts his factious readers to mutual understanding and concord but himself tries—through the deployment of the genre—to be an instrument of irenic mediation. It is in this context that Erasmus pushes irenic discourse to its limits: whereas Anselm takes meditative discourse on the grammar of faith to its mystical limits, while Diderot takes his Socratically-inspired experimental discourse to the limits of criticism, and where Lucian and Hume flirt with the edges of irony, Erasmus speaks from the shaky middle ground—always in danger of collapse—between the sharp hostility of religious antagonists. The fourth section will turn to examine "The Godly Feast," a uniquely utopian dialogue in which Erasmus imaginatively paints the contours of a fully humane and thoughtful conversation over religion.

(1) The Dialogue of Christian Humanism

Two distinctive, yet inseparable and finally complementary currents cut across Erasmus' lifework. On one hand, as can be seen from his earliest correspondence, Erasmus reveres what he calls "the ancient style of eloquence and learning."[26] The young Erasmus cherished ancient literature;[27] he sought to emulate the rhetoric of the classics especially in the composition of letters; and he sought out the company of leading humanist scholars (Lorenza Valla through his books, and Robert Gaguin in Paris, for instance). These same concerns fill the pages of Erasmus' correspondence again in later years—as when, in a typical letter, he warns of the venomous frenzy of those organized against "the classical languages and the liberal arts."[28] Attending to the classics entails, for Erasmus, a unique way of being in the world. Most broadly, it demands a commitment to critical self-reflection and a search for self-knowledge; in rhetoric, it mandates the polished practice of civil and elegant speech; and, morally, "to read the classics" means, as James D. Tracy puts it, "to foster in oneself a spirit of generosity, gentleness and other qualities" that make up "*humanitas*."[29] On the other hand, Erasmus is—very simply but also profoundly—a man of Christian faith. Though many in his own day doubted his faith and though some scholars persist to this day in dismissing the current of Christian piety in his life and work, something fundamental is missed in the interpretation of Erasmus without attending to "the profoundly Christian melody" at work in his writings.[30]

Basic to Erasmus' entire literary enterprise—indeed, the foundation for the all the rest—is his insistence that these two currents—classical scholarship and Christian faith—belong together in fruitful dialogue. He hoped, in short, to carve out space for humanist discourse shaped by, and yet also ultimately serving, the ends of Christian faith. The two currents merge in almost everything Erasmus wrote. Of course, not everyone agreed to this dialogue of classical and Christian wisdom. Some decried the use of anything non-Christian (Erasmus calls them barbarians); while others—wanting to keep scholarship pure and undefiled—wished to avoid anything that would contaminate the classics (he labels them Ciceronians). If Erasmus is to succeed in bringing faith and scholarship together, therefore, he must contend with both parties who would hold the two poles apart. A case must be made, in sum, for the legitimate and fruitful use of classical sources by Christian authors. The rest of this section will look at two extended dialogues in which Erasmus does precisely this: "The Antibarbarians" (a dialogue lambasting the ignorance and narrow-mindedness of religious anti-intellectuals),[31] and "The Ciceronian: A Dialogue on the Ideal Latin Style" (a full length dialogue challenging the cockeyed desire for absolute intellectual purity).[32]

(a) Though "The Antibarbarians" shows the signs of its youthful origin, the thirty-three year generation of this work says even more about the constancy of Erasmus' passion to fuse humanist sensibilities and Christian faith. Initially written as a speech in 1487–1488 (while he was an Augustinian canon at Steyn), Erasmus recast the piece as a dialogue ("to make it easier reading")[33] while at his bishop's country house at Halsteren in 1494 or 1495. He edited the work again in 1495 after the Parisian humanist Robert Gaguin advised him to follow the lead of Plato and Cicero in avoiding long, boring speeches in dialogues.[34] He revised it once more at Bologna in 1506–1507. Then, sadly, Erasmus lost control of his text until much later in Louvain, where he again revised the piece and published it with Johann Froben in 1520. Given this time span, a number of changes understandably exist between the early and later manuscripts—including stylistic changes, new references to church fathers, a little added irony, and, most importantly, some daring attacks on religious orders and their theologians. But what is more startling, as Phillips notes, is that "the basic attitude is unchanged."[35] Erasmus stands steadfast against what he regards as the willful stupidity and anti-intellectual hostility of unlettered (really, uncritical) religion, while defending the right and extolling the virtue of thoughtful, self-critical, and learned religious life. What has changed is the nature and the organization of his anti-intellectual foes: if the opponent in his youth was the general "stupidity and ignorance" so common in religion, the opposition in 1520 was the "more acrimonious, more informed perhaps, more localized, and infinitely more dangerous" group of orthodox theologians at the University of Louvain. It is these adversaries, it should be noted, who hounded Erasmus for his translation of the New Testament, who opposed the institution of the trilingual college Erasmus supported, who increasingly linked Erasmus with Luther in their charges of heresy, and who, only recently, had been stung by a satirical dialogue (wrongly attributed to Erasmus) aimed at them.[36] "The Antibarbarians" represents, therefore, not only an ongoing effort to speak out against anti-intellectual tendencies endemic to the religious world, but also a timely (if very risky) response to the university-based, orthodox opposition to the scholarship of Christian humanism.

The dialogue opens with five friends gathered in the "fresh air and quietude" of a country retreat for three days of "pure amusement" in conversation.[37] The bucolic setting (far from the "raging sea of public affairs") and the intimate gathering of friends (who share a "comradeship based on shared studies") illustrate Erasmus' desire to replicate a classical dialogue "on the model of Plato" or Cicero.[38] Erasmus the character, in fact, hopes to outdo these masters of dialogue! For his part, Erasmus the author seeks to create what Phillips aptly calls "a picture of civilization."[39] That means, of course, that the conversation within the dialogue takes place between friends who are of like mind; only the printed text directly engages the so-called "barbarians." Together these interlocutors explore what has caused the "literature of the ancients" to be so ignored and forgotten in the present age. A number of answers are put forth—one blames the stars, another indicts Christianity's "horror of worldly learning," and a third points to the aging of nature—but none of these explanations prove entirely satisfactory. This prologue then leads to an extended speech against the "barbarians" by Jacob Batt, who is interrupted only for redirection and literary relief. The fact that Erasmus hands the lead voice over to his friend Batt is significant, for, as readers learn in the text, Batt had waged an unsuccessful battle against the local "masters of unlearning," who, with "their bitter hatred, their dedicated band of supporters, [and] their gladiatorial fury," had forced him to resign as a teacher at Bergen for daring to teach the boys humanistic studies.[40] Erasmus thereby gives his friend a bit of literary revenge, while subtly dissociating himself (as author) from the stinging language he puts in Batt's mouth.[41]

The largest mass of anti-intellectual voices consists of ordinary people and the teachers who keep them that way. The "uneducated crowd," Batt claims, has a natural dislike of letters, and they can no more appreciate knowledge than a pig can delight in roses. Consequently, this "slavish herd of sneerers" condemns learning without any knowledge of what they condemn.[42] But common people are less to blame than the would-be teachers who teach nothing but their own fatuity. These "pernicious rulers of youth" (who don't speak but "hee-haw") work to unteach "everything which concerns Good Letters."[43] Indeed, Batt observes, they train the young (quite unsocratically) "to know nothing and yet to think they know everything."[44] Recalling his own bitter dismissal at the hands of "these undoctoral doctors and counselless counsellors," Batt works himself up into a lather:

> Ye gods! What nonsense, what inanities, what mockery, what barbarism, what thorns and brambles, what dregs had been forced upon the unhappy schoolboys by those men who had taught them to know nothing.[45]

One need look no further than the local school, in short, to discover why classical learning (and all it represents) is ignored. "What can you expect from a brutish teacher," Batt asks his friends, "but a more brutish pupil?"[46]

The most dangerous source of hostility to learning, however, has its source in the religious world. Anti-intellectual preachers "cry their wares by claiming to be men of religion," yet "think it the height of piety to know nothing."[47] They assume that "pure religion and consummate learning" are incompatible, since the former rests on faith while the latter rests on questions and argument. It is the religious orders, however, which receive Batt's (hence, Erasmus') most forceful blast. Monks oppose learning by dressing up in "the mask of religion"—the best of all things, but also "the most convenient cloak for any vice you like to name."[48] Indeed, Batt claims, they use "the same cloak for their crass ignorance as for the other shameful things in their lives," like their concubines.[49] "How cunningly," he muses, "they mask their sluggishness, their envy, and the pride under the attractive names of simplicity and religion." But dangerous they can be, as they "throw themselves into [the battle] like ravening wild beasts."[50] "Beware," they say, "he's a poet, he's no Christian."[51] Abbots oversee this monastic culture of ignorance; they "refuse to allow any of their monks to put a finger on Good Letters, the better to impose on them whatever commands they wish."[52] That way, it seems, they bolster their own rule by making sure no one can correct their ignorance.[53] Worst of all is the campaign against the humanities, waged by the scholastic theologians who represent the religious orders. But Batt admits that he is unable to read the works of these modern theologians ("dialecticians"), for they are mere "shadows" when compared with the church fathers who he loves. In addition, reading their "barbarous style and confusion of thought" makes him nauseous.[54]

Batt proceeds to set out a number of arguments designed to undercut the pretensions of these religious antagonists of learning, and to defend the use of classical wisdom by Christian scholars. It is, to begin with, sheer hypocrisy for this "doltish herd of scorners" to turn in disgust from the mention of girls in the poets' stories, while feeling no embarrassment (or guilt) at all about "forcing other men's wives, even Vestal virgins."[55] Perhaps, he surmises, they are moved by envy; or maybe they simply are "frightened by the difficulty of the work"; or it could be that the barbarians have "an innate uncouthness which makes them hate the elegance of literary study."[56] Whatever the motives, Batt finds it the height of absurdity when the barbarians insist that no Christian can use pagan learning without ceasing to be Christian. If we are to take nothing from the pagan world, he argues, then much of Western culture (including the applied arts) will be lost.[57] Frequently, however, he takes a more offensive tack, boldly noting that the scholar's defense of the faith in times of stress has contributed more to the growth of the Christian religion than the blood of martyrs.[58] In another vein, Batt sarcastically belittles the suggestion that people abandon intellectual activities and "leave everything to the Holy Spirit"; this appeal to knowledge from heaven is nothing but a lame excuse for the lack of "diligent effort."[59] Finally, he bluntly challenges the defense of ignorance based on the example of "apostolic rusticity." This appeal might be tolerable, he admits, if the people making it "were to possess the virtues of the apostles." In fact, these barbarians spend their "days and nights" eating, drinking, dancing, and in prurient pursuits; "when the wine makes them begin to stutter," Batt imagines, "they think themselves to be copying the un-polished speech of the apostles."[60]

As the dust clears from these jabs and counter thrusts, readers begin to discern the outline of Erasmus' positive proposal regarding the connection of Christian faith and the scholarly life. Batt concedes to his anti-intellectual foes that "none of the liberal disciplines is Christian, because they neither treat of Christ nor were invented by Christians."[61] Indeed, he insists that there is no such thing as "Christian erudition," since all "systems of learning" were invented in ancient (non-Christian) cultures. This concession comes with a twist, however, for while the liberal arts may not be Christian, they nonetheless "all concern Christ."[62] What Batt means by this is partially explained by his Augustinian language. Echoing Augustine's sweeping argument for world-historical providence in the *City of God*, Batt asserts that "all things, whether hostile or heathen or in any other way far removed from him, must be drawn, even if they do not follow, even against their own will, to the service of Christ."[63] Indeed, he argues, "everything in the pagan world that was valiantly done, brilliantly said, ingeniously thought, diligently transmitted, had been prepared by Christ for his society," so that Christians may make free use of the wisdom and speech of non-Christian culture.[64] Christians are free to use what is good and leave what is bad from non-Christian culture, though, as Batt observes, most people tend to do the opposite.[65]

Despite the sound of these passages, however, Erasmus intends a stronger advocacy of the academic disciplines than Augustine had in mind. In fact, for Erasmus, the Christian not only "may" but "should" turn to pagan learning, since classical wisdom is fully Christ's work.[66] There is no hint in the Erasmian line of argument, for instance, that classical learning was "stolen from the Hebrews" (as in Augustine's *On Christian Doctrine*) or that it is a propadeutic, merely passing stage of revelation (as Augustine argues in *The City of God*). Against the anti-intellectuals of his day, Erasmus fully affirms the value of the secular disciplines for Christian reflection. Thus we find Batt arguing that the study of letters actually leads to "a more humane type of life." As he puts it, letters "quiet our passions, check our uncontrolled impulses, [and] give mildness to our mind in place of savagery." It is the barbarians, conversely, who are pumped up with pride, for "they have no doubts; they settle everything; [and] they dispense instruction wholesale."[67] Erasmus' rule for approaching classical sources, therefore, is compatible with Augustine's even while extending it. Christians may properly use pagan learning, Batt concludes, "if only the pagan teaches me more excellent things than a Christian."[68] And Erasmus is convinced that the classic literature of Greece and Rome do indeed teach us excellent things. The trick for thinking, educated Christians, therefore, is to "reflect the moral virtues of the apostles and at the same time the learning of Jerome."[69] The two streams can and should combine in Christian life.

(b) Erasmus aims at the same convergence in "The Ciceronian: A Dialogue on the Ideal Latin Style," though now he must contend with a new adversary, who comes at him from a new and opposing angle. While in "The Antibarbarians" Erasmus fashions a world of discourse designed to show—against the ignorance and narrow-mindedness of the Christian barbarians—that Christians should be open and appreciative of secular learning, in "The Ciceronian" he must contend with another group (a "new sect," as he calls it), which will countenance nothing but a secular source of knowledge. His foe this time, as the title would indicate, is a group of mainly Italian scholars who (as Betty Knott puts it) revere Cicero as "the only model of correct and stylish Latinity, the only prose author to be imitated by those who wished to use Latin for civilized communication."[70] These opponents, clearly, are not anti-intellectuals, like the school-masters and monks of "The Antibarbarians"; they are, rather, hyper-intellectuals who identify themselves exclusively with one school of classical thought and who demand unqualified fidelity to the rhetorical style of one master. In Erasmus' own words, taken from one of his dedicatory letters, "they reject with intolerable arrogance any literary work which does not reproduce Cicero's stylistic characteristics."[71]

As ludicrous (but familiar) as this narrowly focused agenda may be for the study of literature and the practice of rhetoric, there are more serious questions of a theological nature at stake in the Ciceronian position. There can be no question, of course, about Erasmus' own devotion to classical literature and rhetoric. And he was, to the say the least, filled with admiration for the practical wisdom taught by Cicero, of whom he writes:

> What justice, what purity, what sincerity, what truth in his rules for living!—all is in harmony with nature, nothing glossed over or half asleep. What a spirit he demands from those at the head of public affairs! What a notable and lovable picture of virtue he paints before our eyes! How many lessons he teaches, and how like a saint—even a deity!—on how we should do good to all men even without reward. . . .[72]

And yet Erasmus also had long recognized that one of the main temptations of the scholarly life, besides the formation of exclusive cliques and narrow canons of wisdom, is the pompous rejection of religion. Thus we find Erasmus expressing to Wolfgang Capito (whose mastery of languages proved helpful to Erasmus in his work on the New Testament) his misgiving that "under the cover of the reborn literature of antiquity, paganism may try to rear its ugly head."[73] Some years later Erasmus again asserts his hope that the newly revived humanities at the University of Paris not "overwhelm [other] subjects of which the acquisition is essential." "We must not," he writes, "spend our time on polite literature and nothing else, as some people do in Italy, behaving too much like gentiles."[74] These concerns come to a head in Erasmus' opposition to the Ciceronians, who he felt were especially brazen and insolent in their rejection of Christianity and theological studies. "Good letters," Erasmus insists, should "proclaim the glory of Christ," while the Ciceronians are out "to make us pagans instead of Christians." The purpose of this dialogue, therefore, is to "show how we can genuinely represent Cicero, and combine his supreme powers of expression with faith in Christ."[75] Good letters and sound faith, once again, belong in dialogue.

When the dialogue opens we find Hypologus (Back-up) asking why his "old friend and fellow student" Nosoponus ("Work-mad") now appears so ghost-like, when he once was "the life and soul of our set." Bulephorus ("Giver of counsel") responds that poor Nosoponus suffers from a rather severe case of *zelodulea* ("style addiction").[76] Burdened with a "tenacious passion" for Ciceronian eloquence, he has dedicated himself to achieving perfect and complete fidelity to Cicero's Latin style. As he describes it to his two Erasmian interlocutors (not without some pride), "for seven whole years now I have touched no books but Ciceronian ones, abstaining from all the rest as religiously as a Carthusian from meat."[77] What he craves above all is the honor of being called Ciceronian by the Italian Latinists he reveres; but to receive this title, he must maintain—totally and in every detail—"the pure sheen" of his "Ciceronian diction."[78] Indeed, he declares, "no one will be Ciceronian if even the tiniest word is found in his works which can't be pointed to in Cicero's *opus*."[79] He strives, therefore, to imitate Cicero in every bit of speech and every scrap of writing. Nothing could be worse, after all, than "contamination" from a non-Ciceronian source or conversation. To this end, the obsessed Nosoponus keeps a picture of Cicero before him—in his chapel, in his study, on all the doors, and on his person—so that he will never see anything but Cicero in his dreams. So fastidious is he in this "sacred vocation," he remains a bachelor so as not to be distracted by family concerns.[80] His devotion admits of "no exceptions," but under the rigors of this discipline, he has become a shadow of his former self.

In response to this pathetic devotion, Bulephorus (who is later called "Dr. Word") and Hypologus conspire to play along with Nosoponus for the purpose of healing their sick friend. Slowly but surely, in fine Socratic fashion, Bulephorus leads Nosoponus to see that such an ideal is neither possible nor desirable. How, he inquires, can one hope to wholly imitate Cicero, when the "whole Cicero" which he seeks to replicate is not even present in Cicero's extant corpus?[81] How are we supposed to imitate the missing Ciceronian works? And how might one go about imitating Cicero on subjects which he did not address? Moreover, since no one author surpasses every other in every way, would it not be wiser to "choose from each individual speaker the feature in which he surpassed all the rest?"[82] And what about the rhetorical excesses and "inexcusable solecisms" in Cicero— must we imitate them as well?[83] In fact, the whole endeavor is unfaithful to Cicero, since Cicero was an orator who adapted his speech to the subject and to the situation—how can one exactly copy Cicero's style if one must also (to be Ciceronian) adapt one's rhetoric to meet circumstance that Cicero never faced?[84] If we follow this path, he concludes, we shall not only fail to be Ciceronian, but "Cicero himself would think us out of our minds."[85] Indeed, the whole dream of "Cicero's apes"—craving "total similarity in the very wording"—is simply foolish: "It's impossible, even if it were any use; and it wouldn't be any use if it were possible."[86] This kind of imitation yields, in the end, "nothing but a veneer, a reflection, a faint aura of him."[87] The whole venture, in sum, is impossible, useless, shallow, and dangerous to one's health.

Eventually it begins to dawn on Nosoponus (he is not quick) that Bulephorus' line of questioning is undermining his resolution to be the perfect Ciceronian. At which point, Bulephorus gives a more constructive bent in his counsel. One must begin, the counselor advises, by granting that Cicero was blessed with "a happy facility . . . and an inborn lucidity of expression," and that not everyone—plainly—can lay claim to these natural gifts.[88] Cicero was great, in other words, in large part because of his native abilities and natural gifts. Given this, it is pointless for someone like Nosoponus to attempt "to copy Cicero if his natural bent is totally different from Cicero's."[89] The only way to be authentically Ciceronian, therefore, is to work to develop—as far as possible—the same kind of "oratorical virtues," beginning with sound understanding and good judgment, but also "lucidity, clarity, correctness of language, good arrangement, and so on."[90] With this foundation, the student of Cicero "must learn how to imitate Cicero from Cicero himself." The true imitator of Cicero, in other words, will "imitate him as he imitated others"; he will "read all the best writers and extract from the best the best they have to offer."[91] Then, digesting their wisdom critically, he or she will speak creatively from the heart "in the best and most appropriate way, even though . . . in a manner very different from Cicero's." Indeed, Bulephorus says, the real Ciceronian may be "the one least like Cicero."[92] The key in all of this is a different notion of imitation. One must move beyond unimaginative imitation (copying, really), for "it's inevitable that imitation falls short when it tries only to follow a model, not to surpass it."[93] Far superior to the "hidebound, slavish" imitation of the Ciceronians, Bulephorus concludes, is the attempt "to produce something equally good after the pattern set by him, or, if we can, something even better."[94]

Erasmus finds Nosoponus' Ciceronian ideal narrow and suffocating. More importantly, as a habit of mind and as a policy for speaking, he regards this intellectual narrowness as thoroughly inappropriate for serious Christian thinking. Indeed, Bulephorus exclaims, "it's paganism, believe me, Nosoponus, sheer paganism, that makes our ears and minds accept such an idea."[95] In making this charge, Erasmus is not rejecting Cicero because he is pagan, for as we have seen, he affirms the inherent value of classical learning. What he rejects is not the paganism of Cicero, but the paganism of these so-called Ciceronians. At its most basic level, the Ciceronian's paganism entails a spirit of aesthetic and literary correctness, the parameters of which make it impossible for them to find anything interesting or worthy of attention in the Christian world. Bulephorus takes a mocking shot at this classicist arrogance, when he muses, "how we gasp and gaze in admiration if we get hold of a statue of one of the gods of the ancient world, even a bit of statue; but the image of Christ and his saints get hardly a glance from our prejudiced eyes."[96] These people's uncritical and unimaginative devotion to Cicero's rhetoric also blinds them from appreciating wisdom from Christian literature; there is no room in their canon of great books, for instance, for authors who "dare at some points to move outside Cicero's prescribed boundaries."[97] Ironically, their obeisance to Cicero even prevents them from profiting from Cicero, since they are afraid to adapt his wisdom usefully and persuasively to the needs of the Christian world in which they live. Cicero knew that to speak well meant adapting speech with sensitivity to changing circumstances; but these would-be Ciceronians, Bulephorus observes, refuse to admit new words and terms into their canon of properly Ciceronian rhetoric; indeed, he says, they "positively despise and recoil from" the language of Christian scriptures and doctrine. By so doing, however, they cease being truly Ciceronian, for "anyone who can be Ciceronian only by being unchristian is not even Ciceronian."[98]

The true Ciceronian, Bulephorus counsels, is the one who creatively adapts Cicero's ideals to Christian audiences, as Cicero would himself do "if he were living today as a Christian among Christians."[99] The Ciceronians are guilty, therefore, of keeping apart what most properly belongs together—the excellence of Cicero's rhetoric and the wisdom of Christian faith. Indeed, he says, the Christian thinker should aspire to combine Cicero's "supreme powers of expression with the faith of Christ."[100] But to retrieve the best of Cicero for the sake of Christian rhetoric means overcoming the neo-pagan prejudice of the Ciceronians. As Bulephorus puts it in one of his bluntest statements,

> This idea that everything that diverges from Cicero is a disgusting example of bad Latin is a pernicious hallucination which we must banish from our minds if we are to win among Christians the reputation that Cicero won among his contemporaries.[101]

And that is precisely what Erasmus hopes for: a rich appreciation of the classic rhetoric of ancient Rome within the orbit of Christian faith. Through the Socratic dialogue of Bulephorus and his confused Ciceronian friend, Erasmus proffers the ideal of what Knott aptly calls, a "Christian Ciceronianism"—"a Ciceronianism subservient to Christian thinking and responding to Christian needs."[102] At the dialogue's end, Nosoponus is "nearly cured"; should he require any additional therapy, Bulephorus promises to "fetch Dr. Word again."[103]

The dialogue of Christian humanism—the mutually informative and complementary conversation of Christian faith and tradition with the wisdom, rhetoric, and wit of classical Greece and Rome—stands as the most enduring and fundamental agenda of Erasmus' literary career. But this high ideal is anything but an accomplished fact, as Erasmus well knew. Indeed it must be secured and defended in constant discourse with two quite different adversaries who reject the confluence of faith and scholarship. Erasmus, consequently, must stand "in between" two sets of opponents, somewhat as Hume did when he sought to be the "ambassador" between the protagonists and the antagonists of religion. He must speak with and against two extremes: on one side, the anti-intellectual barbarians who question the propriety of serious intellectual inquiry in Christian life; and on the other, the hyper-intellectual Ciceronians who exclusively and uncritically adopt one favored conceptual system and its methods at the expense of everything else. Against each of these uncompromising opponents, Erasmus must establish middle ground where faith and scholarship are fruitfully reconciled. To this end, as we have seen, Erasmus uses the literary dialogue to create two pictures of civilized, Christian discourse—one commending the critical turn of mind in classical literature for the purposes of Christian self-understanding and another practicing Christian "therapy of the word" for those entranced by the luster of pure scholarship at the expense of piety.[104] To the anti-intellectual, he must show the necessity and utility of critical inquiry, and to the loyal party-intellectual, he must show the virtue of evangelical awareness. In a manner which anticipates Diderot, Erasmian dialogues are cosmopolitan, eclectic, and fully open to critical (Socratic) examination; and yet, in a manner more reminiscent of Anselm, these same dialogues subordinate critical inquiry for the purposes of faith's quest for understanding.

(2) Dialogues of Folly

In his *Satires* Horace points up the utility of conveying truth by way of a little folly and comical diversion:

> But tell me what law is violated if someone laughs
> while speaking truth? You know how teachers sometimes give
> their pupils little cakes, to help them learn their ABC's.[105]

Erasmus knew the truth of this pedagogical device, both from Horace and from his own experience. Indeed, he frequently speaks of his works as "trifles," though he quickly adds that these trifles might prompt thoughts of a more serious nature. It is in this vein, for instance, that he speaks of his *Praise of Folly* as "my bit of nonsense," something filled with "frivolity and fun," but it is (he hopes) "trifling [that] may lead to something more serious."[106] And he expressly defends his *Colloquies* against its detractors by appealing to the usefulness of entertainment and games to make weighty subjects palatable for young people.[107] Even "The Ciceronian" (with its exaggerated lampoon of Italian Latinists) is described by Erasmus as a piece of entertaining "nonsense," but (again quoting Horace) with a "serious outcome."[108] In the same spirit, "The Antibarbarians" is presented as three days of conversation spent in "pure amusement," though the dialogue does serious battle with the opponents to the humanities.[109] As these few references illustrate, Erasmus is especially fond of seasoning his writing with comic diversions and humorous irony. He loves to play with the hidden complexities of meaning, and he revels in the ironic interplay of the grave and the comic. And, key for the purposes of this study, this penchant for the serio-comic carries over to Erasmus' literary discourse on religion. As Walter Gordon aptly writes, in Erasmus "the humour casts light on his faith, and the faith lends substance to the deft, gentle touch of his wit."[110]

In crafting his own serio-comic works, Erasmus learned a great deal from the satirical writings of Lucian. He was, in fact, quite familiar with Lucian's wit and irony, not only from the ongoing work on the *Adages* (in which Lucian is ubiquitous), but also from his collaborative venture with Thomas More to translate many of Lucian's works.[111] Pointing up the comic side of Lucian, he describes the set of translated dialogues which he sends to the Archbishop of Canterbury as "scholarly trifles, [but] such indeed as may make you laugh."[112] Lucian's dialogues, however, are also good for serious criticism. Though he is a "rascal," Erasmus writes, Lucian is "most serviceable for the detection and refutation of the impostures of certain persons who even today cheat the populace, either by conjuring up miracles, or with a pretence of holiness, or by feigned indulgences and other tricks of the kind."[113] It is this dimension of Lucian's serio-comedy that stood out in our reading of Lucian's dialogues in chapter five. Lucian is indeed a master of detecting hypocrisy and undermining false pretensions, especially those having to do with religion. But what Erasmus appreciates about Lucian more than anything else is the manner in which his knack for serio-comedy and his prowess at satiric criticism find such simple, graceful, yet pointed literary expression. As he puts it in a letter prefacing one volume of Lucian's dialogues,

> He possesses such grace and style, such felicity of invention, such a charming sense of humour, and such pointedness in satire; his sallies arouse such interest; and by his mixture of fun and earnest, gaiety and accurate observation, he so effectively portrays the manners, emotions, and pursuits of men, as if with a painter's vivid brush, not so much inviting us to read about them as to see them with our own eyes, that whether you look for pleasure or edification there is not a comedy, or a satire, that challenges comparison with his dialogues.[114]

Such qualities, of course, could aptly be praised in Erasmus' own dialogues. And indeed they were, by one admiring reader who remarked that Erasmus' "brilliant declamations" surpassed even those of Lucian, "most famous of stylists and satirists."[115]

What is crucial here is not simply Erasmus' debt to Lucian's serio-comic style (something Erasmus willingly acknowledges), but the manner in which he creatively adapts and applies the Lucianic genre to his own work on religious issues. Nowhere is Erasmus' talent for conveying the "mixture of fun and earnest" in and through the genre of his writing more apparent than in the *Praise of Folly*—a work in which Erasmus ironically blends (a) a comical look at the follies of the human condition, with (b) searing criticism of the destructive work of professional fools (including theologians, priests, bishops, and so on), topped off with (c) a delightful tribute to the exalted folly of Christ-like love. But the same three-leveled, serio-comic theology also shines through Erasmus' *Colloquies*, a collection of charming—but sometimes very pointed—dialogues that enjoyed immense popularity throughout Erasmus' lifetime, while also provoking severe attacks from the various centers of theological orthodoxy.[116] Though originally designed as simple exercises to help schoolboys master Latin grammar, the later colloquies are highly developed in both literary style and theological substance. Readers find conversations between well-defined characters that are familiar, down to earth, playful, and frequently hilarious. Erasmus brags that while "Socrates brought philosophy down from heaven to earth; I have brought it even into games, informal conversations, and drinking parties. For the very amusements of Christians ought to have a philosophical flavour."[117] But like the *Praise of Folly*, Erasmus also uses these little dialogues to confront readers with ethical and theological questions which are anything but trivial. Some colloquies (a) invite readers to take a good hard laugh at the common, but mostly innocent, folly in everyday religious life; others (b) mix comedy with (what Phillips calls) "the dissolving agent of ridicule," yielding stinging (but still civil) satire of official corruption and organized exploitation practiced in religion's name; and finally, (c) many put forward "positive suggestions and constructive plans" for authentic Christian faith and life.[118]

The remainder of this section will take a brief look at several of Erasmus' *Colloquies* which deal with religious questions. The first group focuses on common distortions and illusions of popular religion; here Erasmus maintains a stance of comic criticism akin to the first section of the *Praise of Folly*. In the second group Erasmus' serio-comic style turns satirical, as he takes aim at monastic corruption and the methods of scholastic theology. In the closing section of this chapter, I will look at one more colloquy, "The Godly Feast," in which Erasmus turns away from comedy and satire to praise the kind of learned, pious, and irenic discourse he considered ideal for Christian life.

(a) Many of the *Colloquies* work to expose and laugh down the illusions and superstitions that pervade popular religion. "Exorcism, or The Specter," for instance, narrates the story of an elaborate hoax played on a superstitious and gullible priest named Faunus. The tale begins with Polus (who is "naturally fond of playing trick's on people's stupidity") pretending to see a dragon-like spirit in the sky.[119] Anxious not to seem unobservant, others (including Faunus) leap headlong into agreement, claiming to have seen the specter too. One night, Faunus is made to hear the spirit groaning (really Polus in the bushes); soon afterward, Polus enjoins the priest to attempt an exorcism, something he undertakes eagerly, armed with special locutions ("by the bowels of the Blessed Virgin"), an Agnus Dei, and lots of holy water. Another night Polus and an assistant mount horses and charge Faunus armed with fire; and on a following evening, Polus' son-in-law (probably Thomas More) dons a linen sheet and converses with the would-be exorcist. After each session Faunus "embroiders" the story to make it more impressive to those who will listen. He is—to say the least—hooked on the marvelous and the fantastic. Indeed, as the narrator tells it, the story "grew in the telling," while the pranksters relished every bit of the priest's "folly." On a third occasion, Polus (who plays the devil) charges the exorcist and exclaims that Faunus is rightfully his, since the priest has had "dealings with a girl." To his surprise, this wild shot in the dark "chanced to hit upon the truth, for the exorcist was silenced by this utterance."[120] Comments one speaker, "they're men, and to err is human," though apparently this priest had erred three times, since his penance was to say the Lord's Prayer three times.[121] In no time, Faunus is completely obsessed with these nocturnal encounters: "he prattled of nothing else" and "he dreamt of nothing but specters and evil spirits."[122] In the end, he is freed from the madness of his superstition only when the designers of his folly arrange for him to receive a letter from the spirit, who thanks him for his efforts. Though still caught in the web of his needful imagination, Faunus remains mad, but now in "a more pleasant way."[123]

"Alchemy," similarly, takes a laugh at the need to believe in the marvelous, only now the superstition in question is driven by greed. As with "Exorcism," here again two interlocutors share the story of someone else's folly. In this tale, a "learned [and] much esteemed gentleman" named Balbinus is approached by a priest who, with deference and heaps of flattery, asks that Balbinus share with him his great knowledge of alchemy. The priest, he tells Balbinus, has mastered the long method of this "sacred science," but has failed to learn the quick method ("curtation") which he hears Balbinus knows well.[124] Put at ease by the flattery, enticed by the opportunity for quick gain, and knowing absolutely nothing about alchemy, Balbinus is hooked; together they agree to practice the long method (it's safer), with the priest doing the work and Balbinus putting up the money. Funds are handed over for the purchase of "pots, glasses, charcoal, and other equipment," which "our alchemist squanders enjoyably on whores, dice, and drink." "That's changing the species of things, all right," one of the interlocutors quips.[125] A series of errors requires more and more monies to fund the project. At one point it is concluded that an offering to the Virgin Mother might secure the needed "blessing from heaven"; so the priest spends "the votive in riotous living."[126] Balbinus gives over yet more money—ostensibly to bribe the police—when the alchemist falsely warns that the authorities will soon arrest them both. But when

Balbinus hears that the priest has been caught with another man's wife, he accuses him of ruining their alchemy scheme with his sinful conduct. The alchemist, however, again capitalizes on Balbinus' piety and greed, telling him that the offering to the Virgin was not wasted after all, for the "Most Holy Virgin" widened the window to help the sinful priest escape the clutches of the angry husband.[127] Finally, after the alchemist's scam is exposed by an old acquaintance, Balbinus gives the priest yet more money to leave town in order to save face in the community. Blind greed made the unbelievable believable, to Balbinus' great loss. Speaking for Erasmus, one of the interlocutors concludes, "I might feel sorry for Balbinus if he himself didn't enjoy being gulled."[128]

Other colloquies take a good hard laugh at the folly of pilgrimages, a religious practice Erasmus considered wasteful, dangerous, and irresponsible. In "Rash Vows," first published in 1522, we find two interlocutors discussing the merits of pilgrimages to Jerusalem. Having just returned from the holy land, Cornelius admits that his trip didn't produce any religious benefits.

> **Arnold:** So what did you see?
> **Cornelius:** A great deal of barbarity everywhere.
> **Arnold:** You don't return any the holier?
> **Cornelius:** Oh, no—worse in every respect.
> **Arnold:** Richer, then?
> **Cornelius:** No—purse emptier than an old snakeskin.
> **Arnold:** Then don't you regret having undertaken such a long and useless journey?
> **Cornelius:** I'm not ashamed, because I've so much company in my folly; and I've no regrets, because they would do no good now.[129]

The only real benefit, Cornelius adds, is that he will have "the vast pleasure" of impressing himself and others "at gatherings or parties by telling lies about my travels"; it will be great fun, as well, to listen to "others lie about things they never heard or saw."[130] Arnold agrees, even though it was an excess of wine that led to his own rash vow to take a wasteful and dangerous pilgrimage to Rome and Compostella. Both men—down to earth, without pretension, and prone to tip the bottle—clearly enjoy (as does Erasmus) laughing "at the foolishness of [their] fellow drinker," which means, in this case, laughing at themselves. And that is where the dialogue ends, with a pledge to gather at yet another drinking party, to laugh at the absurd illusions they share, and to take turns "telling whoppers."[131] When Erasmus comments on this colloquy in "The Usefulness of the *Colloquies*," he is a good bit more passionate in his criticism of pilgrimages.[132] The colloquy itself, however, maintains a thoroughly comic touch, largely, it seems, because Erasmus lets those who have participated in this folly do the laughing. By making his point indirectly, through the dialogue of this kind of interlocutor, Erasmus gently prompts his readers to chuckle at a folly that has crept into popular religious piety.

There is, however, a more positive side to Erasmus' serio-comic criticism. As John Dewey points out, criticism is "not for its own sake, but for the sake of instituting and perpetuating more enduring and extensive values."[133] Erasmus agrees, and many of his dialogues on popular religion portray conversations in which an ideal is held up as a beacon for converting superstitious piety back to what is essential in Christian life. "The Shipwreck" is a perfect example. In this colloquy, we hear the frightening tale of a ship helplessly caught in a terrifying storm. The desperate crew and passengers take refuge in a host of superstitions: the sailors pray to the Virgin Mother (who has succeeded Venus as "protectress of sailors"), calling her "Star of the Sea, Queen of Heaven, Mistress of the World, Port of Salvation," along with "other titles the Sacred Scriptures nowhere assign to her."[134] Others make incantations to the sea, which, it turns out, is deaf. Many make rash vows: one man offers "heaps of gold to the Virgin of Walsingham if he reached shore alive"; some promise to become Carthusians; others pledge to make pilgrimages; another offers a huge wax taper (which, he admits, he won't give if he is spared); and a Dominican entreats the aid of the saints (since "Christ didn't come to mind").[135] "How devout men are made by suffering," marvels one of the interlocutors.[136] In the midst of this superstitious panic, however, two alternative examples of piety emerge: first, Adolf (the narrator) prays directly to God, since "no saint hears sooner than he"; and, second, a woman with child, "the only one who didn't scream, weep, or make promises," simply prays in silence, holding her child close, and making no bargains with saints or other spirits.[137] Both of these figures serve as exemplars for true piety, and, interestingly, both survive the ordeal. In this and similar dialogues, Erasmus not only parodies the inverted values of common superstition, where trivial and secondary features of religious life are deemed more important than the essential life of faith, he also holds up ideal models for conversion back to authentic piety. Readers thereby are given the chance to glean the difference between authentic faith and the creeping trifles that all too often take over common religious life.[138]

(b) In other *Colloquies* Erasmus' criticism moves from gentle comedy to tough-minded satire. Instead of laughing with his readers, Erasmus now laughs *at* more formidable and destructive forms of religious folly. In "The Abbot and the Learned Lady," for instance, Erasmus takes a good laugh at the anti-intellectual tendencies found in the monastic world, something we saw already in "The Antibarbarians." The reader enters the dialogue as Antronius the abbot is voicing his stern disapproval that a woman like Magdalia (probably a pseudonym for Margaret Roper, Thomas More's eldest daughter) would read books, and Greek and Latin ones at that. In the abbot's narrow little world, "it's not feminine [for women] to be brainy. A lady's business is to have a good time."[139] Latin, he insists, is not a fitting language for women. First printed in 1524 by Froben, this dialogue is one of Erasmus' most Socratic of dialogues. Through rapid-fire interrogation, this learned woman undoes the ignorant abbot's confidence and exposes (at least to readers) his narrow-mindedness. The abbot, it turns out, only values "sleep, dinner parties, doing as one likes, money, [and] honours"; and he wants nothing to do with the "goods of mind."[140] Eventually, however, the abbot grows irritated with this intelligent woman's line of questioning:

Magdalia: Do you think one is human if he's neither wise nor wants to be wise?
Antronius: I'm wise enough—so far as I'm concerned.
Magdalia: And swine are wise enough as far as *they're* concerned.
Antronius: You strike me as a sophistress, so keenly do you dispute.[141]

"The world's a stage that's topsy-turvy," she says to the abbot, and Erasmus says to readers. By the dialogue's end, the abbot appears as what he is (a narrow-minded, bigoted hedonist hiding behind a religious mask), while the woman proves a perfect model of Socratic wisdom.[142]

More pointed satire is reserved for those religious professionals whose greed and deceit constitutes an organized force of public exploitation. Nowhere is Erasmus' critical edge sharper (and more successful) than in "A Pilgrimage for Religion's Sake," a dialogue filled with humorous but mocking derision for the cult of relics and the thievery of the monks who run the pilgrimage shrines. Unlike the previous *Colloquies*, here we listen in on the dialogue between a pious and enthralled pilgrim (Ogygius) and a civil but ironic speaker (Menedemus). Throughout the dialogue, enthusiastic accounts are offset with doubt and ridicule, either from Menedemus or from Ogygius' somewhat irreverent traveling companion (Gratian). Among the many, many marvels are a statue of St. James (who seems to smile and nod in thanks for Ogygius' prayers), a letter from "Mary from the Rock" (who thanks Luther for putting an end to all the lurid petitions people bring to her), a set of Peter's knuckles (which Ogygius kisses, while Gratian snickers), a vast quantity of the Virgin's milk (the authenticity of which is verified by elaborate hearsay), and a sacred piece of wood that cures a man gone mad (though he may have just dried out). At many of these sights, Gratian cannot restrain his incredulity, an impropriety which Ogygius pays for, literally, with coins for the irritated monks. "To make fun of the saints is neither reverent nor prudent," warns Ogygius.[143] But Gratian (and Erasmus) cannot help laughing. When, later, at a shrine for a martyred saint, the resident monks bring forth an arm "with the blood-stained flesh still on it," Gratian shrinks from kissing it, and as a result, offends his hosts once more.[144] Gratian "display[s] something less than graciousness" again, when the prior kindly offers him some linen rags which were used by the saint to wipe "the sweat from his face or neck, the dirt from his nose, or whatever other kinds of filth human bodies have."[145] "Puckering his lips as though whistling,"

Gratian provides an excellent vehicle for Erasmus' laughing criticism, though Ogygius' reverence is an equally effective tool with which to critically expose these absurdities.

Though Erasmus' satirical lampoon of relics is funny in its own right, "A Pilgrimage for Religion's Sake" also takes aim at the corruption of the religious professionals who amass great sums of wealth at the expense of the poor. The shrine to Thomas, for instance, is said to contain "a golden chest" filled with "inestimable treasures." In Ogygius' words, "everything shone and dazzled with rare and surpassingly large jewels, some bigger than a goose egg."[146] The monks, it seems, have made a good profit selling religious superstition. In response to this wealth, Gratian (and hence, Erasmus) asks,

> Since . . . the saint was so liberal towards the needy, though he was still poor himself and lacked money to provide for the necessities of life, don't you think he'd gladly consent, now that he's so rich and needs nothing, if some poor wretched woman with hungry children at home, or daughters in danger of losing their virtue because they have no money for dowries, or a husband sick in bed and penniless—if, after begging the saint's forgiveness, she carried off a bit of all this wealth to rescue her family . . . ?[147]

The custodians of the shrine are incensed, of course, by the very question; but their indignation quickly subsides—as usual—when Ogygius apologizes for Gratian and gives them some more coins. On the return trip the pilgrims avoid the route by the shore, since that area is "notorious for frauds and robberies." "It's extraordinary," Menedemus quips with irony, that these thieves "should dare to commit such a serious crime in the presence of so many witnesses"—which, of course, is exactly what those who capitalize on the veneration of relics are doing.[148] Instead the two travelers have to pass through a gauntlet of beggars who harass them for money. At the close of the dialogue, Erasmus ironically poses this critical question to readers: are these monks who profit from the sale of religion any different from thieves and beggars?

At times, however, Erasmus' critical satire aims higher than mere monks and abbots. Indeed, in "Julius Excluded from Heaven," a dialogue between Saint Peter and the recently deceased Pope Julius II, Erasmus examines (though without taking public credit)[149] the corruption of the papacy. Erasmus had witnessed the triumphant march of this "warrior pope" into Bologna in 1506; and, as Michael J. Heath remarks, the "spectacle of Julius' pontificate" helped to crystalize both Erasmus' pacifism and his "commitment to the reform of the church."[150] Reminiscent of Lucian's dialogues of the dead, the dialogue takes place at the gates of heaven, a forum where (as we saw in chapter five) "only truth counts."[151] Julius arrogantly demands entrance for himself and his army of "seasoned cutthroats," threatening Peter with his "thunderbolt of excommunication" for not letting him enter at once.[152] Wondering how such threats could come from a man of Christ, Peter questions what kind of life this pope has led. In response, Julius brags of his shady procurement of the papacy, he touts the riches he accumulated, he speaks with pride of his military conquests, and he boasts of his maneuvers to neutralize a council that dared to criticize him.[153] As this testimony proceeds, the contrast between Julius' papacy and the life of a true disciple of Christ is magnified: "Is this the role of the shepherd, the most holy Father, the vicar of Christ?"[154] Clearly not, Peter concludes, for this man "who wishes to be thought the closest to Christ, and even his equal, is involved with all the most sordid things, money, power, armies, treaties, not to mention vices." Julius is "the furthest from Christ"; he is "truly Christ's enemy."[155] In this dialogue, we see the full negative force of satirical criticism at work; indeed, Erasmus may have been a bit embarrassed that he had actually named his target—the "all-too-mighty Julius" as he calls him elsewhere.[156] But the contrast between Julius' decadent, fraudulent papacy and Peter's ideal of apostolic simplicity and virtue nonetheless provides perfect leverage with which to expose papal failures and shortcomings, without, however, giving up all hope that the ideal may be realized by his successor.[157]

Some of Erasmus' most persistent and formidable opponents were the orthodox theologians of the Sorbonne and Louvain. Though many of his *Colloquies* triggered hostility and censure, only a few of these dialogues satirize the highly trained folly of these theologians, and none of these are nearly as sophisticated as "A Pilgrimage for Religion's Sake." A set of Erasmus' "Formulae" probably written in 1497–1498, the precursor to the *Colloquies* that provided students with exercises in speaking and writing Latin, takes a comic shot at the Scotist theologians of the day. In "All's New," Peter tells of "a certain Cretan" named Epimenides, who fell asleep in a cave and remained asleep for "forty-seven whole years."[158] "I Don't Believe It" follows, with Peter raising a question that links the legend with contemporary theology: "Just what do you think a theologian— as Epimenides was said to be—dreamt about for so many years?" "Answer" gives the answer: as Peter puts it, "what else than what Scotus and men of his ilk produced later on."[59] The key difference between Epimenides and later theologians, and the only thing which makes this grouping of formulae interesting, is that Epimenides enjoyed the happy ending of waking up: "*he* finally came to his senses! Many theologians never wake up from their dreams."[160] As Erasmus put the same point in a letter written while studying at Paris, "Most of our present-day theologians never wake up at all, and believe themselves quite wide-awake when in fact they are drugged with mandrake." The Scotists are dead to the world around them! With such comical jabs, Erasmus entertained himself while "sitting agape among those glorified Scotists" in Paris.[161]

Erasmus makes fun of the scholastic theologians at Louvain in a colloquy titled "The Epithalamium of Peter Gilles." Originally written to congratulate an old friend (Peter Gilles) on his marriage, Erasmus added a prologue in 1517 or 1518 designed to praise Jerome Busleiden's generous funding of the Trilingual College at the University of Louvain.[162] At the dialogue's start we find the Erasmian Alypius marveling at the "lovely spectacle" of "the nine Muses and the three Graces." His interlocutor (a Scotist named Balbinus) can see nothing of the Muses; he thinks Alypius is mad.

> **Balbinus:** But I've never heard anyone more raving than you.
> **Alypius:** On the contrary, you've seen no one happier than I.
> **Balbinus:** Why do you alone have eyes here?
> **Alypius:** Because you haven't drunk from the fountain of the Muses. For only those who have done so can be aware of the Muses.
> **Balbinus:** As for me, I've drank plentifully from Scotus' fountain.
> **Alypius:** That's not the fountain of the Muses but a frog pond.[163]

Alypius tries to give Balbinus his vision by sprinkling his eyes with water, but to no avail. "How deep the darkness that blinds your eyes," Alypius exclaims. The prologue closes with the Muses lambasting the University of Louvain: "what have we to do with that place where so many swine grunt, asses bray, camels bleat, daws scream, magpies chatter?"[164] They promise to take up residence there in the future, however, after Jerome Busleiden sponsors "a college at Louvain, where men of vast learning will give free public instruction in the three languages."[165] Though the Scotists blindly reign today, the study of languages will soon replace them at Louvain.

Somewhat surprisingly, Erasmus rarely returns to satirize his theological adversaries in the *Colloquies*. Perhaps Erasmus is following his own advice that it is better to avoid needless controversy by not stirring the hornet's nest. What comments he does make are dropped into the flow of other dialogues. In "A Fish Diet," for instance, the butcher reminds the fishmonger that one can't trust the judgment of someone simply because they have a "doctor's degree." Besides, he adds, there is so much "extraordinary disagreement among the most learned men" that they help little in resolving difficult religious questions.[166] Erasmus returns to ridicule the pretensions to sacred knowledge and the useless bickering between religious orders in "The Funeral." The most constant item for criticism, however, is the ignorance of languages among academic theologians. In "The Sermon, or Merdardus," for example, an Erasmian speaker complains that

> many theologians have neglected the cultivation of languages and the study of Latin diction, as well as the ancient Doctors of the church, who cannot be fully understood without these helps—a condition very hard to rectify, moreover, once it is firmly fixed in one's mind. You can find some who pay such deference to scholastic opinions that they'd rather distort Scripture than correct human judgments by the rule of Scripture.[167]

Convinced they are correct, there is no point laboring over language skills which can only discount their own claims. Academic obscurantism and dogmatism are again the butt of Erasmian humor in "A Meeting of the Philological Society." There we find seven academic authorities entertaining some of the most far-fetched and unfounded etymologies imaginable to explain the meaning of the word *anticomarita*. Each outpaces the other in obscurity, but in the end, they conclude that anyone who disagrees with them will be labeled "HERETIC IN GRAMMAR."[168] Ignorance and dogmatism, it seems, walk hand in hand. It is not without significance, therefore, that the more trustworthy sources of theological knowledge in Erasmus' *Colloquies* are usually lay people, as we will see shortly in "The Godly Feast."

In each of the *Colloquies* discussed here we find Erasmus blending serious inquiry and pointed criticism with playful humor and lighthearted fun. Clearly, for Erasmus, Horace was right: no law is violated if someone laughs at religion while speaking the truth. And, indeed, the truth about religious life may be spoken more honestly, more incisively, and more effectively, if it is laced with fun and humor. A comic touch helps to promote self-knowledge, as when Erasmus invites his readers to chuckle at the folly of their own superstition. Here everyone is included and the tone is lighthearted. Further, comic genres of writing facilitate criticism of everything that is false and base in religion—including, as we have seen, monastic corruption, papal militarism, and scholastic dogmatism. Here the target is quite specific and the tone becomes satirical in the style of Lucian. The aim of these dialogues, as we have seen, is to help readers penetrate the appearances of official religion, and, thereby, to detect and undermine the destructive hypocrisy that has taken up residence at the heart of religion. Whether operating in a comic or satiric vein, Erasmus' dialogues of folly artfully create scenes of discourse which poke and prod readers into serious reflection on what is ideal—hence, on what is all too often missing—in Christian life. In sum, Erasmian criticism moves indirectly by way of the interlocutors' discourse; it develops playfully, in a manner that allows readers to consider freely the questions at hand; it speaks with humor, since serious truths are more readily faced with a little laughter; it works ironically, trying to expose the gaping contrasts between authentic Christian life and what goes for "Christian"; and, it concludes with a hortatory twist, inviting readers to a life that is faith-filled, learned, honest, humble, and, above all, peaceful. These qualities, but especially the irenic handling of disputes, comprise Erasmus' ethic of discourse. The next two sections will take a look at this ethic.

(3) At the Limits of Irenicism

Erasmus frequently sang the praise of peace. Indeed, as Phillips remarks, "no topic aroused so passionate a defense under his pen."[169] Defend it he did—

repeatedly—in correspondence with friends and allies, and notably in a letter to Wolfgang Capito in February of 1517, in which he allows himself to dream and hope that the "greatest princes of the world" soon will uproot the "nurseries of war" and establish a permanent peace across Europe.[170] At other times Erasmus confidently directed letters to people who he thought might exert some helpful influence at royal courts, sending, for example, a protest against war to Antoon van Bergen, who Erasmus hoped might advise Prince Charles, as well as Maximilian, against the building tides of war.[171] Far more boldly, Erasmus also took occasion to disseminate his horror of war and his praise of peace directly to monarchs and popes through the prefaces dedicating his *Paraphrases*. Thus we find Erasmus lecturing Charles, king of France, on the benefits of peace, the terrible costs of war, and the sacred duties of Christian leaders in securing concord between peoples.[172] And he takes the opportunity to advise Prince Ferdinand (Archduke of Austria and brother to the Emperor Charles) against the "evil counsellors" who suggest the prince's religious duties are fulfilled by attending mass and saying the "hour-offices," rather than looking forward "to forestall the storms of war before they rise."[173] Imagine also the effect on Pope Clement VII of having Erasmus exhort him to administer the medicine of concord to the "chaotic enmities" raging between Charles V and Francis I.[174] In the *Colloquies*, too, Erasmus dares to challenge those who perpetrate the violence and destruction of warfare: the kings and princes, who, "in deadly hatred, clash to their mutual destruction," dragging all of Christendom into "the ravages of war";[175] the popes, like Julius II, who divide the body of Christ by waging "holy war" against the French (and others) in pursuit of worldly glory;[176] the generals, like the one portrayed in the "The Funeral," who grows wealthy from "robberies, sacrileges, and extortions";[177] and finally, the soldiers, those "reckless, rapacious, and impious adventurers," who bring death and disease to themselves and to all they encounter.[178] When it comes to war, Erasmus' critical edge is at its sharpest; and appropriately, his words of exhortation are their boldest and most compelling when he is praising peace.

Erasmus could also draft more systematic reflections on war and peace, as he did in the exquisite and powerful adage titled "War is sweet to those who have not tried it,"[179] and again, in "A Complaint of Peace Spurned and Rejected by the Whole World," which Betty Radice rightly calls his "most explicit and celebrated plea for general peace."[180] In both works, Erasmus seeks to awaken his readers to the evils and insanity of warfare with three separate, yet complementary, lines of appeal. First, he argues in a manner reminiscent of the Stoics, that war constitutes an inversion of Nature's design. How preposterous that "a peaceful creature, whom nature made for peace and loving-kindness (the only one, indeed, whom she intended for the safety of all), should rush with savage insanity, with such mad commotion, to mutual slaughter."[181] Nature gave humankind all the tools required to maintain peace and harmony—a gentle appearance; "friendly eyes"; "embracing arms"; the kiss (by which "soul meets soul"); "laughter, the sign of merriment"; "tears, the mark of mercy"; "the use of speech and reason, the thing above all which would serve to create and preserve goodwill"; a hatred of solitude and love of companionship; the "love of learning" which yields "the greatest power of knitting up friendships"; and finally, "a spark of the mind of God, so that without having any reward in view, he might take a disinterested delight in being of service to all."[182] All these gifts (it turns out) are wasted on their recipients, who rush headlong into "wholesale butchery," leaving "the slaughtered lying in heaps, the fields running with gore, the rivers dyed with human blood."[183] As Erasmus wryly notes, no group of animals can match the ferocious violence organized by human beings. Nature can only wonder (and lament), therefore, what evil genius has spoiled her work.

Second, Erasmus appeals to the disastrous (and disproportionate) consequences of engaging in armed conflict. In "times of peace," Erasmus observes,

> fields are tilled, gardens grow green, flocks graze in contentment, buildings go up on country estates and in the towns, . . . wealth increases, . . . the laws are in full strength, statecraft flourishes, religious fervour glows, justice holds sway, humanity is influential, arts and crafts are carried on with enthusiasm, the poor earn more and the opulence of the rich is more splendid.

But in gross contrast, "as soon as the wild storm of war breaks out, . . . what a tidal wave of misfortune rushes in":

> Flocks are driven away, crops trampled underfoot, peasants slaughtered, farms burnt, flourishing cities which took centuries to build are overturned by a single squall. . . . The citizens' wealth falls into the hands of accursed brigands and mercenaries. Homes mourn, everywhere there is fear, sorrow, wailing and lamentation.[184]

The human agony is only worsened, Erasmus adds, by the deployment of newly devised weapons (artillery). Since the costs (political, financial, cultural, human, and moral) far outweigh the gains (a bit of land, a smattering of honor, a taste of revenge), no rational—certainly, no Christian—person can be considered in their right mind who prefers the damages to the benefits of war. "Make some calculations" of the costs and benefits, Erasmus counsels the political leaders of Europe; "do not think only of what you wish to gain, but think of what you will lose to gain it—the sacrifice of so much that is good, the danger and disasters you will incur."[185]

Erasmus' third, and most passionate, line of criticism stems directly from the philosophy of Christ. Examine Christ's teaching, Erasmus challenges his readers, and you will find "nothing anywhere which does not breathe the spirit of peace, which does not savour of love." Indeed, "just as the whole of [Christ's] teaching spelt tolerance and love, so his entire life was a lesson in compassion."[186] And yet,

Erasmus observes in horror and indignation, Christians everywhere plunge themselves into the fury of armed conflict, not only against common enemies (e.g., the Turks), but also against other Christians; and not only for debatably legitimate reasons (to defend the common good), but for the most petty and self-serving interests (e.g., the childish feuds between princes). Worse, "no one is astonished, no one is horrified,"[187] mainly because "warmongering priests" and ignorant theologians dare to bless the warrior's efforts—and on both sides of the battle at that![188] In all of this, Erasmus observes with sadness, everything is mixed up. Everything is inverted. Everything about Christ is lost. Christ taught love—"what could be more opposed to this than war? He greets his friends with blessed salutation of peace." Why, then, do Christians "rush to butcher each other," all the while "making Christ the witness and authority for so criminal a thing?"[189] Erasmus' questions here are extremely pointed: "What has a mitre to do with a helmet, a crozier with a sword, the Gospel with a shield?"[190] And the answer, plainly, is nothing at all.

Authentic Christian life, conversely, has everything to do with peace and harmony between peoples. As Erasmus puts it in his adage on war and peace, three qualities should adhere to those who "deserve the name of Christian":

> innocence, that is to be pure from vice; charity, to do good to all as far as we may; and patience, to tolerate evildoers and where possible overwhelm the evil with good.[191]

These three virtues comprise, for Erasmus, the conditions for a life actively committed to peace and concord. Though it surely will look foolish to those enamored of the world's wisdom, Christian life is, in the first place, meant to be free of the vices which generate conflict and hostility—most prominently the desire for glory and power, mixed with "anger, ambition, and folly."[192] Second, Christian life is supposed to be marked with love and kindness, not only for those of one's own fold but across group lines, to embrace all people.[193] Finally, living a true Christian life means being patient and tolerant, even of wrong-doers (heretics) and enemies (the Turks). It would be both more Christian and more effective, Erasmus suggests, if Christians fought the Turks with Christ-like virtues rather than unChristian weapons. "If language fails us," he advises, let "conduct worthy of the Gospel" be our "mighty eloquence." And for Erasmus, there is no method more persuasive in reconciling adversaries than "a blameless life, the wish to do good even to our enemies, a tolerance which will withstand all injuries, contempt of money, heedlessness of glory, [and] life held lightly." The most truly Christian response to error and hostility, in short, is loving persuasion and "mild reasoning"; as Erasmus puts it, "concord will be more easily maintained if on most questions each is free to understand things in his own way, so long as it is without contention."[194] These virtues—innocent purity, loving kindness, and tolerance—

comprise the Erasmian antidote to violent conflict and war; and they constitute a lifestyle conducive to a more humane and peaceful existence.

What Erasmus says about war and peace carries over directly to human affairs and to the whole gamut of human discourse. Indeed, as Erasmus observes in "The Tongue," so much of human discourse is full of poison and frenzy. Strife and tumult appear ubiquitous. Though nature designed human speech to be the "governor of human life, ready for its responsibility to care for human advantage and assistance," and though venomous discourse inevitably "brings about the private and public ruin of the human race," people everywhere debase the powers of the tongue not only by excesses of speech (chattering and indiscretion), but especially through deceptive speech (lying, flattery, and perjury) and aggressive talk (slander, backbiting, and calumny).[195] There is "no corner of the world" to which one can flee, Erasmus laments, to be safe from "an evil tongue."[196] Christians are no exception; indeed, Erasmus observes, they hurl themselves into contention and dispute, "battling to the death with so many conflicting dogmas."[197] What a confusion of tongues, as each Christian claims to be something else; one man a Scotist, another a Thomist, a third a Lutheran, yet another a follower of Karlstadt, and so on. It is as if they want to rebuild Babel, that "tower of pride and strife," as they "attack each other's lives and teachings."[198] And there is no shortage among Christians of poisonous discourse: witness the habit of churchmen "criticizing and slandering perfectly correct behavior, distorting by a malicious interpretation honest words, wielding heresy as a charge, where there was a praiseworthy act of piety."[199] Conflict flourishes across the board of human discourse.

But if Christians are (as they say) "tendrils of the same vine," all joined together in Christ, then they should "mark the nature of Christ's tongue" and "imitate this tongue with all [their] might."[200] And that means, for Erasmus, first and foremost that every individual Christian must become "modest" (what he calls having a "tongue that confesses all"), and by so doing, turn toward others with language that is healing, mild, and conciliatory.[201] The first step toward authentic Christian discourse, consequently, is the renunciation of the "self-seeking and arrogance with which we are puffed up"; instead of accusing others, one should— with modesty—concentrate on "confessions of our own evils." Concretely, this means shunning "excess of talking" and learning to "love silence"; it means replacing "cheap jests" with "good conversation" which "conduces to the edification of the faith"; and it means replacing covetous speech with words of thanksgiving.[202] In the context of social relations, it means putting aside "all bitterness and anger and indignation and clamour and blasphemy"—the very things that stir up the poisons of controversy and conflict. In place of slander and denigration, the one who practices Christ-like speech is to offer "brotherly rebuke" and "a mild and honest reproof." Gentle criticism, Erasmus counsels, is far superior to punitive measures: would it not be far more effective (and humane) if one who has erred or sinned were to feel that, in receiving the bishop's reproof, "he is being handled by a doctor, not a butcher"?[203] Christian speech, in sum, should be conciliatory. "When shall we recall our brother from error," Erasmus asks, "if he sees he is dealing with enemies" who do nothing but "bark abuse" and threaten with condemnations? The "tongue of the good shepherd," alternatively, is to imitate God's eloquent word in Christ, and with trust and love "bind up what is broken, to make firm what is frail. . . ."[204]

Every one of these points—the critique of quarrelsome and divisive speech and the eulogy of modest and irenic discourse—is evident throughout Erasmus' own life and career. Indeed, Erasmus knew from years of experience the depth and the vehemence of theological hostility—first from his never-ending controversies with theologians of Catholic orthodoxy (notably with the Carmelite Nicolaus Baechem and Jabous Latomus at Louvain, but also Edward Lee over the New Testament translations, and with the Sorbonnist theologians who repeatedly censured Erasmus), and later from various reformers (including not only Luther, but also Hutten and Oecolampadius). Despite the frequency and the severity of polemics directed against him, Erasmus continued to value, to teach, to advance, and (more often than not) to practice a kind of discourse that is critical and ironic, yet modest and irenic. This is the most central, enduring, and remarkable feature of Erasmus' project in Christian humanism. His writings (including the dialogues) feature the practice of modest, loving, and irenic discourse as the defining measure of authentic Christian life. When, for instance, someone is encountered who is different—a Jew, a superstitious man, or perhaps an adversary—Erasmus counsels "gentleness and courtesy." Persuasion "will come about more readily through goodwill than through contentious arguing," he insists.

> In order that peace and concord exist everywhere among you, some things must be ignored, some endured, some interpreted with more kindness. This forbearance and sincerity has great force to produce mutual fellowship of life. Peace will never remain firm among many unless in some things one gives way in turn to another, inasmuch as there are various opinions among people.[205]

Thus, Erasmus argues again and again, only "the modesty proper to a Christian" can begin to temper "the war between scholars now carried on with tongue and pen." Saying this, however, does not rule out criticism, for disagreement is not the same thing as insult; and the emphatic expression of indignation also is not unwarranted, Erasmus insists, where the gospel is trampled under the "deep lethargy" of theological opinion.[206] But, in major storms of controversy (like that surrounding Martin Luther, for instance), Erasmus felt that the "mutual fellowship" of authentic Christian life could only be restored though a return to modesty, tolerance, and discourse steeped in conciliatory love. We thus find Erasmus advising Luther to take a more moderate tone, while encouraging Luther's critics (like

Cuthbert Tunstall, and, through him, Thomas More) to take a more sober, scholarly, and honest look at Luther's principles.[207] The key to authentic Christian life, Erasmus insists, is actual practice of humane and peaceful discourse, but to approximate this ideal means abandoning the antagonistic rhetoric of opposition, while standing firm on the Christ-like principles of modesty, charity, and patience. Such is the centrality and the constancy of his "irenic spirit."

This is not to suggest that Erasmus was noble and virtuous on every occasion. He clearly was not. As Schoeck observes, though Erasmus consistently maintained the "goal of peace," he nonetheless "engaged in a great deal of controversial writing, some of it petty and personal."[208] His ironic criticism of religious folly—in the *Colloquies*, for instance—did not always appear so humorous to those who were the butt of his jokes. Edward Lee, to take but one example, was incensed with the barbs Erasmus sent his way. Two passages of a colloquy (which he took to be aimed at him) proved especially irksome—one that brands a "famous Scotist" as arrogant and bitter; the other suggesting this man's work would be better used for "wiping the buttocks." Is this "that famous modesty" of Erasmus, Lee asks? Are these the words of the world's "great theologian, its moral critic, its monk, its paragon of humility"? "Could one say anything filthier, more revolting, more poisonous? Is there a noisy ruffian, a buffoon, a low comedian, the keeper of a privy who could have voided anything so foul on anyone?"[209] Clearly, Lee is upset. He has been stung by Erasmus.

The latter's correspondence on these matters reveals that Erasmus knew he had overstepped his usual bounds. He thus writes to a friend: "I, the familiar champion and preacher of peace and tranquility, have entered the ring; I deal out black eyes and receive them in turn."[210] Erasmus is aware, in short, that he has violated his own standards through his laughing criticism. But he also is quick to defend himself—first with a concession and then with a more practical statement of his ethic of discourse. From the beginning of his career, Erasmus writes to Martin Dorp, he had sought never to "attack any mortal in print by name."[211] That self-imposed directive, however, proved impossible to maintain. It is just too tempting to strike back at narrow-minded and hostile opponents by making them the target of a good joke. As he laments elsewhere, "some evil genius grudged me this enviable reputation"; he could not, in other words, remain perfectly irenic.[212] Despite this short-fall, Erasmus proudly claims a record of modesty and forbearance. He has never written, he claims in 1523,

> to hurt to the extent of never drawing sword against anyone except under insufferable provocation; nor have I ever answered anyone without overcoming by forbearance an adversary who had the advantage of me in scurrility.[213]

Erasmus is not a saint and does not claim to be one. And though he has written immodestly in the heat of controversy—to Lee, for instance—Erasmus clings tenaciously to a policy of modesty, respect, and conciliation. "Who can you show me in the whole range of authors," he asks, who is "so modest that he never wrote with acrimony of anyone?"[214] That much is only human. However, even with the expected lapses, (indeed, precisely because they are lapses,) Erasmus is note-worthy in his persistent effort to take the high road by promoting modest, tolerant, and irenic discourse. There is, in sum, a consistently irenic trajectory in Erasmus' discourse over religious issues.

The most important and distinctive feature of Erasmus' discourse on religion is the far-reaching extent to which he takes irenic discourse. Indeed, in practice and in texts, Erasmus takes irenic discourse to its limits. Hounded by the theologians of Catholic orthodoxy and peppered by assaults through pamphlets by Luther's friends,[215] Erasmus finds himself in the crossfire of two antagonists. Looking to the right and to the left, he notes how "each side draws unto itself the rope of con-tention."[216] And with that rope stretched taught, Erasmus' plea—that "both sides pursue Christ's business on Christian principles"—cannot but sound odd, unsup-portive, even disingenuous to both antagonists. Pressured by both sides to join and scorned by both parties for his refusal, Erasmus' position—and his discourse of peace—becomes increasingly precarious. As he puts it, somewhat blithely, "my misdeeds amount to this: I am all for moderation, and the reason why I have a bad name with both sides is that I exhort both parties to adopt a more peaceable policy."[217] His refusal to participate in the rhetoric of a "side" and his persistent calls for reconciliation make the middle ground upon which he speaks increas-ingly shaky. Irenic discourse is stretched and strained to the breaking point by the expectations and criticism of his opponents. What is most important here is that Erasmus' stance—which his opponents inevitably regard as shallow and cowardly neutrality—is founded on a basic commitment to a Christian ethic of discourse. Erasmus is anything but neutral with respect to *how* people speak with each other.

In the remainder of this section, I want to look at three dialogues that illus-trate the limits of Erasmian irenicism: one dialogue that responds to the inhumane treatment of Johannes Reuchlin (a lawyer, a scholar of Jewish languages and mysticism, and a humanist who argued, against the tide of Christian anti-Semitism for tolerance and loving respect of European Jews), and two dialogues dealing with Martin Luther.

(a) In "The Apotheosis of That Incomparably Worthy, John Reuchlin," Eras-mus works to vindicate the scholarly achievement of the period's greatest student of Hebrew languages and literature (especially the Kabbalah) against the narrow-minded and hot-headed theologians at Cologne who hounded Reuchlin relent-lessly with accusations, inquisitions, trials, and condemnations. Shortly after Reuchlin's death, the dialogue tells us, an "exceptionally holy" Franciscan had a vision in which Reuchlin (clad in a "dazzlingly white, marvelously shining robe") passes over a bridge into heaven, all the while being chased by grotesque "black-feathered" birds (i.e., Dominicans) who "were as big as vultures, with crests, hooked beaks, and talons, and puffed-up bellies."[218] After Reuchlin banishes these furies with a simple sign of the cross—leaving "a stench that would make dung seem sweet marjoram or spinekard by comparison"—St. Jerome greets his "most holy colleague," embraces him, and escorts him upon "a great pillar of fire" into the sky, both clad in gowns decorated with tongues of bronze, emerald, and sapphire—jewels meant to signify the "three languages in which they excelled."[219] So as not to leave any doubt about his support of Reuchlin's scholarship, Erasmus caps off this charming encomium by making Reuchlin a saint—a point that earned him the rebuke of the theological faculty in Paris some four years later.[220] The dialogue closes with words of prayer designed to eulogize serious linguistic studies, while (again) slamming the barbarians who slander such efforts: "O sacred spirit, bless languages and those who study them; prosper godly speech; bring to nought evil speech, infected by the poison of hell."[221]

This dialogue represents, in the first place, an unqualified support for the line of scholarship pursued by Reuchlin. Indeed, as Erasmus' letters show, he greatly respected Reuchlin's "range of literatures and languages" and he praised his "courtesy and personal charm."[222] In addition, he strongly endorsed Reuchlin's stand against the burning of all Hebrew books (something proposed by Johann Pfefferkorn to the emperor Maxmillian); and later he was genuinely appreciative of Reuchlin's cooperation in preparing a scholarly edition of Jerome.[223] Secondly, the dialogue provides a ringing denunciation of Reuchlin's opponents—and some of Erasmus' to boot.

What does not appear in the dialogue, however, is the unease (and increasing ambivalence) he felt over entering the public fray on Reuchlin's behalf. Indeed, as he would distance himself from Luther in years to come, Erasmus seems to distance himself from Reuchlin, something which earned the rebuke of Ulrich von Hutten.[224] Thus we find Erasmus declaring to Willibald Pirckheimer (a leading patron of letters in Nürnberg) that, though he is friends with Reuchlin, he has nothing to do with his case.[225] Elsewhere, he insists that, while he supports Reuchlin, he wants no quarrel with Jacob van Hoogstroten, the leader of the Cologne Dominicans who were attacking him.[226] In 1519, after his letters to Reuchlin were published without his approval, Erasmus claimed that he is "no Reuchlinist."[227] Finally, Erasmus complains to Thomas Wolsey that his opponents "confound the cause of the humanities with the business of Reuchlin and Luther, though there is no connection between them."[228] Given these statements, how are we to read the unqualified tribute to Reuchlin in "The Apotheosis"?

Admittedly, Erasmus' letters give the impression of abandoning Reuchlin in his time of need. To those eager and willing for a fight (as Hutten was, for instance), Erasmus can only appear to be weak in character with his claims of neutrality. A more careful glance, however, reveals an Erasmus who is not forsaking Reuchlin, but simply and consistently taking his stand in a manner which he believes will best uphold and sustain the dialogue of learning and faith. When, therefore, Erasmus says that he is not involved in Reuchlin's case, he means (very precisely) that he has not participated in the "venomous conflicts" between Reuchlin and the supporters of Jacob of Hoogstraten;[229] indeed the bitter tone of Reuchlin's supporters (in the famous *Letters of Unknown Men*, for instance) deeply disturbed Erasmus.[230] "Both sides are using paper with teeth in it," he laments to John Fisher.[231] For his part, as we would come to expect, Erasmus counsels "civilized restraint" and abstinence from personal attacks.[232]

When, moreover, he backs away from conflict with Reuchlin's foes, he is acting on a very practical perception that it is extremely distasteful (and futile) to enter into a controversy from which one "can derive nothing, win or lose, but poison, pox, and mischief."[233] Erasmus prefers, in contrast, to take the "high-minded line" by not condescending to "a conflict with all those swarms of hornets, armed with poison as well as stings."[234] When, therefore, he renounces the label "Reuchlinist," he is not rejecting Reuchlin but the idea that good scholarship and sound Christian faith will be furthered by joining a faction. Thus Erasmus declares, "I am no 'Reuchlinist'. I belong to no man's party, and detest these factious labels. I am a Christian, and I know what 'Christian' means; I will not tolerate 'Erasmists,' and 'Reuchlinists' is not a word I know."[235] Finally, when he separates the cause of humanities from that of Reuchlin and Luther, he simply is stating the obvious: Reuchlin is a scholar of Hebrew literature and Luther is an activist in church reform, and neither of these falls readily into the dialogue of learning and faith Erasmus hopes to advance. It is better, Erasmus contends, to pursue the matter by soliciting the support of church authorities and magistrates[236]— which is why he wrote to two cardinals and to Pope Leo X to gain powerful support for Reuchlin.[237] Erasmus is anything but silent and neutral in this case; he speaks in a manner and through channels by which he can hope reasonably for success.

In substance, therefore, Erasmus sides with Reuchlin, but when it comes to the bitter style of controversial discourse (even for a good cause like Reuchlin's) he will not endorse it. Nor will he participate in it. And because of this, Erasmus appears (in his correspondence surrounding this dialogue) to stand alone, detached, and on neutral ground. In fact, Erasmus' stand is anything but neutral. Rather, his position rests on the fundamental perception that the actual practice of love and concord are the decisive factors shaping authentic Christian life. Hostility for religion's sake simply makes no sense for Erasmus, even if it is intended for an ostensibly good cause. The primacy Erasmus gives to the virtues of Christian discourse is bolstered by a second, very practical perception—namely, that it is absolutely futile to engage raving monsters in debate. No good can come from such talk. What Erasmus fears most in this regard is that serious damage will be done to the dialogue of faith and learning—either because scholarship will become an ever more susceptible target for anti-intellectual aggression, or because good scholars will be distracted from their work and infected in their character by participating in the invective common to such conflicts. But this does *not* mean that he will not support Reuchlin. It means, rather, that he will pursue the cause of this embattled scholar through the most opportune outlets available—that is, by soliciting support for Reuchlin from people of power. Erasmus' true position is crystallized in the counsel he sends by letter to Reuchlin: "Let us, my dear Reuchlin, forget these monsters, let us take our joy in Christ, and pursue honourable studies."[238] It is this convergence of patient forbearance, faith in Christ, and scholarly study, which Erasmus fancies in "The Apotheosis" and expresses in the related correspondence.

(b) Similar issues and questions arise for Erasmus in the whirlwind of controversies surrounding the reform activities of Martin Luther. In this case, however, the textual evidence is more massive, the sentiments expressed by Erasmus are more complex and dynamic (his views of 1518, understandably, are not those of 1525), and the layers of interpretation that have settled around his controversy make it extremely difficult to discern Erasmus' stance. Clearly, however, Erasmus struggles to pursue the same policy of moderation and reconciliation, and in so doing, he reaches the same precarious limits of irenic discourse as he did in the Reuchlin case.

In a famous catalogue of his works, written to Johann von Botzheim in 1523, Erasmus calls attention to three (as yet unfinished) dialogues in which he attempts a "discussion rather than a confrontation" on the "question of Martin Luther."[239] These dialogues, he tells Botzheim, will represent the exchange between three characters: Thrasymachus (taking "Luther's part"), Eubulus (representing "the other side"), and Philalethes (who will "act as arbiter," presumably in the style of Erasmus). The description of each dialogue's content is very cryptic, but nonetheless conveys Erasmus' intentions. The first text will investigate whether "this approach" (that of 'discussion' rather than 'confrontation') will be "expedient"; the second will take up some of Luther's doctrines; and the third is to "display a method of bringing this conflict to a peaceful end in such a way that it cannot break out again in the future."[240] Most importantly, for the purposes of this discussion, Erasmus specifies the tone and style of the interlocutors' discourse:

> The question will be discussed between the two of them without scurrilities, with no wrangling and no disguise; the bare truth only will be put forward, in a simple and countrified way, with such fairness and moderation that there will be more danger, I think, from the indignation of the opposite party, who will interpret my mildness as collusion with the enemy, than from Luther himself, if he has any grain of the sense with which many people credit him—and I for one wish him joy if he has it, and hope he may acquire it if not.[241]

Here we see in simple outline the kind of ideal discourse Erasmus hoped would transpire between Catholic orthodoxy and Luther. In his preferred world of discourse, open and fair discussion would replace scurrility and wrangling. It is interesting to note, here, that Erasmus expects (and seems to get a certain pleasure from the idea) that the Catholic party will be 'indignant' with the 'mildness' of these dialogues, and, consequently, will regard his indulgence as 'collusion.' He expects less hostility from Luther, though he is uncertain how sensible Luther's response will be. Perhaps that is why Luther is named after Thrasymachus—the character from Plato's *Republic* who defines justice by the self-interest of the powerful. What is crucial, however, is the insistence that mildness is preferable to severity in reconciling the differences of these adversaries.

It is regrettable, indeed, that these dialogues were never written, since they would have given us a graphic and well-rounded literary expression of Erasmus' ideal of modest and peaceful discourse. But because "both parties are now so hot," as Erasmus explains elsewhere, he thought it "better to keep quiet."[242] As Craig R. Thompson suggests, another dialogue by Erasmus—"An Examination Concerning Faith"—may be "an abbreviated version" of the second of these unwritten dialogues.[243] Probably written in late 1523 or early 1524, and first published by Froben in March 1524—at the same time that Erasmus was drafting and circulating his challenge to Luther in "Diatribe on Free Will"—the "Examination" exposes the misunderstandings (mainly on the Catholic side) that infect the discourse between Luther and Catholic orthodoxy.

The dialogue opens with the Catholic speaker (Aulus) nervously greeting the Lutheran (Barbatius). He is afraid, it seems, to stand too close to Barbatius, for fear that God (or his vicar) might strike him down with a thunderbolt; and he worries again about being spiritually infected by Barbatius' heretical contagion. When the latter assures Aulus that there is no risk involved, and, indeed, that there may even be "hope of improvement," Aulus agrees to risk a conversation. In the rest of the dialogue, Aulus interrogates his Lutheran interlocutor to see if he is orthodox according to the Apostles' Creed. Much to Aulus' surprise, Barbatius proves himself of sound doctrine; his beliefs about God, the incarnation, redemption, the resurrection, eschatology, and the trinity all appear to contain nothing heretical. The only substantive point of dissension concerns Barbatius' attitude toward the "holy church"—in his view, it is not proper to "believe *in* the holy church" because "though it consists of none except the good, nevertheless [it] consists of human beings, who can change from good to bad, deceive and be deceived."[244] Despite this disagreement, Aulus finds Barbatius' explanations to be those of a sound believer. So orthodox is he, in fact, he confuses Aulus:

> **Aulus**: When I was at Rome, I did not find everyone so sincere in belief.
> **Barbatius**: No, and if you look around you'll find many elsewhere, too, who aren't equally convinced of these matters.

Aulus: Since you agree with us in so many and so difficult questions, what prevents you from being wholly on our side?

Barbatius: I want to hear about that from you, for I think I'm orthodox. Even if I wouldn't vouch for my life, still I try diligently to make it correspond to what I profess.

Aulus: Then why is there such conflict between you and the orthodox?[245]

That question need not be answered, for Erasmus' point lies in the question itself. It is an open, irenic question to Catholic and Lutheran, challenging both parties to discover how much they have in common, and cautioning them not to let disputes over less important matters needlessly divide them. Such a question is daring indeed, as Thompson notes, for Luther was excommunicated three years earlier.[246]

Though "The Examination" may not be one of Erasmus' most sophisticated literary pieces, the simplicity and brevity of the dialogue contribute mightily to its effect. On one hand, the dialogue is directed primarily at Catholic orthodoxy; it is, after all, Aulus' cockiness and disdain for what he takes to be heterodox that is shown up as hollow and baseless. He is moved from fear and loathing for his Lutheran counterpart to the point of agreeing to dine together. On the other hand, Erasmus makes a point—more subtle, but perhaps also more important—to Luther and his followers. This message emerges when we consider where Erasmus places himself within the dialogue. As Thompson reports, Erasmus elsewhere identifies himself with the character of Aulus, while "his real opinions are put into the mouth of Barbatius."[247] The identification with Aulus may be a sop thrown to orthodox readers (perhaps for defensive purposes) or it may be a joke, but the fact that Erasmus' real views—and, more importantly, his preferred and ideal style of discourse—are put in the mouth of Barbatius must be taken as a message for the Lutheran party. It cannot be for orthodox consumption, since they would be unlikely to find the idea of an irenic Lutheran very credible. It must, therefore, be taken as a subtle correction of Lutheran rhetoric. Not only does the dialogue tell orthodox readers that the Lutheran believes more than enough to be considered orthodox, it also performs the kind of modest and irenic discourse required of the Lutherans if they are to stay in friendly communion with those who would drive them out.

In "The Examination," therefore, we see Erasmus standing in the middle—and at a time when the middle has all but collapsed—chiding those who would claim orthodoxy for themselves at the exclusion of others; and subtly correcting the dissenting group, who would perpetuate their own alienation by harping on the factors of disagreement and persisting with heated rhetoric. He speaks, in short, to both groups at once (even while they cannot speak with each other), challenging and inviting the parties to renounce their animosities for the sake of peace and friendship. What "The Examination" shows, as the basis of these challenges, is the double definition Erasmus gives to the middle ground. First, the ground

upon which all Christians can dwell in an amicable and fruitful manner is determined doctrinally by nothing more than the Creed. As many scholars have noted,
Erasmus always stressed piety and practice over theology and doctrine, and consequently held that church authorities should place less emphasis on defining
articles of belief. Second, the middle ground between orthodox and Lutheran is
defined discursively by the actual practice of modesty, forbearance, and conciliatory love. For Erasmus, the prior standard is intentionally minimal; but the latter is
absolutely essential for Christian life.

The views conveyed by Erasmus through "The Examination," like those
regarding the Reuchlin affair, must be reconciled with what else he wrote on the
same questions.[248] In many cases, such reconciliation is not difficult. First, there
is no conflict between this dialogue and Erasmus' early statements to and about
Luther. Early mention of Luther in Erasmus' correspondence is either neutral (in
as much as Luther's work is not concerned with the kind of scholarship Erasmus
pursues), positive (insofar as Erasmus concurs with Luther's criticism of corruption in the church), laudatory (especially with regard to Luther's integrity), or protective (in that he feels Luther is being savaged by uncritical and unfair charges of
heresy).[249] Second, crucial documents written in the years of Luther's condemnation yield clear evidence of the same kind of sentiments. In his advice to Elector
Frederick the Wise on how to respond to the papal bull against Luther, Erasmus
rejects the un-Christian means (filled with "wrangling, conspiracies, bitter passions, and poisonous libels") by which Luther is dealt with.[250] In another piece
from the same period, Erasmus defends Luther's view on indulgences and papal
power as legitimately "stirred by righteous indignation and zeal for the Christian
faith." Those charged with judging Luther should approach him humanely and
with "brotherly advice," always remembering "the peace of the Christian community," and offering judgment only after a careful study and face-to-face hearing
of Luther's views.[251] All of these recommendations live on, as we have seen,
in Erasmus' dialogue. Finally, "The Examination" squares well with those many
occasions—up through the year of the dialogue's publication—on which Erasmus
levels a criticism of Luther's immoderate rhetoric, while chiding Luther's opponents for the ruthless and unprincipled manner in which they attack him.

Other statements by Erasmus are somewhat more difficult to reconcile with the
balanced irenicism of "The Examination." When, for instance, Erasmus seeks to
distance himself from association with Luther—claiming to Leo X that he does
not know Luther's works—it is hard to avoid the impression that Erasmus is dis-
sembling.[252] He may not know all of Luther's works, but it is unlikely that a
scholar of Erasmus' ilk would not have been familiar with Luther's key writings.
He appears evasive, once again, when he writes to Albert of Brandenburg that
he neither attacks, nor defends, nor answers to Luther.[253] To anyone firmly taking
a side—Lutheran or Romanist—this range of verbs must suggest that Erasmus is

afraid to act, to take a stand. Perhaps he is playing a scholar's game, splitting words; or perhaps he simply lacks nerve. The latter charge seems to receive support from key letters in which Erasmus concedes that he lacks the spirit and the strength to risk his life for Luther.[254] Given these statements, Erasmus' evenhandedness may seem to issue more from weakness than from virtue. The fact that he puts his pen to work against Luther—in the "Diatribe Concerning Free Will," for instance—also appears to undermine the balanced irenicism of "The Examination," as does the hostility directed Luther's way in Erasmus' later correspondence. The question, therefore, is how these other bits of evidence connect to the ethic of discourse acted out in "The Examination."

The answer must begin with a concession and end with a defense. On one hand, Erasmus at times does speak in a hesitant and waffling manner, largely, it seems, out of a natural concern for his own welfare and reputation. One need not deny this very human element in Erasmus' maneuverings. On the other hand, Erasmus' apparent waffling with regard to Luther does not mitigate his dedication to the irenic ethic of discourse projected in "The Examination." When he adopts a heavily qualified position regarding Luther (as he does to Albert, for instance), Erasmus is constructing and prudently defending an independent position; resisting the call to be confined to a "side" in these controversies. What he abhors is the fracture of church life and the rancor exchanged by both parties. And thus, what is called for is a clear religious focus (centered on Christ) and nuanced judgment—and that is precisely what Erasmus seeks to articulate, despite the efforts of each side either to enlist him or to brand him a partisan of the enemy camp. In this vein, he writes to William Blount, that

> The Germans are indignant with me as being, they say, an opponent of Luther; and in your country, I perceive, I am of his party, am I? I must be a proper weathercock, one thing here and something quite different with you. Neither the tricks of some men I could name, nor the promises or hostility of others, have ever been able, or ever shall be, to make me a member of any party but Christ's. A curse on all who rejoice in these factious labels![255]

Erasmus is a Christian, not a weathercock—and the commitments entailed in this identity yield a distance from the factions; and this transcendence, in turn, allows for precisely the kind of nuanced evaluation of both groups that is evident in "The Examination." As he put it in the same letter to Blount, "the teaching of the Gospel, the glory of Christ" draws his work; and he has been a "supporter of the humanities so far as they might serve Christ's glory." Therefore, when Erasmus complains (as he does repeatedly) that the turmoil surrounding Luther has hurt the cause of humane letters—claiming that both Luther's adversaries and his supporters are out to derail serious scholarship—this signals an important distinction of purpose from that of both parties, and thus an important mark of independence that allows for criticism of both sides. Erasmus can see truth and falsity on either side of the fray. This perspective makes it possible to relativize the significance of each party's agenda: in "contests of this kind," he tells Blount, "when the turmoil and the bloodshed are over and the facts are clear, we sometimes find that both parties held the same opinion, and the struggle was only over words." For his part, Erasmus admits, he would "rather go wrong on some points than fight valiantly for the truth and set the world by the ears."[256] In saying this, Erasmus is not being indifferent to truth; rather, he is, once again, giving expression to the evangelical modesty at the heart of the philosophy of Christ. His admission, consequently, that he lacks the spirit and strength to risk his life for Luther, is not so much a lack of moral nerve, as it is a sincere statement of self-knowledge, mixed with a modest confession that the cause of the gospels transcends that of any individual. In sum, nuanced perception, independent judgment, evangelical modesty, and balanced criticism are the crucial ingredients in Erasmus' irenicism. They are at work both in "The Examination" and in Erasmus' correspondence dealing with Luther.

Erasmus' later statements regarding Luther are remarkably consistent with the trajectory of this ethic of discourse. When, for instance, after years of pressure to write "against" Luther, Erasmus finally published his "Diatribe Concerning Free Will" in which he challenges Luther on a specific point of controversy, he does not contradict his position of independence and balance in "The Examination." Indeed, Erasmus considered the "Diatribe" to be a "courteous disputation," written (as Schoeck puts it) in a "moderate and avuncular mode," entirely in keeping with the moderation of his dialogue.[257] The problem, unfortunately, is that neither Luther nor Rome saw it this way, and, consequently, neither could Erasmus for very long. When, in the end, Erasmus becomes increasingly hostile toward Luther in later years—blaming Luther's "arrogant, impudent, seditious temperament" for "shattering the whole globe in ruinous discord"—this certainly does signal an end to his irenic hopes for Luther and the church.[258] As he put it in 1525, the remedy (Luther) has become worse than the disease (church corruption).[259] But this shift does not put an end to his efforts to promote concord and peace. Throughout the reformation controversies in which Erasmus was involved, he struggles to stand on that same ground—at once modest, critical, and irenic— he claimed in "The Examination." Other motives play a role, certainly, but they do not abrogate the underlying and fundamental commitments which he sought to express and to realize.

Indeed, another of Erasmus' *Colloquies*—"The Epicurean"—reveals that Erasmus clung to the same irenic ground for many years. Making its first appearance in March of 1533, this dialogue returns in tone and topic to the basis of Erasmus' philosophy of Christ, but it does so in the context of the ongoing dispute with Luther. It manages, in short, to accomplish three things in one stroke. First, "The

Epicurean" re-affirms Erasmus' life-long commitment to the dialogue of Christian faith and the study of non-Christian literature and philosophy, meant to engender an intelligent, faithful, and humane form of existence. Second, it retrieves these old concerns of Erasmus in a direct, though tacit, debate with Luther. As Boyle rightly observes, "The Epicurean" is Erasmus' response to Luther's repeated charge that Erasmus is drunk with the "folly of Epicurus," a phrase Luther used for those who did not believe in the word of God.[260] Third, though Luther's charge evidently rankled Erasmus, his response through dialogue rekindles a tone that is calm, moderate, and lightly ironic—in short, precisely the kind of discourse evident in Erasmus' *Colloquies*, including "The Examination." This dialogue constitutes a most remarkable convergence of Erasmus' most basic commitment (the dialogue of faith and scholarship) with his most consuming and trying controversy (with Luther) and with the ethic of irenic discourse.

As the conversation opens, we find Spudaeus ("earnest") more confused than ever after his study of Cicero's *On the Ends of Goods;* as he tells Hedonius ("devotee of pleasure"), "I can't get over the fact that on so important a subject [as the ends of human life] there was so much conflicting opinion among such eminent men." Hedonius (who speaks for Erasmus) confesses that he is most attracted to the Epicurean philosophy. Though they have gained a bad reputation, he claims, "there are no people more Epicurean than godly Christians." This correlation stuns Spudaeus; for him Christians seem closer to Cynics, "because they wear themselves out by fasting and bewailing their sins." Religious people, he insists, surely miss out on a lot of good pleasures.[261] In response, Hedonius leads his interlocutor—through a carefully constructed series of questions and answers— to consider a hierarchy of pleasures: those of the mind, they agree, are higher than physical pleasures, but the highest pleasure comes only from living righteously before God, "the supreme good, than which nothing is more beauteous, more lovely, more dear." As he puts it, "only righteousness renders a man blessed— only righteousness, which alone reconciles God, the source of the supreme good, to man." In contrast, Hedonius observes, with a Platonic note, that most people neglect "the real pleasures of the mind" for the sake of "shadows and illusions of pleasures."[262] Common life "embrace[s] empty shadows of goods" instead of "true goods," but the delight taken in these deceptions, Hedonius warns, ends "not in a laugh but in eternal grief." Calculate the balance, therefore, and see how much "bitterness" is mixed in with "shameless love, unlawful passion, and excessive wining and dining." Directing the same point to the heavy drinker, Hedonius asks, "when fever, headache, colic, fuzzy mindedness, disgrace, loss of memory, vomiting, ruined digestion, and palsy follow too much drinking, would even Epicurus think that a pleasure worth seeking?" The ultimate price, however, for a life lived in pursuit of false pleasures is "torments of conscience, enmity with

God, [and] expectation of eternal punishment."[263] And this, as Erasmus sees it, is the agony and predicament of human existence—a judgment he shares with Luther.

For Erasmus, however, true Christian life is relieved by Christ of the torment of bad conscience, and consequently, Christians rightly (and most properly) are called "Epicurean," since no life is more agreeable and more filled with pleasure than the life filled with piety and righteousness. As Hedonius puts it, "wherever is a pure heart, there God is. Wherever God is, there is paradise, heaven, happiness. Where happiness is, there is true gladness and unfeigned cheerfulness."[264] Christian life, therefore, is full of delight—a far cry from the way of the cross projected in Luther—and this life of righteous pleasure has its source in Christ. In Hedonius' words,

> no one better deserves the name of Epicurean than the revered founder and head of the Christian philosophy, for in Greek "*epikurus*" means "helper.". . . Completely mistaken, therefore, are those who talk in their foolish fashion about Christ's having been sad and gloomy in character and calling upon us to follow a dismal mode of life. On the contrary, he shows the most enjoyable life of all and the one most full of true pleasure. . . .[265]

Christ re-orders the hierarchy of pleasures, and in so doing, teaches the way to blissful righteousness. As a result, when people are rightly focused on God, they can endure any of the torments life may throw at them, for (as Hedonius puts it) there is "no analogy" between finite pains and the infinite pleasure of delight in God. When, therefore, the Christian beholds creation, this "godly man" regards "with reverent, innocent eyes, and with surpassing inward delight, the works of his Lord and Father."[266] Pleasure abounds through Christ, for the one who takes delight in the most real good. What's more, Hedonius adds, those who live righteously take greater delight in earthly pleasures, since they are seen as gifts of God. The dialogue ends on a hopeful note, for as long as there is life and breath left, then the one plagued by a "bad conscience" can appeal with passionate cry to God's mercy—for "the mercy of the Lord knows neither bound nor limit."[267]

In this little colloquy, Erasmus returns, after a decade's time, to a dialogue with Luther. Whether or not "The Epicurean" was ever intended to convey the points Erasmus had promised to make in his three unwritten dialogues cannot be decided, but, as Boyle observes, "it serves that purpose, for it is a conversation with Luther."[268] More importantly, it is the *kind* of conversation Erasmus would like to have had with Luther. In "The Examination," Erasmus takes his ideal of irenic discourse to the limits, and those limits (as we have seen) are drawn out of the middle that is created by the conflict perpetrated by two mutually disparaging antagonists. In "The Epicurean," however, Erasmus steps away from that tenuous situation, and instead recasts the debate with Luther on a topic and in a style that issues consistently from his philosophy of Christ. Here, in the first place, is a dialogue that expresses Erasmus' basic commitment to the dialogue of faith and learning—witness the interweaving of scriptural, Epicurean, and Platonic motifs throughout the conversation. As Boyle notes, the debate with Luther, for Erasmus, was not a matter of defending church doctrine, but—once again—of justifying and advocating the value of non-Christian wisdom for Christian self-understanding.[269] The centerpiece of this dialogue of faith and learning, however, is an ethic of discourse that focuses on modest, humane, and irenic speech—as we have seen throughout this section. Here, then, in the second place, is a dialogue that performs in genre the sort of amicable and peaceful discourse which, Erasmus argues, should emerge from authentic Christian life. In this regard, then, Erasmus takes irenic discourse to the limits once more, though this time the limits are defined by the peaceful and productive dialogue between faith and philosophy, rather than by the heat of battle.

(4) A Utopian Banquet

In March and August of 1522 Froben released new and much expanded editions of the *Colloquies*. For the first time, as Craig R. Thompson comments, Erasmus gave his readers full-fledged "dialogues rather than sets of formulae" designed for schoolboys.[270] Three of the *Colloquies* discussed above first appeared in these editions, including the serio-comic treatment of pilgrimages in "Rash Vows," the humorous satire of soldiers in "Military Affairs," and the imaginative lampoon of Reuchlin's enemies in "The Apotheosis." These exercises in serio-comic criticism, however, triggered immediate and harsh blows from Nicholas Baechem at Louvain. In response, Erasmus complained to Jeroen van der Noot, the chancellor of Brabant and minister to Charles V, that

> Baechem is attacking me everywhere at social gatherings and in public sermons, and frequently calls me a heretic, and . . . he is taking steps to secure from the emperor's court to burn my book entitled *Colloquia*, on the ground that in it on the subjects of confession, of fasting, and of man-made legislation I think as Luther does.[271]

As Erasmus later observed, once his book became "useful in many ways," "it could not escape the poison-fangs of slander."[272] This was especially true given that his adversary was driven by hatred to find heresies where none existed.[273] Despite his low regard for Baechem—he considered him "physically purblind and mentally even more so"[274]—it was necessary for Erasmus to make quick and sure defenses against these charges. Clearly Erasmus was discovering that serio-comic criticism is never well-received by the self-serious and the humorless.

Consequently, as we saw with regard to the cases of Reuchlin and Luther, his rhetorical agility would be required to fend off the assaults, while he continued trying to promote more peaceful, humane, and fruitful conversation.

Along with these serio-comic pieces, the 1522 editions of the *Colloquies* include a dialogue of a very different and unique sort—a symposium titled "The Godly Feast." Unlike any of the imaginary conversations of Erasmus we have looked at thus far, this text stands aside from the fray of theological controversy. Gone is the comic treatment of assorted religious follies; gone also the sting of satirical criticism. In their stead appears an imaginative vision of ideal discourse. Distinctive among the *Colloquies*, the "Godly Feast" is a utopian dialogue: its conversation does not take place in the midst of human follies (at a pilgrimage site); it is not (for the most part) concerned with the ignorance, corruption, and aggression of religious professionals; it is not directed to a group of adversaries; and, interestingly, its language does not provoke the fury of a polemical response. Rather, in a moment of literary tranquility, Erasmus casts his vision toward the limit-case of a discourse in which all things are reconciled in balanced and fruitful harmony. This dialogue, therefore, provides a complete literary expression of that "mellow, balanced sanity" we saw Erasmus struggling to preserve in the midst the controversies surrounding Reuchlin and Luther.[275]

"The Godly Feast" opens at the country villa of Eusebius—a "modest [place] but well cared for," far removed from the "smoky cities"—where a small circle of lay, Christian philosophers have come to enjoy a common meal and some fine conversation.[276] The guests (and the reader) are first introduced to the charming beauty of Eusebius' "Epicurean gardens," where the great variety of plants and flowers yield nothing but pleasure—"to feast the eyes, refresh the nostrils, [and] restore the soul."[277] Where nature leaves off, painted murals take over, filling the house with a "varied spectacle" of plants, flowers, and animals. In Eusebius' house, the "cleverness of Nature" and the "inventiveness of the painter" complement each other in a balanced, yet competing harmony. "Good heavens," exclaims one interlocutor, "who could possibly become bored in this changing scene?"[278]

What makes this "wonderful variety" even more interesting, however, is that there is nothing "that's not doing or saying something."[279] In this home, everything speaks: murals, plants, even the wine cups bear inscriptions with wise counsel for the guests and celebrate the "goodness of God, who gives all these things for our use."[280] "The charming countenance of verdant Nature" speaks of God's wisdom and goodness; the garden at the entrance to Eusebius' house "greets those who enter"; the fresco of Peter (more appropriate than a "filthy Priapus") speaks in Greek, Hebrew, and Latin (an Erasmian touch) of the life of faith; the herbs carry banners that indicate the "special virtue" of each kind; and the painted owls, scorpion, and serpents offer their "royal sayings" to those who listen.[281] In fact, even the wine cups speak—reminding the drinker that "no one is harmed [by wine] but by himself."[282] This setting—free from the affairs of the city, overflowing with natural and artistic beauty, and teeming with "plenty of talk"—provides Eusebius with an idyllic setting for "conversing with [himself] or some close friend."[283] On this day, in fact, it proves to be a most fitting environment for the philosophical conversation among a group of friends.

And conversation abounds, especially at the banquet, where the nine guests ("equal the number of the Muses")[284] join in cooperative interpretation of passages from biblical and classical literature. Besides the host Eusebius, there are four main speakers, plus the four "shadows" who accompany the four friends to Eusebius' home.[285] In order not to squander their time together, the group agrees to season their dinner with a few readings from scripture, which they will try to interpret in turn. It will be best, Eusebius declares for the whole group, if

> we avoid foolish yarns and enjoy profitable conversation. I disagree with those who think a dinner party isn't fun unless it overflows with silly, bawdy stories and rings with dirty songs. True gaiety comes from a clean, sincere conscience. And truly enjoyable conversations are those which are always pleasant to have held or heard and always delightful to recall, not those which soon cause one to be ashamed and conscience-stricken.[286]

In agreeing to this, the group realizes another Erasmian balance—this time between the body and the mind. Just as nature and art provided complementary sources of revelation in Eusebius' home, so, too, here at the feast: "when the whole man is refreshed," both the body and its partner the mind, "this is abundant refreshment indeed."[287] In this dinner colloquy, the interlocutors refresh themselves with hearty fare and sumptuous interpretations of a Hebrew proverb: Eusebius puts forth a moral interpretation; Timothy offers a symbolic reading of the same verse; Sophronius (the only shadow to speak) draws a comparison to a Pauline text; Theophilus focuses on the contextually determined meaning of central terms; and Eulalius delves into various perplexities contained in Paul. In this Erasmian symposium, the participants revel not only in the plenteous number of dishes, but also in the plurality of interpretations.

Being Erasmian creations, however, these characters cannot rest with biblical wisdom alone. Though scripture is, as Eusebius puts it, "the basic authority in everything," it is hard to believe that God is not speaking also through the hearts of pagan authors. Indeed, he wonders, in a perfectly Erasmian sentiment, if "perhaps the spirit of Christ is more widespread than we understand, and the company of saints includes many not in our calendar."[288] In a line that continues to resonate, he notes how inferior contemporary authors are in comparison with writers like Cicero—"Good Lord, how dull they are by comparison!"[289] The key difference for Eusebius is the effect they have on people's lives. As he states it, the secular classics instruct him in the virtuous life, whereas he rises "from the reading of those others"—he is thinking of Scotus—"somehow less enthusiastic about true virtue, but more contentious."[290] With this lead, the guests jump into the conversation. Chrysoglottus is quite taken with Cicero's book on old age, especially where Tully writes that we "depart from this life as from an inn, not from a home." "What could a Christian have said more reverently?"[291] Uranius agrees, but wonders how many Christians have lived well enough to share Cicero's confidence about his life? Nephalius then adds the equivalent words from Socrates—"The human soul is placed in this body as if in a garrison"—which Uranius finds quite similar to what Paul writes to the Corinthians, and which Nephalius compares favorably with the language of Peter.[292]

But there is a critical, not just a complementary, lesson to be learned from juxtaposing pagan and scriptural authors. The ancients are to be read with a discriminating eye, shaped by Christian charity, while actual Christian life can (and should) absorb a great deal from these sources of wisdom. Both Uranius and Nephalius, for example, find Socrates' humility more appropriate for Christian life than Cicero's self-confidence before death. Socrates "conceived a strong hope that God in his goodness would accept them, because he had endeavored to live righteously."[293] What an "admirable spirit," exclaimed Nephalius. Thus, though "the spirit of Christ" certainly shines through the wisdom and eloquence of Cicero, making him a worthy tutor for Christian readers, there is more of the divine in Socrates—a point Nephalius caps off with an exuberant "St. Socrates, pray for us."[294] But the force of criticism cuts the other way as well. When, for instance, Crysoglottus proclaims his belief that other ancient writers (Horace and Virgil) are also "sanctified," his admiration for these authors uncovers a sad (but instructive) contrast with the way most Christians live and die. "How many Christians have I seen die ever so bitterly," laments Nephalius.[295] Christians have good reason, and every right, therefore, to read and learn from these saintly authors. As Eusebius puts it, "whatever is devout and contributes to good morals" is worthy of serious attention and appreciation.[296]

It is at this point in the dialogue that the reader must step back and attend not only to what the characters are saying, but also to the larger point Erasmus is making by way of their conversation. If we focus momentarily on the structure of Erasmus' literary performance, then it becomes clear that what Erasmus is doing in this text is enacting a Christian liturgy of word and bread. "The Godly Feast," in short, is a eucharistic banquet, though not—clearly—in a churchy sense. The participants first wash, so as to "approach the table with hands and heart both clean."[297] They then bless the food and give thanks to God, in imitation of the example given by Jesus. Eusebius follows with an invocation: "may Christ, who makes all men to rejoice, and without whom nothing is truly pleasing, deign to attend our feast and rejoice our hearts by his presence."[298] They proceed with their feast of food and conversation over biblical and philosophical texts. It is in the activity of their conversation, however, that the "godly" meaning of their feast comes to the fore. As Erasmus writes in another colloquy, reading amounts to conversation with an author, and in the act of reading the Gospels, one hears the "enchanting speech" of that "eloquent companion" who conversed with "the two disciples on the road to Emmaus."[299] Reading scripture, in other words, is a conversation with Christ. But, as Boyle rightly notes, this conversation is never for Erasmus a solitary pursuit; it is, rather, a social enterprise, done in "the imitation of the holy colloquy."[300] In Boyle's words,

> The theologian is a colloquial man [sic]. He converses with the Text and with its best commentaries. In imitation of Christ, God's own eloquent oration, he shares discourse with others in a renaissance of life and letters. The scholarship of Erasmus, standing bent over his manuscripts alone, is not solitary, but an imitative *sermo*, a textual conversation with ancient and contemporary men. It flowers into a "godly feast," a colloquy of devout men wisely explaining Scripture to one another.[301]

The unspoken blueprint for Erasmus' dialogue, therefore, manifests itself in and through the hermeneutical process of reading and conversing. Erasmus' own dialogue with God's word in scriptural and pagan texts yields a conversation in a text ("The Godly Feast"), which, when published, purchased, read, and talked about, creates a larger colloquial process centered on Christ's word. In producing such a dialogue, the point of which Erasmus performs but does not explicitly state, he invites his readers to partake in the purity and perfection of ideal Christian discourse.

In this sense, "The Godly Feast" is also a utopian banquet. Through its literary performance, Erasmus relocates discourse over religion, he introduces new speakers into the world of theology, and he puts on display what he takes to be the most desirable and the most responsible style of discourse for talking about religious questions. With regard to location, Erasmus was never satisfied with (and frequently was openly critical of) theology as it was practiced in the universities. As we saw earlier, the young Erasmus found scholastic lectures and disputations at Paris to be empty of life and filled with contention;[302] later, he thought little better of Louvain, in no small part because of the fierce antagonism to the humanities and the study of languages he discovered among theologians. Though he briefly was affiliated with Cambridge (1511–1514), Erasmus preferred the freedom of the non-attached scholar, even though this made the solicitation of funds a continual burden. Turning from the universities, he gravitated to the small, familial "academies" like Aldus Manutius' Venetian publishing house (and later, in Basel, to the house and shop of Johannes Froben), where he enjoyed the support, friendship, and competence in languages of other like-minded scholars. These little communities of inquiry, however, were not at all inward looking; in fact, these centers of literary activity and publication made it possible for Erasmus to converse with friends and foes across the European continent. Indeed, as Johan Huizinga correctly remarks, Erasmus "wrote for all the world, that is to say, for all educated people."[303] Through publications, but also through his voluminous correspondence, Erasmus facilitated the relocation of theological discourse from the universities to the "interlocking" world of educated people.[304] "The Godly Feast" participates in precisely this move. In miniature form, it sets biblical interpretation and theological conversation in the midst of ordinary life—in a circle of educated friends gathered in a home.

In giving theology this new residence, of course, Erasmus also opens the door to a new set of participants in theological inquiry. He was, in fact, quite hopeful that his own labors had contributed to making theology "much more accessible than it used to be."[305] In "The Godly Feast" he embraces the notion (and the value) of lay participation in theology. Early on in the feast, the host wonders whether it is "permissible for us simple laymen to discuss these topics"; he wishes that he and his guests had "a good theologian" in their midst to help them understand the meaning of the scriptural passage they have just read.[306] With the question raised, Erasmus gives a resounding answer through Timothy's voice: "Permissible even for sailors, in my opinion, provided there is no attempt at formal definition."[307] The requirements for sound interpretation of scripture, Erasmus suggests, are everywhere (and for everyone) the same—piety, learning, humility, and the grace of Christ. And all four elements are evident as these laymen take their turns interpreting verses from scripture. After Eusebius' initial reading, for instance, Timothy needles his host for his lack of courage: "what do you mean, 'layman'? Were I a bachelor of divinity I'd be very little ashamed of this interpretation."[308] But Eusebius is modest still (not wanting to claim too much for his own viewpoint), though he applauds Timothy's interpretive efforts: "Truly, Timothy, you're venerable not in years alone but in pure learning as well."[309] The spirit of Christ, Erasmus hopes to show, is very much present among these laymen who are "gathered together in his name."[310] Theological conversation, in sum, is not the exclusive prerogative of the clerics and professional doctors who reign over the universities. At Erasmus' utopian banquet, not one of the nine is a professional theologian or a cleric. In their place, the voices of ordinary laymen take center stage. The only guests lacking a theological voice are women; though Erasmus calls attention to this exclusion in a manner which insinuates that men are the cause of their voicelessness.[311]

Finally, "The Godly Feast" enacts what for Erasmus is the ideal style of discourse over religious topics. It is Erasmus' utopia, an imaginative vision of the "ideal Christian society informed by theological eloquence."[312] All the key qualities of speech Erasmus values are consistently and fruitfully present. The characters' discussion is broad-minded; as we have seen, they have no hesitancy to appreciate and learn from non-Christian sources. Their dialogue, moreover, balances faith and intellect; as Eusebius puts it when thanking his guests for attending the banquet, their conversation was "equally learned and devout."[313] And there is a strongly pluralistic quality to their conversation. On one hand, Erasmus' interlocutors are completely free to offer their own interpretations; there are no external constraints on their voices and (with the minor exception of Eusebius' modesty) they do not appear inhibited to speak. On the other hand, their discourse is quintessentially cooperative. Each voice complements the other; there is no hint of competition among the speakers. The interlocutors work together, and by collaborative means assist each other in arriving at a common and richer appreciation of scripture.[314] Most importantly, their discourse is thoroughly irenic. There are no factions or divisions; no animosities or resentments undermine their efforts; there is not the slightest hint of bickering or sniping; no aggression or violent rhetoric sullies the mood. Rather, their voices gather in friendship, in concord, and with mutual respect. This character of discourse constitutes the culmination of Erasmus' utopian vision.

One more Erasmian balance comes into play at the close of "The Godly Feast." The lunch discussion has just taken up the issue of the excessive amount of money spent on religious shrines and ceremonies, when one speaker wonders about the expense of Eusebius' home. Perhaps, Erasmus is asking, such civilized discourse is only the reflection of Eusebius' wealth and leisure, which allow him to live comfortably while nicely isolated from the worries of the world. Two answers appear to this question. First, Eusebius assures his guests that his house is actually quite moderate, even if it is elegant; in contrast, "mendicants build more splendidly" and many "adorn monasteries or churches at excessive cost," while ignoring the "immediate needs of our neighbor."[315] For his part, Eusebius claims to have economized in the construction and decoration of his home in order to be "more bountiful towards the poor."[316] Second, while it is true that "The Godly Feast" takes place in a quiet retreat, far removed from the divisions and conflicts of public life, this does not mean that the civil and irenic standards of rationality which emerge in this symposium are the exclusive prerogative of a leisured life. On the contrary, this colloquy ends with Eusebius leaving his isle of rich conversation to minister to public needs and conflicts. He must leave, he tells them, to visit a sick friend and to settle a conflict between two stubborn men. He turns, in short, from text to life, "from the study to the village," as Boyle puts it.[317] This colloquy leaves off, in other words, where the rest of Erasmus' *Colloquies* begin, in the scattered and quarrelsome discourse of everyday life. And this, I take it, is precisely Erasmus' point: the virtues of discourse that flower splendidly in Eusebius' country villa remain the imperatives for theological conversation in all spheres of life. Those who enter into discourse over religion are charged by

Erasmus to leave their godly feast in order to engage a variety of voices in serious conversation, and in so doing, to open and sustain working ground for amicable but critical dialogue with all interlocutors.

This colloquy truly is a "compendium of almost all of Erasmus' theories and preferences."[318] It portrays in miniature the kind of speech Erasmus took to be essential to good theological conversation. The speakers meet in friendship, they work together cooperatively, their inquiry is learned and critical, and, together, they build a living community of inquiry. This banquet has eucharistic significance, as we have seen, for in amicable and productive conversation, they "recapitulate humanly the economy of Christ, drawing men (sic) together in a bond of charity."[319] The interlocutors' work together institutes, therefore, a "microcosm of the Christian commonwealth,"[320] a vibrant community that fuses faith and learning together such that both are enhanced, which balances strong (and frequently ironic) criticism (e.g., of ceremonialism) with an irenic spirit, and that weds intellectual inquiry to a passion for justice. Straight to the point and with her characteristically Erasmian flavor, Boyle concludes: "this colloquy is a cameo of the human imitation of Christ, the archetypal conversation, civilizing the commonwealth through language."[321] And it is this blend of communicative virtues—what Phillips aptly calls Erasmus' "mellow, balanced sanity"[322]—that Erasmus exhibits through dialogue in "The Godly Feast." Those who venture into discourse about religion are challenged by Erasmus to practice the standards of critical rationality and the ideals of cooperative, irenic civility evident in this dialogue.

But, of course, in "The Godly Feast" this ethic of discourse is portrayed at the outer limits of human reach. This dialogue, clearly, is a *utopian* banquet. In actual practice, such ideals remain fragile and fleeting, as other forms of speech dilute them or obstruct their realization. The human tongue is, as Erasmus learned from the classics and from experience, an "ambivalent organ": it promises great benefits ("if anyone directed it as they should"), yet what a "great plague of life" can spring from it.[323] Unfortunately, even to venture an ethic of discourse is to participate in the ambiguity of human language. As Erasmus observes, "friendly, salutary, [and] well-timed words" exhorting us to civil and irenic discourse can be a "powerful and prompt remedy" for sick spirits; but all too easily, speech that is "ill-intentioned or corrupting or out of season" turns into a "deadly poison."[324] A good dose of caution and self-criticism is required, therefore, of anyone who wishes to speak about ethical norms for human discourse. To further examine the possibilities and the limits of an ethic of discourse, I turn in the final chapter of this book to a consideration of Plato's *Phaedrus*.

Notes

[1] Roland H. Bainton, *Erasmus of Christendom* (New York: Charles Scribner's Sons, 1969) 24.

[2] Isocrates, "Nicocles or the Cyprians," trans. George Norlin, *Isocrates* (New York: G. P. Putnam's Sons, 1928) 5–9.

[3] Cicero, *De Inventione*, trans. H. M. Hubbell (Cambridge, Mass.: Harvard University, 1949) Bk. I. ii. 2–3.

[4] Cicero, *De Inventione*, Bk. I. iii. 3.

[5] Cicero, *De Inventione*, Bk. I. iii. 4.

[6] Cicero, *De Inventione*, Bk. I. iv. 5.

[7] Isocrates, "To Nicocles," 12–14.

[8] Erasmus, "A Complaint of Peace Spurned and Rejected by the Whole World," trans. Betty Radice, ed. A. H. T. Levi, *Collected Works of Erasmus*, vol. 27 (Toronto: University of Toronto, 1986) 295. In a dialogue on rhetoric and education, Erasmus has "Bear" tell "Lion" that he has "learnt from Galen that what differentiates man from the other animals, or brutes as they are called, is not reason, but speech." Erasmus, "The Right Way of Speaking Latin and Greek," trans. Maurice Pope, ed. J. K. Sowards, *Collected Works of Erasmus*, vol. 26 (Toronto, University of Toronto, 1985) 369.

[9] Erasmus, "The Tongue," trans. Elaine Fantham, ed. Elaine Fantham and Erika Rummell, *Collected Works of Erasmus*, vol. 29 (Toronto: University of Toronto, 1989) 262.

[10] Erasmus, "The Tongue," vol. 29, 260.

[11] Erasmus, "The Right Way of Speaking," vol. 26, 369.

[12] Erasmus, "A Complaint of Peace," vol. 27, 294–296.

[13] Erasmus, "The Tongue," vol. 29, 259–260.

[14] Erasmus, "The Tongue," vol. 29, 404. As Elaine Fantham notes, Erasmus has a tradition of theological literature on the "sins of language" as a precedent. See her Introduction to "The Tongue," 251–252. For a classic example, see *The Summa Theologica of St. Thomas Aquinas* (New York: Benziger Brothers, n.d.) 2. 2. 72–76 (on reviling, backbiting, tale-bearing, derision, and cursing) and 2. 2. 110–116 (on lying, hypocrisy, boasting, false modesty, flattery and quarreling).

[15] Erasmus, "The Tongue," vol. 29, 406. Erasmus asks his Christian readers: "why is there no sound from us of the sober, sparing, modest, decent, careful, truthful, mild, peaceable, kindly, honest tongue, able to beseech, console, exhort, confess, and give thanks?" In her Introduction to her translation of "The Tongue," Fantham complains that Erasmus over

stresses the negative while giving so little attention to the positive Christian ideal of loving speech. In contrast to Fantham's criticism, Margaret Mann Phillips calls "The Tongue" a "complete example of the Erasmian approach." See Phillips, "Erasmus on the Tongue," *Erasmus of Rotterdam Society Yearbook*, vol. 1 (1981): 125. Indeed, Erasmus follows roughly the same structure in "The Tongue" as he does in *Praise of Folly*: there too, the majority of space is given to general (and comic) folly and professional (and vicious) forms of folly, with only a small, but crucial, portion given to Christian (ideal) folly.

[16] Erasmus, "The Tongue," vol. 29, 410.

[17] See, for instance, Erasmus, "The Tongue," vol. 29, 349–360.

[18] Erasmus, "The Handbook of the Christian Soldier," trans. Charles Fantazzi, ed. John W. O'Malley, *Collected Works of Erasmus*, vol. 66 (Toronto: University of Toronto, 1988) 29.

[19] See the insightful discussion of language in Erasmus' theological method in Marjorie O'Rourke Boyle, *Erasmus on Language and Method in Theology* (Toronto: University of Toronto, 1977) 40–47.

[20] R. J. Schoeck, *Erasmus of Europe; The Prince of the Humanists, 1501–1536* (Edinburgh: Edinburgh University, 1993) 368.

[21] See R. J. Schoeck, *Erasmus of Europe; The Making of a Humanist, 1467–1500* (Edinburgh: Edinburgh University, 1990) 133; and Schoeck, *Erasmus of Europe; The Prince of the Humanists*, 256. For Erasmus' thoughts on the art of letter writing, see "On the Writing of Letters," trans. Charles Fantazzi, ed. J. K. Sowards, *Collected Works of Erasmus*, vol 25 (Toronto: University of Toronto, 1985) 10–267.

[22] See Margaret Mann Phillips, *The "Adages" of Erasmus; A Study with Translations*, (Cambridge: Cambridge University, 1964) 3–34. See also Schoeck, *Erasmus of Europe; The Prince of the Humanists*, 74–85.

[23] See John B. Payne, Albert Rabil, Jr., and Warren S. Smith, Jr., "The *Paraphrases* of Erasmus: Origin and Character," ed. Robert D. Sider, *Collected Works of Erasmus*, vol. 42 (Toronto: University of Toronto, 1984) xi–xix.

[24] Martha C. Nussbaum, *Love's Knowledge; Essays in Philosophy and Literature* (New York and Oxford: Oxford University, 1990) 3. Recall the discussion of a genre's "statement-making function" in chapter one of this book.

[25] Erasmus, "The Tongue," vol. 29, 326 and 404. See also Erasmus, "The Handbook of the Christian Soldier," 29. The same point is made with classical grounding in the adage titled "As the man is, so is his talk" (I. vi. 50), in which Erasmus writes: "a complete image of a man's way of life and the whole force of his character is reflected in his style as in a mirror, and the very secrets of his bosom can be detected from clues, as it were, that lie beneath the surface." Erasmus, "As the man is, so is his talk," trans. R. A. B. Mynors, *Collected Works of Erasmus*, vol. 32 (Toronto: University of Toronto, 1989) 36–37. See also Erasmus, "The Ciceronian: A Dialogue on The Ideal Latin Style," trans. Betty I. Knott, ed. A. H. T. Levi,

Collected Works of Erasmus, vol. 28 (Toronto: University of Toronto, 1986) 441. For an application of this point, see "Fools in their folly speak" (I. i. 98), trans. Margaret Mann Phillips, *Collected Works of Erasmus*, vol. 31 (Toronto: University of Toronto, 1982) 141–142.

[26] Erasmus, "Letter to Jacob Canter" (letter 32), trans. R. A. B. Mynors and D. F. S. Thomson, *Collected Works of Erasmus*, vol. 1 (Toronto: University of Toronto, 1974) 62.

[27] Terence is praised and Horace called "our favourite." See Erasmus, "To a Friend" (letter 31), and "To Servatius Rogerus" (letter 15), *Collected Works of Erasmus*, vol. 1, 57–60 and 20.

[28] Erasmus, "To Petrus Mosellanus" (letter 948), trans. R. A. B. Mynors and D. F. S. Thomson *Collected Works of Erasmus*, vol. 6 (Toronto: University of Toronto, 1982) 310–318.

[29] James D. Tracy, *Erasmus; The Growth of a Mind* (Genève: Droz, 1972) 168. On Erasmus' reading of the classics, see Erika Rummel, "Erasmus and the Greek Classics," and Elaine Fantham, "Erasmus and the Latin Classics," both in *Collected Works of Erasmus*, vol. 29, xxi–l.

[30] Schoeck, *Erasmus of Europe; The Prince of the Humanists*, ix–x.

[31] Erasmus, "The Antibarbarians," trans. Margaret Mann Phillips, ed. Craig R. Thompson, *Collected Works of Erasmus*, vol. 23 (Toronto: University of Toronto, 1978) 18–122.

[32] Erasmus, "The Ciceronian," vol. 28, 342–448.

[33] Erasmus, "Erasmus of Rotterdam to His Friend Johann Witz," prefatory letter to "The Antibarbarians," *Collected Works of Erasmus*, vol. 23, 16.

[34] "Letter from Robert Gaguin" (letter 46), *Collected Works of Erasmus*, vol. 1, 93.

[35] Margaret Mann Phillips, Introduction to "The Antibarbarians," vol. 23, 23.

[36] Phillips, Introduction to "The Antibarbarians," vol. 23, 13–14. The dialogue in question is titled "The Dialogue of the Two-tongued and the Trilinguals," trans. Paul Pascal, *Collected Works of Erasmus*, vol. 7 (Toronto: University of Toronto, 1987) 335–347. See the Introduction by Pascal, 330–333.

[37] Erasmus, "The Antibarbarians," vol. 23, 19–23.

[38] Erasmus, "The Antibarbarians," vol. 23, 19–23 and 39–40.

[39] Phillips, Introduction to "The Antibarbarians," vol. 23, 14.

[40] Erasmus, "The Antibarbarians," vol. 23, 28 and 35–37. See Schoeck, *Erasmus of Europe; The Prince of the Humanists*, 138. On Jacob Batt, see ed. Peter G. Bietenholz, *Contemporaries of Erasmus; A Biographical Register of the Renaissance and Reformation*, vol. 1 (Toronto: University of Toronto, 1985) 100–101.

[41] Meeting with the barbarians, Erasmus tells us, "often made him [Batt] vomit or go hot with rage." "The Antibarbarians," vol. 23, 27. Elsewhere Batt wishes that "Ate" be "dragged along by a hook like a criminal and thrown straight into the public sewer." Ate is the classical "personification of blind folly" who renders her victims "incapable of rational choice"; she also is the daughter of Eris ("spirit of turmoil"). See Michael Grant and John Hazel, *Gods and Mortals in Classical Mythology; A Dictionary* (New York: Dorset, 1979) 59. As Phillips shows, Ate is an ironic allusion to Jan Briart (known as Atensis). See Phillips' Introduction to "The Antibarbarians," vol. 23, 13–14.

[42] Erasmus, "The Antibarbarians," vol. 23, 47.

[43] Erasmus, "The Antibarbarians," vol. 23, 28.

[44] Erasmus, "The Antibarbarians," vol. 23, 33.

[45] Erasmus, "The Antibarbarians," vol. 23, 34–35.

[46] Erasmus, "The Antibarbarians," vol. 23, 31.

[47] Erasmus, "The Antibarbarians," vol. 23, 32.

[48] Erasmus, "The Antibarbarians," vol. 23, 33 and 48.

[49] Erasmus, "The Antibarbarians," vol, 23, 49. Erasmus (or Batt) slips in a low blow when he notes how these "select fat bulls [are] uncommonly well provided, genitally speaking." See 33.

[50] Erasmus, "The Antibarbarians," vol. 23, 43.

[51] Erasmus, "The Antibarbarians," vol. 23, 34.

[52] Erasmus, "The Antibarbarians," vol., 23, 80. See Erasmus, "The Abbot and the Learned Lady," trans. Craig R. Thompson, *Collected Works of Erasmus*, vol. 39 (Toronto: University of Toronto, 1997) 499–505.

[53] Erasmus, "The Antibarbarians," vol. 23, 63 and 68.

[54] Erasmus, "The Antibarbarians," vol. 23, 108 and 74.

[55] Erasmus, "The Antibarbarians," vol. 23, 51 and 54.

[56] Erasmus, "The Antibarbarians," vol. 23, 55.

[57] Erasmus, "The Antibarbarians," vol. 23, 56–57.

[58] Erasmus, "The Antibarbarians," vol. 23, 83.

[59] Erasmus, "The Antibarbarians," vol. 23, 114–117.

60 Erasmus, "The Antibarbarians," vol. 23, 104–105.

61 Erasmus, "The Antibarbarians," vol. 23, 90.

62 Erasmus, "The Antibarbarians," vol. 23, 90.

63 Erasmus, "The Antibarbarians," vol. 23, 59.

64 Erasmus, "The Antibarbarians," vol. 23, 60 and 97.

65 Erasmus, "The Antibarbarians," vol. 23, 58.

66 Erasmus, "The Antibarbarians," vol. 23, 60–61. See Marjorie O'Rourke Boyle, *Christening Pagan Mysteries; Erasmus in Pursuit of Wisdom* (Toronto: University of Toronto, 1981) 10–23.

67 Erasmus, "The Antibarbarians," vol. 23, 64 and 67.

68 Erasmus, "The Antibarbarians," vol. 23, 58.

69 Erasmus, "The Antibarbarians," vol. 23, 112.

70 Betty I. Knott , Introduction to "The Ciceronian," vol. 28, 324.

71 Erasmus, "The Ciceronian," vol. 28, 337.

72 Erasmus, "To Jacob de Voecht" (Letter 1519) , trans. R. A. B. Mynors, *Collected Works of Erasmus*, vol. 7 (Toronto: University of Toronto, 1987) 72.

73 Erasmus, "To Wolfgang Capito" (Letter 541), trans. R. A. B. Mynors and D. F. S. Thomson, *Collected Works of Erasmus*, vol. 4 (Toronto: University of Toronto, 1977) 266.

74 Erasmus, "To Juan Luis Vives" (Letter 1111), *Collected Works of Erasmus*, vol. 7, 307.

75 Erasmus, "The Ciceronian," vol. 28, 337 and 338.

76 Erasmus, "The Ciceronian," vol. 28, 342.

77 Erasmus, "The Ciceronian," vol. 28, 346.

78 Erasmus, "The Ciceronian," vol. 28, 346.

79 Erasmus, "The Ciceronian," vol. 28, 349.

80 Erasmus, "The Ciceronian," vol. 28, 352.

81 Erasmus, "The Ciceronian," vol. 28, 363 and 369.

82 Erasmus, "The Ciceronian," vol. 28, 361–362.

[83] Erasmus, "The Ciceronian," vol. 28, 364–366 and 369.

[84] Erasmus, "The Ciceronian," vol. 28, 396; 407; and 383.

[85] Erasmus, "The Ciceronian," vol. 28, 363.

[86] Erasmus, "The Ciceronian," vol. 28, 399.

[87] Erasmus, "The Ciceronian," vol. 28, 404. See Erasmus' spoof on the Ciceronians in "The Echo," trans. Craig R. Thompson, *Collected Works of Erasmus*, vol. 40 (Toronto: University of Toronto, 1997) 796–800.

[88] Erasmus, "The Ciceronian," vol. 28, 497 and 396.

[89] Erasmus, "The Ciceronian," vol. 28, 396.

[90] Erasmus, "The Ciceronian," vol. 28, 375; 402; and 397.

[91] Erasmus, "The Ciceronian," vol. 28, 401 and 446. Compare with 402.

[92] Erasmus, "The Ciceronian," vol. 28, 399.

[93] Erasmus, "The Ciceronian," vol. 28, 377. See also 399 and 406.

[94] Erasmus, "The Ciceronian," vol. 28, 399.

[95] Erasmus, "The Ciceronian," vol. 28, 394.

[96] Erasmus, "The Ciceronian," vol. 28, 395.

[97] Erasmus, "The Ciceronian," vol. 28, 443.

[98] Erasmus, "The Ciceronian," vol. 28, 447.

[99] Erasmus, "The Ciceronian," vol. 28, 392.

[100] Erasmus, "The Ciceronian," vol. 28, 338. Compare with 400. See Geraldine Thompson, *Under Pretext of Praise: Satiric Mode in Erasmus' Fiction* (Toronto: University of Toronto, 1973) 147.

[101] Erasmus, "The Ciceronian," vol. 28, 401.

[102] Betty I. Knott, Introduction to "The Ciceronian," vol. 28, 328–329. See also Geraldine Thompson, *Under Pretext of Praise; Satiric Mode in Erasmus' Fiction*, 137–147.

[103] Erasmus, "The Ciceronian," vol. 28, 448.

[104] See Erasmus, "To a sick spirit speech is a physician" (Adage III. 1. 100), trans. R. A. B. Mynors, *Collected Works of Erasmus*, vol. 34 (Toronto: University of Toronto, 1992)

223–224. For classical references, see Pedro Laín Entralgo, *The Therapy of the Word in Classical Antiquity*, trans. L. J. Rather and John M. Sharp (New Haven: Yale University, 1970).

[105] *Horace's Satires and Epistles*, trans. Jacob Fuchs (New York: Norton, 1977) Book I, satire 1, lines 24–26.

[106] Erasmus, "Praise of Folly," trans. Betty Radice, ed. A. H. T. Levi, *Collected Works of Erasmus*, vol. 27 (Toronto: University of Toronto, 1986) 83–84. Erasmus returns to the Horatian fusion of the humorous and the serious in his famous letter "To Maarten van Dorp" (Letter 337), trans. R. A. B. Mynors and D. F. S. Thomson, *Collected Works of Erasmus*, vol. 3 (Toronto: University of Toronto, 1976) 115.

[107] Erasmus, "The Usefulness of the *Colloquies*," in *Collected Works of Erasmus*, vol. 40, 1098.

[108] Erasmus, "First Dedicatory Letter" to "The Ciceronian," vol. 28, 337.

[109] Erasmus, "The Antibarbarians," vol. 23, 23.

[110] Walter M. Gordon, *Humanist Play and Belief; The Seriocomic Art of Desiderius Erasmus* (Toronto: University of Toronto, 1990) 3.

[111] See Craig R. Thompson, *The Translations of Lucian by Erasmus and St. Thomas More* (Ithaca, 1940); and Schoeck, *Erasmus of Europe; The Prince of the Humanists*, 57–58 and 170–171.

[112] Erasmus, "To William Warham" (Letter 261), trans. R. A. B. Mynors and D. F. S. Thomson, *Collected Works of Erasmus*, vol. 2 (Toronto: University of Toronto, 1975) 229. Compare letter 187 dedicating an earlier volume of Lucian translations.

[113] Erasmus, "To René d'Illiers" (Letter 199), in *Collected Works of Erasmus*, vol. 2, 122. On Erasmus' use of Lucian, see Christopher Robinson, *Lucian and His Influence in Europe* (London: Duckworth, 1979) 165–197.

[114] See Erasmus' letter to Christophe Urswick written in June of 1506, *The Collected Works of Erasmus*, vol. 2, 115–116.

[115] "From Udalricus Zasius" (Letter 344), *Collected Works of Erasmus*, vol. 3, 148. For Erasmus' estimation of Zasius, see letter 305, 31.

[116] On the numerous editions and printings of the *Colloquies*, see Craig R. Thompson's Introduction to *Collected Works of Erasmus*, vol. 39, xx–xxvii; and Preserved Smith, *A Key to the Colloquies of Erasmus* (Cambridge: Harvard, 1927) 2–27. See also *Collected Works of Erasmus*, vol. 40, 1137–1138 for a list of editions. While supporters found them instructive and witty, critics called them indecent and irreverent. Major sections of the *Colloquies*, for instance, were censured by the Sorbonne as "erroneous, scandalous, or impious"; and the author was described as "a pagan who mocks at the Christian religion and its sacred

rites and customs." See Thompson, *The Colloquies of Erasmus*, (Chicago: University of Chicago, 1965), xxx–xxxi. Soon after Erasmus died, the *Colloquies* were repeatedly condemned by Rome.

[117] Erasmus, "The Usefulness of the *Colloquies*," vol. 40, 1102–1103.

[118] Margaret Mann Phillips, *Erasmus and the Northern Renaissance* (New York: Collier, 1965) 125. For an extended discussion of satire in Erasmus' *Colloquies*, see Thompson, *Under Pretext of Praise*, 87–151.

[119] Erasmus, "Exorcism, or The Specter," *Collected Works of Erasmus*, vol. 39, 535.

[120] Erasmus, "Exorcism, or The Specter," vol. 39, 539.

[121] Erasmus, "Exorcism, or The Specter," vol. 39, 539.

[122] Erasmus, "Exorcism, or The Specter," vol. 39, 540.

[123] Erasmus, "Exorcism, or The Specter," vol. 39, 541. See Erasmus' ironic interpretation of this dialogue in "The Usefulness of the *Colloquies*," vol. 40, 1103.

[124] Erasmus, "Alchemy," *Collected Works of Erasmus*, vol. 39, 547.

[125] Erasmus, "Alchemy," vol. 39, 549.

[126] Erasmus, "Alchemy," vol. 39, 550.

[127] Erasmus, "Alchemy," vol. 39, 552.

[128] Erasmus, "Alchemy," vol. 39, 553.

[129] Erasmus, "Rash Vows," *Collected Works of Erasmus*, vol 39, 37.

[130] Erasmus, "Rash Vows," vol. 39, 38.

[131] Erasmus, "Rash Vows," vol. 39, 39.

[132] Erasmus, "The Usefulness of the *Colloquies*," vol. 40, 1098.

[133] John Dewey, *Experience and Nature* (New York: Dover, 1958) 403.

[134] Erasmus, "The Shipwreck," *Collected Works of Erasmus*, vol.39, 355.

[135] Erasmus, "The Shipwreck," vol. 39, 355–359.

[136] Erasmus, "The Shipwreck," vol. 39, 356. Compare the similar scenes and points in Rabelais. See *The Complete Works of Rabelais* (Bibliophilist, n.d.) Book IV. 17–24.

[137] Erasmus, "The Shipwreck," vol. 39, 356 and 357.

[138] Erasmus' "The Funeral" generates a similar contrast of pious and impious ways of life (and of death). See *Collected Works of Erasmus*, vol. 40, 763–779.

[139] Erasmus, "The Abbot and the Learned Lady," *Collected Works of Erasmus*, vol. 39, 501.

[140] Erasmus, "The Abbot and the Learned Lady," vol. 39, 501.

[141] Erasmus, "The Abbot and the Learned Lady," vol. 39, 502. On Erasmus' attitudes toward women, see Anne M. O'Donnell, "Contemporary Women in the Letters of Erasmus," *Erasmus of Rotterdam Society Yearbook*, ed. Richard L. Demolen, vol. 9 (1989): 34–72. See Elizabeth McCutcheon, "'Tongues as Ready as Men's': Erasmus' Representation of Women and Their Discourse," *Erasmus of Rotterdam Society Yearbook*, vol. 12 (1992): 64–86. See also Thompson's notes 32 and 33 in *Collected Works of Erasmus*, vol. 39, 512–514.

[142] Erasmus, "The Abbot and the Learned Lady," vol. 39, 505.

[143] Erasmus, "A Pilgrimage for Religion's Sake," *Collected Works of Erasmus*, vol. 40, 641.

[144] Erasmus, "A Pilgrimage for Religion's Sake," vol. 40, 643.

[145] Erasmus, "A Pilgrimage for Religion's Sake," vol. 40, 647.

[146] Erasmus, "A Pilgrimage for Religion's Sake," vol. 40, 645.

[147] Erasmus, "A Pilgrimage for Religion's Sake," vol. 40, 644.

[148] Erasmus, "A Pilgrimage for Religion's Sake," vol. 40, 647.

[149] A swirl of debate over authorship has surrounded this dialogue ever since its appearance, in large part, no doubt, because of Erasmus' words denying involvement. On the epistolary and manuscript evidence that links Erasmus to the "Julius," see Michael J. Heath, Introduction to "Julius Excluded from Heaven: A Dialogue," trans. Michael J. Heath, ed. A. H. T. Levi, *Collected Works of Erasmus*, vol. 27 (Toronto: University of Toronto, 1986) 156–163.

[150] Michael J. Heath, Introduction to "Julius Excluded from Heaven," vol. 27, 162.

[151] Erasmus, "Julius Excluded from Heaven," vol. 27, 170. On the Lucianic form, see Heath's Introduction, 164–165.

[152] Erasmus, "Julius Excluded from Heaven," vol. 27, 170.

[153] Erasmus, "Julius Excluded from Heaven," vol. 27, 192; 174–177; 189–190; and 180–184.

[154] Erasmus, "Julius Excluded from Heaven," vol. 27, 191.

[155] Erasmus, "Julius Excluded from Heaven," vol. 27, 195.

[156] Erasmus, "To Andrea Ammonio" (Letter 245), *Collected Works of Erasmus*, vol. 2, 205.

[157] As Heath argues, this dialogue is "inspired by a real desire for reform rather than by political opportunism or mere animosity." The dialogue ends, therefore, on a hopeful note—that the office will survive Julius. See Heath's Introduction, vol. 27, 162.

[158] Erasmus, "Additional Formulae," in *Collected Works of Erasmus*, vol. 39, 121.

[159] Erasmus, "Additional Formulae," vol. 39, 121. In a letter "To Thomas Grey," Erasmus claimed that Epimenides dreamt of "those very super-subtle subtleties that today are the boast of the sons of Scotus; for I should be prepared to swear that Epimenides was reincarnated in Scotus." See Erasmus, "To Thomas Grey" (Letter 64), *Collected Works of Erasmus*, vol. 1, 137. Elsewhere, Erasmus makes a similar point, writing that "there can be no doubt that the soul of this theologian Epimenides has migrated into our sophistical theologians, who have brought so many empty dreams into the world that two hundred years' unbroken sleep would hardly suffice for them." See Erasmus, "You sleep longer than Epimenides" (I. ix. 64), *Collected Works of Erasmus*, vol. 32, 217–218.

[160] Erasmus, "Additional Formulae," vol., 39, 121.

[161] Erasmus, "To Thomas Grey" (Letter 64), *Collected Works of Erasmus*, vol. 1, 137. In the colloquy titled "Echo," a youth asks, "what do those do who spend their lives in quibbling only?" Echo answers: "Only spin." "They spin cobwebs, maybe." Echo: May be." See Erasmus, "Echo," vol. 40, 798.

[162] Craig R. Thompson, Introduction to "The Epithalamium of Peter Gilles," *Collected Works of Erasmus*, vol. 39, 520. See also note 19 on 527–528.

[163] Erasmus, "The Epithalamium of Peter Gilles," vol. 39, 521–522.

[164] Erasmus, "The Epithalamium of Peter Gilles," vol. 39, 522.

[165] Erasmus, "The Epithalamium of Peter Gilles," vol. 39, 522.

[166] Erasmus, "A Fish Diet," *Collected Works of Erasmus*, vol. 40, 691.

[167] Erasmus, "The Sermon, or Merdardus," *Collected Works of Erasmus*, vol. 40, 948.

[168] Erasmus, "A Meeting of the Philological Society," *Collected Works of Erasmus*, vol. 40, 836.

[169] Phillips, *Erasmus and the Northern Renaissance*, 139. On the ways in which Erasmus' thoughts on peace are bound up with the critique of ceremonialism and the promotion of humanistic values, see Tracy, *Erasmus, The Growth of a Mind*, 133–162.

[170] Erasmus, "To Wolfgang Capito" (letter 541), *Collected Works of Erasmus*, vol. 4, 261–262.

[171] Erasmus, "To Antoon van Bergen" (letter 288), *Collected Works of Erasmus*, vol. 2, 278–283.

[172] Erasmus, "Dedicatory Letter" to *Paraphrase on Mark*, trans. Erika Rummel, *Collected Works of Erasmus*, vol. 49 (Toronto: University of Toronto, 1988) 2–12.

[173] Erasmus, "Dedicatory Letter" to *Paraphrase on John*, trans. Jane E. Phillips, *Collected Works of Erasmus*, vol. 46 (Toronto: University of Toronto, 1991) 9–10.

[174] Erasmus, "Dedicatory Letter" to *Paraphrase on Acts*, trans. Robert D. Sider, in ed. John J. Bateman, *Collected Works of Erasmus*, vol. 50 (Toronto: University of Toronto, 1995) 2–4.

[175] Erasmus, "Charon," *Collected Works of Erasmus*, vol. 40, 821.

[176] Erasmus, "The Old Men's Chat, or The Carriage," *Collected Works of Erasmus*, vol. 39, 459.

[177] Erasmus, "The Funeral," vol. 40, 770.

[178] Craig R. Thompson, Introduction to "Military Affairs," *Collected Works of Erasmus*, vol. 39, 53.

[179] Phillips, *The "Adages" of Erasmus*, 308–353.

[180] Betty Radice, Introductory Note to Erasmus, "A Complaint of Peace," vol. 27, 290.

[181] Erasmus, "War is sweet to those who have not tried it," Phillips, *The "Adages" of Erasmus*, 310.

[182] Erasmus, "War is sweet," 311–312. Compare Erasmus, "The Complaint of Peace," vol. 27, 295.

[183] Erasmus, "War is sweet," 313.

[184] Erasmus, "War is sweet," 323–324.

[185] Erasmus, "War is sweet," 350 and 343. See also Erasmus, "A Complaint of Peace," vol. 27, 310–311.

[186] Phillips, *The Adages of Erasmus*, 328. Compare with Erasmus, "The Complaint of Peace," vol. 27, 299.

[187] Erasmus, "War is sweet," 321.

[188] Erasmus, "A Complaint of Peace," vol. 27, 309. Compare with Erasmus, "War is sweet," 321. Thus Erasmus exclaims in horror of the clerical sanctification of war: "How foul is the tongue of priests who preach war." Erasmus, "A Complaint of Peace," vol. 27, 308.

[189] Erasmus, "War is sweet," 327 and 321–322.

[190] Erasmus, "A Complaint of Peace," vol. 27, 307.

[191] Erasmus, "War is sweet," 352.

[192] Erasmus, "A Complaint of Peace," vol. 27, 305–306 and 310.

[193] Erasmus, "A Complaint of Peace," vol. 27, 314–315.

[194] Erasmus, "War is sweet," 344–348.

[195] Erasmus, "The Tongue," vol. 29, 268 and 314.

[196] Erasmus, "The Tongue," vol. 29, 321.

[197] Erasmus, "The Tongue," vol. 29, 406–408.

[198] Erasmus, "The Tongue," vol. 29, 406–408. Compare with "A Complaint of Peace," vol. 27, 298.

[199] Erasmus, "The Tongue," vol. 29, 320. See 349.

[200] Erasmus, "The Tongue," vol. 29, 406.

[201] Erasmus, "The Tongue," vol. 29, 408.

[202] Erasmus, "The Tongue," vol. 29, 409–410.

[203] Erasmus, "The Tongue," vol. 29, 410.

[204] Erasmus, "The Tongue," vol. 29, 411 and 323.

[205] Erasmus, "Paraphrases on Romans and Galatians," trans. John B. Payne, Albert Rabil, Jr., and Warren S. Smith, Jr., ed. Robert D. Sider, *Collected Works of Erasmus*, vol. 42 (Toronto: University of Toronto, 1984) 77.

[206] Erasmus, "To Thomas Lupset" (letter 1053), *Collected Works of Erasmus*, vol. 7, 160–161.

[207] Erasmus, "To Martin Luther" (letter 1127a), *Collected Works of Erasmus*, vol. 8, 21; and "To Cuthbert Tunstall" (letter 1369), *Collected Works of Erasmus*, vol. 10, 31.

[208] Schoeck, *Erasmus of Europe; The Prince of the Humanists*, 372.

[209] "From Edward Lee" (letter 1061), *Collected Works of Erasmus*, vol. 7, 181–182.

[210] Erasmus, "To Hermann von Neuenahr," *Collected Works of Erasmus*, vol. 7, 228.

[211] Erasmus, "To Martin Dorp" (letter 337), *Collected Works of Erasmus*, vol. 3, 113–114.

[212] Erasmus, "To Johann von Botzheim" (letter 1341a), *Collected Works of Erasmus*, vol. 9, 325.

[213] Erasmus, "To Johann von Botzheim" (letter 1341a), vol. 9, 325.

[214] Erasmus, "To Martin Dorp" (letter 337), vol. 3, 113–114.

[215] Erasmus, "To Willibald Pirckheimer" (letter 1268), *Collected Works of Erasmus*, vol. 9, 49; and "To Joost Lauwereyns" (letter 1299), vol. 9, 122.

[216] Erasmus, "To Cuthbert Tunstall" (letter 1369), trans. R. A. B. Mynors and Alexander Dalzell, *Collected Works of Erasmus*, vol. 10 (Toronto: University of Toronto, 1992) 33.

[217] Erasmus, "To Johann von Botzheim" (letter 1341a), vol. 9, 340–341.

[218] Erasmus, "The Apotheosis of That Incomparable Worthy, John Reuchlin," *Collected Works of Erasmus*, vol. 39, 248.

[219] Erasmus, "The Apotheosis of That Incomparable Worthy, John Reuchlin," vol. 39, 249–250.

[220] Erasmus, "The Apotheosis of That Incomparable Worthy, John Reuchlin," vol. 39, 250–251. See Heinz Scheible's entry on Reuchlin in *Contemporaries of Erasmus*, vol. 3, 145–150.

[221] Erasmus, "The Apotheosis of That Incomparable Worthy, John Reuchlin," vol. 39, 251.

[222] Erasmus, "To Jakob Wimpfeling" (letter 305), *Collected Works of Erasmus*, vol. 3, 33; and "To Jakob Wimpfeling" (letter 326b), vol. 3, 76–77. See also "To Leo X," in the same volume, 109. For references to Erasmus' letters I am indebted to Heinz Scheible's entry on Reuchlin in *Contemporaries of Erasmus*, vol. 3, 145–150. See also Schoeck, *Erasmus of Europe; The Prince of the Humanists*, 132–134.

[223] Erasmus, "To Johann Reuchlin" (letter 324), *Collected Works of Erasmus*, vol. 3, 62–63.

[224] Erasmus, "From Ulrich von Hutten" (letter 1135), trans. R. A. B. Mynors, *Collected Works of Erasmus*, vol. 8 (Toronto: University of Toronto, 1988) 32–34.

[225] Erasmus, "To Willibald Pirkheimer" (letter 856), *Collected Works of Erasmus*, vol. 6, 67.

[226] Erasmus, "To Hermann von Neuenahr" (letter 636), trans. R. A. B. Mynors and D. F. S. Thomson, *Collected Works of Erasmus*, vol. 5 (Toronto: University of Toronto, 1979) 84–85.

[227] Erasmus, "To the Reader" (letter 1041), *Collected Works of Erasmus*, vol. 7, 129.

[228] Erasmus, "To Thomas Wolsey" (letter 967), *Collected Works of Erasmus*, vol. 6, 368–369.

[229] Erasmus, "To Albert of Brandenburg" (letter 1033), *Collected Works of Erasmus*, vol. 7, 110.

[230] Erasmus, "To Hermann von Neuenahr" (letter 636), *Collected Works of Erasmus*, vol. 5, 84. Erasmus felt that the backers of Reuchlin frequently acted "with more zeal than discretion." See "To the Reader" (letter 1041), *Collected Works of Erasmus*, vol. 7, 129.

[231] Erasmus, "To John Fisher" (letter 824), *Collected Works of Erasmus*, vol. 5, 396.

[232] See Erasmus, "To Johann Reuchlin" (letter 1155), *Collected Works of Erasmus*, vol. 8, 79.

[233] Erasmus, "To Jacopo Bannisio" (letter 700), *Collected Works of Erasmus*, vol. 5, 179. Compare with "To Johannes Caesarius" (letter 808), vol. 5, 358–359: "It seems to me to be the depths of misfortune to struggle with monsters like that, from whom you can win no trophies but the pox." Besides, Erasmus cautions Willibald Pirckheimer, "this foul-mouthed villain [Pfefferkorn] cannot be defeated, for he is entirely made up of malignancy and has so many wicked angels to provide him with new strength when he is tired." See "To Willibald Pirckheimer" (letter 694), vol. 5, 170.

[234] Erasmus, "To Hermann von Neuenahr" (letter 703), *Collected Works of Erasmus*, vol. 5, 183.

[235] Erasmus, "To the Reader" (letter 1041), *Collected Works of Erasmus*, vol. 7, 129. Compare with "To the Theologians of Louvain" (letter 1217), *Collected Works of Erasmus*, vol. 8, 255.

[236] Erasmus, "To Willibald Pirckheimer" (letter 694), *Collected Works of Erasmus*, vol. 5, 170.

[237] See Erasmus, "To Raffaele Riario, Cardinal of San Giorgio" (letter 333), "To Domenico Grimani" (letter 334), and "To Leo X" (letter 335), *Collected Works of Erasmus*, vol. 3, 85–110.

[238] Erasmus, "To Johann Reuchlin" (letter 713), *Collected Works of Erasmus*, vol. 5, 204.

[239] Erasmus, "To Johann von Botzheim" (letter 1314a), *Collected Works of Erasmus*, vol. 9, 347.

[240] Erasmus, "To Johann von Botzheim" (letter 1314a), 347.

[241] Erasmus, "To Johann von Botzheim" (letter 1314a), 347. See Phillips, *Erasmus and the Northern Renaissance*, 177.

[242] Erasmus, "To Willibald Pirckheimer" (letter 1268), *Collected Works of Erasmus*, vol. 9, 49.

243 Erasmus, *Inquisitio De Fide*, ed. Craig R. Thompson, second edition (Hamden, Connecticut: Archon, 1975) 37.

244 Erasmus, "An Examination Concerning Faith," *Collected Works of Erasmus*, vol. 39, 429.

245 Erasmus, "An Examination Concerning Faith," vol. 39, 430.

246 Thompson, Introduction to Erasmus, *Inquisitio De Fide*, 39.

247 Thompson, Introduction to Erasmus, *Inquisitio De Fide*, 39.

248 On the development of Erasmus' perception of Luther, see Thompson's Introduction to Erasmus, *Inquisitio de Fide*, 4–34.

249 See, for instance, Erasmus, "To the Elector Frederick of Saxony" (letter 939), *Collected Works of Erasmus*, vol. 6, 297.

250 Erasmus, "Brief Notes of Erasmus of Rotterdam for the Cause of the Theologian Martin Luther," trans. Martin Lowry, ed. J. K. Sowards, *Collected Works of Erasmus*, vol. 71 (Toronto: University of Toronto, 1993) 106.

251 Erasmus, "Minute Composed by a Person who Seriously Wishes Provisions to be Made for the Reputation of the Roman Pontiff and the Peace of the Church," trans. Martin Lowry, *Collected Works of Erasmus*, vol. 71, 109–111.

252 Erasmus, "To Leo X" (letter 1143), *Collected Works of Erasmus*, vol. 8, 50–52.

253 Erasmus, "To Albert of Brandenburg" (letter 1033), *Collected Works of Erasmus*, vol. 7, 108.

254 Erasmus, "To Richard Pace" (letter 1218), *Collected Works of Erasmus*, vol. 8, 259. Compare with "To Lorenzo Campeggi" (letter 1167), vol. 8, 120–121.

255 Erasmus, "To William Blount" (letter 1219), *Collected Works of Erasmus*, vol. 8, 261.

256 Erasmus, "To William Blount," vol. 8, 260–261.

257 Schoeck, *Erasmus of Europe; The Prince of the Humanists*, 299.

258 Erasmus, "To Martin Luther" (April 11, 1526), in Johan Huizinga, *Erasmus and the Age of Reformation* (New York: Harper and Row, 1957) 241.

259 Erasmus, "To Conrad Pellicanus" (letter 1640), *Collected Works of Erasmus*, vol. 11, 365.

260 Boyle, *Christening Pagan Mysteries*, 63–95.

261 Erasmus, "The Epicurean," *Collected Works of Erasmus*, vol. 40, 1073–1075.

[262] Erasmus, "The Epicurean," vol. 40, 1077–1079.

[263] Erasmus, "The Epicurean," vol. 40, 1079–1080.

[264] Erasmus, "The Epicurean," vol. 40, 1083.

[265] Erasmus, "The Epicurean," vol. 40, 1086.

[266] Erasmus, "The Epicurean," vol. 40, 1084.

[267] Erasmus, "The Epicurean," vol. 40, 1087.

[268] Boyle, *Christening Pagan Mysteries*, 74–75.

[269] Boyle, *Christening Pagan Mysteries*, 84–87.

[270] Thompson, *The Colloquies of Erasmus*, xxv.

[271] Erasmus, "To Jeroen van der Noot" (letter 1300), trans. R. A. B. Mynors, *Collected Works of Erasmus*, vol. 9 (Toronto: University of Toronto, 1989) 126.

[272] Erasmus, "To Johann Von Botzheim" (letter 1341a), *Collected Works of Erasmus*, vol. 9, 305.

[273] Erasmus twice mentions hatred as his adversary's motive. See "To Jeroen van der Noot" (letter 1300) and "To Joost Lauwereyns" (letter 1299), *Collected Works of Erasmus*, vol. 9, 126 and 123.

[274] Erasmus, "To Johann Von Botzheim" (letter 1341a), *Collected Works of Erasmus*, vol. 9, 305.

[275] Phillips, *Erasmus and the Northern Renaissance*, 206.

[276] Erasmus, "The Godly Feast," *Collected Works of Erasmus*, vol. 39, 175–176.

[277] Erasmus, "The Godly Feast," vol. 39, 178.

[278] Erasmus, "The Godly Feast," vol. 39, 179–181.

[279] Erasmus, "The Godly Feast," vol. 39, 180.

[280] Erasmus, "The Godly Feast," vol. 39, 179. As Thompson notes, Erasmus surely had classical models in mind when he fashioned Eusebius' home, most notably "Horace's Sabine farm or Cicero's villa at Tusculum"; but he probably also was tapping his experience of actual homes, including the country house at Anderlecht where he lived for six months in 1521. See Thompson's Introduction to "The Godly Feast," vol. 39, 171–172. On Erasmus' time at Anderlecht, see Schoeck, *Erasmus of Europe; The Prince of the Humanists*, 206–207. As Thompson also observes, Erasmus may well have been calling upon his memories of the house belonging to his friend Johann von Botzheim; in a letter, "To

Marcus Laurinus" (letter 1342), Erasmus speaks of this home as "a real home of the Muses; no part of it but displays something in the way of polish and elegance, no part without a voice—all speaks in paintings that attract and retain the attention." *Collected Works of Erasmus*, vol. 9, 378.

[281] Erasmus, "The Godly Feast," vol. 39, 175; 176; 177–178; 178; and 181.

[282] Erasmus, "The Godly Feast," vol. 39, 189.

[283] Erasmus, "The Godly Feast," vol. 39, 178 and 179.

[284] Erasmus, "The Godly Feast," vol. 39, 176. Opting to imitate the Muses, Erasmus ignores another piece of classical wisdom. See "Seven makes a feast, nine makes a fray" (Adage I. iii. 97) in *Collected Works of Erasmus*, vol. 31, 315–316.

[285] See Erasmus, "Shadows" (Adage I. iii.97) in *Collected Works of Erasmus*, vol. 31, 58–59.

[286] Erasmus, "The Godly Feast," vol. 39, 183.

[287] Erasmus, "The Godly Feast," vol. 39, 189.

[288] Erasmus, "The Godly Feast," vol. 39, 192.

[289] Erasmus, "The Godly Feast," vol. 39, 192.

[290] Erasmus, "The Godly Feast," vol. 39, 192.

[291] Erasmus, "The Godly Feast," vol. 39, 193.

[292] Erasmus, "The Godly Feast," vol. 39, 194.

[293] Erasmus, "The Godly Feast," vol. 39, 194.

[294] Erasmus, "The Godly Feast," vol. 39, 194.

[295] Erasmus, "The Godly Feast," vol. 39, 194. Recall the general's death in the "The Funeral," vol. 39, 192.

[296] Erasmus, "The Godly Feast," vol. 39, 192.

[297] Erasmus, "The Godly Feast," vol. 39, 182.

[298] Erasmus, "The Godly Feast," vol. 39, 183.

[299] Erasmus, "The Soldier and the Carthusian," *Collected Works of Erasmus*, vol. 39, 332.

[300] Boyle, *Erasmus on Language and Method in Theology*, 101.

[301] Boyle, *Erasmus on Language and Method in Theology*, 130.

[302] In a letter to Thomas Grey written in 1497 (letter 64), Erasmus speaks of those "quasi-theologians of our day" as those "whose brains are the most addled, tongues the most uncultured, wits the dullest, teachings the thorniest, characters the least attractive, lives the most hypocritical, talk the most slanderous, and hearts the blackest on earth." See *Collected Works of Erasmus*, vol. 1, 138. On the shape of scholasticism at Paris in Erasmus' day, see Schoeck, *Erasmus of Europe; The Making of a Humanist*, 174–178.

[303] Huizinga, *Erasmus and the Age of Reformation*, 191.

[304] See Schoeck, *Erasmus of Europe; The Prince of the Humanists*, 257.

[305] Erasmus, "To Wolfgang Capito" (letter 541), *Collected Works of Erasmus*, vol. 4, 265.

[306] Erasmus, "The Godly Feast," vol. 39, 184.

[307] Erasmus, "The Godly Feast," vol. 39, 184.

[308] Erasmus, "The Godly Feast," vol. 39, 185.

[309] Erasmus, "The Godly Feast," vol. 39, 186.

[310] Erasmus, "The Godly Feast," vol. 39, 184.

[311] See Erasmus, "The Godly Feast," vol. 39, 187.

[312] Boyle, *Erasmus on Language and Method in Theology*, 131.

[313] Erasmus, "The Godly Feast," vol. 39, 204.

[314] Boyle, *Erasmus on Language and Method in Theology*, 136.

[315] Erasmus, "The Godly Feast," vol. 39, 198–200.

[316] Erasmus, "The Godly Feast," vol. 39, 200.

[317] Boyle, *Erasmus on Language and Method in Theology*, 140.

[318] Geraldine Thompson, *Under Pretext of Praise*, 34.

[319] Boyle, *Erasmus on Language and Method in Theology*, 136.

[320] Boyle, *Erasmus on Language and Method in Theology*, 140.

[321] Boyle, *Erasmus on Language and Method in Theology*, 141.

[322] Phillips, *Erasmus and the Northern Renaissance*, 206.

[323] Erasmus, "The Tongue," vol. 29, 365.

[324] Erasmus, "To a sick spirit speech is a physician" (Adage III.i.100), *Collected Works of Erasmus*, vol. 34, 224.

7
At Play with *Pharmaceia:*
Plato's *Phaedrus* as Ethic of Discourse

Phaedrus: What sort of discourse have you now in mind, and what is its origin?

Socrates: The sort that goes together with knowledge, and is written in the soul of the learner: that can defend itself, and knows to whom it should speak and to whom it should say nothing.

Phaedrus: You mean no dead discourse, but the living speech, the original of which the written discourse may fairly be called a kind of image.

—Plato's *Phaedrus*, 276a

Religious language—it would appear—is affected by deep-seated moral ambiguities. While efforts to speak about religious topics can and do break through to wondrous discovery and emancipating insight, they are just as likely to degenerate into rancor and raillery. Recall, for instance, how tenuously Philo's dialogue with Cleanthes and Demea hangs in the balance between civility and acrimony; remember also how fragile and fleeting are the glimmers of understanding between the stable philosopher and the crazed nephew in Diderot's dialogue; or mark how tempting it is to transform the ironic wit of Lucianic or Erasmian serio-comedy into invective and polemic. Such discourse—these dialogues tell us—is a delicate moral affair. Its outcome hangs in the balance. Those who engage in such discourse, therefore, face a number of difficult questions. Is there an intelligible and credible way to draft normative judgments regarding the practice of religious discourse? Is an ethic of discourse possible, and if so, what would it tell us? Moreover, how would the discourse that takes up these ethical questions itself proceed to speak?

Answers to these questions are up for grabs in current philosophical debates. On one hand, Richard Rorty questions the very possibility of an ethic of discourse. For Rorty there are no "final vocabularies" for measuring the truth or the goodness of specific languages. He counsels readers, therefore, to give up the dream (variously called "Platonic," "Kantian," and "metaphysical") of measuring discursive claims by checking them against objective reality. In his dreams, alternatively, Rorty envisions a society of "liberal ironists."[1] Fully aware that their own commitments and "languages of moral deliberation" are contingent, these ironists' most fundamental hope would be "to keep the conversation going rather than to find [some] objective truth" which would commensurate variant experiences of the world.[2] There is, in Rorty's scheme, no discourse that can speak *about* the ethical fiber of discourse. Jürgen Habermas, on the other hand, holds out hope for a rationally grounded ethic of discourse. Like Rorty, Habermas construes knowledge as something social and "communicatively mediated." Rationality, for him, is the "capacity of responsible participants in interaction to orient themselves in relation to validity claims geared to intersubjective recognition."[3] While these claims to validity are inherently bound to a particular "here and now," they also "transcend any local context": the "transcendent moment of universal validity bursts every provinciality asunder."[4] Stressing this "principle of universalization" in the communicative process, Habermas rejects Rorty's suggestion that philosophy should abandon its role as "guardian of rationality."[5] The task of a philosophical ethic of discourse, according to Habermas, is to interpret the "logic of moral argumentation" embedded in communicative actions.[6] Consequently, Habermas, unlike Rorty, holds on to the hope for universalizable judgments about ethical standards for discourse. In the debate between Rorty and Habermas, however, the possibility and the shape of an ethic of discourse remains in question.

I will return to the issues raised in this debate at the end of this chapter. For the time being, I suggest that we stick with the method used throughout this work by taking our bearing for an ethic of discourse from the literary dialogues discussed in previous chapters. Admittedly this may seem questionable, given the mixed and tenuous moral tenor of conversation displayed in many of these texts. A closer look, however, reveals a rich plurality of ethical perspectives at play in the conversational fabric of these works. In each dialogue, what an author perceives to be base (or blameworthy) and normative (or praiseworthy) is embedded in the actual practices of the interlocutors' discourse. Although the ethical note may remain implicit in any given dialogue, the characters' actions and reactions in dialogue signify an author's perceived ideal or norm for the discursive situation at hand. Each dialogue, in other words, embodies an ethic of discourse, and it does so without purifying the discourse of its natural ambiguity and fragility. Thus we find *virtues* like civility (Hume) or honesty (Lucian) struggling to develop in the discursive soil of raillery and deceit. Other dialogues set off certain exemplary qualities of *interaction* against their ignoble opposites—like playful openness against self-serious dogmatism (Schleiermacher), or respect and tolerance versus ethnocentric arrogance (Voltaire), or affirmation and inclusiveness as opposed to hostility or domination (Cardenal). Alternatively, these dialogues leave readers with traces of desirable *ends* for discourse: irenic plurality as opposed to fractured difference (Erasmus), or correctness over against disorder and heterodoxy (Anselm). In varied ways, these dialogues offer pointers for crafting an ethic of discourse. We can make some headway in this direction by heeding the lessons implanted in the practices themselves.

To this end, I suggest that we eavesdrop on one more dialogue—one that makes the normative strains of dialogue its central concern. I am thinking particularly of Plato's *Phaedrus*, without doubt one of the richest and most complex dialogues ever composed. I choose the *Phaedrus* for two reasons. In the first place, it would be unthinkable to end this study of dialogues without turning back to the classic source of this genre in the works of Plato. Though not the first author of dialogues or the sole classical model for later dialogues, Plato has remained paradigmatic for centuries of apprentices and imitators. Second, and more to the point, I turn to the *Phaedrus* because there Plato provides both an ethic of discourse and an actual discourse *on* norms. That is, by providing a discourse on normative discourse through the dialogue form, Plato not only spells out his standards for evaluating discourse, but also shows through the drama of fictional conversation what ideal discourse would look like and consequently what it would take to talk about such ideal talk. The choice of genre is crucial, therefore, because through it Plato creates a form of discourse for developing an ethic of discourse which (a) attempts to live up to the ideals of this ethic, and (b) does not claim exemption from the limitations and contingency common to natural discourse. Careful consideration of this dialogue, therefore, furthers the search for ethical insight into the life of the word, and yields a language for doing so.[7]

I will begin the first section by examining the *Phaedrus*' debate on rhetoric. An initial discussion of this dialogue's fictional and historical context will trace Socrates' effort to move beyond a merely technical evaluation of rhetoric in order to generate ethical questions and standards for the uses of persuasive language. As I will show in the second section, Plato's ethic of discourse pivots on the relation of basic loves (or desires) and rhetorical practices. Following now familiar lines of Plato interpretation, I will outline the ways in which different forms of speech are infused with and shaped by alternative desires (or loves) which undergird human life. How we love (or what we basically desire) shapes how we talk to and with others, and thus determines what kind of life we lead. The third section will muddy the waters of this correlation of love and speech by considering a number of problems—including the dialogue's discordant structure, a condemnation of writing performed in writing, and the enigmatic character of Socrates—that make it difficult to discern Plato's posture with respect to his own ethic of discourse. This has led some interpreters (Jacques Derrida, in particular) to suggest that Plato is caught in the self-destructive tension of his own project. If this is correct, then Plato's love-based ethic of discourse also dissolves itself. In the final section, I will argue that, on the contrary, his use of the dialogue form, with all its structural breaks and internal tensions, signals Plato's dialectical finesse and philosophical imagination, not a self-destructive confusion. In particular, Plato's fusion of rhetorical concerns with normative questions, in such a way that the irrational forces in human life are acknowledged and even embraced, provides an ethical measure for discourse that does not seek to escape from the muddle and ambiguity of actual human discourse. This achievement, I will suggest in closing, represents a coherent and compelling challenge to contemporary perspectives—like those of Rorty and Habermas—on the ethic of discourse.

(1) Beyond a "Life of Mere Words"[8]

When Socrates encounters him, Phaedrus is beginning a walk in the country upon the advice of Acumenus, a well-known physician; he has just spent a long morning listening to a speech on love by Lysias, someone he regards as the "the ablest writer of our day" (228a). A self-described "amateur" in the practice of oratory, Phaedrus is enamored with the power and reputation of professional writers for the courts—so much so that he has taken with him on his promenade a written copy of Lysias' speech to imitate in private. Phaedrus loves fine speeches, but what he fancies most about them is the excellence of their rhetorical technique, the rules of which he has studiously absorbed from the rhetorical manuals of the day (273a6; 266d5–6). His "enthusiasm for discourse" (228b; 242a8), in fact, is purely formal, as is evident in his praise for the rhetorical distinction of both Lysias' oration and Socrates' second speech on love, even though the substantive claims of these two speeches clash diametrically (234c and 257c). Phaedrus is, as one commentator put it, an "intellectual impressario": he "attaches himself to leading thinkers, spurs them to perform, and propagates the latest arguments and trends."[9] It is no surprise, for instance, to find him trailing in the company of the renowned sophist Callias (*Protagoras* 315c) or to discover him present at the house of Agathon, complaining to the distinguished guests that so little praise is sung to the god of love (*Symposium* 177a–d). His one talent lies in the ability to instigate more competent minds to speak—especially, it seems, on the topic of love. In this sense, Eryximachus (Acumenus' son) refers to Phaedrus as "the real author of our discussion" in the *Symposium* (177d), something echoed several times by Socrates in the *Phaedrus*.[10]

As a character, Phaedrus is a remarkably shallow and unimaginative interlocutor for Socrates. It is true that Socrates depicts Phaedrus as wavering between Lysias and himself, unsure whom to follow (257b); indeed, shortly thereafter he prays that Phaedrus will turn to philosophy (261a). Despite the hope sounded in these passages, however, Phaedrus has no real facility for philosophical reflection. His status as intermediary, and consequently his role as Socrates' messenger to Lysias (243d–e and 278b, e), simply point up that Socrates and professional writers like Lysias share something in common. Like these rhetoricians, Socrates takes the power of language seriously. Thus he admits, sometimes dramatically under the inspiration of local deities, but also methodically throughout the dialogue, that he too is "sick with love for discourse" (228b; Fowler trans.). It is only because Socrates is a fellow enthusiast about speeches, after all, that Phaedrus can so easily convince him to continue the conversation (236b–d and 242a–b). In this regard, Phaedrus commands the suasive power of a fellow lover of words, but their common desire for discourse, and consequently the link between Socrates and the likes of Lysias, is also fraught with tension over how language should or should not be used. Phaedrus provides a go-between, a proxy interlocutor for Socrates and the rhetorically oriented sophists of the day. Through the dialogue between Socrates and Phaedrus, Plato engages the sophists and rhetoricians over the ends of discourse and the proper deployments of language.

It is a speech by Lysias that has Phaedrus beaming. Phaedrus is quite taken with the cleverness of Lysias' claim—that one should surrender one's affections only to someone who is not in love rather than to someone who is (227c)—but playing it coy, he conceals his written copy in order to show off his skill at reciting the speech from memory. In his opening response to Phaedrus, Socrates encodes and anticipates several objections to the aims and practices of writers like Lysias. To begin, he mocks the cleverness of Lysias' thesis by farcically extending the claim: let the boy surrender his affections to the poor, the elderly, the ordinary, even to Socrates as well ("what an attractive democratic theory that would be!") (227c–d). By pointing up the absurdity of this "democratic" theory, Socrates takes satiric aim at Lysias, who was an active proponent of Athenian democracy; and Plato indirectly anticipates Socrates' objection to the written word and its uses in the courts, namely that a written speech can be picked up and used by anyone. This, of course, is precisely what Phaedrus has done with Lysias' speech. Socrates sees through Phaedrus' ploy, demanding that he bring forth the actual written speech from "under his cloak" and read it verbatim, remarking that "Lysias himself is here present" in written form. Socrates is not eager to let Phaedrus "practice his oratory" on him (228). This too is an ironic jab at Lysias, who, as a ghostwriter of speeches to be bought and used by litigants at court, was never present except in written form. Athenian law required that all litigants speak for themselves in court, regardless of their abilities. Those with poor speaking skills but with ample financial resources could arrange for a writer like Lysias to write their defense; then they could memorize it for their own delivery, just as Phaedrus practiced the recitation of Lysias' speech on love. Since Lysias was known for his elegant but simple prose, as well as his ability to craft a speech in a natural manner, fitting to the customer's character, he became one of the leading speech-writers of his day.[11] Though Lysias' profession provided a service demanded by the structures of the courts, it was always open to abuse, for a master like Lysias could easily make the worse cause seem the better.[12] Such abuses become a central object of Socrates' criticism.

Phaedrus respects Lysias greatly, partly due to the influence of the teachers of rhetoric, especially those who wrote handbooks for study. The authors of these handbooks (e.g., Tisias, Theodorus, and Thrasymachus) gave instruction on judicial speeches, focusing primarily on the proper arrangement of the different parts of the speech and offering stock devices for persuasive argumentation, including the ability to craft credible arguments from probability. As George Kennedy points out, the democratic court system of ancient Athens was largely responsible for the rhetorical theories and practices of these sophists. They provided "a practical kind of philosophy which taught the techniques of civic life," and this naturally included rhetoric.[13] Through instruction, they offered citizens training in the practical logic required to protect their interests at court. Like the professional speech-writers, however, sophistic rhetoric was open to the charge of training people in the techniques of deceit and the practices of chicanery—once again, of making the worse cause appear the better. Socrates knows these handbooks and their authors well, at one point giving a quick digest of their contents (266d–267d). As the dialogue with Phaedrus shows, he harbors deep suspicions of the entire profession.

While Socrates argues *through* Phaedrus *against* the speech-writers and teachers of rhetoric, Plato as author addresses the dialogue as a whole first and foremost *to* Isocrates, the pre-eminent rhetorician of the day and the director of a rival school to Plato's academy. It is true that Socrates only mentions Isocrates at the end of the dialogue, contrasting him with Lysias as someone of noble character, superior literary achievement and true philosophical potential; indeed, Socrates prophesies, Isocrates will someday make "all his literary predecessors look like very small fry."[14] The paucity of explicit references to Isocrates, however, is misleading, since the dialogue is littered with subterranean allusions to him.[15] Isocrates too is a lover of discourse.[16] It is, he tells us, the "power of speech" which lifts human beings above the "life of wild beasts" in order to create political communities and other institutions;[17] and it is "beautiful and artistic speech"—the "surest sign of culture"—which distinguishes the wise from the ignorant and the Athenian from the barbarian.[18] Although Isocrates wrote and sold court speeches in his early years and may have written a rhetorical handbook, he later renounced these occupations and dedicated himself to teaching "the art of discourse." However, he is quick to distinguish his educational program from that of the teachers of disputation (like those ridiculed in Plato's *Euthydemus*); from that of the sophistic teachers of rhetoric (who pompously pretend to apply a fixed and mechanical method "with hard and fast rules" to the "art of discourse"); and from speculative philosophy (including Platonic dialectic).[19] Anything worthy of the name "philosophy," Isocrates insists, must surely "enable us to govern wisely both our own households and the commonwealth."[20] True philosophy must be practical, for "likely conjecture about useful things is far preferable to exact knowledge of the useless."[21]

Socrates' dialogue with Phaedrus, therefore, stands against the background of a much broader debate concerning the nature and limits of rhetoric. It is the speech-writers, teachers of rhetoric, and especially Isocrates, whom Plato addresses through their conversation. Socrates defines the topic for this debate as "the nature of good and bad speaking and writing" (259e). The problem with this description, unfortunately, is that the qualifiers "good and bad" are equivocal. So too is Socrates' talk of "shameful and bad" speaking and writing (258d). Such terms can be taken in a purely technical sense—referring, for instance, to correct arrangement or to effective persuasion. This is what interests Phaedrus. He cares, above all, about the mastery of rhetorical technique necessary to become a "finished performer" (269d). But another aspect of these terms emerges through Socrates' pushing and prodding: they also can carry moral or normative meanings. Then the question shifts from what is procedurally correct to what is ethically "proper or improper" (274b). How ought human beings go about communicating with each other? What counts as "shameful" (*aischron*) and what counts as praiseworthy in the use of language with others? These questions take their bearing not from a standard of technical precision but from ethical norms and ideals for living and acting. Socrates' aim throughout the second part of the dialogue centers on the emergence of this line of ethical questioning.

(a) Socrates' first move to generate ethical questions about discourse is to broaden the meaning and scope of rhetoric. Following the lead of the sophists and judiciary speech-writers, Phaedrus thinks of the "art of speaking and writing" as applying exclusively to court oratory and the "public harrangues" of politicians (261b). This is too narrow for Socrates, since it pertains only to public forms of discourse. For Socrates rhetoric concerns all kinds of human interaction. The art of rhetoric, he insists, is "a kind of influencing of the mind by means of words" (*eie psychagogia tis dia logos*), and this takes place in both public and in private places; and it can deal with either important or unimportant matters (261a–b). Since Phaedrus loves anything having to do with rhetoric, the generality of this definition appeals to his zeal for the topic, though it is not exactly what he has been told by the teachers of rhetoric. Socrates manages to lead him to a broader understanding of rhetoric only by showing that what public orators *do*—namely, mislead audiences by playing with appearances—has already occurred in the first two speeches on love which they rehearsed together earlier.[22] The techniques of persuasion, in short, are found "wherever men speak" (261e), and as much between lovers as between litigants at court. For Socrates' purposes, conceiving rhetoric this broadly has the result of showing that rhetoric affects all human life. Questions about the proper and improper uses of the art of persuasion, consequently, have a bearing on the kind of life one chooses to live. Rhetoric carries ethical implications.

(b) Socrates wants Phaedrus to feel a sense of shame about devious or underhanded uses of persuasive language. To this end, he undertakes some of the dialogue's most dramatic—even ecstatic—behavior to shock his interlocutor into looking at rhetoric with a conscience. The interlude following Socrates' first speech on love is a good example. Socrates is ashamed of his speech. Strangely, indeed, he begins to hear an inner voice which forbids him to leave the spot without first making atonement for his "offense to heaven" (242b–c). The "divining power" of his mind tells Socrates that his first theory of love was blasphemous; he has sinned against the gods in order to win renown among people (242d). Unlike Phaedrus, moreover, Socrates subscribes to the popular view that Eros is a god. Since he has treated love as if it were something evil, he must surely make amends for his offense (242d–e). To do so, he ritually imitates the example of Stesichorus, the ancient poet who recanted his slur of Helen (243a). As if appeal to the poets is insufficient, Socrates also calls upon the opinion of a hypothetical "man of generous and humane character": wouldn't he "utterly refuse to accept our vilification of Love?" Socrates asks (243c–d). By all these different means, "Phaedrus is meant to learn that even a speech technically superior to that of Lysias should be judged in terms of moral categories as well."[23] Socrates wants him to shift from a merely technical understanding of rhetorical excellence to a moral perspective.[24]

(c) In a more argumentative vein, Socrates turns his attention to the effects of persuasive speech. Phaedrus, of course, is familiar with the power of a good orator (that is what he loves); and thus he readily admits the possibility of deception. A good orator at court, for instance, "can make the same thing appear to the same people now just, now unjust" (261c–d). So too, a politician with honed speaking skills can "make the same thing seem to the community now good, and now the reverse of good" (261d), simply by playing on slight "degrees of resemblance" (262a). Socrates begins by focusing Phaedrus' attention on the consequences of deceptive speech. Think of the disastrous results, he suggests, were a smooth-talking donkey merchant to convince a soldier that a donkey was really a horse and hence the perfect animal to ride into battle (260b–c). Far more serious consequences of deception occur on the political level. Were a charismatic politician to practice the same manipulative and deceptive techniques, for instance, by preying on a community's ignorance of what is good and what is evil, he could move people to commit wicked actions. Thus Socrates asks Phaedrus pointedly, "what kind of crop do you think his oratory is likely to reap from the seed thus sown?" (260d).

Socrates does not develop these examples in any depth. He chooses instead to indict the teachers of deceptive rhetoric, and within that charge, to highlight the pedagogical roots of deception. Behind the practices of deceptive speech, Socrates contends, stands the theory of those "cunning folk" who write "manuals of rhetoric." They "know all about the soul but keep their knowledge out of sight" (271c), dispensing only the techniques for pulling the wool over people's eyes.

Tisias and Gorgias, for instance, "could make trifles seem important and important points trifles by the force of their language"; they could even "dress up novelties as antiques and vice versa" (267a–b). And a teacher like Thrasymachus was so powerful a speaker that he could "rouse a crowd to anger and then sooth them down again with his spells"; no one was more deft, moreover, at "casting aspersions and dissipating them" (267c–d). These teachers and their handbooks are worse than the orators, for they train others in the habits of deceit, thereby propagating lives based on cunning and manipulation. They disseminate the art of deception, and thus wreak havoc on people's lives.[25]

At the root of the sophists' teaching, Socrates tells Phaedrus, is a fundamental disregard for truth. "Budding orators" are taught to ignore questions of what is true or good; they need only pay attention to what people think is true, and based on that, make a plausible case for their cause. Sarcastically imitating the advice of an unscrupulous teacher, Socrates counsels Phaedrus to care

> only about what is plausible. And that is the same as what is probable, and is what must occupy the attention of the would-be master of the art of speech. Even actual facts ought sometimes not to be stated, if they don't tally with probability; they should be replaced by what is probable. . . ; whatever you say, you simply must pursue this probability they talk of, and can say good-bye to the truth for ever. Stick to that all through your speech, and you are equipped with the art complete. (272e–273a)

But saying good-bye to truth, Socrates warns, can only have disastrous effects. A crafty politician, for instance, who capitalizes on the population's prejudices by glossing over any facts to the contrary, is not truly a good orator—in the same sense that the one who preys on another person with seductive talk is not a good lover. Effective persuasion for its own sake, Socrates insists, will surely result in a poor crop of human beings (260c–d). A truly good speaker, therefore, must value the truth and speak accordingly.

Socrates' point here is somewhat more complicated than it might appear, for while he criticizes the sophists for disregarding the truth, he (and hence, Plato) also chides Isocrates for falling into the same trap. At first glance it appears that Isocrates is at one with Socrates: he too ridicules the "professors of education" for promising great things to students but having "utter disregard of the truth"; and he scolds the teachers of rhetoric for having "no interest whatever in the truth," all the while considering themselves "masters of an art" if they attract students and secure their tuition.[26] Socrates certainly would applaud these censures. A closer look, however, reveals that Isocrates shares with many sophists a deep skepticism regarding philosophical claims to exact knowledge of human affairs. Because a certain inadequacy affects every effort to speak on truly interesting and important matters, there is (according to Isocrates) plenty of room left "to improve upon what has been said" by others.[27] For this reason it is desirable for people to speak on one subject from many different angles, even to compete in their efforts to "speak better." They are, Isocrates instructs them, to represent the great as lowly or invest the little with grandeur; to recount the things of old in a new manner or set forth events of recent date in an old fashion.[28] This rhetorical shifting is perfectly appropriate for the practical-minded Isocrates, but from Socrates' view, this exercise is indistinguishable from the art of deception practiced by Tisias and Gorgias. Consequently, he sees no reason not to borrow Isocrates' words to describe the sophists' deception.[29] For Socrates, Isocrates' skeptical hesitancy regarding philosophical truth leaves the door open to deceptive rhetoric. The ability to speak eloquently and in a novel manner (what Phaedrus requests of Socrates following Lysias' speech) does not make a good orator; for that, Socrates insists, one must keep an eye fixed on the truth.

(d) Socrates amplifies this point by engaging in a debate current with his contemporaries over the kind of personal qualifications necessary to be a good orator. In "Against the Sophists," Isocrates heaps abuse on the sophists' promise to make their students into "clever orators." These teachers, he tells us, are "so stupid and conceive others to be so dull" that they claim to transmit the "science of discourse as simply as they would teach the letters of the alphabet." Learning to be a good orator is for them a rote matter of memorization. They ignore the pivotal part played by "practical experience" and the "native ability of the student," Isocrates observes; and they quickly avoid taking the "trouble to examine into the nature of each kind of knowledge," relying instead on the "extravagance of their promises."[30] The sophists make the art of eloquent and persuasive speech into a mechanical, step by step program. It is simple, inexpensive, and comes with a guarantee! No qualifications are required. In opposition to the sophists, Isocrates struggles to establish a fuller sense of what is required for good writing and speaking. To be a good orator, he writes,

> [a student] must, first of all, have a natural aptitude for that which they have elected to do; secondly, they must submit to training and master the knowledge of their particular subject, whatever it may be in each case; and, finally, they must become versed and practiced in the use and application of their art; for only on these conditions can they become fully competent and pre-eminent in any line of endeavor.[31]

Native talent, hard study, and long practice—these are the prerequisites for becoming a finished speaker. Formal training is important, but insufficient in itself. For Isocrates, "natural ability is paramount and comes before all else."[32]

Socrates joins the discussion sounding a great deal like Isocrates. To be a "finished performer," he tells Phaedrus, one must have "an innate capacity," knowledge, and practice (269d). Oddly enough, Socrates agrees with the sophists on the importance of knowing the correct procedures of rhetoric. He is at one with them, for example, concerning the arrangement of good speeches. In his words, "any discourse ought to be constructed like a living creature, with its own body, as it were" (264c). As he goes on to explain, every speech must have its parts (e.g., head, feet, arms, etc.) in the correct place. Order is a virtue in good speech. As an example of his point, Socrates mocks Lysias' speech on love as being like the epitaph on the tomb of Midas the Phrygian—where "it makes no difference what order the lines come in" (264c–e). In one way, Socrates insists on even greater rhetorical precision; namely, in his demand that speeches begin with conceptual clarity or definition. Lysias' speech, once again, fails Socrates' test: "he doesn't seem to get anywhere near what we are looking for: he goes about it like a man swimming on his back, in reverse, and starts from the end instead of the beginning" (264a).

Despite his criticisms of the sophists, Socrates is not insensitive to the demands of rhetorical excellence.[33] For Socrates, however, a good orator must know more than standard rhetorical devices. As he puts it to Phaedrus, all the great arts need "supplementing by a study of Nature"; your artist must "cultivate garrulity and high-flown speculation" to achieve "finished execution" in speaking (270a). It is imperative, therefore, that the would-be orator go beyond mere book knowledge of rhetorical technique to investigate in a thorough-going way the nature of the human soul. Since it is the "function of oratory . . . to influence men's souls," the aspiring orator must know "what types of soul there are," must be able to recognize each type, and must apply the appropriate arguments to each person (271d–272a). Just as medicine deals with the body and depends for its successes on a scientific study of the body's workings, so too rhetoric deals with the soul and properly rests on a thorough and methodical study of the soul (270b). Anyone who thinks himself a doctor "by picking up something out of a book . . . without any real knowledge of medicine" is mad and dangerous (268a–c). Such a person has mastered only the antecedents of medicine, but not the art itself. The same is true, Socrates argues, for rhetoric. A good orator is one who knows more than a few rhetorical tricks; he is, instead, one who has studied human character in an exact and scientific manner.

Socrates demands, in short, that speaking and writing be grounded in careful and precise knowledge. If rhetoric is truly an art—rather than "a knack" (260e)—then it must be scientific. To this end, he proposes a rigorous method (really, a new "*techne*") for sorting through the similarities and differences which characterize the things of experience. He calls this method "dialectic" (*dialectikos*), by which he means the rigorous practice of collecting pluralities under a "single form, seeing it all together," and dividing unities into a plurality of forms or types (265d–266a). As a method for speaking, dialectic provides a rigorous means for coming to understand the way things are connected to or distinguished from each other. Whereas orderly collection (conceptual definition) enables discourse "to achieve lucidity and consistency," careful division (analysis) yields clear-cut distinctions, unlike the hackings of a "clumsy butcher" (265d–e). Because the dialectician knows how things do and do not fit together, he can speak appropriately and with precision. Dialectic is the *techne* of the good orator. Speech becomes artful, for Socrates, only when it is methodically (and "scientifically") oriented to the truth of the matter under discussion. While Socrates happily claims to be a "lover of these divisions and collections" (266b), Phaedrus complains about how much work would be involved in following these procedures, and wonders if there is not a "shorter way of arriving at the art" (272b–c). Clearly, he is still under the spell of the quick and easy methods peddled by the teachers of rhetoric, and thus, Socrates' norms for good speaking appear to him as far too demanding.

Ignorance of the knowledge born by dialectic is responsible, Socrates claims, for the misguided notions of rhetoric taught by the sophists, and consequently for the poor oratory of their students. Socrates is concerned especially with what he perceives to be the connection between deceitful oratory and rhetoric uninformed by knowledge of the truth. In his view, a "good and successful" discourse "presupposes a knowledge in the mind of the speaker of the truth about his subject" (259d). Phaedrus demurs at this, for effective persuasion certainly does not require the kind of exact knowledge Socrates expects. Socrates argues, however, that knowledge of the subject matter (rather than simple familiarity with an audience's opinions) is the only antidote to the kind of deception taught by the sophist rhetoricians and practiced in the courts. "The art of speech displayed by one who has gone chasing after beliefs, instead of knowing the truth, will be a comical sort of art, in fact no art at all" (262c). Both the speaker and the audience can be led to the wildest judgments. For them, the only antidote to deception is knowledge (262b). Dialectical knowledge is the backbone of truthful discourse, and consequently, the mainstay of Socrates' ethic of discourse.

It is more than a little confusing, therefore, when Socrates reverses his line of approach to argue that even the intentionally deceitful orator must possess knowledge of the subject at hand. In order to beguile his listeners, Socrates argues, the deceiver must surely "know the truth about the given thing" (262a, 273d). This concern for what makes someone "good" at deception lacks cogency, and works at cross-purposes with Socrates' efforts to link knowledge with morally "good" discourse. I will return to this (and similar) confusions in the third section of this chapter. For the present, however, note that Socrates demands dialectical knowledge both because it makes oratory "artful" and because it protects people from the harmful consequences of deception.

(e) Socrates makes enormous claims for his dialectically informed rhetoric. It is dialectic, he tells Phaedrus, that gives him "the power to speak and to think" (266b). And when Phaedrus complains about how much work is involved (272b), Socrates encourages him with an even grander promise. Though it may be a "long detour," the goal is "glorious," for unlike the would-be methods of Tisias and Thrasymachus whose only aim is "the gratification of their fellow-slaves" (274a), Socrates' art makes it possible "to speak what is pleasing to the gods" (273e). Dialectic yields speech for the gods.

Curiously, just when Socrates has claimed this as a result of his rhetorical method, he introduces a note of caution. Five times he spells out the "art of dialectic" required for scientifically rigorous rhetoric (270e, 271a, 271d, 273d–e and 277b–c), but on the last occasion he hesitates, acknowledging that there are limits to the extent to which speech can be controlled by *techne*. Immediately after this unobtrusive hesitation, Socrates' focus and tone shift dramatically. He now turns critically to consider the knowledge claimed by a good speaker, and consequently also, to questions of a speaker's character. Any speech—"whether by Lysias or anyone else"—is a "reproach to its author," Socrates declares, if he regards it as "containing important truths of permanent validity" (277d). A good orator will, alternatively, consider his compositions as full of fancy, having no value except as a pointer to the truth (277e–278a). Such notes of humility regarding knowledge stand in stark contrast to Socrates' ostentatious claims for dialectic; I will return to consider the significance of this shift in the third section. At this point, however, it is sufficient to note that Socrates includes a posture of humility and self-limitation as a norm for good speaking and writing.

It is with this norm in mind that Socrates disparages the sophist rhetoricians and speech-writers as arrogant and pretentious. They are the "learned" who reject out of hand any religious language for love (245c) and the "clever" who undercut mythic discourse with their rationalistic explanations (229c–230a). Socrates is thinking of those bookish intellectuals who, in their addiction to texts, take on the semblance of wisdom. Pumped up with an air of intelligence, they are filled with a self-proclaimed "conceit of wisdom," making them truly a "burden to their fellows" (275a–b).

In contrast to these would-be wise men, Socrates introduces three characteristics that should be found in the good orator. First, since it is only proper for a god to be called wise, the good speaker who practices dialectic would more appropriately be called a "lover of wisdom" (278d). Anything more would be unseemly. Second, and more significantly, Socrates insists that a speech is praiseworthy only if it is regarded as "containing much that is fanciful," very little serious, and is at the best "a means of reminding those who [already] know the truth" (277e–278a). Discourse is finite, and the good speaker claims no more for it. Interestingly, this is how Socrates speaks about his second speech on love, even though this discourse is filled with claims about the nature of the soul and the abode of the gods. In that speech, Socrates confides to Phaedrus, "we attained some degree of truth, though we may well have sometimes gone astray." Though the speech may lay "some claim to plausibility," it really has been "just a festive entertainment"

(265b–c). This is not an incidental gesture on Socrates' part; nor is it a rejection of the mythic language that pervades his second speech. Quite the opposite is the case, for in labeling his most profound and eloquent speech as limited and merely plausible, Socrates is showing his openness to mythic discourse and stating outright that it accords well with the norms for good speech.

Along the same lines, Socrates adds a third note of caution and humility to the evaluation of discourse. The good orator, Socrates tells Phaedrus, must be able to "demonstrate the inferiority of his writings out of his own mouth" (278c). For a discourse to be good, in other words, its author must be able to engage in vigorous self-criticism—surely the best antidote to the arrogance and pomposity of someone who loves his own words too much. It is important, at this juncture, to note that this principle of self-criticism applies fully to Socrates' own claims for dialectic. *No* discourse should be immune to self-criticism. Without this corrective, the speaker can become forgetful of the real limits of his knowledge (275a). As will become clear shortly, this standard for good discourse feeds directly into Socrates' preference for living dialogue and indirectly into Plato's option for writing in dialogue form.

(f) Finally, Socrates generates ethical concerns for the kind of interaction that takes place between speakers and listeners. This discussion is concentrated on the myth of Theuth and Thamus, wherein Socrates presents his critique of writing. What Socrates initially objects to about writing is the absence of the speaker from the audience. A speech-writer like Lysias illustrates paradigmatically what happens in all writing, according to Socrates: since the speaker is not present with the audience, the words "drift all over the place, getting into the hands not only of those who understand it, but equally of those who have no business with it" (275e). This is literally the case with Lysias' speeches, but it applies equally to all written words. The absence of the speaker, and hence the independence of the words, makes the discourse fundamentally impersonal. The words themselves don't "know how to address the right people, and not address the wrong" (275e). So too it is impossible for them to defend themselves against challenges— they always need their "parents" to come to their aid (275e; 276c). Written words, Socrates continues in the same vein, are dead imitations. Like paintings, they "stand before us as though they were alive: but if you question them, they maintain a most majestic silence. . . ." There is no dialogue with words divorced from their origin: "they seem to talk to you as though they were intelligent, but if you ask them anything about what they say, for a desire to be instructed, they go on telling you the same thing forever" (275d). Consequently, such words will not bear fruit for the listener.

The good orator, on the other hand, opts for "living speech," of which writing is only a faint image (276a). Such discourse, Socrates argues, is "the sort that goes together with knowledge, and is written in the soul of the learner: [it] can defend itself, and knows to whom it should speak and to whom it should say nothing" (276a). Ideal discourse requires the knowledge born of dialectic, and part of such knowledge is the intelligence to apply words appropriately to different audiences or listeners (271b, d; 273d, 277b–c). On this point, Socrates echoes Isocrates, who repeatedly stresses that effective oratory demands "fitness for the occasion."[34] But what Socrates eulogizes here also has a distinctively dialogical purpose. In his words,

> the dialectician selects a soul of the right type, and in it he plants and sows his words founded on knowledge, words which can defend both themselves and him who planted them, words which instead of remaining barren contain a seed whence new words grow up. . . . (276e–277a)

In Socrates' living discourse, the other person becomes the text upon which the speaker writes his words, but, unlike other texts, this one grows and responds. What Socrates promotes here is living dialogue. Though he does not rule out written speech altogether, it is more important for him that speakers face other people with immediacy and response. The irony, of course, as has been pointed out often, is that Plato continues to write Socratic dialogues; indeed, he includes Socrates' critique of writing *in* his own writings. As will become clear later, however, Plato's choice of the genre of dialogue attempts to measure up to the Socratic demands of living words by fostering a text which instantiates the process of dialogue.

In sum, Socrates struggles in his exchange with Phaedrus to generate ethical questions about speaking and writing. Oratory and rhetoric can be morally shameful or ethically inappropriate, as well as technically incorrect. His efforts reviewed in this section, aim to help Phaedrus see the distinction between technical and ethical standards for speaking and writing. The *Phaedrus*, however, seeks to do more: it also works to anchor the debate over ethical standards for discourse in a comprehensive theory of the human soul and its fundamental desires. It is here that Plato provides the framework for an ethic of discourse. The next section takes up this more constructive topic.

(2) Plato's Ethic of Discourse

Throughout their discussion of rhetoric, Socrates pushes Phaedrus to look beyond the surface of oratorical performance. There are ethical—not just procedural—standards to be taken into consideration when evaluating good and bad speaking. It is imperative, he argues, to conceive of rhetoric broadly; to orient speech productively toward the truth; to speak thoughtfully and with knowledge; to be humble and self-critical; and to preserve the immediacy and vitality of dialogue. Before their explicit examination of rhetorical standards, Socrates has implicitly laid the groundwork for an ethic of discourse in the three speeches on love that open the dialogue. In this section I will explore the significance of these speeches for Plato's ethical reflections on rhetoric.

What Plato has done in the *Phaedrus* is suggest how different forms of love (*eros*) undergird and express variant rhetorical practices. The ways we love (or what and how we most basically desire) shape our habits of relating to others, and this includes discursive relations through speaking and writing. There is, in other words, a natural and substantive connection between love and speech; they are respectively the motion and action of the soul in relation with others. To reflect on love, therefore, is already to be concerned with a fundamental discursive relation of desire, or what Socrates calls the motion of the soul. This intimate connection between love and speech also is evident in what lovers do. As a lover, one's interest lies in touching the other with affection, and in leading the other to move toward one with intimacy; and this "leading" is achieved through words. The rhetoric of love, then, is the art of influencing another person (*psychogogia*) through words (*dia logos*) for the fulfillment of desire (*eros*).[35]

The connection between love and rhetoric escapes Phaedrus' attention, but this is not entirely his fault. Socrates lets their conversation shift from speeches on love to dialogue on speech without hinting at the deeper correspondence. As a result, Plato's ethic of discourse remains in the background of Socrates' dialogue with Phaedrus. Only passing allusions (both are lovers of words, which just happen to be lovers' words) and playful banter (Socrates addresses Phaedrus as if he were the "boy") (243e) alert the reader that the halves of the dialogue converge to make a larger point. In this regard, Plato demands that the reader make the connections, and, by doing so, rise to a higher level of reflection on linguistic life. The three speeches on love, therefore, comprise the framework for Plato's typology. The way each lover speaks of love is subsequently echoed in corresponding rhetorical theories and practices.[36] Through these analogies, which the reader comes to see retrospectively, Plato constructs a typology of ethical postures for discursive interaction with others. The rest of this section will outline Plato's typology of lovers and draw the rhetorical analogy for each.

(a) The speech credited to Lysias purports to be an address spoken to a beautiful young boy, in which the speaker claims to be the best sexual match for the boy precisely because he does not love him.[37] Lovers are irrational, undependable, and hence dangerous. It is better—so the speech argues—for the boy to yield sexually to a nonlover; that is, to someone who is self-controlled and disinterested. The nonlover is master of his own desires and not the "victim of love" (233c). Therefore, he will be better for the boy. Since he is not possessive, the boy will not be subjected to the grips of jealousy, and since he is controlled ("a free agent under no constraint") (231a), the boy will be protected from the dangers of public gossip. Distant and unaffected, the nonlover proclaims himself the ideal sexual partner.

Phaedrus loves Lysias' speech. He finds it "extraordinarily fine, especially in point of language" (234c). Playfully, Socrates feigns appreciation of Lysias' rhetoric, but soon he shows his aversion to Lysias' work. Not only does the speech not say "what it ought," but it also is rhetorically deformed. While Phaedrus treasures it for its unsurpassable thoroughness, Socrates finds it an "extravagant performance," something that "even Lysias would deem . . . inadequate" (234e–235b). Socrates does not pause to articulate his criticisms of Lysias' speech, but he returns later with complaints about its technical inadequacy (263d). He is thinking of more than poor arrangement, however, when he compares it to the words on a tombstone (264c–d); as one recent commentator put it, "Lysias' text is paradigmatically dead."[38] Strikingly, the speech lacks both a speaker and a specific other, for the would-be speaker lacks personal identity (it could be read by anyone) and the boy remains a surd (nameless and undescribed). The text is, therefore, dormant and immobile; its speech lacks all passion and possibility for moving another. This is, of course, Socrates' reproach against writing in general; to his mind, reliance on written texts inevitably produces impersonal and lifeless discourse. This is, more specifically, his charge against the impersonal, totally available writing of speech-writers like Lysias, whose words could be repeated without a distinct speaker or listener. Strange as this practice may be in the courts, it is doubly odd in the intimate exchanges of lovers. Undoubtedly, Socrates would level the same charge against the rhetoric of greeting cards in our own day.

In juxtaposing the attitude of the nonlover with the rhetoric of speech-writers like Lysias, Plato challenges his readers to face squarely the basic human posture entailed in abstract and "semantically purified" language. Such discourse is "like a thrifty burgher," as Richard Weaver observes, for "it has no romanticism about it; and it distrusts any departure from the literal and prosaic."[39] In its desire to purge language of all contour and identity, its rhetoric becomes cold, prudential, and distant. To speak like this is to regard others in the same manner— indifferently and with abstraction. Where words become interchangeable, so do persons. In such a framework, it is all too easy for a speaker who knows what is going on to "play an oratorical joke" on the listener. This is the case, Socrates suggests, in Lysias' speech on love (262d). It is only "a comical sort of art," after all, that can pretend to seek intimate sexual involvement with the icy rhetoric of the nonlover. And since the nonlover does in fact desire sexual satisfaction, his discourse is deceptive as well.[40] He solicits passion but conceals his real desires behind controlled and passionless language. Socrates, therefore, rejects Lysias' nonlover and the corresponding rhetoric.

(b) Having criticized Lysias' speech, however, Socrates is obliged to give one of his own. In some of the most delightful exchanges in the dialogue, Phaedrus prods Socrates to compete with Lysias by giving a speech that starts from the same premise—namely, "that the lover is less sane than the nonlover" (236b). When Socrates voices reluctance, Phaedrus compels him with mock threats to come up with a speech (236c–e). It is only when Phaedrus threatens to with-hold reports of "any other speech by any other author whatsoever" (236e), that Socrates succumbs. The manner in which he yields, however, provides a clue that he is not being entirely serious.

> **Socrates**: Aha, you rogue! How clever of you to discover the means of compelling a lover of discourse to do your bidding!
> **Phaedrus**: Then why all this twisting?
> **Socrates**: I give it up, in view of what you've sworn. For how could I possibly do without such entertainment?
> **Phaedrus**: Then proceed.
> **Socrates**: Well, do you know what I'm going to do?
> **Phaedrus**: Do about what?
> **Socrates**: I shall cover my head before I begin: then I can rush through my speech at top speed without looking at you and breaking down for shame.
> **Phaedrus**: You can do anything else you like, provided you make your speech. (236e–237a)

As usual Phaedrus misses Socrates' point. Socrates knows in advance that a better speech starting from Lysias' premise will bring shame (*aischunes*) upon him; and he understands that engaging in such a competition (which, ironically, Isocrates deemed valuable) will provide no more than idle entertainment.[41] His strange act of covering his head, moreover, imitates Phaedrus' act of reading, which was also done "without looking at" his interlocutor.

Socrates' tale (*mythos*) (241e) narrates the efforts of a wily young man to persuade a "handsome young boy" that he ought to "favor a nonlover rather than a lover" (237b). Concealing his own desires for the boy, Socrates' nonlover casti-gates everything about a person in love. In his eyes, love is an "irrational desire" which tramples good judgment as it "strains [relentlessly] toward bodily beauty" (238b–c). "Dominated by desire and enslaved to pleasure," the man in love aims to make the boy "totally ignorant and totally dependent on his lover, by way of se-curing the maximum of pleasure for himself, and the maximum of damage to the other" (239b). Love, therefore, is fundamentally exploitative, interested only in the lover's pleasure at the expense of the bodily, intellectual, and spiritual devel-opment of the beloved. Totally dedicated to his own self-interest, the lover will do everything in his power to keep the beloved weak and effeminate, slow of mind, and financially dependent. It would have been far better, the speaker argues, had the boy yielded to "one possessed of reason and not in love" (241b–c). Surrender to a lover means falling victim to a "faithless, peevish, jealous and offensive captor, to one who would ruin his property, ruin his physique, and above all ruin his spiritual development. . . ." (241c). The attentions of a lover "carry no good-will," despite their appearances, for as the wolf devours the lamb, so the lover smothers the beloved. If Lysias' nonlover was inhuman in his cold abstraction, Socrates' nonlover is a crafty predator.[42]

Phaedrus, not unexpectedly, is enthused with Socrates' performance. Socrates, on the other hand, is ashamed and self-critical. This view of love—which he blames on Phaedrus (242b, e)—is foolish and blasphemous. Both speeches, in fact, are an "offense towards [the god of] Love" (242e). What does a wolf know about love? Moreover, the authors of these speeches are guilty of "the most exquisite folly of parading their pernicious rubbish as though it were good sense because it might deceive a few miserable people and win their applause" (242e–243a). The transgression, in other words, lies in competing for oratorical fame by giving fanciful speeches that willfully dismiss any regard for truth. Socrates, too, is guilty of making "an oratorical joke" out of a serious topic, and thereby deceiving anyone who would be influenced by his rhetorical fabrications. Indeed, Socrates is aware that his "quite unusual eloquence" (238c) is all in jest, when he assures Phaedrus that if he had continued any further with this praise of a sober, self-controlled lover, he would have gone beyond enthusiasm and lost his self-control altogether.[43] Surely, Socrates exclaims, a noble lover would reject "our vilification of Love" (243c). And just as certainly, a noble rhetor would reject the deception and concealment practiced by both Lysias and Socrates.

The concealed love of Socrates' first speech corresponds to the "base rhetoric" of oppression and exploitation.[44] Speech driven by this kind of "love" seeks to dominate all other speakers, suppressing their voices and smothering their understanding of the world. Such a speaker deceives a listener about his real purposes, or exploits an interlocutor's weaknesses for the sake of intellectual victory, or simply overwhelms the other person dogmatically with the sheer weight of authority. Think, for instance, of the oppressive designs of ruling political parties or of the authoritarian policies of orthodox religious institutions. Dressed up in the deceptive rhetoric of paternal care, and dogmatically claiming privileged access to certainty, charismatic leaders seek above all to keep their people passive and docile. Free and critical thinking is squelched. In its place stands the monologue of official teaching or propaganda. Whether in the personal, political, or religious sphere, Socrates warns that this kind of seductive and manipulative rhetoric must be rejected. It is the destructive result of the attempt to model speech on reason freed from the passion of love.

(c) Socrates is ashamed for having engaged in such an exercise. "False is the tale," he tells Phaedrus, that favor ought to be accorded to the one who does not love, on the ground that the nonlover is "sound of mind" while the lover is mad (244a). Like Stesichorus of old, who regained his sight by recanting his "defamation of Helen," Socrates proceeds to make his own "palinode to Love" (243a–b). Whereas the discourses against love are attributed to Phaedrus, Socrates' "encomium of the lover" is credited to Stesichorus, whom Socrates symbolically imitates by unveiling his head, thereby regaining his sight (243e–244a and 243b).[45]

Not all madness is bad, Socrates tells Phaedrus. "The greatest blessings come by way of madness, indeed of madness that is heaven sent" (244a). The talents of divination, healing, and poetry are examples of madness given by the gods (244–245a), but the "best of all forms of divine possession" belongs to the philosophic lover who "beholds the beauty of this world" and thereby is "reminded of true beauty" (249e). Socrates' second speech, therefore, is directed against those people who "scare us into preferring the friendship of the sane to that of the passionate." He must prove, in short, that "this sort of madness [or love] is a gift of the gods, fraught with the highest bliss" (245b–c3).[46]

Unlike the sober and objective rhetoric of the first two speeches, Socrates delivers his praise of love through a dramatic and elaborate myth of the human soul. For Socrates the human person resembles a charioteer driving two winged steeds. The charioteer (symbolizing reason) must contend with the antagonistic struggle of the two horses (254), one representing wanton sexual desire and the other a moral sense of shame. Unlike the gods, for whom an ascent to contemplate that which is the most real is easy, the human journey is full of "toil and struggling" (247b), due to the "heaviness" of the bad horse's desires (247a–b) and the soul's broken wings (the human "share in the divine nature") (246d–e). Though every human soul originally had a vision of true being, the vast majority are completely forgetful of this experience. In the human estate, it is beauty above all which sparks the memory of that original vision.[47] Most people live bestial lives, Socrates contends, lurching after pleasure not with reverence but "after the fashion of a four-footed beast" (250e). For a few, however, the encounter with "a godlike face or bodily form that truly expresses beauty" causes a near mystical experience. There is

> a shuddering and a measure of that awe which the vision inspired, and then reverence as at the sight of a god: and but for fear of being deemed a very madman he would offer sacrifice to his beloved, as to a holy image of deity. Next, with the passing of the shudder, a strange sweating and fever seizes him: for by reason of the stream of beauty entering in through his eyes there comes a warmth, whereby his soul's wings are melted . . . ; then as the nourishment is poured in the stump of the wing swells and hastens to grow from the root over the whole substance of the soul. . . . Wherefore she gazes upon the boy's beauty, she admits a flood of particles streaming therefrom—that is why we speak of a "flood of passion"—whereby she is warmed and fostered; then has she respite from her anguish, and is filled with joy. (251a–d)

Is it any wonder that most people look on the lover as demented (249e)?

Four things are noteworthy in Socrates' rapturous description of the soul in love: (i) The soul stands between the gods and the beasts, attracted to the "banquet of the gods" (what Griswold calls "the state of perfect objectivity"[48]), yet bound to the contingencies and passions of animal life. There is no escape from this "in between" status. (ii) This is noteworthy because the madness Socrates praises is caused by beholding the "beauty of this world" (249e). Far from advocating a disembodied retreat from the world, Socrates locates the primary place for the revival of memory in the encounter of lovers, bodily beauty and all. As Griswold rightly emphasizes, Socrates' myth is about embodied souls, not disembodied ones. Socrates does not speak about the soul's essence independent of its multitude of passions and works.[49] Recollection takes place in and through the concrete passions of erotic love. (iii) It follows, therefore, that the soul cannot achieve its desired end without other human beings. The erotic relationship of love, in other words, requires a social basis for the soul's recollection of beauty. And this is precisely where rhetoric comes into play. It is rhetoric that provides the discursive tools needed for interaction with others, specifically for the lover's engagement with the beloved. (iv) This intimate tie of love and rhetoric, rooted in the lover's desire to lead the other by means of words, is the fundamental reason for Socrates' commitment to dialogue. In Socrates' hands, rhetoric is the art of dialogue animated by love.

Socrates' myth of love serves as "a complex mirror in which people can recognize not just who they are but who they might become at their best."[50] A person's character, Plato's myth tells us, is largely determined by the life lived in previous incarnations. The "ordinance of Necessity" casts each soul in a life-form according to the choices made in previous lives (248c–249c). A soul becomes its best, Socrates tells Phaedrus, when it achieves the philosophic life. When a soul is struck by the beauty of the beloved, suffering the passionate effects described above, it undergoes an intense, interior struggle—a war between unbridled sensual desire and the prudence of rational judgment (254). In the noble love of Socrates' eulogy, the "evil steed" is subdued and the "soul of the lover follows after the beloved with reverence and awe" (249e). What is so striking in Socrates' depiction of this ideal love is the conjunction of the language of control and desire. The lovers have achieved both "self-mastery and inward peace" in leading "the ordered rule of the philosophic life" (256a–b); but at the same time their life together is filled with powerful erotic passions, leaving them speechless and uncomprehending (255c–d). Put differently, the noble lover is both free and compelled. He is compelled by the beauty of the other, yet free and capable in his deliberations over "what desires should move him."[51] Socrates' ideal love, therefore, does not supplant reason with passion or passion with reason. In this kind of love, the soul is fully a lover (driven by the horses and animated by the wings) *and* a nonlover (under the prudent control of the charioteer).[52] What Socrates lauds, in sum, is the harmonious wedding of passion and reason. As Ferrari aptly puts it, "Socrates succeeds not by dismissing the voices [of *eros* or reason], but by integrating them . . . into his polyphonic song of the charioteer's success."[53]

This portrait of love differs in almost every respect from the way love is described in the first two speeches. Noble love is, first of all, highly personalized. The noble lover is unlike Lysias' nonlover, in that the objects of his desire are not interchangeable. He is attracted to and follows after one who bears the image of his god: "the followers of Zeus seek a beloved who is Zeus-like in soul," and so on (252e). The noble lover seeks above all to cast the beloved in "the closest possible likeness to the god they worship," for "every lover is fain that his beloved should be of a nature like to his own god" (253a–b). Love in this context wishes to ennoble and divinize the other. Though a great deal of Socrates' language emphasizes the extent to which the lover molds the boy into a divine image (like a statue), there is still an element of mutuality in their love. For as the lover reaches out after his god,

> [he is] possessed by him, and from him they take their ways and manners of life, in so far as a man can partake of a god. But all this, mark you, they attribute to the beloved, and the draughts which they draw from Zeus they pour out, like Bacchants, into the soul of the beloved. . . . (253a; compare 255c–d)

The lover's remembrance of the transcendent is, after all, only possible through the concrete, personal mediation of the beloved. Thus, though the lover is without question the more active player in the relationship, he is in an important sense responding to the beauty of the other. It follows from this that the noble lover genuinely seeks the bodily, intellectual, and spiritual good of the beloved. Unlike Lysias' nonlover and Socrates' concealed lover, the noble lover generously cares for the welfare of the boy.

Socrates' "fairest recantation"—predictably—meets with praise from Phaedrus, who finds it a far "finer achievement than the one you made before" (257c). Phaedrus' acclamation is surprising, indeed, given his negative attitude toward the mythic language that runs throughout Socrates' discourse. At the opening of the dialogue, for example, Phaedrus appears astonished that Socrates might believe the myth of Boreas, which is said to have occurred near the spot where they are sitting (229c). Later, he will protest Socrates' fabrication of the myth of Theus and Thamus, only to be scolded by Socrates for narrow-minded rationalism (275b–c). Socrates' reliance on mythic language, however, proves very appropriate for his praise of love. As a genre, myth provides a vehicle for the imagination to soar beyond the mundane and the conventional; yet simultaneously, it concedes its own limitations. In Ferrari's words, myth "illuminates . . . what happens when philosophers cope with contingency by attempting to gain the cosmic or impersonal perspective while maintaining their personal sense of who they are. . . ."[54] Mythic discourse accomplishes both for Socrates. It allows him to explore the personal depths of erotic love while placing such relationships in the cosmic context of their ultimate significance; at the same time, it assures that his speech will live up to his own demand that praiseworthy discourse be self-critical (278c), containing "much that is fanciful" (277e) and avoiding the temptation to claim

dogmatically any "truth of permanent validity" (277d). Mythic discourse, therefore, provides an excellent rhetorical vehicle for Socrates' palinode.

More broadly conceived, the noble love of Socrates' second speech corresponds to the rhetoric of living dialogue. To speak as Socrates' noble lover loves
is to engage the other person in lively and fruitful conversation, the kind which
serves, for Socrates, as the standard for evaluating all other forms of rhetoric.[55] In
its ideal form, dialogue should fuse the erotic and the rational in a playful but productive balance. This means that dialogue ought to reflect a passion for unity of
insight. Socrates represents this unity in the highly erotic language of spiritual intercourse represented in the social zenith of the philosophic life. As Hans-Georg
Gadamer puts it,

> [in] the successful conversation they both come under the influence of the truth
> of the object and are thus bound to one another in a new community. To reach an
> understanding with one's partner in a dialogue is not merely a matter of total self-
> expression and the successful assertion of one's own point of view, but a trans-
> formation into a communion, in which we do not remain what we were.[56]

At the same time, dialogue compensates for the passion of communion by
maintaining rational direction and movement. In Socrates' "erotic art" such control
is preserved through the methodical "power of questioning" which drives the dialogue forward.[57] The movement of the dialogue, moreover, should reflect a playful
spirit, both in the lightheartedness of their exchanges (e.g., the banter of Socrates
and Phaedrus) and in the self-critical, even ironic, regard for their achievements.
Dialogue, finally, should be productive, leading the interlocutors to fresh insight.
Good speech, Socrates tells us, plants seeds in the listener, giving birth to a living
quest for wisdom. It is speech that seeks to divinize the listener, causing the
other's wings to grow once again, so he or she may soar in memory to a vision
of the good and beautiful. Only then does speech imprint wisdom in "the soul of
the learner" (276a), planting a "seed whence new words grow up in new characters" (277a).

The rhetoric which reflects a noble love contrasts like night and day with
the rhetorical practices corresponding to either Lysias' nonlover or Socrates'
concealed lover. What Plato has accomplished in juxtaposing these three forms
of "love" with their analogous forms of speech is to point up "the congruence of
rhetoric with the soul."[58] The way we speak, in other words, reflects our most fundamental desires and our habitual ways of handling them. The way we speak
shapes the character we assume. Plato offers his readers an ethic of discourse by
pointing up the ways that shameful or exemplary stances are embodied in actual
practices of discourse. He forces his readers to reflect back on the ways of life (the
"habits of the heart") that undergird and motivate the most ordinary uses of

language. Plato's aim, clearly, is to dissuade his readers from the life and the discourse reflected in the first two speeches, and to exhort them to pursue the noble life of philosophy and dialogue.

Despite the considerable value of this typology, a number of things in Plato's text make an adequate interpretation of his project much more complicated than I have suggested thus far. Indeed, to insist too much on the analogies of love and speech as the framework for an ethic of discourse would be to ignore other, more subtle and more problematic, facets of Plato's work—namely, its interlocking levels of meaning, the many jarring transitions, and the subtle nuances that are sprinkled throughout the dialogue. The next section turns to examine these features of the *Phaedrus*, to see whether they undercut or contribute to the ethic of discourse outlined in this section.

(3) A Self-Propagating Artifact

The *Phaedrus* is a most complicated dialogue. In it Plato confronts the reader with a dizzying array of recognizably Platonic topics and a disorienting fluctuation in literary styles. It has, as one commentator puts it, "the appearance of a tapestry that has come partially unraveled into a tangled skein of themes and images."[59] Schleiermacher, for one, found the *Phaedrus* so burdened with undeveloped philosophical topics and unpracticed method that he regarded it as the first literary product of Plato's youth. "Even in the outward form," he comments, "this youthful spirit betrays itself, in the constantly renewed luxuriance of the secondary subjects introduced at every resting point," not to mention the affected style, "the immoderate introduction of the religious," and the "awkwardness in the transitions" from topic to topic.[60] In addition to the fractured structure of the dialogue, there is the character of Socrates, which, though consistent in many ways with what we see of him in other Platonic dialogues, is far stranger and more puzzling than is the case elsewhere. Moreover, there are numerous places where Plato seems to be making points at odds with Socrates, or even at odds with his own philosophy. These three points—the broken structure, Socrates' character, and Plato's voice—raise difficult questions for any interpretation of the *Phaedrus*, including the one put forth in the previous section.

Why does Plato muddy the waters of his dialogue? Here we come face to face with a sensitive hermeneutical issue: are these textual difficulties deliberately introduced (making them marks of artistic sophistication) or are they inadvertent blunders? Any discussion of authorial intention is frowned upon in many of today's fashionable scholarly circles, but the issue here cannot be avoided. No reading of the *Phaedrus* can pass over these textual oddities, hence no interpreter can escape deciding whether or not these are deliberate effects. If the *Phaedrus* advances a unified thesis—an exhortation to philosophical rhetoric built on the correlation of love and speech—then why does Plato confuse the issue by conspicuously littering the dialogue with structural breaks and substantive inconsistencies?

This section will review the three major problems that stir this debate about the *Phaedrus*. In the final section I will address possible answers to the questions raised here.

(a) *Socrates' Typhonic Character.* The Socrates we encounter in the *Phaedrus* is an exceedingly odd character. Phaedrus, in fact, calls him "the oddest of men": for one who never leaves the city (hence, a stranger to the country), he is enthralled with the beauty and freshness of the natural surroundings where the two settle to talk (230c–d). He is odd, too, in rejecting the "scientific accounts" of mythical oddities current among the intellectual in-crowd (229c–e). Socrates, it seems, doesn't fit in where he is most at home (the city), and yet appears to know and appreciate the world where he is said to be a stranger (the country). As Griswold puts it, he is "both most out of place and quite at home" simultaneously.[61]

There are other oppositions in Socrates' character that make him odd. As Ferrari notes, for example, Socrates is neither a professional rhetorician nor a layman. Yet, curiously, he seems to be both. Socrates is neither a speech-writer like Lysias nor a teacher of rhetoric like Tisias or Thrasymachus; yet, just as he knows the exact location along the river where Boreas is said to have seized Oreithuia (229c), he is thoroughly knowledgeable in current theories of rhetorical education (262a–264e). Though it is not his business, he is eager to put a discussion of speeches with Phaedrus "above all business" (227b). Socrates is odd, indeed. Though a stranger in need of a guide (he calls Phaedrus "the stranger's perfect guide") (230c), it is Socrates who guides Phaedrus through the complex topics before them. Socrates is the master of discourse, the "discursive erotician par excellence,"[62] the one who possesses the art of influencing others through words, but he is not a professional rhetorician.

To a certain extent, these curious oppositions within Socrates' character are ironic. More adept than his interlocutor, he relishes the playful banter and the ironic reversals made possible by a dialogue with Phaedrus. Yet there is something else at stake here, and Socrates knows it. He is concerned, above all, with his own identity: he wants to know whether he really is "a more complex creature and more puffed up with pride than Typhon, or a simpler, gentler being whom heaven has blessed with a quiet, un-Typhonic nature" (230a). Typhon, it seems, was a prehistoric monster. In Apollodorus' account, Typhon is described as

> half man and half wild beast. He was the largest and most powerful of Earth's offspring, so huge up to his thighs (which were of human form), that he towered above all the mountains. His head touched the stars and his hands, when outstretched, reached the one to the west, the other to the east. From his shoulders extended a hundred snake heads. From his thighs down he had huge coils of vipers which, when

stretched out, reached all the way to his head and hissed loudly. His entire body was covered with wings and his hair and beard were unkempt and blew in the wind. Fire flashed from his eyes.[63]

Hesiod adds an eerie note about Typhon's multiplicity of voices:

> Astounding voices came from those weird heads,
> All kinds of voices: sometimes speech which the gods
> Would understand, and sometime bellowings. . . ."[64]

Truly a grotesque and frightening image. Why would Socrates compare himself to a monster like this? *Is* Socrates typhonic?

The answer is yes. On one hand, of course, this means no more than that Socrates is human. Recall, for instance, Socrates' portrait of the soul as a charioteer guiding two winged horses; there, too, we find an image of a monster. Though more positively portrayed, this certainly is an unnatural fusion in its own right. Typhon, therefore, is simply a monstrous expression of Socrates' likeness of the soul. On the other hand, unlike human beings in general, Socrates is peculiarly and intensely typhonic. In the language of the *Phaedrus*, he combines both the mad passion of the lover and the cool detachment of the nonlover. He speaks, alternatively, with the zeal of an enthusiast inspired by the local deities and with the methodical precision of a scientific scholar of rhetoric. Throughout the discussion of rhetorical education, for example, he is the dialectician proceeding carefully through his distinctions between good and bad rhetoric. But we are just as likely to find him sounding like a religious prophet or seer. Repeatedly he regards himself as one who is inspired: the wisdom of ancient authors is poured into him and wells up within his breast (235c–d); he calls upon Muses for assistance in delivering his first speech (237a); he gives his first speech "as one possessed" (238d); he calls himself a "seer" whose "familiar divine sign" warns him when he sins (242b–c); and so on. Socrates is just as likely to express himself through myth as through dialectic, and he is just as serious in prayers (e.g., to love or to Pan) (257a–b and 279b–c) as in technical analysis. Like Typhon, Socrates combines different natures. He is complex, filled with tensions, and he speaks with many voices.

Being typhonic, Socrates can, and frequently does, change his voice. In this regard, it is highly appropriate that Socrates and Phaedrus converse under the eye of statues dedicated to Achelous (230c), since Achelous was known for his ability to change appearances.[65] Indeed, Socrates has changed significantly from other dialogues: while in other contexts he loathes lengthy speeches, we now find him giving not one but two speeches of considerable length.[66] He similarly shifts about and reverses himself within the *Phaedrus*. While Socrates appears especially critical of deceptive oratory, for instance, he is not afraid to engage in his own concealment when he ironically claims to have "forgotten how, and from whom" he has heard some wise words spoken on love (235d); or, more seriously, when he participates in Phaedrus' competition of love speeches by giving an oration praising a love that is "simply sick."[67] There is, as Ferrari notes, something of the nonlover in Socrates—despite his attempt to blame Phaedrus for "putting a spell" (*katapharmakeuthentos*) on his lips (242e). There is also something of the lover in him—despite his theatrical attempt to cloak his voice under the guise of Stesichorus (244a). Socrates is like a *silenus*, as Alcibiades observes with great eloquence in the *Symposium*. When you open him up, there is yet another figure inside.[68] He never stops changing.

Consistent with other Platonic dialogues, the Socrates of the *Phaedrus* prizes self-knowledge above all else. Everything else is extraneous (230a). Given this commitment, Socrates looks remarkably disfigured and out of sorts. He sounds more than a little naive, as Ferrari points out, in his criticisms of Lysias' speech. He demands that Lysias begin his speech with a definition, for instance, when Lysias probably avoided this intentionally; and he complains that Lysias' speech is disorganized, when, once again, Lysias might have intended this in order to imitate living discourse more successfully.[69] More grievously, some of Socrates' arguments look exceptionally weak—as when he insists that deceptive orators need knowledge of the truth in order to deceive an audience (e.g., 262a–b). In the same context, Socrates appears to miss the point of the little speech put forth by "Rhetoric": possession of truth is well and good, she concedes to Socrates, but rhetoric is needed as well for effective persuasion to take place (260d). Truth is good, but it is insufficient for persuasion. She is right, of course, but Socrates somehow misses her point, turning immediately to question whether rhetoric is an art. Socrates appears, moreover, to suffer lapses of memory, as when he refers back to his speeches as illustrations of dialectical technique (265a–b and 265e–266a, for example). He has, it seems, forgotten how his speeches proceeded: in recalling them, he makes his oratorical procedure look smoother and more systematic than it was in fact.[70]

The Socrates of the *Phaedrus* is enigmatic indeed. One need not share Nietzsche's hostility to Socrates to appreciate the aptness of his summary characterization: "Everything about him is exaggerated, buffo, caricature, everything is at the same time hidden, reserved, subterranean."[71] The question, of course, is why? Why, in particular, does Plato portray Socrates in this manner? Given that Socrates is Plato's advocate for an ethically noble discourse, what impact does Socrates' confused and confusing character have on Plato's ethic?

(b) *The* Phaedrus *as Self-Propagating Artifact.* The waters become even murkier if we stop to consider the development of topics and genre in the *Phaedrus*. When Socrates completes his second speech on love, he prays to the "God of Love" that his speech will have made sufficient atonement for the blasphemous speeches that preceded it. Then, without warning, the dialogue with Phaedrus

shifts in both topic and genre. Whereas the first part consists of rhetorical monologues on the philosophical topic of love, the second part turns to examine rhetoric through philosophical dialogue.[72] In Griswold's words, the "enthusiastic and
erotic idiom of the first half seems replaced by a detached and analytic idiom" in
the second half.[73] Kennedy offers an intriguing historical explanation for these
structural breaks when he observes that the *Phaedrus* itself is written as a kind
of rhetorical manual. The two parts "correspond strikingly to the two methods
of rhetorical instruction current in classical Greece"; namely, a collection of specimen speeches for imitation and then a theoretical discussion of precepts and
techniques.[74] Kennedy goes on to note, that, in structuring the *Phaedrus* in this
manner, Plato constructs a mirror image of Isocrates' *Helen*, a text which first in-
spects current rhetorical theories and then turns to give a specimen speech on
beauty. These historical insights help to explain Plato's reasons for giving the
Phaedrus its "broken-backed structure."[75] And they corroborate in part the correlation of love (response to beauty) and speech (rhetorical theory) suggested in the
previous section.

As helpful as these points are in explaining the *Phaedrus'* structure, they do
not account for the repeated shifts and reversals injected into the course of the
dialogue's development. As Griswold aptly puts it, "the development of the *Phaedrus* is palinodic"—meaning that, "in typically Socratic fashion, various points of
view are presented as though they were final and are then purposely undercut to
reveal a further, unanticipated, meaning."[76] With each recantation, a previous view
is placed in a larger context that serves to diminish its apparent value in order to
make a yet larger point.

(i) The most obvious act of recantation appears in Socrates' second speech.
He must, he tells Phaedrus, purify himself as Stesichorus did, for "when Stesichorus lost the sight of his eyes because of his declamation of Helen, he was not, like
Homer, at a loss to know why. As a true artist he understood the reason," and
promptly composed his "Palinode" to purify himself. In imitation of Stesichorus,
Socrates sets out to make his own "palinode to Love" before any harm comes to
him (243b–c). Making amends to love, Socrates declares the tale (*mythos*) false
which regards love as dominating and concealing. In delivering his palinode
Socrates reverses himself both in style and message: where the first two speeches
used a controlled idiom for the purpose of castigating susceptibility to passion and
eulogizing detached (and ultimately deceptive) reason, Socrates' palinode revels
in mythic speculation and poetic experimentation in order to give balanced status
to passion and reason in the life of love.[77] He recants, in other words, both the love
of and the language of empty and deceptive oratory.

(ii) But no sooner is Socrates finished with his palinode than he feels the need
to disavow it and move on to a more sober level. In his myth, it seems, Socrates
has lost control of himself, giving an account of things that no mere mortal could
possibly know, given the myth's account of the human estate. As Griswold nicely

puts it, "Socrates goes beyond the grave and returns knowing all—an impossibility according to the myth itself."[78] Although Socrates speaks humbly about his knowledge of the soul (246a), he quickly forgets his limitations, deigning to speak "of that place beyond the heavens [where] none of our earthly poets has yet sung" (247c). Socrates simply knows too much. Apparently, he has become self-forgetful. Ironically, this is precisely what Socrates feared was happening to him in the midst of his first speech, when he praised the self-control of the nonlover (241e). *That* self-forgetfulness called forth an apology for blasphemy (his first palinode), which now, in turn, requires yet another palinode—this time for his "hubristic self-promotion to the rank of divine poet."[79]

The shift to the second palinode is effected partly by Socrates' prayer for pardon (257a–b), and partly by Phaedrus' reliable fixation on rhetorical form (257c). Together they demand that the reader stop and reflect back on Socrates' speech *as* a piece of rhetoric. The madness (or poetic passion) of the myth becomes the object of a controlled, analytical examination of rhetorical forms. Thereby, "we are compelled to think about the myth self-consciously and so to understand its limitations."[80] This more analytical perspective stands in sharp contrast to the poetic frenzy of Socrates' first palinode. But the shift also concerns substance: whereas the myth pointed forward to the ultimate ends of human discourse, the second palinode retracts the uninhibited speculation of myth by demanding a dialogue on the means or techniques of discourse. There are limits to the madness of mythic speculation, and Socrates, becoming aware of this, steers his dialogue with Phaedrus toward more sedate waters. What follows is a comparatively dry appraisal of current rhetorical theories and practices.

(iii) Plato's palinodic movement is not finished, however. Before the dialogue ends, Socrates turns to recant his claims for *techne*. In his efforts to articulate the dialectic technique necessary for good oratory, Socrates has moved to an extremely abstract level of discourse. Through this part of the dialogue, "we are treated to speech [dialogue] about speaking [the method of division and collection] about speeches [the discourses earlier in the *Phaedrus*]."[81] But the move to talk about talking—something demanded by the extravagance and uncontrollability of Socrates' myth in comparison with the measured rhetoric of the first two speeches—takes on its own brand of *hubris* and forgetfulness. Recall, for instance, Socrates' lofty claims for a scientifically complete rhetoric (e.g., 277b–c). It is only the orator informed by the *techne* of dialectic, he tells Phaedrus, who strives "not for the sake of speaking to and dealing with his fellow-men, but that he may be able to speak what is pleasing to the gods" (273e). Now Socrates must also make amends for the excesses of this technical blasphemy. He does so, interestingly, by shifting back to mythic discourse.

It is in the myth of Theus and Thamus that Socrates recants his excessive accolade for rhetorical technique. Although this story commonly is read as attacking writing in general, it makes more sense to interpret Socrates' critique in relation to the more immediate referents indicated earlier in the dialogue. And that means speech-writers like Lysias and those who manufacture and consume rhetorical textbooks. These are the most immediate targets of Socrates' critique of writing, even if grander targets lie beyond them. In Socrates' words, the object of his critique is "anyone who leaves behind him a written manual, and likewise anyone who takes it over from him" (275c). But he is also making amends for his own self-absorption in technical precision. Engaging the sophists over the most adequate technique for good oratory, Socrates has let the ends of discourse slip from his mind. The myth on writing, therefore, makes amends for this short-sightedness—first by introducing notes of humility and self-criticism (e.g., "within human limits," "much that is fanciful," "at the best, a means of reminding those who know the truth") (277c, 277e–278a); and second, by returning the focus of the dialogue with Phaedrus to the proper ends of discourse (conversation "written in the soul of the learner") (278a). Socrates' third palinode, therefore, rescinds the excessive claims made for dialectic by subordinating *techne* to *telos*.

Indeed, the whole discussion of rhetorical technique is framed by warnings about forgetfulness. While the myth of Theus and Thamus closes the excursus on technique, Socrates prefaces the discussion of *techne* with another story—the myth of the cicadas. The cicadas—"singing after their wont in the hot sun and conversing with one another" (258e)—are descendants of an ancient people who became so completely possessed by the pleasure of music that they "forgot to eat and drink until they actually died without noticing it" (259c). They now sing and chirp endlessly, while watching over the activities of human beings in order to give reports to the Muses (259b–d). Though they may appear innocent, Socrates warns Phaedrus to steer clear of "their bewitching siren-song" (259a–b). They must, by all means, stay alert and wakeful in their conversation, lest they be lulled to sleep like a "pair of slaves." What appears good may also be deadly. The fact that Socrates links the cicadas with the inspiration of the Muses is significant, for Phaedrus is a "lover of the Muses" (259b), and Socrates ascribes the first two speeches (Lysias' and his own) to the inspiration received from "those mouth-pieces of the Muses that are chirping over our heads" (262d). Philosophers also are said to be "followers of the Muses" (248d). The Muses' inspiration, therefore, can be dangerous. It can leave a speaker oblivious and forgetful. But while Socrates' warning appears to be directed at the danger of inspired oratory (e.g., the poetic flights of his second speech), its placement before the discussion of rhetorical technique projects an echo regarding the deadly forgetfulness wrought by technique alone.

Beware the siren-song of pure technique! That is Plato's warning. That Plato intentionally underscores the limitations of *techne* is evident from several other factors in the dialogue. To begin, it is strange, indeed, that while the method of collection and division is supposed to be very exact and precise, it nowhere receives anything like an exact description.[82] The reader cannot help wondering, along with Phaedrus, how Socrates' technical prescription for good oratory will work. But, of more importance, the descriptions of dialectical technique are directed only to the monologues in the first half of the *Phaedrus*, and as Griswold notes, "even these it distorts." As the reader can see retrospectively, Socrates' speeches "did not proceed in the way" of dialectic. It is especially odd—given Socrates' encomium of dialectic—that his technical method is so insensitive to the critical transition from his first "base speech" to the second, noble one. And, with reference to Plato, it is surely significant that the *Phaedrus* itself is not composed according to "the standards of the art of division and collection."[83] As Griswold observes, once again, Plato is by these means intentionally underscoring the limitations of dialectical *techne*. Though the art of dialectic truly is helpful in conducting thoughtful and careful analysis, the method itself holds a "subservient" place within the dialogue as a whole. It is "not in itself a means by which one may rejoin the gods at the divine banquet."[84]

In sum, the *Phaedrus'* structure is marked by a series of breaks or recantations—places where Plato suddenly, and with little if any comment, turns away from one topic, claim, and genre to another. From a strictly logical point of view, therefore, the *Phaedrus* makes no sense, "since Socrates is continually reaching conclusions, which he subsequently, and without comment, abandons."[85] The reader is not allowed to settle in with any given conclusion or style of speech. Plato has, in short, provided a bumpy road for his readers to follow. He has written what Stanley Fish calls a "self-consuming artifact": a "mimetic enactment in the reader's experience of the Platonic ladder in which each rung, as it is negotiated, is kicked away."[86] The dialogue devours itself in its development. But, as Fish notes, the dialogue's palinodic structure also is a boon, since it "provides [the reader] a series of stimuli to intellectual growth that is in some sense progressive. . . ." For the reader, the "moments of blurring become invitations to examine closely premises too easily acquiesced in." Plato's self-consuming artifact, therefore, serves to "refine its reader's vision."[87] More properly put, the *Phaedrus* is a self-propagating artifact: it casts forth seeds of discourse which take root in the reader. Not all interpreters of Plato agree with Fish, however. In the final section of this chapter, I will turn to consider Derrida's reading of the *Phaedrus*, where the dialogue's palinodic structure is taken as a symptom of Plato's failure.

(c) *Plato's Anonymity: Dialogue and Irony.* There are, in addition, at least two other palinodic moments to the *Phaedrus*, but they are not spoken by Socrates. The fourth belongs solely to Plato, who, in writing the *Phaedrus*, rescinds Socrates' critique of writing. It is as if Plato is saying, "False is the tale that writing causes forgetfulness"; but, of course, he nowhere says this, since he never speaks *in* the dialogue. In and through his act of writing, however, we hear Plato redressing the stridency of Socrates' critique of writing. The *Phaedrus* as a text, then, might be read as yet another palinode.

Socrates' primary complaint about writing is that it induces forgetfulness. In the words of king Thamus,

> If men learn this [writing], it will implant forgetfulness in their souls: they will cease to exercise memory because they rely on that which is written, calling things to remembrance no longer from within themselves, but by means of external marks; what you have discovered [Theuth] is a recipe [*pharmakon*] not for memory, but for reminder. (275a)

A *pharmakon*, as Derrida observes, is something essentially ambiguous. Its drugging power is at once a remedy and a poison, it can heal and it can kill. Lysias' speech is such a drug, as Socrates concedes, when he calls it a "recipe [*pharmakon*] for drawing me out" (230d). As Derrida rightly argues, the notion is central to Socrates' critique of writing; for him, indeed, the wisdom carried in a book is comparable to a drug (268c). The *pharmakon* of writing hypnotizes memory, "fascinating it, taking it out of itself by putting it to sleep in a monument."[88] Writing is "the mime of memory"; it gives readers "not memory but memorials."[89] No wonder then that Phaedrus baits Socrates to compete with Lysias' written speech with the promise of a monument dedicated to him (235d–e). Those who rely on written texts, Socrates argues, are mere imitators of life: authors are but "self-proclaimed wise men" (sophists) and readers consequently get swept away by "the appearances which enable it to pass for truth," just as Orithyia was swept away by Boreas when playing with *Pharmaceia* (229c).[90] The great danger, as the history of religions bears out, is what Griswold calls the "canonization of a *biblio*": "the written word lets us persuade ourselves too easily that we are in irrefutable possession of the truth, while in fact we are not."[91]

In writing the *Phaedrus*, Plato participates in the *pharmakon* of writing. As Derrida puts it, "Plato imitates the imitators in order to restore the truth of what they imitate: namely, truth itself."[92] He takes up writing as a remedy for the deadening effects of writing. But the height of irony here is not that Plato writes, but that he writes in precisely the same ways as those whom Socrates criticizes within the dialogue. Thus, in writing the *Phaedrus*, he competes in writing with Isocrates' *Helen*. And though he has Socrates lambast speech-writers like Lysias, it is Plato who ghostwrites a speech on love for Lysias—a ghostwriter whom he criticizes through a ghostwritten speech! Moreover, Plato outdoes Lysias by ghostwriting Socrates' critique of writing. In writing the *Phaedrus*, therefore, Plato participates very much in the same *pharmakon* as his opponents. In so doing, he recants Socrates' austere and puritanical rejection of writing; and he stands in danger of falling prey to the deadly discourse of the sophists.

Here again we come across an odd, but interesting, feature of this dialogue: namely, that Plato frequently seems to be at odds with Socrates. It is at these points that we as readers begin to hear the difference between Socrates' voice within the dialogue and Plato's anonymous voice as author of the dialogue. Plato speaks, in other words, not only through Socrates' voice (which he does a great deal) but also through Socrates' errors and lapses. When, therefore, Socrates forwards weak arguments against rhetoric, or similarly when he appears oblivious to "Rhetoric's" insistence that technique is needed in addition to truth, Plato is letting Socrates' limitations speak for him. As Ferrari puts it, "the limitation of his arguments are as thematically important . . . as what can positively be claimed for them." For Ferrari, Plato is not simply criticizing Lysias, but also "dramatizing the very elusiveness of the common argumentative ground between Socrates and Lysias upon which direct criticism could be built."[93] Ferrari's point is sound, but there is another side to it. In fact, the typhonic character of Socrates is of a piece with the palinodic structure Plato gives to the *Phaedrus*. Through these literary devices, Plato can *assert* the difference between Socrates' philosophic dialogue and the rhetoric of speech-writers like Lysias, at the same time *showing* how the alternatives they represent converge as well. In his critique of writing, Socrates establishes the difference between himself and the sophistic rhetoricians; but in writing the *Phaedrus* Plato pulls back from this critique, thereby acknowledging that any challenge to the sophists must also proceed through the *pharmakon* of writing. Plato says, therefore, precisely what he does; writing is dangerous (as Socrates says) but necessary (as Plato shows).

Turned around, however, Plato seems to be at odds with himself as well. For by letting Socrates' critique of writing stand, indeed by leaving it stand at the consummation of the dialogue, Plato leaves himself open to criticism from his lead character. In this sense, he seems to negate his own work. This act of self-criticism, as Griswold notes, is Plato's final palinode. Here Plato makes amends for writing *while* manifesting the necessity of writing for this purpose. The irony, of course, is that what Plato has written is supposed to be a living (nonwritten) dialogue.[94] His palinode for writing, therefore, takes place in writing under the ironic cover of nonwritten dialogue. In this most indirect of manners, Plato appears to work against his own project.

The *Phaedrus* is—as this section suggests—an astoundingly intricate if not confused text. Its complexities generate a number of questions. Why is Plato—of all people—saying something that seems to unsay itself even as he speaks? If he is—as I have claimed—trying to say something about the ethics of saying, then what does this add? Or does it nullify his efforts to speak coherently and persuasively about the ethical standards for discourse? The final section of this chapter will address three responses to these questions.

(4) Embracing the *Pharmakon*

Why did Plato write the *Phaedrus* in the manner described in the last section? What can a self-critical and ironic discourse contribute to an ethic of discourse? Why would Plato work ironically against his protagonist and self-critically against his own project?

There are three main responses to these questions. First, Schleiermacher's route explains the textual morass as an accident of Plato's youth. This view proves untenable, however, given a modern consensus, which dates the *Phaedrus* as late as 365 B.C., making it the mature work of an experienced author.[95] Second, Derrida's deconstructionist reading takes the difficulties in the *Phaedrus* as symptoms of subterranean faults in Plato's philosophical venture; faults which ultimately unravel and self-destruct. Alternatively, a positive reading (forwarded primarily by Griswold) looks on the many breaks and tensions within the *Phaedrus* as contributing to a philosophically richer and more nuanced understanding of the nature and limits of discourse. Indeed, as I will argue, the breaks and conflicts that dominate the *Phaedrus* illustrate Plato's literary sophistication in crafting a dialogue that seeks to portray—with irony and self-critical finesse—the possibilities and limits for talking about the ethic of discourse.

Derrida's reading of the *Phaedrus* centers on the concept of the *pharmakon* in Plato's critique of writing. The *pharmakon*, as we have seen, is an inherently two-pronged drug: it is at once a medicine and a poison. As Socrates confesses to Phaedrus, the written word is such a drug for him. With its "power of fascination," the book seduces Socrates and leads him astray from his normal routine.[96] Writing is not authentic. It is a substitute for living discourse. In Derrida's words, it is "something secondary, external, and compensatory, and something that substitutes, violates and usurps."[97] At best a convenient reminder, the written word elides true memory while giving the appearance of the real thing. In writing, therefore, the sign reigns. Everything else drifts into oblivion. In choosing to write, "the author of the written speech is already entrenched in the posture of the sophist: the man of non-presence and of non-truth."[98] The same is true from the other side—when a reader comes to depend on the written word, the sign becomes central while the author slips from presence into the background. Dependence on the written word, therefore, belies "a desire for orphanhood and patricidal subversion."[99] The author—or what Socrates calls the father of a speech (261a and 275b)—is subverted, leaving the words as orphans with no one to defend them. Writing leads people into irreality and leaves them forgetful. In Derrida's characteristically dramatic language (in writing, I should note), "the powers of *lethe* simultaneously increase the domains of death, of nontruth, of nonknowledge."[100]

Interestingly, Derrida observes, "Socrates in the dialogues of Plato often has the face of a *pharmakeus*": a sophist, a magician, a sorcerer, and even a poisoner.[101] Agathon, for example, accuses Socrates of trying to bewitch him (*pharmatein*) in the *Symposium* (194a). Meno similarly complains that Socrates is "exercising magic and witchcraft" upon him; under Socrates' spell, Meno is reduced to a "mass of helplessness." Like a stingray, Socrates has numbed Meno's mind and lips, to such a degree he can't remember what virtue is. Warning Socrates, Meno says: "If you behaved like this as a foreigner in another country, you would most likely be arrested as a wizard" (80a–b). But Socrates is also a doctor of the soul, whose medicine is temperance (*Charmides*); and he is the one seeking the "best of medicines" (*ariston pharmakon*)—namely, knowledge (*Critias* 106b). His counter spell is dialectic (*Phaedo* 77e–78b). Socrates' *pharmakon*, evidently, is equivocal: it "petrifies and vivifies, anesthetizes and sensitizes, appeases and anguishes."[102] What Socrates tries to do, according to Derrida, is to oppose his *pharmakon* (called knowledge, dialectic, philosophy) against "the *pharmakon* of the sophists."[103] The danger, of course, is that he is playing with a poison—which ultimately will kill him.[104]

Here, for Derrida, is the nub of Plato's project. Plato dreams of memory without a sign, or, alternatively, of philosophy without a text.[105] But the adversaries he faces are speech-writers and sophists, and to overcome their poisonous methods, he must call upon the very thing he seeks to expel—namely, the *pharmakon* of written discourse. Through the ironic discourse of Socrates (which Plato writes from a distance), Plato "precipitates out one *pharmakon* by bringing it in contact with another *pharmakon*."[106] At Plato's pen, therefore, "philosophy thus opposes to its other [the sophists] this transmutation of the drug into a remedy, of the poison into a counterpoison."[107] The danger, once again, is that Socrates' counter spell for sophistic forgetfulness remains a spell (*pharmakon*); and it too can numb the mind and the lips, as Meno testifies. Plato's quest is to separate out the therapeutic dimension of the *pharmakon*, without falling prey to its lethal side. He seeks, in other words, to distinguish honorable writing from shameful writing. This, Derrida asserts, is the "great fold which divides the dialogue."[108]

For Derrida, Plato's grand venture fails. Despite the apparent nobility of his intentions, Plato falls preys to the ineluctably ambiguous character of the *pharmakon*. In Derrida's words, "the pharmacy has no foundation."[109] It is a "bottomless fund" of ambiguity (*fonds sans fond*); and there is no way to exempt oneself from the tensions and oppositions at work within it.[110] To write at all, accordingly, is to dwell within the *pharmakon*, and consequently to succumb to its crosscurrents. As Derrida conceives it, the *pharmakon* "constitutes the medium in which opposites are opposed, the movement and the play that links them among themselves, reverses them or makes one side cross over into the other (soul, good, inside, memory, speech, etc.)." Or, "the *pharmakon* is the movement, the locus, the play: (the production of) [these] difference[s]."[111] To write, therefore, is to throw oneself into the play of these oppositions. To participate in the written repetition of life, which Plato does in writing the *Phaedrus*, is to put oneself at the mercy of "the very movement of non-truth." There is no escape, Derrida claims, for to repeat Socrates' criticism of repetition in writing is—obviously—already to repeat. To oppose the alienation of author and text in the sophists, and to do so in writing, is already to assume the opposition which is being criticized. Or, more dramatically, "when read from the viewpoint of Socrates' death," Plato's writing is "in the situation of writing as it is indicted in the *Phaedrus*."[112] For in a very real sense, Plato writes out of Socrates' death: "while condemning writing as a lost or parricidal son, Plato behaves like a son writing this condemnation, at once repairing and confirming the death of Socrates."[113] In taking up the *pharmakon*, consequently, Plato succumbs to that which he most opposes.

For Derrida, Plato ultimately is an unwitting victim of linguistic ambiguities. As he sees it, the word *pharmakon* (with all its associations) is bound up in a long "chain of significations"; the concept traverses age-old "corridors of meaning," which shape the language Plato takes up when he writes. In one passage, Derrida concedes that Plato sometimes "voluntarily" plays with the oppositions within the *pharmakon*; but he quickly adds that even this is "only a mode of 'submission' to the necessities of a given 'language'." Most fundamentally, Plato "cannot see the links, can leave them in the shadows or break them up. And yet these links go on working of themselves."[114] In a parallel context, Derrida is more evasive on the question of how aware Plato is of the dialectical tensions at play within his writing. It is, he insists, "impossible to say to what extent he manipulates it voluntarily or consciously, and at what point he is subject to constraints weighing upon his discourse from 'language'." But despite these words of indecision, Derrida is convinced that Plato is caught up in linguistic patterns beyond his control, which—in the end—unravel his philosophical project. "It is in the back room," he writes, "in the shadows of the pharmacy, prior to the opposition between conscious and unconscious, freedom and constraint, voluntary and involuntary, speech and language, that these textual 'operations' occur."[115] Derrida has—despite the obscurity of his language—designated Plato a casualty of the *pharmakon*.

If Derrida is correct in his critique of the *Phaedrus*, then Plato's philosophical project, including the ethic of discourse discussed in section two of this chapter, unravels of its own inner ambiguity. It self-destructs, as it were, because it cannot escape the negative poles of the *pharmakon*. Plato praises philosophical knowledge and living memory in opposition to the sophists, but, in choosing to write, he implicates himself in the deception and forgetfulness propagated by his opponents. Socrates' counter spell is itself a spell, just as Plato's writing is itself a form of writing. Neither can claim exemption from the *pharmakon*'s poisonous effects. Plato's ethic of discourse, therefore, perishes by the ambiguity of its own remedy.

A great deal of evidence supports Derrida's reading of the *Phaedrus*. The fact that Plato's dialogue devours itself even as it progresses seems to illustrate Derrida's contention that Plato's project is doomed of its own internal tensions. If, as Derrida claims, the conceptual framework within which Plato works is a "bottomless fund" of ambiguity, then all we are left with is discourses about other discourses. As Griswold puts it, paraphrasing Derrida, "each discourse seems to undermine itself in a way that generates yet another discourse."[116] Since the entire dialogue concerns "disputable" issues (like love) (263a–d), there appears to be no way to settle the conflicting claims of the different discourses. If this is true, as Griswold notes, then we find ourselves very much in the position described by Richard Rorty, where no discourse is available to bridge the gaps between alternative moral perspectives. Moreover, we have no recourse to the typical foundations associated with Plato's philosophy; the vision of the Forms or the method of dialectic, for example. Even these recant themselves. If Derrida is correct in this, then the reader is left in the position of Phaedrus: "a solitary promeneur" absorbed in the "World of the Text" with no recourse for substantive judgments about truth. The *Phaedrus*, therefore, turns out to be "a defense of Phaedrus," despite Plato's intentions to the contrary.[117] And that, according to Derrida, is where Plato leaves us.

Or is that just where *Derrida* leaves us? This is the question Griswold asks in his reading of the *Phaedrus*. Griswold begins from the same facts: namely, that the dialogue recants itself as it develops, and that Socrates (like the dialogue itself) appears unstable and contradictory. If anything, Griswold is far more thorough and incisive in charting these features of Plato's text. While Derrida concentrates exclusively on Socrates' critique of writing, Griswold surveys the entire dialogue. Unlike Derrida, moreover, Griswold approaches the dialogue with the assumption that Plato is in control of the ambiguities and dialectical tensions at work in his text.[118] Plato is aware, in other words, of the deconstructive features of his dialogue. In fact, as Griswold notes, Plato intentionally constructs his texts in a way that invites Derridean conclusions, while providing an escape hatch for the diligent and perceptive reader. Plato is in control of the ambiguities and confusions within the *Phaedrus;* confident and ironic, he composed a text which, on many levels, concedes the ambiguous nature and deconstructive power of the *pharmakon* of philosophical discourse. In my own language, Plato embraces the *pharmakon*.

In the *Phaedrus*, Plato discovered and perfected the possibilities for a form of writing—namely, the genre of dialogue—that at one and the same time can entertain the dialectical tensions of philosophical discourse, and point beyond the self-destructive tendencies entailed in such discourse. The dialogue form provides Plato a means (ultimately, a post-Socratic *techne*) for engaging the merits *and* the dangers inherent within writing. As Griswold puts it, Plato, in choosing to write at all, signals his disagreement with Socrates' critique. It is possible, after all, he declares through his act of writing, to escape the impersonal nature of composition, to avoid the self-seriousness which comes with authorship, and to retain the vital memory possible in living discourse. In choosing to write a dialogue, however, he signals his agreement with Socrates that "dialogue ought to be the ruling medium of all forms of philosophical rhetoric."[119] Simultaneously, the option to write in dialogue form also concedes, ironically, the truth of Socrates' protest. The virtue of the dialogue is that it allows Plato to convey this intricately complex message.[120]

Dialogue allows Plato to speak in a manner that is optimally fruitful and yet fully self-critical. Through the fiction of dialogue, Plato can (through Socrates' voice) forward strong (even immoderate) claims for both mythic imagination and dialectic. The first of these describes the abode of the gods, while the second promises speech fitting for the gods. Each mode of discourse promises a great deal, but, as we have seen, each suffers from forgetfulness. As Griswold puts it, "the palinode's myth was an inspired, deep, but finally self-forgetful monologue; the *techne* of division and collection is an uninspired effort at accountability, which seems purchased at the price of superficiality."[121] The dialogue form makes it possible for Plato to affirm the strengths while highlighting the weaknesses of both forms of discourse. His handling of them, indeed, foreshadows the movement typical of Hegelian dialectic: in praising both myth and dialectic, Plato tempers the excesses of each, without, however, emptying them of value. Through their self-negating but productive opposition, both are sublated into a larger whole. And it is the dialogue form which makes it possible for Plato to say (by showing) this two-fold relationship and movement.

The option for dialogue also makes it possible for Plato to speak indirectly and obliquely. Doing so permits him to write in a manner that satisfies a number of Socrates' demands for good speech, even as it distances him from the views of his protagonist. As is the case in all of his dialogues, Plato never speaks directly—in his own voice—within the *Phaedrus*. His points are always mediated through the words of a character. The unsystematic (even disorganized) character of the dialogue form (something accentuated in the *Phaedrus*) serves to alert the reader that Plato's message is not the same as Socrates'. As Griswold writes, "by writing a dialogue that seems shockingly disunified and in which unified writing is defined and praised by someone who refused to write, Plato thrusts the point at the reader."[122] One cannot equate Plato's voice with Socrates'. Plato's silence—the fact that he only speaks obliquely, often through Socrates' mistakes, or even in conflict with him—provides Plato a means of avoiding all pretensions to dogmatic self-assurance in writing.[123] Since Plato never speaks within the dialogue, *his* words are not set up as permanent artifacts. Indeed, they remain interactive, unstable, and elastic. Moreover, because Plato speaks on so many levels, at once serious and jocular, his words speak with sensitivity to different audiences; they know when to speak and when not to speak, and thus, in a sense, they have the power to ask questions of and propose answers to different readers.[124] The dialogue, in sum, allows Plato's voice to remain nimble and responsive to its audience.

That Plato speaks by showing (rather than directly by saying) allows a great deal of ironic inflection. One must, as Ferrari nicely puts it, listen carefully to the chirping of the cicadas, for what happens in the background of Plato's text ultimately is more important than what occurs in the foreground.[125] That certainly holds for Plato's central philosophical concerns—including his ethical judgments on proper and improper rhetoric effected through the correlation of love and speech. As Gadamer writes,

> [the dialogues] shroud all of what they say in the ambiguous twilight of irony. And in this way Plato is able to escape the trap of the ever so vulnerable written work, which cannot come to its own defense, and to create a truly philosophical poetry which points beyond itself to what is of real consequence. His dialogues are nothing more than playful allusions which say something only to him who finds meanings beyond what is expressly stated in them and allows these meanings to take effect within him.[126]

Whereas the dialogue's palinodic, yet fruitful rhythms keep Plato attuned to variations among his readers, the ironic tone demands that readers conversing with Plato through the *Phaedrus* also remain fully alert and responsive to the author's shifts in meaning. Nowhere is this more striking than when Plato ghostwrites speeches for Socrates, who in turn lambasts ghostwriters like Lysias. The dialogue form conceals but later reveals this odd turn of events—demanding thereby that the reader come to terms with Plato's indirect and ironic voice. In such ironic concessions, Plato confesses his own implication in the *pharmakon* of writing. Laced with irony, however, Plato's *pharmakon* turns out to be dialogue.

Plato embraces the *pharmakon* of writing knowingly and voluntarily. Through writing a dialogue, in other words, Plato concedes the ambivalence of his voice; his writing too can animate lively memory *and* it can drug the reader into forgetfulness. Plato, in short, does not claim exemption from the ambiguity of the *pharmakon*. Indeed, he seems to revel in demonstrating its destructive effects on every form of discourse. Much of the *Phaedrus*, as we have seen, is dedicated to showing the self-negating potential buried in every effort to speak or write. Oration, myth, dialectic, even dialogue are all contingent; they unravel themselves even as they contribute their insights. Plato embraces precisely this fact of discursive life with all its internal tensions. This is the heart of the *Phaedrus*. Contrary to Derrida's interpretation, Plato does not claim exemption from the poisonous side of the *pharmakon*; neither is his project dismantled by it. What Plato offers is a self-consuming—but self-propagating—form of discourse. And *that* form of discourse is dialogue; a form of writing (*pharmakon*) that propagates lively inquiry even as it concedes its own limitations. Plato's ironic recantations demand, therefore, the genre of dialogue—a form of writing through which he can "demonstrate the inferiority of his [own] writings out of his own mouth" (278c). This is Plato's dialogical *pharmakon*.

What is important about Griswold's reading of the *Phaedrus*, in contrast to the Derridean interpretation, is that it highlights the ethical message attached to Plato's use of the dialogue form. As he puts it, the *Phaedrus* begins not with "metaphysical or epistemological doctrines" (vision of the Forms is a luxury reserved for the gods), but with "an exercise in the art of rhetoric."[127] More specifically, the dialogue opens with Phaedrus' passion for "novel and possibly absurd discourses." Through Socrates' voice, it then proceeds to "describe the dialectical development of this passion." What Socrates exposes in the process is that Phaedrus has lost himself in the "World of the Text"; his "passion for beautiful speeches" has left him oblivious to the Delphic "Know thyself."[128] It is true that Plato's playful unraveling of Phaedrus appears "very similar in execution" to Derrida's dismantling of Plato's text. But the differences are more striking, for where Platonic dialogue opens and closes by trusting the "ethical dimension of the Delphic imperative," Derridean deconstruction is entirely without direction. In Griswold's words, Derridean "philosophizing would seem to be the imaginative play of the mind whose fruit is an endless interplay of discourses."[129] Thus, while Derrida's deconstructive play may resemble the palinodic movement of Platonic dialogue, his real equivalent is Phaedrus. In the end, Griswold suggests, Derrida's dialectical performances "resemble merely sophisticated poems of the 'clever'," a charge leveled by Socrates at Phaedrus' friends (229d and 245c).[130] Derrida does in fact leave us with Phaedrus, for the two are kindred souls.

In choosing to write in dialogue form, and in doing so in the highly self-critical and ironic manner described above, Plato prods his readers to look beyond Phaedrus (the character), and to think beyond the *Phaedrus* (the text). As Griswold puts it, "the literary or dramatic aspect of Plato's artifacts is intended to prevent readers from becoming absorbed in them in the way that Phaedrus does in Lysias' text."[131] It is impossible to become too comfortable with any particular perspective within Plato's text due to "the jarring effect that governs the dialogue as a whole."[132] Readers are forced onward by the peculiarly restless structure. In turn, they are forced backward to reflect on the kinds of love and speech which shape their lives. Plato uses the dialogue, in other words, not simply to represent a dialogue between Socrates and Phaedrus, but to engage readers dialogically in the restless, intensely self-critical search for self-understanding. Readers become interlocutors in as lively a manner as possible. To the extent that they become attuned to the palinodic movement of Plato's dialogue, they absorb Plato's rhetorical "seeds" and come to have Plato's "dialogical *pharmakon*" written in their souls (278a).

The *Phaedrus*, in the end, offers its readers "an intensely reflexive defense of dialogue."[133] It is dialogue—as shown to us through Plato's written performance—that provides a form of discourse uniquely suited to reflecting discursively on ethical standards for discourse. In leading his readers to engage in dialogue, Plato encourages us to take our discursive lives seriously, but to do so in a fully self-critical manner. He encourages us to make substantive claims (e.g., about love), while insisting that every claim face the limiting pressure of alternative views. He offers us a glimpse of an ideal form of life (embodied in philosophical *eros*), but insists that there are no privileged, purely objective perspectives on the ends of life. He even suggests a means to this ideal (dialogue), but immediately notes how every form of discourse is susceptible to deception and forgetfulness. In the end, Plato shows us something about the possibilities and the limits of ethical discourse. Any and every attempt to speak ethically about the way we talk with each other—including Erasmus' praise of irenic discourse, and Plato's own correlation of forms of love and forms of speech—should proceed with the confident passion of a philosophical lover (leading and luring the other with questions, possible answers, and new questions), while never forgetting that every form of discourse stands in danger of deception, forgetfulness, and domination. Plato's *Phaedrus*, therefore, proposes an ethic of discourse appropriate for typhonic creatures like ourselves—who, while striving for the pure vision of the gods, remain bound to the complex passion of the beasts.

Notes

[1] Richard Rorty, *Contingency, Irony, and Solidarity* (Cambridge: Cambridge University, 1989,) 61.

[2] Richard Rorty, *Philosophy and the Mirror of Nature* (Princeton: Princeton University, 1979) 376–78.

[3] Jürgen Habermas, *The Philosophical Discourse of Modernity*, trans. Frederick Lawrence (Cambridge, Massachusetts: MIT Press, 1987) 314 and 322. Habermas writes: "Reason is by its very nature incarnated in contexts of communicative action and in structures of the lifeworld." See 322.

[4] Jürgen Habermas, *Moral Consciousness and Communicative Action,* trans. Christian Lenhardt and Shierry Weber Nicholsen (Cambridge, Massachusetts: MIT Press, 1990) 57.

[5] Habermas, *Moral Consciousness*, 20.

[6] Habermas, *Moral Consciousness*, 14–19 and 57.

[7] Except where noted, all quotations from the *Phaedrus* are taken from R. Hackforth's translation, *Plato's Phaedrus* (New York: Liberal Arts, 1952). In order to preserve certain key wordplays or associations, I occasionally will quote from H. N. Fowler's translation, *Plato* (London: William Heinemann, 1919). Passages from other Platonic dialogues are from *The Collected Dialogues of Plato*, ed. Edith Hamilton and Huntington Cairns (Princeton: Princeton University, 1961). References to the *Phaedrus* will be placed parenthetically within the text.

[8] G. R. F. Ferrari, *Listening to the Cicadas; A Study of Plato's Phaedrus* (Cambridge: Cambridge University, 1987) 6.

[9] Ferrari, *Listening to the Cicadas*, 5. For another discussion of Phaedrus' character, see Ronna Burger, *Plato's Phaedrus; A Defense of a Philosophic Art of Writing* (University, Alabama: University of Alabama, 1980) 8–18.

[10] Phaedrus is said to be "blessed in his offspring" for instigating so many speeches from others (261a). Complaining of Phaedrus' effect on himself, Socrates exclaims: "Of the discourses pronounced during your lifetime no one, I fancy, has been responsible for more than you, whether by delivering them yourself or by compelling others to do so by one means or another—with one exception, Simmias of Thebes: you are well ahead of all the rest. And now it seems that once more you are the cause of my having to deliver myself" (242a–b). See Plato, *Phaedo* 108d–e where Simmias prods Socrates to speak further on the nature of the earth and the heavens. See also *Phaedrus* 242e and 243e–244a, where Socrates attributes his first speech on love to Phaedrus.

[11] Cicero reports that Lysias offered a written defense to Socrates (*De Oratore* 1.231), but, according to Diogenes Laertius, Socrates refused it. *Diogenes Laertius; Lives of the Eminent Philosophers*, vol. 2, trans. R. D. Hicks (Cambridge, Mass.: Harvard University, 1938) 40–41.

¹² Occasionally it seems Lysias practiced dissemblance in his speeches. See, for instance, "On the Refusal of a Pension to the Invalid" and "Before the Council: In Defense of Mantitheus at his Scrutiny." *Lysias*, trans. W. R. M. Lamb (Cambridge, Mass.: Harvard University, 1943) 519–533 and 375–387. See George Kennedy, *The Art of Persuasion in Ancient Greece* (Princeton: Princeton University, 1963) 140.

¹³ Kennedy, *The Art of Persuasion*, 26.

¹⁴ As R. Hackforth notes, this may be a "conciliatory gesture" on Plato's part, making amends for the possible reference to Isocrates in *Republic* 500b. R. Hackforth, *Plato's Phaedrus*, 168. Granting this possibility, it also seems likely that Plato is mimicking Isocrates' own hope to rise far above his rivals so that "it will seem as if no word had ever been spoken . . . upon this subject." Isocrates, "Panegyricus," *Isocrates*, vol. 2, trans. George Norlin (London: William Heinemann, 1928). For this suggestion, see Burger, *Plato's Phaedrus*, 115–116. Because Plato's prophecy of literary achievement already is fulfilled when Plato wrote the *Phaedrus*, it rings with irony. For background on Isocrates, see R. C. Jebb, *The Attic Orators from Antiphon to Isaeos*, vol. 2 (London: Macmillan, 1876).

¹⁵ Ronna Burger suggests that the description of Phaedrus as "wavering" back and forth between Lysias and Socrates is a coded reference to Isocrates. This holds, if, as seems likely, *Euthydemus* 305–306 refers to Isocrates. There Socrates criticizes those "frontiersmen between philosophy and politics." It is true that they are "moderately well up in philosophy, and moderately well up in politics," and thus they do "come near to wisdom," but because they mix things with different ends, their wisdom is more an appearance than a reality. See Burger, *Plato's Phaedrus*, 115.

¹⁶ Isocrates, "Antidosis," *Isocrates*, vol 2, trans. George Norlin (London: William Heinemann, 1928) 311.

¹⁷ Isocrates, "Nicocles or the Cyprians," *Isocrates*, vol. 1, 6–7; and "Antidosis," vol. 2, 254.

¹⁸ Isocrates, "Panegyricus," vol. 1, 48–49; compare "Antidosis," vol. 2, 293–294.

¹⁹ Isocrates, "Against the Sophists," *Isocrates*, vol. 2, 160–180.

²⁰ Isocrates, "Antidosis," vol. 2, 285.

²¹ Isocrates, "Helen," *Isocrates*, vol. 3, trans. La Rue Van Hook (London: William Heinemann, 1928) 5.

²² R. Hackforth takes Socrates' reference to "the two speeches" that illustrate deceitful rhetoric (262d) as applying to all three speeches on love. It refers, he argues, first to Lysias' oration, and then to Socrates' two speeches taken together as one. See Hackforth, *Plato's Phaedrus*, 125, note. While Plato's reference certainly lacks clarity, Hackforth's reading seems forced. Since the "two speeches" are used as examples of deceptive oratory, it seems more likely that Plato is thinking only of Lysias' speech and the first of Socrates' two speeches. When, in 264e, Socrates and Phaedrus "pass to the other speeches," the reference

is to both of Socrates' speeches. The confusion and ambiguity of these references is created deliberately by Plato. See Charles L. Griswold, Jr., *Self-Knowledge in Plato's Phaedrus* (New Haven: Yale University, 1986) 277, note 19.

²³ Griswold, *Self-Knowledge in Plato's Phaedrus*, 56.

²⁴ Griswold, *Self-Knowledge in Plato's Phaedrus*, 70–72.

²⁵ What Socrates ascribes to the rhetoricians was by Plato's time a stock charge against the sophists. Just how widespread it was is indicated in Aristophanes' satirical assault on such teachers in *The Clouds*. Ironically, Aristophanes casts Socrates as such a teacher. It is the art of deception that Strepsiades hopes to secure from Socrates' "Thinkery" in order to deflect his creditors' lawsuits. He seeks the sophists' skill of "taking what might appear to be the worse argument and nonetheless winning the case." Aristophanes, "The Clouds," *Four Plays by Aristophanes*, trans. William Arrowsmith, Richmond Lattimore, and Douglass Parker (New York: New American Library, 1962) 103. The power of deception—making "an utter mockery of the truth" (90)—boomerangs on Strepsiades when his son is able "to prove beyond the shadow of a doubt the philosophical propriety of beating [his] Father" (135). Ironically, Plato's Socrates shares Aristophanes' concern that, in Ferrari's words, the "orators are indifferent to morality and that this is a bad thing for a society in which ethical decisions are arrived at under their influence." Ferrari, *Listening to the Cicadas*, 40–1.

²⁶ Isocrates, "Against the Sophists," vol. 2, 1 and 9.

²⁷ Isocrates, "Panegyricus," vol. 1, 5–6.

²⁸ Isocrates, "Panegyricus," vol. 1, 8.

²⁹ R. Hackforth rightly suggests that Socrates is quoting Isocrates' words when he describes Tisias and Gorgias, "who could make trifles seem important and important points trifles by the force of their language, who dressed up novelties as antiques and vice versa . . ." (267a–b). See Hackforth, *Plato's Phaedrus*, 143–44.

³⁰ Isocrates, "Against the Sophists," vol. 2, 9–10.

³¹ Isocrates, "Antidosis," vol. 2, 187–88. Compare with "Against the Sophists," vol. 2, 10.

³² Isocrates, "Antidosis," vol. 2, 189.

³³ As George Kennedy points out, Socrates' first speech is a "very credible composition" according to the standards of Greek oratory, notably in "rhetorical form" or arrangement. Kennedy, *Art of Persuasion*, 77.

³⁴ Isocrates, "Against the Sophists," vol. 2, 13. Compare with "Panegyricus," vol. 1, 9.

³⁵ The common denominator between rhetoric and *eros* is the beautiful (*kalon*). Meaning "admirable, fair, noble, suitable, appropriate, [or] measured," *kalon* applies equally to the object of erotic longing and to the fine quality of a good speech. It means a great deal more,

as Griswold notes, than "mere pleasing"—what Phaedrus expects in a good speech and what Lysias' lover wants in a sexual partner. See Griswold, *Self-Knowledge in Plato's Phaedrus*, 117. On the contrast of the good (*agathon*) with pleasure in the *Phaedrus*, see Ferrari, *Listening to the Cicadas*, 96.

[36] For this correlation of love and rhetoric in brief outline, see Richard Weaver, *The Ethics of Rhetoric* (South Bend: Regnery and Gateway, 1953) 3–26. Interestingly, Gadamer draws an exact, three-fold typology of basic attitudes and interpretive practices. See Hans Georg Gadamer, *Truth and Method* (New York: Crossroad, 1982) 321–325.

[37] It is doubtful that this speech is written by Lysias, although a good deal of debate has been given to the question. See Hackforth, *Plato's Phaedrus*, 17. For a brief review of this debate, see G. J. De Vries, *A Commentary on the Phaedrus of Plato* (Amsterdam: Adolf M. Hakkert, 1969) 11–14.

[38] Griswold, *Self-Knowledge in Plato's Phaedrus*, 50.

[39] Richard Weaver, *The Ethics of Rhetoric*, 7 and 8.

[40] Griswold, *Self-Knowledge in Plato's Phaedrus*, 48. Nussbaum suggests that Phaedrus' attraction to Lysias' defense of the non-lover over the lover makes some sense, if considered as analogous to what a young professional woman faces when entering an all-male academic world. She would, Nussbaum seems to say, find the clarity of the non-lover far safer (leaving her to "live and work on reasonable and non-threatening terms with the people with whom she works") than the passionate intrusions of colleague suitors. See Martha C. Nussbaum, *The Fragility of Goodness* (Cambridge: Cambridge University, 1986) 207–208. While Nussbaum's hypothetical young woman may be right to mistrust the passion of her admirers, she would (I think) have even more reason to fear the self-serving deception of Lysias' non-lover or Socrates' concealed lover.

[41] This contrasts with Socrates' words at 227b where he wants to put listening to discourses "above all business." Later, in a different sense, Socrates refers to his second speech on noble love as no more than a "festive entertainment" (265c).

[42] This part of the *Phaedrus* has proved especially difficult to interpret, and for good reason. Why is it that Socrates puts this speech in the mouth of a wily one (*aimulos tis*), someone only pretending to be a nonlover? Hackforth suggests that the speaker "shows a real concern for the welfare, especially the moral welfare, of the boy, a concern which it would have been unconvincing to attribute to a genuine cold-blooded sensualist." Trusting the speaker as he does, Hackforth sees here a glimpse of the ideal lover, Socrates himself. See Hackforth, *Plato's Phaedrus*, 40. Other interpreters have seen more irony in Socrates' performance. Ferrari, for instance, regards Socrates' willingness to participate in Phaedrus' contest of speeches as a symptom of the danger of Socrates' philosophical love of discourse degenerating into a "life of mere words." See Ferrari, *Listening to the Cicadas*, 103–112.

[43] Griswold, *Self-Knowledge in Plato's Phaedrus*, 69.

[44] Weaver, *Ethics of Rhetoric*, 11.

[45] Nussbaum notes Plato's wordplay. Socrates' second speech is credited to "Stesichorus, son of Euphemus, from Himera" (244a). "Euphemus" means "reverent in speech," while Himera (deriving from *himeros* meaning passionate desire) "might well be called Desire Town or Passionville." Plato is having great fun! See Nussbaum, *Fragility of Goodness*, 211.

[46] For a discussion of the types of madness, see Josef Pieper, *Enthusiasm and Divine Madness; On the Platonic Dialogue Phaedrus*, trans. Richard and Clara Winston (New York: Harcourt, Brace and World, 1964) 47–71. On the significance of Plato's shifting attitude toward *mania* (and the non-intellectual elements of the human personality), see Nussbaum, *The Fragility of Goodness*, 200–233.

[47] On the special status of beauty, see Ferrari, *Listening to the Cicadas*, 147–49. See also Hans-Georg Gadamer, *The Relevance of the Beautiful and Other Essays*, trans. by Nicholas Walker (Cambridge: Cambridge University, 1986) 13–15.

[48] Griswold, *Self-Knowledge in Plato's Phaedrus*, 104.

[49] Griswold, *Self-Knowledge in Plato's Phaedrus*, 148–150.

[50] Griswold, *Self-Knowledge in Plato's Phaedrus*, 147.

[51] Ferrari, *Listening to the Cicadas*, 195.

[52] Griswold, *Self-Knowledge in Plato's Phaedrus*, 96.

[53] Ferrari, *Listening to the Cicadas*, 199–200.

[54] Ferrari, *Listening to the Cicadas*, 129.

[55] Griswold, *Self-Knowledge in Plato's Phaedrus*, 204. Gadamer's discussion of Platonic dialectic as a model for ideal conversation provides a hermeneutical parallel to the philosophical rhetoric guided by noble love. See Gadamer, *Truth and Method*, 325–333.

[56] Gadamer, *Truth and Method*, 341.

[57] Griswold, *Self-Knowledge in Plato's Phaedrus*, 116.

[58] Weaver, *Ethics of Rhetoric*, 17.

[59] Griswold, *Self-Knowledge in Plato's Phaedrus*, 1.

[60] Friedrich Schleiermacher, *Schleiermacher's Introductions to the Dialogues of Plato*, trans. William Dobson (New York: Arno Press, 1973) 59–60.

[61] Griswold, *Self-Knowledge in Plato's Phaedrus*, 36. For evidence of the conflicting interpretations given to Socrates, see H. Spiegelberg, *The Socratic Enigma* (Indianapolis: Bobbs-Merrill, 1964).

[62] Griswold, *Self-Knowledge in Plato's Phaedrus*, 136.

[63] Apollodorus, *Gods and Heroes of the Greeks; The Library of Apollodorus*, trans. Michael Simpson (Amherst: University of Massachusetts, 1976) 19.

[64] Hesiod, *Theogony*, 831–833, trans. Dorothea Wender (London and New York: Penguin, 1973) 50. For a discussion of Socrates' typhonic character, see Griswold, *Self-Knowledge in Plato's Phaedrus*, 39–42.

[65] The association with Achelous is bolstered by the fact that Achelous was the father of Castalia, nymph of the spring at Delphi, the location of Socrates' oracle. Pointing up the danger buried even in sources of inspiration, Castalia is also the nymph of the Sirens. See Apollodorus, *Gods and Heroes*, 103. In the *Symposium* of Plato, Alcibiades compares Socrates to a Siren. See *Symposium*, 216b.

[66] See Plato, *Protagoras*, 334d, and *Gorgias*, 449b.

[67] Ferrari, *Listening to the Cicadas*, 105.

[68] Plato, *Symposium*, 215b.

[69] Ferrari, *Listening to the Cicadas*, 50–53.

[70] See Ferrari, *Listening to the Cicadas*, 60–61.

[71] Friedrich Nietzsche, *Twilight of the Idols*, trans. R. J. Hollingdale (New York and London: Penguin, 1968) par. 4, 31. I owe the reference to Griswold.

[72] See Ferrari, *Listening to the Cicadas*, 31.

[73] Griswold, *Self-Knowledge in Plato's Phaedrus*, 157.

[74] Kennedy, *The Art of Persuasion in Ancient Greece*, 74. Despite his famous critique of rhetoric in the *Gorgias*, Plato later acknowledges the importance of rhetorical education. In a parody of Isocrates' concession that disputation (probably including Platonic dialectic) may serve some practical purposes, Plato concedes in *Philebus* 58c–d that the art of rhetoric is "of paramount service to mankind," while the art of dialectic possesses the "fullest measure [of] reason and intelligence." Plato's rhetorically exact practice of judiciary oratory is evident in the *Apology*. In the *Menexenus*, for example, Plato's rhetorical abilities are evident when he has Socrates whip off a funeral oration by stringing commonplaces together. Kennedy calls this dialogue "a model of proper oration," something like the second speech in the *Phaedrus*. See Kennedy's discussion, 158–64.

[75] Ferrari, *Listening to the Cicadas*, 230.

[76] Griswold, *Self-Knowledge in Plato's Phaedrus*, 218.

[77] If Nussbaum is right, Socrates' palinode also counts as Plato's recantation of his own earlier philosophical views on madness and the passions. See Nussbaum, *The Fragility of Goodness*, 200–233.

[78] Griswold, *Self-Knowledge in Plato's Phaedrus*, 152.

[79] Griswold, *Self-Knowledge in Plato's Phaedrus*, 152.

[80] Griswold, *Self-Knowledge in Plato's Phaedrus*, 153.

[81] Griswold, *Self-Knowledge in Plato's Phaedrus*, 163.

[82] See Griswold, *Self-Knowledge in Plato's Phaedrus*, 189. On the concept of dialectic in the *Phaedrus*, see Herman L. Sinaiko, *Love, Knowledge, and Discourse in Plato; Dialogue and Dialectic in Phaedrus, Republic, Parmenides* (Chicago: University of Chicago, 1965) 22–118.

[83] See Griswold, *Self-Knowledge in Plato's Phaedrus*, 178–179.

[84] Griswold, *Self-Knowledge in Plato's Phaedrus*, 182.

[85] Stanley Fish, *Self-Consuming Artifacts* (Berkeley: University of California, 1972) 12.

[86] Fish, *Self-Consuming Artifacts*, 13.

[87] Fish, *Self-Consuming Artifacts*, 12.

[88] Jacques Derrida, *Dissemination*, trans. Barbara Johnson (Chicago: University of Chicago, 1981) 105.

[89] Derrida, *Dissemination*, 105 and 107.

[90] Derrida, *Dissemination*, 105 and 103. In Plato's *Sophist*, Socrates calls the sophist "the imitator of him who knows" (268c).

[91] Griswold, *Self-Knowledge in Plato's Phaedrus*, 207.

[92] Derrida, *Dissemination*, 112.

[93] Ferrari, *Listening to the Cicadas*, 86 and 56.

[94] See Griswold, *Self-Knowledge in Plato's Phaedrus*, 13.

[95] On the dating of the *Phaedrus'* composition, see Hackforth, *Plato's Phaedrus*, 3–7; De Vries, *A Commentary on the Phaedrus of Plato*, 7–11; and Nussbaum, *The Fragility of Goodness*, 470, note 5. Hackforth dates the dialogue around 370 B.C.; De Vries probably between 369–367; and Nussbaum around 365.

[96] Derrida, *Dissemination*, 70.

[97] Derrida, *Dissemination*, 110.

[98] Derrida, *Dissemination*, 68.

[99] Derrida, *Dissemination*, 77.

[100] Derrida, *Dissemination*, 105.

[101] Derrida, *Dissemination*, 117.

[102] Derrida, *Dissemination*, 119 note.

[103] Derrida, *Dissemination*, 124.

[104] The hemlock is called a *pharmakon* in the opening line of Plato's *Phaedo* (57a).

[105] Derrida, *Dissemination*, 109.

[106] Derrida, *Dissemination*, 119.

[107] Derrida, *Dissemination*, 125.

[108] Derrida, *Dissemination*, 68.

[109] Derrida, *Dissemination*, 148.

[110] Derrida, *Dissemination*, 127.

[111] Derrida, *Dissemination*, 127.

[112] Derrida, *Dissemination*, 148.

[113] Derrida, *Dissemination*, 153.

[114] Derrida, *Dissemination*, 96.

[115] Derrida, *Dissemination*, 129.

[116] Griswold, *Self-Knowledge in Plato's Phaedrus*, 233.

[117] Griswold, *Self-Knowledge in Plato's Phaedrus*, 233.

[118] Griswold suggests that an author of a dialogue possesses "absolute control" over "the conversation presented in it." See Griswold, *Self-Knowledge in Plato's Phaedrus*, 225. Here he follows Leo Strauss, *The City and Man* (Chicago: University of Chicago, 1964). Strauss writes: "one cannot take seriously enough the law of logographic necessity. Nothing is accidental in a Platonic dialogue; everything is necessary at the place where it occurs" (60). While it is true that the *Phaedrus* is crafted with extreme care—down to the very smallest detail—Griswold and Strauss' claim seems extravagant. Griswold's point—that Plato is not a victim of language, as Derrida has it—holds without ascribing infallible control over the forces of language to Plato.

[119] Griswold, *Self-Knowledge in Plato's Phaedrus*, 204.

[120] On Plato's use of the dialogue form, see Paul Friedländer, *Plato; An Introduction*, trans. Hans Meyerhoff (Princeton: Princeton University, 1969) 154–170; Kenneth Seeskin, *Dialogue and Discovery; A Study of Socratic Method* (Albany: State University of New York, 1987); Kenneth M. Sayre, *Plato's Literary Garden: How to Read a Platonic Dialogue* (Notre Dame: University of Notre Dame, 1995); and Charles L. Griswold, Jr., "Plato's Metaphilosophy: Why Plato Wrote Dialogues," ed. Charles L. Griswold, Jr., *Platonic Writings; Platonic Readings* (New York and London: Routledge, 1988) 143–167.

[121] Griswold, *Self-Knowledge in Plato's Phaedrus*, 192.

[122] Griswold, *Self-Knowledge in Plato's Phaedrus*, 219–220.

[123] As Gadamer writes, "the literary form of the dialogue places language and concept back within the original movement of the conversation. This protects words from all dogmatic abuse." See Gadamer, *Truth and Method*, 332.

[124] Griswold, *Self-Knowledge in Plato's Phaedrus*, 221–222.

[125] Ferrari, *Listening to the Cicadas*, 3 and 30–31.

[126] Hans-Georg Gadamer, *Dialogue and Dialectic; Eight Hermeneutical Studies on Plato*, trans. P. Christopher Smith (New Haven: Yale University, 1980) 70–71.

[127] Griswold, *Self-Knowledge in Plato's Phaedrus*, 238.

[128] Griswold, *Self-Knowledge in Plato's Phaedrus*, 237 and 238.

[129] Griswold, *Self-Knowledge in Plato's Phaedrus*, 239 and 236.

[130] Griswold, *Self-Knowledge in Plato's Phaedrus*, 239. The same charge fits Rorty's work, according to Griswold. See 234–239.

[131] Griswold, *Self-Knowledge in Plato's Phaedrus*, 239.

[132] Ferrari, *Listening to the Cicadas*, 119.

[133] Griswold, *Self-Knowledge in Plato's Phaedrus*, 241.

Index of Names